S0-BGM-364

1985
SEASON

THE COMPLETE HANDBOOK OF
PRO HOCKEY

Super Sports Books from SIGNET

(0451)

☐ **THE ILLUSTRATED SPORTS RECORD BOOK by Zander Hollander and David Schulz.** Here, in a single book, are 350 records with stories and photos so vivid they'll make you feel that "you are there." Once and for all you'll be able to settle your sports debates on who holds what records and how he, or she, did it. (111818—$2.50)*

☐ **EVERYTHING YOU ALWAYS WANTED TO KNOW ABOUT SPORTS* *and didn't know where to ask by Mickey Herskowitz and Steve Perkins.** Here is the book that answers every question a sports fan ever had in the back of his mind and tells the truth about all the whispered rumors of the sports world. (124715—$2.75)*

☐ **INSTANT REPLAY: THE GREEN BAY DIARY OF JERRY KRAMER edited by Dick Schapp.** From the locker room to the goal line, from the training field to the Super Bowl, this is the inside story of a great pro football team ... "The best behind-the-scenes glimpse of pro football ever produced."—*The New York Times* (096576—$2.50)

☐ **EVEN BIG GUYS CRY by Alex Karras with Herb Gluck.** The nationwide bestseller by the former Detroit Lions tackle who's big enough to tell it like it really was. "Marvelous ... one of the best!"—*Los Angeles Times* (125290—$2.95)

*Prices slightly higher in Canada

Buy them at your local bookstore or use this convenient coupon for ordering.

NEW AMERICAN LIBRARY
P.O. Box 999, Bergenfield, New Jersey 07621

Please send me the books I have checked above. I am enclosing $_____
(please add $1.00 to this order to cover postage and handling). Send check or money order—no cash or C.O.D.'s. Prices and numbers are subject to change without notice.

Name_____

Address_____

City _____ State _____ Zip Code _____

Allow 4-6 weeks for delivery.
This offer is subject to withdrawal without notice.

1985
SEASON

THE COMPLETE HANDBOOK OF
PRO HOCKEY

EDITED BY ZANDER HOLLANDER

A SIGNET BOOK
NEW AMERICAN LIBRARY

ACKNOWLEDGMENTS

Canada's game returned home—fittingly to Wayne Gretzky and his Oilers—but will Edmonton quaff champagne again in 1984-85? Will the Islanders rise anew? Will touted Pittsburgh rookie Mario Lemieux be as good as his press clippings? It is these and all the other unknowns that make for an intriguing new season and set the stage for this 14th edition of *The Complete Handbook of Pro Hockey*. We acknowledge with appreciation the many hands who figured in the making of the book: Frank Kelly, Hugh Delano, Frank Orr, Pat Calabria, Dick Chubey, John Halligan, Dick Johnston, Jeff Shermack, Mark Ruskie, Bob Carter, Phyllis Hollander, Peter Hollander, Steve Wisniewski, Richard Rossiter, Benny Ercolani, Dot Gordineer, Beri Greenwald, the corps at Westchester Book Composition and the NHL team publicity directors.

Zander Hollander

PHOTO CREDITS: Front cover—Paul Bereswell; back cover—Richard Pilling; inside photos—Bruce Bennett, Richard Pilling, Scotty Kilpatrick, Universal Pictures, UPI, and the NHL team photographers.

Copyright © 1984 by Associated Features Inc. All rights reserved.

SIGNET TRADEMARK REG. U.S. PAT. OFF. AND FOREIGN COUNTRIES REGISTERED TRADEMARK—MARCA REGISTRADA HECHO EN CHICAGO, U.S.A.

SIGNET, SIGNET CLASSICS, MENTOR, PLUME, MERIDIAN AND NAL BOOKS are published by The New American Library Inc. 1633 Broadway New York, New York 10019

First Printing, October 1984

1 2 3 4 5 6 7 8 9

PRINTED IN THE UNITED STATES OF AMERICA

CONTENTS

Editor's Note: The material herein includes trades and rosters up to final printing deadline.

Mark Messier Emerges from Gretzky's Shadow

By DICK CHUBEY

The night of May 15, 1984 will burn brightly for years in the memories of the 17,498 who regularly congregate at the North-lands Coliseum in Edmonton.

What's so monumental about the 15th?

After all, the record shows it was four nights later when the upstart Edmonton Oilers turned this northwestern outpost into a frenzy by unceremoniously dethroning the four-time champion New York Islanders for the Stanley Cup. The Oilers required but a scant five games to become the first refugee from the World Hockey Association to capture Lord Stanley's oversized beer stein, accomplishing this remarkable feat in only their fifth National Hockey League campaign.

But, take away one individual accomplishment on the 15th and the Stanley Cup might not be residing in Western Canada for the first time since the Victoria Cougars won three of four games from the Montreal Canadiens in 1925. Such was the snowballing effect of an absolutely brilliant goal by Mark Messier at 8:38 of the second period in the pivotal Game 3 against the Islanders.

With the Oilers on the defensive, a pass by Islander center Brent Sutter was tipped at the Edmonton blue line by defenseman Lee Fogolin. Messier scooped the puck and wheeled in the other direction in one powerful skating motion. He hit the Isles' blue line where he spied veteran Denis Potvin and rookie Gord Dineen. Not surprisingly, he opted for the freshman. But the manner in which he left Dineen corkscrewed to the ice has the folks still giggling in these parts. Then Messier uncorked a 20-foot wrist

Dick Chubey has covered hockey in Alberta since 1964 — the past six years as beat man on the Edmonton Oilers for the Edmonton Sun.

MVP Mark Messier whoops it up after Oilers' Cup triumph.

shot that had Isles' goalie, the despised Billy Smith, staring into far away places.

The goal, first of two by Messier, pulled the Oilers into a 2-2 tie and Edmonton went on to triumph, 7-2. Never again were they to trail in the series. And, to further underline the impact upon Messier's teammates, of the final 22 goals in the series, 18 came off Edmonton sticks.

Messier, who produced the game-winner on an almost equally

sensational solo effort in Game 4, wound up with the Conn Smythe Trophy as the Most Valuable Player of the Stanley Cup playoffs. Almost as significant, perhaps for the first time in the 23-year-old's five-year NHL career, people outside of Edmonton began recognizing his emergence out of Wayne Gretzky's shadow.

For it was Messier, not Gretzky, who ignited the stagnant Oilers' offense against the Isles. Oh sure, Gretzky, who is un-paralleled among hockey performers on this planet and probably any other, did his fair share in the end—two goals in each of the final two games, including the all-important first goal in each match. When Gretzky staked the Oilers to a 2-0 lead in the final game, Smith—Public Enemy No. 1 in these parts—was sum-moned to the bench after the first period as the Oilers went on to a Cup-winning 5-2 triumph.

But, it was Messier—known as "The Other Kid" ever since his arrival in 1979—who provided the one spark that was required to make the Oilers total believers in themselves.

"When he made it 2-2 in Game 3, that was where we started to turn things around," said defenseman Kevin Lowe, who along with goalie Grant Fuhr also received consideration for the Smythe Trophy. "It was a classic Oiler goal. He beat the defense and he beat the goalie. From that point on, we never looked back."

"If Gretzky and Mark aren't one-two right now as the best players in the world, I don't know who is," said Oilers' right winger Dave Lumley in another ultimate compliment.

Lumley is understandably biased. But Messier's talents—whether they are displayed at left wing or center—are widely recognized by hockey people, if certain fans and cocoon-dwelling members of the media are only now beginning to see the light.

In the summer of 1983, New York-based agent Art Kaminsky lumped him with Gretzky and Islander right winger Mike Bossy as the only players in the NHL who could "run past compensation" where free-agency is concerned. "That's a pretty high compli-ment . . . I don't know if it's true or not," shrugged Messier when informed of Kaminsky's high assessment.

Despite intermittent reports to the contrary throughout last win-ter, Messier was staying put in Edmonton, the site of his birth. Therefore it hardly came as a surprise when owner Peter Pock-lington proudly announced on March 1 that the big forward had signed a new five-year-deal—speculated to run in excess of $300,000 annually. Pocklington made the announcement on the occasion of the Oilers' annual Junior Achievement Dinner—an affair of fun, food and frivolity that generally carries the news value of a campaign speech. The timing, however, had newsmen scampering to telephones.

"It never entered my mind to go anywhere else," said Messier, whose father Doug has managed and coached the Oilers' farm team in Moncton, N.B., for the past two years. "I started my career in my home town and I'd like to end it here."

Commenting on the free-agency route common in other sports, Messier shrugged: "This isn't baseball or football. This league doesn't have a U.S. national TV contract, doesn't produce the revenue other sports do. We have to be realistic about it."

He is equally as level-headed when it comes to drawing comparisons to Gretzky's salary, which is approaching $1 million annually.

While others in his position may regard a tag such as "The Other Kid" a burden, Messier obviously considers it for what it is worth.

Mark Douglas Messier was born in Edmonton on Jan. 18, 1961—the second son to Doug and Mary-Jean Messier. His brother, Paul Edmond, had been born three years earlier in London, England, where dad played a year as a rugged defenseman. By the time Mark, along with sisters Jennifer and Mary-Kay were born, the family was back in Edmonton, where dad played for the old pro Western Hockey League Flyers—in the final years of the No. 1 farm team of the Detroit Red Wings.

Doug took a crack at Detroit's training camp on two occasions back during the six-team NHL. Both times he wound up on the farm in Pittsburgh, finally concluding his minor-league career with seven years in Portland, Ore. Paul, a third-round pick of the Colorado Rockies (now the New Jersey Devils), had a brief NHL fling and performed in the West German first division in 1983-84.

It was left for young Mark to carve the family's niche in the NHL.

The big raw-boned youngster didn't exactly break into the pro hockey ranks with the publicity-laden impact of a Gretzky, to say the least. Countless duds were welcomed with more printers' ink than the 1984 Conn Smythe Trophy winner.

Actually, however, there was a Gretzky connection—even back then. When Pocklington pulled off the famed Indianapolis Purchase (Gretzky, Peter Driscoll and goalie Eddie Mio for $850,000—$350,000 which was paid in cash) back in November, 1978, the WHA Racers were on their deathbed. Owner Nelson Skalbania, previously Pocklington's partner with the Oilers and the man who later moved the Atlanta Flames to Calgary, sought out another 17-year-old phenom on which to pin his fading Indianapolis hopes, if only for a couple of weeks.

Enter Mark Messier from the St. Albert Saints, a Tier Two

junior team in a suburb north of Edmonton in which he was raised. In fact, his dad coached the team.

Even if it didn't show initially, give Skalbania credit for smarts. Messier played five games with the Racers and after they folded he appeared in 47 games with the Cincinnati Stingers. Output: one goal, 10 assists, 58 minutes in penalties.

But the Oilers, operating on the same wavelength as Skalbania, saw something in Messier the other 20 NHL teams didn't. They made him their second pick (behind Kevin Lowe and in the third round) of their first NHL amateur draft in 1979.

As the Oilers' rookie camp opened in 1979, Mark undoubtedly set an NHL record for being the youngest holdout in history. "It was kind of difficult to believe at the time," recalled Dave Lumley, an Oilers' recruit from the Montreal Canadiens' organization. "It was the team's first training camp and we heard there was a holdout, which was no big deal. But then we heard he was 18 and had one goal the year before..."

Coach Glen Sather wasn't exactly doing cartwheels. "Mark and his dad are looking at it the way guys could have gotten paid two years ago," said Sather at the time. "But times have changed now that we're down to one league again. And, remember, here's a guy who scored only one goal the previous year."

Messier's holdout—however brief it turned out to be—was one in a series of incidents that had this mischievious teenager continually immersed in hot water as he launched his NHL career.

Twenty days into his first NHL season, Messier was in the minors as a result of a disciplinary move for missing a flight to St. Louis. Previously, this adolescent was late for a bus departure for the airport in Vancouver during preseason play and was also late for a practice at home. Three strikes and go straight to Houston.

"Missing a plane is not all of it, but you could bet it had something to do with it," said Sather, having a difficult time concealing his disappointment at the time. "I also want Mark to go down there and have a chance to play regularly and not screw up his chances, because I think he could be an excellent pro...once he learns how to catch buses on time, be at the airport and discipline himself.

"He's got to learn hockey is the most important thing in his life right now and he must make the sacrifices."

Over three years later Messier revealed the circumstances behind missing the flight that netted him four Central League games in Houston.

"That's a big omelette that I don't think I've ever told anybody before," sheeplishly grinned Messier as he finally came clean midway through the 1982-83 campaign. "I went to the wrong airport. I looked at the itinerary and it said we were returning to the Industrial Airport [near downtown Edmonton]. That's where I figured we left from and that's where I had my mother drop me off. When I went inside, I knew something was wrong. I didn't see any of the guys and I jumped in a cab [for the International, 25 miles away]. The cabbie turned it on, but when I got there, the plane was taxiing out."

Hello Houston!

Innocence aside, there's little doubt the big, brawny teenager didn't approach the game in his younger years with the dedication and discipline demanded by Sather. At that stage Messier was so far left of center, his ambition was to be a rock singer. Mick Jagger, not Bobby Hull, was his idol.

For Messier's first couple of NHL seasons (12 and 23 goals), Sather spent considerable time on his case. Word traveled fast, even in a 21-team far-flung NHL. The trade offers were many. The Islanders attempted to put together a package for Messier and Glenn Anderson, but Sather laughed. The New York Rangers offered Ron Duguay, goalie Doug Soetaert and another Ranger for Messier. Sather again nixed the deal.

Instead the Oilers' GM-coach toughed it out with the 6-foot, 205-pounder. "I probably deserved it," said Messier of the heat received from the boss. "It was not only for the good of the team, but also for me as a person. It helped me get my priorities straight. That hockey was No. 1. There was a time when I didn't know anything was. I just wasn't ready for the commitment.

"Today I'm still having fun, but I realize you're only as good as your last shift. You must prove yourself game after game. Back then I'd be high on the hog for one game, but I'd go into the tank for two or three. Now I don't let my highs get too high . . . or my lows too low."

Actually, things started to fall into place for Messier in mid-February of 1981—his second NHL season. Over the final 27 games 20-year-old Mark accounted for 13 goals and 35 points.

He was tough, loud, boisterous and epitomized the Oilers' Kiddie Korps that went on to upset the Montreal Canadiens in the first round of the 1981 playoffs and to extend the Islanders to six games in the quarterfinals. He was all these things that people frown upon, but he also was a multitalented young man. In short, he was able to back his abrasiveness.

There was an occasion when the Oilers arrived for a practice session at the Montreal Forum—hockey's high cathedral, where Henri Richard said he wouldn't dare shave until he spent five years with the Canadiens. Messier, in a voice that caused a disturbing quiver among the 22 Stanley Cup pennants that normally hang limp in the NHL shrine, was hardly shy in proclaiming the arrival of the young Oilers.

"Let's beat the piss out of these guys!" he bellowed in a tone loud enough to cause the frozen earth to move in and around Howie Morenz' grave. The impact of Messier's thunderclap voice, it was reported, resulted in the shattering of glasses in Henri Richard's tavern. Suddenly 78 regulars up and bolted out of Toe Blake's joint. Rocket Richard's Grecian Formula kicked out. Jean Beliveau, Le Gros Bill, developed an earache.

"I may as well let them know what I think," quipped Messier.

In 1981 the Islanders lost one game at home during the playoffs. Yup, 4-3, to the new kids on the block, who on that night were into singing on the bench:

Here we go Oil-ers, here we go.
Here we go Oil-ers, here we go.
Here we go Oil-ers, here we go.
Here we go Oil-ers, here we go.

You-know-who was playing the part of Mitch Miller. "Aw, what the hell," grinned maestro Messier, "it takes your mind off the pressure of the game."

Throughout it all Messier developed into the premier left winger in the game today. In 1981-82, he cracked the charmed 50-goal circle and added 38 assists for a first All-Star team berth at the season's end. Forty-eight goals and 106 points netted him another first-team nomination the following year. Last season his goal-scoring production dipped (37), but he still broke the 100-point barrier (101) after moving to center ice for the final 22 regular-season games and the playoffs.

As evidenced by his gangbuster performance against the Islanders in the final this time around, the Isles were damned fortunate Messier was far from 100 percent in 1982-83.

With 14 goals through three playoff rounds, he had suffered a first-degree shoulder separation in a collision with fellow Edmonton product Keith Brown during Game 3 of the Oilers' four-game, semifinal sweep of the Chicago Black Hawks. As is custom in such situations, the Oilers downplayed the injury, terming it no more than a "bruise" as Messier struggled in pain through the first three games of the final.

Messier played along with the bluff, too. In Game 1 he delivered a couple of crunching, if illegal, elbow checks at Tomas Jonsson and Anders Kallur. "I was more or less trying to show them I wasn't hurt so they wouldn't keep hitting my shoulder," said Messier after Sather leaked the news between Games 3 and 4. "I almost wish it hadn't come out. This is not the time of year of excuses. I don't want to give anyone a reason to think I need an excuse. I'm not concerned about it. It's just something I have to live with."

Ironically, the healing of the injury—sufficiently for Sather to finally reveal its seriousness—coincided with Messier scoring his only goal of the 1983 series, Edmonton's second in the Isles' Cup-winning triumph in Game 4.

When the season concluded, Messier, his brother Paul and two other hockey-playing bachelors (Darryl Morrow, Vince Magnan) headed to the Far East for six weeks. "I like playing hockey and I enjoy the fringe benefits, but eight months is long enough," he explained. "I have to get far away from it during the offseason. Maybe not mileage-wise but certainly in my mind. I think it took a month for my shoulder to heal and two months for my mind to get back to normal. There are so many little mind games played throughout the season you don't know what has to be in better shape—your body or your mind."

Was Thailand far enough removed from the maddening hockey crowd?

"Was it ever wild?" slyly smiled Messier. "We rode bikes everywhere we went—to beaches where the sand was as white as the paper you're writing on. Every day was a hair-raising experience. The four of us, we kind of cruise together. We pretty well got the whole world covered now, but Bangkok has got to be the wildest place I've ever been."

So, how wild was it?

"I think I'll leave that to the peoples' imagination . . ."

C'mon, Mark?

"Well . . . Put it this way. You could see the most beautiful temples in the world, to the poorest slum areas, to the most outrageous sexual fantasies imaginable. That pretty well covers the whole infield right there."

Ahem, yes, one would think so . . .

The video machine in the coaches' office at the Northlands Coliseum was serving another painful reminder of the 1983 Stanley Cup finals a week into training camp last autumn. "Our team has more character than any other in professional sport," proudly said Isles' coach Al Arbour after New York's fourth Cup triumph. A perturbed Messier suddenly peeled down to nothing but a frown. He whipped a towel from around his waist and snapped it in the direction of the TV screen. "Little does he know!" snorted Messier, storming away.

Eight months later the message was delivered loud and clear to Arbour, Billy Smith, the Islanders, the NHL and fans throughout North America.

The Schoolboy Goalie Who Made It To the NHL

By DICK JOHNSTON

Just a year before, Tom Barrasso had been preparing for graduation from Acton-Boxboro High School, in a Boston suburb.

Now, here he was, on June 4, 1984, at a glittering ceremony

Buffalo's Tom Barrasso

A hockey and newspaper institution in himself, Dick Johnston has covered hockey for a quarter of a century for the Buffalo Evening News. *He was on the scene at the birth of the Buffalo Sabres in 1970 and he was there when rookie Tom Barrasso came to play in 1983. But when the 1984-85 season begins, Dick will be hard put to find any ice in Naples, Fla., where he has retired after 43 years on one newspaper.*

in Toronto, being honored as winner of two major awards—the Vezina Trophy for best goaltender in the NHL and the Calder Trophy for the league's outstanding rookie.

During the previous eight months while his high-school classmates were becoming oriented to college life, Barrasso was in the Montreal Forum, in the Spectrum in Philadelphia, in Boston Garden and in other celebrated arenas, blocking shots propelled at nearly 100 miles an hour by some of the best players in hockey.

When Barrasso started against the Hartford Whalers in Buffalo's 1983-84 opener, he was the youngest player to tend goal in the NHL in 40 years. Back in 1943, an apple-cheeked 17-year-old named Harry Lumley had a two-game tryout with the Detroit Red Wings. Lumley lost both games.

In the intervening years, no one as young as Barrasso had played goal in an NHL game. Lumley, it might be noted, returned the following season to become a regular with Detroit and went on, still known as "Apple Cheeks," to be voted into the Hockey Hall of Fame.

Who knows what's ahead for Barrasso? A youthful product of the U.S., tributed as one of the best professionals at his position in this predominantly Canadian game, Barrasso already is also one of its most controversial figures.

When Scotty Bowman, highly-respected general manager and coach of the Buffalo Sabres, chose Barrasso as his first pick, fifth overall, in the 1983 NHL draft, people took notice—they sure did—but nobody expected the youngster to have such an immediate impact on big-league hockey.

That includes Bowman.

"Barrasso has exceeded our expectations," Bowman said late in the season.

No goaltender ever had been selected higher than fifth in the draft and no goaltender from the U.S. ever had gone in the first round before. And right out of high school.

Sure, Barrasso had an 0.73 goals-against average but it was in only 23 games and not even against Canadian junior competition, from whence most NHL rookies come, but against schoolboy teams in Massachusetts.

The big kid (6-3, 195) showed them that Bowman, again, knew what he was doing.

Barrasso started the Sabres' first exhibition game in hallowed Montreal Forum; started the season opener, before the home fans in Memorial Auditorium, and won it; alternated all season with veteran netminder Bob Sauve, and ended up with the second best goals-against average in the league, 2.84.

Washington's Pat Riggin was first, with 2.66. Riggin had a

21-14-2 won-lost-tied record; Barrasso was 26-12-3.

Pretty heady stuff for a teenager, eh?

Well, this teenager is, as the expression goes, 19 going on 40.

Self-assured, confident, poised, Tom Barrasso is one cool customer. He handles interviews as though he had been in the league for 15 years.

That is, probably, one reason he is such a good goaltender at such a tender age.

There are many who say that Tom has too much confidence. Cocky, brash, even arrogant, he has been called by the media.

Adverse comment surrounded Barrasso even before he joined the Buffalo organization. Barrasso went to the Olympic tryouts of Team USA but left training camp after playing two exhibition games to turn pro with the Sabres.

There were many published reports that the rest of the U.S. team stood up and cheered when it was announced that Barrasso had left. The implication, obviously, was that he was not exactly popular.

Then, there was Barrasso's first game in Boston Garden, where only a few months before he had goaled in a schoolboy tournament. Tom was in the nets in Buffalo's first game of the season against the Bruins. Buffalo lost. And Barrasso ducked the Boston press afterward.

In the Stanley Cup playoffs, when the Sabres did a nose dive after having a great season, Barrasso again avoided the press on one or two occasions. And, during the season he had made some comments that weren't accepted too well.

Some writers excused him. "He's only a teenager, under heavy pressure. And a goaltender besides. Other goaltenders have refused to talk to the press after losing," they said.

Others retorted: "Yeah, but this kid is making a six-figure salary. With hockey players making the money they do these days, part of their job is public relations. They wouldn't be making that money if it wasn't for media coverage. They are like show business celebrities, right?"

Barrasso agrees that part of his job is public relations. And, he says, he enjoys being center of attention.

"I love it," he has said. "Little kids asking me for autographs, stuff like that. It's just great. That's what I always dreamed about doing when I was younger. I am glad to talk to people and to stay around after a game to talk to the press. I know that it helps me."

Asked after the season, if he would have done differently in his dealings with the press if he had it to do over, Barrasso replied, "No, I'd still say the same things. I received a lot of knocks from the press but what I say, that's me. I don't enjoy being knocked

Barrasso was voted NHL's top rookie and No. 1 goaltender.

but I'm not going to change, just to look good in the newspaper. I will tell you what I think. And I will be consistent. I won't tell you one thing and tell somebody else something else."

As to the story about the Olympic team, Barrasso shrugs it off. "I didn't really want to play on the Olympic team," he explained.

"Always my goal had been playing in the NHL. I was sort of talked into going to the Olympic training camp. After all, it is a big chance, to play in the Olympics.

"But when I got there, I found I just didn't want to be there. I didn't want to play and I didn't want to practice. I didn't feel I was working toward my goal. I wasn't happy there at all.

"I stayed by myself most of the time because of the way I felt.

I knew some of the Olympic players were teed off at me toward the end, but I didn't care what they thought. I still don't care.

"I made my up my mind to leave Team USA and sign with Buffalo, get started working toward an NHL career right away. I was just happy to be with the Buffalo Sabres."

Barrasso's Buffalo teammates backed him in his decision. "Why didn't the Olympic guys like him? Because he was the best," said veteran right winger Mike Foligno. "He was getting a big contract and they were jealous. When he left Team USA for the Sabres he was thinking about his future. I'm sure most of them would do the same, if they had the chance."

As to the Boston incident, Barrasso explained that he was seeing his family, who came to Boston for the game, and the Sabres' bus was leaving shortly for a chartered flight back to Buffalo, so he was in a hurry.

He undoubtedly handled it badly. "All he had to do was take five seconds to explain that he only had a little time and wanted to spend it with his family," said one Boston writer.

In subsequent visits, Barrasso always was available to the Boston press. He tended goal in two more Boston Garden games, winning one and losing one, both by 5-3 scores.

The other Sabres have observed Barrasso's trouble with the press with amusement combined with sympathy. They realize he was only 18 when he was thrust into the spotlight without much preparation. They kid him in the dressing room, as they kid with each other. He gets the needle and he retorts in kind.

Rip Simonick, assistant to trainer Frank Christie, is around the club every day, at home and away. He says, "Barrasso's okay. The guys like him. The day he is to play, he likes to be left alone. But that's nothing unusual for a goaltender."

Craig Ramsay, who has been with the Sabres since their second year in the NHL, said that Barrasso was accepted right away, perhaps because there are so many other young players on the club, and the big goaltender's attitude never has been a problem for his teammates.

"Barrasso was very quiet, at the start," said Ramsay. "He just played hockey, did his job. During training camp he went out with the other guys. He never was pushy, never talked too much. He did his best to join in and our club makes it easy for rookies to join in. We make them welcome. He never asked for too much from anybody.

"We couldn't help but be pleased with the way he played, right from the start. We were looking for a goaltender to complement Bobby Sauve and Barrasso seemed to be the man to do it.

"I must say, it certainly surprised me that he came in with such confidence, at his age, and played so well. He could give up an early goal and still play great the rest of the way. That's not the case with all goalies. He doesn't ever seem to get rattled and he's aggressive; stands in there, no matter what."

As to Barrasso's cocky attitude, his teammates think that is good in a goaltender.

"We love it," said Foligno. "There's nothing better for a team than a cocky goaltender. Tommy's cocky in a very positive manner. Some people are cocky in a negative way and hurt the team.

"He talks like a winner and acts like a winner. That's the kind of people you want on your team."

Defenseman Jerry Korab, who at 35 rejoined the Sabres last season after a term of duty in Los Angeles, was just one year short of twice Barrasso's age when the young goaltender made his debut.

"Tom doesn't bother anybody here. He's a nice guy. Sharp, mature, you can talk to him about anything, not just hockey."

Barrasso's single-minded approach to his profession might upset some. He wanted to play, to tend goal, in the NHL since he was eight.

"That always was my ambition. Never any other," he said.

He was on skates first when he was four and played organized hockey at five, as a defenseman against kids nine and 10 years old.

"We played on Saturdays," he recalled, "and after the games I would go to another rink to attend goalie school. I wanted to be a goalie even then but my father wanted me to become a good skater first, so I played defense that first year."

The following winter he became a goaltender and has been one ever since.

Barrasso grew up in Stow, a small town about 25 miles west of Boston. His entire family was crazy about hockey, so the young goaltender not only was allowed to pursue his dream, he was helped along the way by his father and mother.

At one time, the Barrasso family had season tickets to the Bruins, the New England Whalers of the World Hockey Association and the Bruins' farm club in the American Hockey League, the Braves, who also played in Boston Garden for one year.

"I probably saw 100 pro games that season," Barrasso mentioned. "I used to watch all the NHL goalies and try to pick up something from them. But I never patterned myself after any one in particular."

Many have compared Barrasso to Ken Dryden, another big guy Bowman had tending goal for him, in Montreal.

Barrasso says his style differs from that of the Stanley Cup and

Hall of Fame netminder who came out of Cornell University to star in the NHL.

"We go about it differently," Barrasso pointed out. "Dryden tended to stay in his net. He didn't handle the puck very often."

Barrasso moves out of the net frequently, passing the puck to defensemen and, often, to forwards. He does this with remarkable poise for a fellow who has been in the league only a season.

Bowman has said that the way Barrasso clears the puck, "he serves almost as a third defenseman."

"I know I handle the puck well, so I'm not afraid to do it," Barrasso said. "It's easy for me to be comfortable out there, handling the puck. I try to do it as much as I can. But I don't want to get carried away with it. I just play the puck when I can and when I should."

Always a goalie in youth hockey around Boston, where the sport is well organized for youngsters, Barrasso was a polished performer when he reached Acton-Boxboro High School.

"He was 14 when I got him and there wasn't much I could teach him," recalled Tom Fleming, Barrasso's high-school coach. "He had it all—good reflexes, good form. He knew how to handle his stick and he had all the confidence in the world."

When he was 15, NHL scouts predicted Barrasso would be a first-round pick in the league draft when he became eligible at 18.

At least half a dozen NHL scouts attended every game he goaled his senior year in high school.

Barrasso knew they were there and he knew what he had to do to impress them. Hockey was first in his life and he concentrated on it with a fierceness few possess.

"On the ice Tom Barrasso was one of the best team players I've ever seen," his high-school coach once said, "but off the ice he pretty much went his own way."

One of the NHL scouts watching Barrasso was Bucky Kane, a Bostonian who now is Bowman's right-hand man with the Sabres. Kane followed Barrasso to Leningrad when the goaltender played for Team USA in the 1982 World Tournament. Barrasso lost to the Russian team, 5-3, but the final goal was into an empty net and he blocked more than 40 shots.

Kane recommended—even pushed—the big youngster to Bowman as a first-round draft pick. The game against the Soviets convinced Bowman. The rest, as they say, is history.

How did Barrasso take all the honors he earned in his freshman NHL season?

"I'm really, really happy about it," he said, shortly after returning to Stow for the summer. "I never would have expected so much."

This was said in the same measured, self-assured tones he answered all questions in interviews.

His mother, however, let on—when Tom wasn't present—that her son genuinely was excited inside, "really thrilled," at all that had happened.

"Only a mother can tell," she said. "Tom doesn't let himself get excited because he's afraid of disappointment. During the season he didn't want to talk about how things were going. He didn't want to think ahead, didn't want to lose his concentration. He just wanted to do the best job possible. He's been like that since he was eight years old. Before an important game he didn't want to talk."

Even though he was an NHL star, Barrasso was, after all, only 18 most of the season, and living away from home for the first time.

He always has been close to his family—they drove him all over to hockey tournaments until he turned pro—and living alone in an apartment in a Buffalo suburb was lonely. His monthly phone bill, Tom says, ran about $500 a month.

Phil Housley, Buffalo's first draft pick of 1982, also out of a U.S. high school (St. Paul, Minn.), lived in the same apartment complex. They traveled around together quite a bit, eating lunch out and sometimes dinner.

"I did my own cooking a lot of the time," Barrasso mentioned. "It was a completely different life for me. Besides the cooking, there was the laundry, cleaning the house, paying the bills, all things I never had to think about before."

He bought himself a Porsche 944 but otherwise didn't live it up much.

As to the coming season, well, Tom Barrasso knows that's going to be another challenge.

"There's going to be lots of pressure, I know that," he stated. "I have to prove that the first year wasn't a fluke."

JOHN HALLIGAN'S ALL-TIME HOCKEY TRIVIA LISTS

For nearly three decades, John Halligan has been collecting anything and everything about the game he loves best—hockey. His first file said "Hockey Stuff," the second "Trivia," the third "Minutiae." Now it's "Lists."

Currently Director of Communications for the National Hockey League, Halligan spent 20-plus years as publicity and public relations director for the New York Rangers.

9 FAVORITE HOCKEY FLAKES

1. **Gilles Gratton**: Reincarnated as a goalie after being a soldier in Spanish Inquisition; hockey's first streaker and first concert pianist.
2. **Derek Sanderson**: There are those who could have made a living on the $100 bills he burned.
3. **Phil Watson**: Said to a group of reporters: "Gentlemen, I have nothing to say. Any questions?"
4. **Fern Gauthier**: They said he couldn't put the puck in the ocean and, legend has it, he proved them correct. From New York's Battery Park, his first shot hit a parking sign.
5. **Howie Young**: His madcap career covered 13 seasons, countless penalty boxes, and reams of newspaper copy.
6. **Eddie Shore**: When players on his team didn't play, he sold popcorn or changed light bulbs in the arena.
7. **Jerry Mitchell**: The *New York Post* reporter who once described a penalty shot as "a drink with a bar pest."
8. **Bob Plager**: Modern-day hockey's premier practical joker.
9. **Gary Simmons**: He once bought an expensive saddle, although he didn't own a horse.

Boston's colorful Eddie Shore: Player, coach, owner.

WAYNE GRETZKY'S
FAVORITE MUSICIANS

1. **Anne Murray**
2. **David Foster** (Canadian songwriter/producer)
3. **James Young** (Styx)
4. **Paul Anka**

SIX PLAYERS WITH MOST CAREER
PLAYOFF HAT TRICKS

1. **Maurice Richard**, Montreal, 7
2. **Phil Esposito**, Boston, 4
3. **Bernie Geoffrion**, Montreal, 3
4. **Norm Ullman**, Detroit, 3
5. **Johnny Bucyk**, Boston, 3
6. **Rick MacLeish**, Philadelphia, 3

FAMOUS QUOTES

1. "I went to the fights the other night, and a hockey game broke out."—**Rodney Dangerfield**
2. "If hockey fights were fixed, I'd have been in more of them."—**Rod Gilbert**
3. "You hockey puck!"—**Don Rickles**
4. "If you can't beat 'em in the alley, you can't beat 'em on ice."—**Connie Smythe**

10 FAMOUS FANS

1. **Tiny Tim**: He loved hockey even before Miss Vickie.
2. **Charles Schulz**: On ice with Charlie Brown, Snoopy and Woodstock.
3. **Tony Bennett**: Regular at old Garden.
4. **John Mitchell**: Played college hockey at Fordham.
5. **Yogi Berra/Joe Garagiola** (entry): Saw NHL hockey in St. Louis, 1934.
6. **Andy Warhol**: Takes pictures at MSG games.
7. **Steve Allen**
8. **Billy Joel**
9. **Peggy Cass**
10. **Monte Hall**

Maurice (Rocket) Richard: Piercing eyes, piercing shots.

8 ANNOUNCER'S TRADEMARKS

1. "He Shoots . . . He *SCORES*!!!"—Originated by **Foster Hewitt**, imitated by countless others.
2. "That guy handles the puck like a cow handles a gun."—**Bill Chadwick**, New York Rangers
3. "What a Bonanza!"—**Joe Starkey**, California Seals and Pittsburgh Penguins
4. "There's the bell, the game is . . . *OVER*!"—**Foster Hewitt**; Maple Leaf Gardens the only arena to signal the end of a period with a bell.
5. "Great Balls of Fire"—**Mike Lange**, Pittsburgh Penguins
6. "Over to you, 18"—**Jiggs McDonald**, New York Islanders, turning microphone over to Eddie Westfall.
7. "Lookout, Loretta"—**Mike Lange**, Pittsburgh Penguins
8. "This is *NEW* Jersey Devils Hockey!"—**Larry Hirsch**, New Jersey Devils

PHIL ESPOSITO'S 5 FAVORITE FOODS

1. **Pasta e Fagiola** (beans and macaroni)
2. **Banana Cream Pie**
3. **Spaghetti and Meatballs**
4. **Steak and Baked Potato**
5. **Dandelion Salad**

BOBBY CLARKE'S 6 FAVORITE GOLFERS

1. **Tom Watson**
2. **Arnold Palmer**
3. **Jack Nicklaus**
4. **Raymond Floyd**
5. **Gene Sarazen**
6. **Calvin Peete**

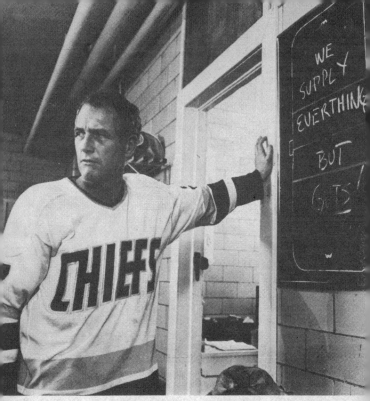

Paul Newman: Star of "Slapshot."

10 MOVIES
WITH HOCKEY THEME

1. **King of Hockey/1939**: Grade B at best.
2. **It's a Pleasure/1945**: Sonja Henie, Michael O'Shea
3. **Love Story/1970**: Ryan O'Neal, Ali MacGraw
4. **Slapshot/1977**: Paul Newman
5. **Ice Castles/1979**: Robby Benson
6. **Idol of the Crowds/1937**: John Wayne is a hockey player.
7. **Hell's Kitchen/1939**: The Dead-End Kids and Ronald Reagan go to the old Madison Square Garden.
8. **Hockey Homicide/1975**: Disney animation. Goofy on skates.
9. **Paperback Hero/1974**: Keir Dullea
10. **Duke of West Point/1936:** Louis Hayward

THE ALL-BOTANICAL TEAM

Goal: **Jacques Plante**
Defense: **Brad Park**
Defense: **Al Arbour**
Left Wing: **Claude Larose**
Center: **Doug Berry**
Right Wing: **Guy Lafleur**
Coach: **Don Cherry**

8 MOST DRAMATIC GAMES

(Editor's note: These are in no particular order and are based on games that John Halligan has seen in person or on television.)

1. **Team Canada 6, Soviet Union 5, Sept. 28, 1972**: Possibly the most dramatic international game ever. Paul Henderson's goal won it with 34 seconds left.
2. **Montreal Canadiens 3, Detroit Red Wings 2, May 5, 1966**: My first Stanley Cup-deciding game in person. Roger Crozier wins Conn Smythe Trophy despite being on losing team. Toe Blake sends entire team on ice at conclusion to add to confusion over controversial winning goal.
3. **United States 4, Finland 2, Feb. 24, 1980**: Broadcaster Al Michaels: "Do you believe in miracles? . . . YESSS!"
4. **Philadelphia Flyers 1, Boston Bruins 0, May 19, 1974**: The Flyers' first Stanley Cup. The Kate Smith promotion, quite simply the most exciting pregame activity ever.
5. **New York Islanders 3, New York Rangers 2, April 10, 1984**: Ken Morrow wins it at 8:56 of sudden death. Columnist Joe Gergen: "This game deserved a parade of its own."
6. **United States 9, Czechoslovakia 4, Feb. 28, 1960**: The *United States*, in living black and white, wins the gold medal at Squaw Valley. Jack McCartan in goal.
7. **New York Rangers 3, Chicago Black Hawks 2, April 29, 1971**: Peter Stemkowski's goal at 11:58 P.M. after 41:29 of overtime ends longest modern-day game in Rangers' history.
8. **New York Rangers 3, Detroit Red Wings 2, March 14, 1962**: Gordie Howe scores his 500th NHL goal against Gump Worsley.

Gordie Howe: A memorable 500th goal.

6 CURRENT NHL FRANCHISES THAT HAVE NEVER HOSTED AN ALL-STAR GAME

1. **Calgary**
2. **Edmonton**
3. **Hartford**
4. **Pittsburgh**
5. **Quebec**
6. **Winnipeg**

5 NHLers WITH NO. 99

1. **Desse Roche**: Montreal Maroons
2. **Joe Lamb**: Ottawa Senators
3. **Leo Bourgault**: Montreal Canadiens
4. **Wayne Gretzky**: Edmonton Oilers
5. **Wilf Paiement**: Toronto Maple Leafs

5 HOCKEY POEMS

1. Give Me Hockey, I'll Take Hockey Anytime!—**John Kieran, 1939**
2. An Ode To Lester's Gallant Stand—**Jim Burchard, 1947**
3. A Little Old Lady Writes A Letter—**Grandma Pearly, 1940**
4. Who Said They Couldn't?—**Jack Filman, 1937**
5. The Cook Brothers—**Harold Burr, 1935**

5 OLDEST NHL ARENAS

1. **Montreal Forum**: 1924
2. **Boston Garden**: 1928
3. **St. Louis Arena**: 1929
4. **Chicago Stadium**: 1931
5. **Maple Leaf Gardens** (Toronto): 1931

5 NEWEST NHL ARENAS

1. **The Saddledome** (Calgary): 1983
2. **Byrne Meadowlands Arena** (N.J.): 1981
3. **Joe Louis Arena** (Detroit): 1981
4. **Hartford Civic Center**: 1980
5. **Northlands Coliseum** (Edmonton): 1975

BERNIE PARENT'S
5 FAVORITE HUNTING SPOTS

1. **Labrador, Newfoundland**: Caribou
2. **Billings, Montana**: Elk
3. **Northeastern Wisconsin**; White-tail deer
4. **Northwestern Pennsylvania**: White-tail deer
5. **Colorado**: Mule deer

5 NHLers WHO
PLAYED IN JAPAN

1. **Randy Gregg**
2. **Curt Bennett**
3. **Darryl Sutter**
4. **Harvey Bennett**
5. **Garry Monahan**

5 GREAT MIDDLE NAMES

1. **Guy DAMIEN Lafleur**
2. **Nicholas EVAMPLIOS Fotiu**
3. **Daniel MIRL Gare**
4. **Marcel ELPHEGE Dionne**
5. **Edward LAVERN Johnstone**

5 GONE, BUT NOT FORGOTTEN,
HOCKEY TEAMS

1. **Macon Whoopies**
2. **California Golden Seals**
3. **Ottawa Silver Seven**
4. **Amarillo Wranglers**
5. **Toronto Arenas**

LaFontaine & Flatley Drive to Recapture Islander Dream

By PAT CALABRIA

Rookie Pat LaFontaine sat squashed between Dave Langevin and Ken Morrow on a bus taking the New York Islanders to New York's LaGuardia Airport. There was a small piece of luggage on LaFontaine's lap and a rumpled raincoat was draped over his shoulder. And LaFontaine said, "Isn't this great?"

He meant it. So did Pat Flatley, who joined LaFontaine in the Islanders' lineup, a Mutt-and-Jeff combination that may help the team regain the Stanley Cup it lost to Edmonton.

Never in the brief but rich history of the New York Islanders had two rookies generated so much anticipation in such a short period. The Islanders already had four Stanley Cups and, at the time, clearly envisioned another. They possessed balanced scoring, solid defense and spectacular goaltending, not to mention a bench that was deep and experienced. About the only thing they didn't have on their side was youth.

"The hardest thing to trade for or draft is what they gave us," Islander general manager Bill Torrey would say later. "You get a goalie or a defenseman or whatever. What you can't buy so easily is enthusiasm."

That, more than anything, is what LaFontaine and Flatley supplied to the Islanders, even as their Drive for Five became stalled in the Stanley Cup finals. They also provided a blitz of publicity the Islanders had not witnessed since the arrival of Denis Potvin 12 years earlier.

"It was nothing like what happened this year," Potvin said.

Potvin, it should be pointed out, was easily the most coveted

---

As a sportswriter for Newsday, *Pat Calabria was an eyewitness to the rise and fall of the New York Islanders.*

Two Pats—Flatley, left, and LaFontaine—launch Isle careers.

junior player of his generation and, as history has shown, by far
and away the most successful No. 1 draft choice of the 1970s.
Yet, he was still unknown to most of the Islander fans, who then
had little knowledge of the Canadian junior leagues and the National Hockey League draft. In fact, no one educated the Islander
fans better than Flatley or LaFontaine.

For one thing, there was the Olympics. The success of the USA
in winning the 1980 gold medal is generally credited for focusing
increased attention on the USA's next version, four years later.
But that clearly is wrong. What happened at Lake Placid turned
the spotlight brighter and hotter on all the Olympic hockey players.
And none stood in the glare as much as LaFontaine and Flatley.

"It always seemed that people were talking about us," Flatley
said. "It wasn't just in the Olympics, it was happening everywhere."

It was happening most of all on Long Island. Flatley was the
Islanders' first draft pick and 21st overall—last in the first round—

in 1982. A big, rugged right wing (6-1, 195) out of the University of Wisconsin, he was immediately hailed by the Islander scouting staff and opponents alike. Jim Devellano, then the Islander chief scout and now general manager of the Detroit Red Wings, had Flatley rated no lower than 14th.

And Tex Ehman, then the Islanders' chief Western scout and now their assistant general manager, said: "We had Flatley rated as the top college prospect without question."

Surely, fans and other players have heard those claims before. But on the day of the draft came this hard, unequivocal statement from Calgary coach Bob Johnson, who was Flatley's college coach: "He can play in the NHL right now."

That was quite a mouthful about a player who had only completed his sophomore season. But it proved to be the first trickle of publicity and expectation that would nearly consume Flatley and later LaFontaine. Flatley, for all his ability, is quiet, somewhat shy—but supremely confident, a typical Islander. That's opposed to LaFontaine, the effervescent 5-10, 177-pound center, who set junior scoring records and played a style that seemed to make him an uncharacteristic pick of the team.

Yet Torrey and his staff knew they needed quickness. They also feared the scoring droughts their club was suffering sporadically was a symptom of something deeper. So going into the 1983 draft, they scrutinized every top player carefully because they had obtained two years earlier the No. 1 pick of the Colorado Rockies for defenseman Bob Lorimer. With LaFontaine blossoming in just his first junior season, it would rank among Torrey's best deals.

No doubt, LaFontaine was swift. Unquestionably, he had a touch around the net. Indisputably, he was a terrific player, destined for stardom, even if he didn't play the defensive style the Islanders are accustomed to demanding. But there were two additional things that LaFontaine had that made him desirable, a combination that no other draft choice in Islander history could claim.

One, he was cute. Two—and even better—he was American.

"I expected a welcome," LaFontaine said shortly after his arrival. "But I didn't expect this."

He didn't expect to immediately become the darling of every female teeny-bopper from Syosset to Southampton. He didn't expect to walk up to Nassau Coliseum each night seeing giggling high-school girls wearing Islander jerseys with the name LAFONTAINE sewn on the back. So complete was his acceptance and his growth into an idol that Potvin, when he heard the squeals of LaFontaine's fans, said: "I remember when they used to do that for me."

LaFontaine faced Cup reality against Oilers' Mark Messier.

Of course, there was a reason for all that. LaFontaine was well-known to hard-core hockey fans when he was a teenager growing up in Waterford Township, Mich., just outside of Detroit. La-Fontaine's father, John, an executive with Chrysler, was Pat's peewee coach and tutored his son on the frozen lake behind their home. When the lake didn't freeze, John would flood a homemade backyard rink. Pat learned quickly.

He scored an astonishing 175 goals in 79 games for his midget team, then decided to leave his home to play Canadian junior hockey for good reason—his high school didn't have a hockey team. LaFontaine arranged to have himself drafted by the Verdun Juniors, outside Montreal, near where his maternal grandmother used to live.

He had 104 goals and 130 assists at age 17 and only 10 penalty minutes. "I haven't gotten in a fight my whole career," he said.

His all-around talent, especially his speed, appealed to the coaches of the 1984 U.S. Olympic team. And LaFontaine was certainly attracted to the Olympics. He had watched on TV as the USA won the gold medal four years before. After the Islanders drafted him third overall, he got it. He became the star of the

The Toronto-born Flatley came by way of the U. of Wisconsin.

U.S. team, with large, puppy-dog eyes to go along with his swift strides.

It was at the Olympics in Sarajevo where the friendship of LaFontaine and Flatley was cemented, despite obvious contrasts. Although Flatley attended the University of Wisconsin, he was Canadian. He was born and raised in Toronto and became known not for sparkling playmaking, but for bruising checks. Flatley, in fact, was nicknamed "white eyes" by college teammates who claimed to have seen his eyes roll back in anger.

Although he scored the unremarkable total of 17 goals in 33 games in his freshman season, Flatley was drafted 21st by the Islanders, who were seeking to shore up the right wing. And like LaFontaine, he welcomed the chance to compete in the Olympics when the opportunity came along. The publicity the players received in Yugoslavia made them Islanders before they ever actually wore the uniform.

It was the Islanders, for instance, who had organized a letter-writing campaign to the two young athletes in the weeks before the Olympics. It was a creative and successful move by the team's public relations staff as Islander fans responded by the hundreds. LaFontaine said: "I couldn't believe it. People I never knew, and they said such nice things. I felt welcomed and I wasn't even here yet."

Torrey couldn't have planned it any better. Newspapers were trumpeting the accomplishments of the two rookies. The Islanders, although they finished an impressive second overall in the regular season, were occasionally showing signs of age, in addition to suffering an unfortunate series of injuries to leading players. Not only were Flatley and LaFontaine ripe for the Islanders, but the Islanders were ripe to have them.

Ideas quickly were manufactured for new bumper stickers. "We Have a Pat Hand," was one slogan.

The Islanders, who had often been slow and reluctant to welcome rookies, took to the two Pats immediately. Certainly, Flatley and LaFontaine did everything they could not to ruffle their teammates. At the press conference that officially announced their signing, Flatley was asked what he expected. He replied: "I expect to work hard just like I know all the other Islanders do, and I hope I can help the team. I think that's what they want, too."

And LaFontaine said, "It's a great team. They've won four Stanley Cups. I don't expect to have things given to me when they already have so many great players."

Maybe those sentiments were not completely true, but it was obvious they were just what the other players wanted to hear. The arrival of the two new players surely disturbed those whose jobs were already in jeopardy, but Mike Bossy put it best when he was asked how he and his teammates were responding to all the hoopla surrounding two players who had yet to take a shift in the NHL.

"I think the only resentment will come from guys who are worried about their jobs, and I don't think it will even be that much of a problem," Bossy said. "As far as everybody else goes, I think that we feel that if these kids can help us win, then I'm all for them."

Any tension was broken at an afternoon practice the day the players joined the team. LaFontaine entered the locker room to find that Clark Gillies had slashed the laces of LaFontaine's skates into spaghetti-like shreds. Then Gillies emerged from a shower wearing a black executioner's hood, demanding: "Where are the rookies?"

Over in another corner, Anders Kallur—who feared losing his right wing position—turned to a circle of teammates and authored one of the great lines of sports introspection. Pointing across the room to the fresh-faced rookie quietly dressing, Kallur said: "He's Flatley. I'm history."

Everyone laughed. And it helped that Flatley and LaFontaine made their presence felt quickly. Flatley scored on his second NHL shift on the first shot of his career, beating Doug Soetaert in Winnipeg. Three nights later, LaFontaine had one of the most memorable performances ever by an Islander rookie. In a game in Toronto, he scored three goals and added two assists. Two stars were born.

They also were appropriately initiated. They had endured, along with their teammates, a grueling day to begin the road trip when the Islanders' flight to Winnipeg was canceled because of bad weather. When the team was rerouted through Minneapolis, Butch Goring took charge of assigning seats. Not surprisingly, he did so on the basis of experience.

"Window?" Goring called out, and handed a boarding pass to Ken Morrow. "Aisle?" he yelled, and handed one to Dave Langevin. Finally, only two passes were left in his hand. He turned to Flatley and LaFontaine and said, "You guys can either have a middle, or a middle."

At a team meal the afternoon of the game in Toronto, the players were seated around a table when Bob Bourne suddenly shouted, "Shoe check." Flatley and LaFontaine looked bewildered as the others lifted up the tablecloth and looked down, as if peering at their feet. So the rookies did the same. But when they looked down, they discovered their shoes had been smeared with ketchup.

"It made us feel welcome," Flatley said. "From the time we arrived, guys kidded with us, took time to help coach us, invited us over for dinner. I couldn't have asked for more."

By the time the pair made their home debut at Nassau Coliseum, they were well-known, well-liked and well-publicized. Despite the club purposely downplaying their presence in the lineup—no special ceremonies or announcements—to ease the mounting pressure, the crowd reacted with long, warm applause when the two had their names announced along with the other 20 players over the public address system.

There was further applause when coach Al Arbour, displaying a stroke of showmanship usually neglected by the staid organization, inserted his rookies in the starting lineup together. "Why not?" he said later. "Isn't that what everyone wanted to see?"

There was no argument. And there was no disputing their effect on a crowd that was more than ready to embrace them. LaFontaine scored twice in the debut, including a goal that sent the Islanders past Philadelphia when he won a faceoff, pushed the puck past

Ron Sutter and, in a blitz of speed and motion, fired a shot into the net.

The fans chanted, "La-font-taine, La-font-taine."

LaFontaine quickly began to show the quickness that made comparisons to Marcel Dionne, also small and swift. He also proved that despite his size he could take a check. Time after time opponents pounded him, half-expecting LaFontaine to fold like a wallet, and then hide the rest of the game. It didn't happen.

If that was a mild surprise, then so was Flatley's ability to handle the puck. He had come with the reputation of being a checker and not a goal-scorer. But he quickly demolished that talk by fitting right into the Islanders' style—crisp forechecking to force a giveaway and then quickly pounding on the mistake and putting the puck in the net.

Still, it was Flatley's bone-rattling checks that made him most valuable. During the first-round playoff series against the Rangers, he slammed into none other than Barry Beck, separating the mountainous defenseman's left shoulder. "It sounded like thunder when it hit," Beck said, acknowledging the check was both hard and clean.

Flatley would go on to score goals in three straight games as the Islanders battled Washington in the second round of the playoffs. LaFontaine, meanwhile, managed assists in four straight games. The Islanders clinched the series with Flatley scoring two more goals and adding an assist and LaFontaine getting an assist. Finally, after a season of joy and production, things began to sour.

LaFontaine twisted his ankle the day before the Islanders were to leave to face Montreal in the Prince of Wales final. He would miss all but one game of the series. Flatley tailed off until he scored goals in each of the last two games as the Islanders again battled from behind. Then, like their teammates, a bruising playoff took its toll in the Stanley Cup finals against Edmonton. Physically and emotionally spent, the Islanders lost in five games, their four-year reign as champions ended.

Flatley had one goal in the series. But Islander fans saw a hopeful omen in the closing period of the final game. Down 4-0, the Islanders scored twice in the first 35 seconds of the third period, both times on goals by LaFontaine. It was almost enough to bring the Islanders back—but not quite. They lost, 5-2, and were left with their memories and peeks at the future.

They mentioned over and over what it would mean to have Flatley and LaFontaine for a full season. "I think it's going to be extremely significant," Torrey noted.

LaFontaine said, "I can hardly wait until next season."

He had plenty of company.

INSIDE THE NHL

By FRANK ORR and HUGH DELANO

PREDICTED ORDER OF FINISH

Adams	Patrick	Smythe	Norris
Buffalo	N.Y. Islanders	Edmonton	Minnesota
Quebec	N.Y. Rangers	Calgary	Chicago
Boston	Washington	Vancouver	St. Louis
Montreal	Philadelphia	Winnipeg	Detroit
Hartford	Pittsburgh	Los Angeles	Toronto
	New Jersey		

Stanley Cup: Edmonton

Mark Messier was seated behind the wheel of a bright red Trans-Am that sparkled in the sunshine outside New York's posh Plaza Hotel on the morning of May 30, 1984.

The Edmonton Oilers' husky forward raised a clenched fist of triumph and let forth a shout of joy as he stepped out of the new car he had been given as MVP in Edmonton's Stanley Cup conquest of the defending champion New York Islanders.

"I don't think it will be that tough for us to keep the drive and intensity going to win the Stanley Cup again," said Messier. "I think winning the Cup the first time is tougher than winning it again. I know we're capable of doing it again."

It was the night of June 1, 1984, and Bob Bourne was relaxing at his home on Long Island. The shock of the Islanders' unsuccessful drive for a record-tying five straight championships still had not fully worn off.

Frank Orr of the Toronto Star *wrote the Norris and Smythe divisions and Hugh Delano of the New York* Post *covered the Adams and Patrick. Delano wrote the introduction after a faceoff with Orr.*

"Islander-style hockey is not dead," said the Islanders' veteran forward. "We'll still keep on winning. We'll be back. We've got the veterans who have won it before and we're developing good, young players—Pat LaFontaine, Pat Flatley, Gord Dineen, Paul Boutilier, Duane and Brent Sutter, Greg Gilbert."

What it all adds up to is a most intriguing 1984-85 season.

Is the Islanders' dynasty dead or merely temporarily interrupted? Is Edmonton on the verge of starting a new dynasty?

Edmonton again is the dominant force in the Smythe Division. Calgary, Vancouver and Winnipeg should be the other playoff teams. Los Angeles seems destined for last place.

The Norris Division could produce a four-team race among Minnesota, St. Louis, Chicago and Detroit, leaving a struggling Toronto to again bring up the rear.

The Rangers, Washington and Philadelphia could challenge the Islanders for first place in the strong Patrick Division. Pittsburgh should be able to escape last place. The New Jersey Devils don't seem to stand a chance for anything but last place.

Buffalo, Quebec and Boston appear best in the strong Adams Division, Montreal can't be counted out. That leaves Hartford in the non-playoff position.

Mario Lemieux' first season in the NHL will be followed with much interest. He's the 6-4, 200-pound, 18-year-old center Pittsburgh made No. 1 in the June draft. He set a Canadian junior hockey record last season with a remarkable 133 goals, 149 assists, 282 points in 70 games for the Laval Voisins of the Quebec Junior League.

"Lemieux reminds me of Jean Beliveau," said former NHL player Ron Harris. "He's going to be a great scorer."

The new season reflects the ongoing revolving-door pattern for coaches. Former Montreal and Los Angeles coach Bob Berry takes command in Pittsburgh. Former Flyers' coach Pat Quinn will be behind the bench in Los Angeles. Former NHL player Dan Mahoney is Toronto's new coach. Three men with no NHL background make their coaching debuts: Mike Keenan in Philadelphia, Doug Carpenter in New Jersey and Bill LaForge, the NHL's youngest coach at 32, in Vancouver.

Jacques Lemaire (Montreal) and Barry Long (Winnipeg), both former NHL players, start their first full seasons of coaching; they took over during 1983-84.

Two respected veteran players retired to become general managers: Bobby Clarke in Philadelphia, Rogie Vachon in Los Angeles.

Who will win the Cup this time? The opinion here is that Edmonton will take it again.

BOSTON BRUINS

TEAM DIRECTORY: Pres.-Gov.: Paul A. Mooney; GM: Harry Sinden; Asst. GM: Tom Johnson; Dir. Pub. Rel.: Nate Greenberg; Coach: Gerry Cheevers. Home ice: Boston Garden (14,451; 195' × 83'). Colors: Gold, black and white. Training camp: Danvers, Mass.

SCOUTING REPORT

OFFENSE: When opposing scouts assess the Bruins, they try to find ways to stop the Big Three of Barry Pederson, Rick Middleton and Ray Bourque.

Pederson (39 goals, 116 points), Middleton (47 goals, 105 points), and Bourque (31 goals, 96 points) are the Bruins' most dominant attacking weapons. Combined, they accounted for 38 power-play goals, 18 winning goals and eight shorthanded goals last season.

Boston ranked third in the NHL standings last season, seventh in offense, sixth in power-play efficiency and won the Adams Division race for the sixth time in nine years. The Bruins need more goal-scoring from some of their other forwards. They hope to get it from Tom Fergus, brothers Keith and Bruce Crowder, and Nevin Markwart.

In trading Mike Krushelnyski to Edmonton for Ken Linseman, GM Harry Sinden and coach Gerry Cheevers got the fast, feisty center they were looking for. Linseman had 18 goals, 67 points for the Stanley Cup champions.

When it comes to hard work and relentless fore-checking leading to goals, the Bruins are one of the best in the NHL. Especially in the confines of their small Boston Garden rink. And when he's healthy, veteran Terry O'Reilly is a master of sustaining or starting scoring plays with his energetic checking.

DEFENSE: Forwards who play hard in both ends of the ice (offense and defense) helped make life pleasant for their defensemen and goalies last season.

Bourque is an outstanding two-way defenseman. He can start scoring plays in one end of the ice and stop enemy attacks at the other end with his skill and quick reactions as a defender. Mike O'Connell is a good two-way defenseman, a vigorous worker who excels at blocking shots and breaking up rivals' playmaking patterns. Few defensemen hit as hard or play with the drive and desire of Mike Milbury. Big Gord Kluzak should begin to reach his potential as a defenseman this season. Randy Hillier is a capable defensive defenseman.

The goaltending is in good hands with No. 1 goalie Pete Peeters and backup goalie Doug Keans.

Boston ranked third in defense and had the second-best penalty-killing record last season.

OUTLOOK: Although they were quickly erased in last season's playoffs, the steady but unspectacular, hard-plugging Bruins should be at or near the top of their division and the NHL standings in 1984-85.

Barry Pederson again topped the Bruins in scoring.

BRUIN ROSTER

No.	Player	Pos.	Ht.	Wt.	Born	1983-84	G	A	Pts.	PIM
	John Blum	D	6-3	205	10-8-59/Detroit, Mich.	Edm.-Bos.	1	2	3	32
						Moncton	3	22	25	202
7	Raymond Bourque	D	5-11	200	12-28-60/Montreal, Que.	Boston	31	65	96	57
12	Lyndon Byers	RW	6-1	185	2-29-64/Saskatoon, Sask.	Boston	2	4	6	32
						Regina	32	57	89	154
34	Geoff Courtnall	LW	5-11	165	8-18-62/Victoria, B.C.	Boston	0	0	0	0
						Hershey	14	12	26	51
32	Bruce Crowder	RW	6-0	180	3-25-57/Essex, Ont.	Boston	6	14	20	44
18	Keith Crowder	RW	6-0	180	1-6-59/Windsor, Ont.	Boston	24	28	52	128
	Brian Curran	D	6-4	210	11-5-63/Toronto, Ont.	Hershey	0	2	2	94
						Boston	1	1	2	57
	Dave Donnelly	LW	6-1	190	2-2-63/Edmonton, Alta.	Boston	3	4	7	2
29	Luc Dufour	LW	5-11	179	2-13-63/Chicoutimi, Que.	Boston	6	4	10	47
						Hershey	9	19	28	51
11	Tom Fergus	C	6-0	179	6-16-62/Chicago, Ill.	Boston	25	36	61	12
14	Mike Gillis	RW-C	6-1	195	12-1-58/Toronto, Ont.	Boston	6	11	17	35
						Hershey	8	21	29	13
33	Greg Johnston	RW	6-1	200	1-14-65/Barrie, Ont.	Boston	2	1	3	2
						Toronto (OHL)	38	35	73	67
23	Randy Hillier	D	6-0	178	3-30-60/Toronto, Ont.	Boston	3	12	15	123
11	Steve Kasper	LW	5-8	160	9-28-61/Montreal, Que.	Boston	3	11	14	19
6	Gord Kluzak	D	6-4	220	3-4-64/Climax, Sask.	Boston	10	27	37	135
	Bob Laforest	RW	5-10	190	5-19-63/Sault Ste. Marie, Ont.	N.H.-Hershey	13	23	36	10
13	Ken Linseman	C	5-10	175	8-11-58/Kingston, Ont.	Edmonton	18	49	67	119
14	Craig MacTavish	C	6-0	185	8-15-58/London, Ont.	Boston	20	23	43	35
17	Nevin Markwart	LW	5-10	170	12-9-64/Toronto, Ont.	Boston	14	16	30	121
16	Rick Middleton	RW	5-11	170	12-4-53/Toronto, Ont.	Boston	47	58	105	14
26	Mike Milbury	D	6-1	202	6-17-52/Brighton, Mass.	Boston	2	17	19	159
23	Doug Morrison	C	5-11	175	2-1-60/Vancouver, B.C.	Hershey	38	40	78	42
8	Jim Nill	D-LW	6-0	175	4-11-58/Hanna, Alta.	Van.-Bos.	12	8	20	159
20	Mike O'Connell	D	5-9	180	11-25-55/Chicago, Ill.	Boston	18	42	60	42
24	Terry O'Reilly	RW	6-1	205	6-7-51/Niagara Falls, Ont.	Boston	12	18	30	124
21	Brad Palmer	LW-RW	6-0	180	9-14-61/Ducan, B.C.	Hershey	25	32	57	16
	Dave Pasin	RW	6-1	185	7-8-66/Edmonton, Alta.	Prince Albert	68	54	122	68
10	Barry Pederson	C	5-11	175	3-13-61/Big River, Sask.	Boston	39	77	116	64
	Ray Podloski	C	6-2	190	1-5-66/Edmonton, Alta.	Portland	46	50	96	44
	Dave Reid	LW	6-1	210	5-5-64/Toronto, Ont.	Boston	1	0	1	2
						Peterborough	33	64	97	12
21	Dave Silk	RW	5-11	190	1-1-58/Scituate, Mass.	Boston	13	17	30	64
						Hershey	11	10	21	22

No.	Player	Pos.	Ht.	Wt.	Born		GP	GA	SO	Avg.
31	Doug Keans	G	5-7	185	1-7-58/Pembroke, Ont.	Boston	33	92	2	3.10
30	Mike Moffat	G	5-10	165	2-4-62/Galt, Ont.	Boston	4	15	0	4.84
						Hershey	30	124	0	4.67
1	Pete Peeters	G	6-0	175	8-1-57/Edmonton, Alta.	Boston	50	151	0	3.16

BRUIN PROFILES

BARRY PEDERSON 23 5-11 175   **Forward**

"He has great natural instincts," says veteran Bruins' GM Harry Sinden... Points have climbed from 92, 107, 116 in three NHL seasons... Led Boston in scoring again last season... Center skilled in all aspects of game... Born March 13, 1961, in Big River, Sask.... Can score goals and set up wingers for goals... Seldom makes bad pass or bad play... Wins most of his faceoffs and is good penalty-killer... Had +27 record and seven winning goals last season... Seven-point game (3-4-7) in 1982 tied Bruins' record shared by Bobby Orr and Phil Esposito.

Year	Club	GP	G	A	Pts.
1980-81	Boston	9	1	4	5
1981-82	Boston	80	44	48	92
1982-83	Boston	77	46	61	107
1983-84	Boston	80	39	77	116
	Totals	246	130	190	320

RICK MIDDLETON 30 5-11 170   **Forward**

Tricky Ricky... Man with a thousand moves... Nicknamed "Nifty" because of his knack for making fancy plays... Can do things with a puck and a stick that only Celtics' Bob Cousy could do with a basketball... Has scored 360 career goals... Only three Bruins have scored more in their careers... Born Dec. 4, 1953, in Toronto... Former Bruins' coach Don Cherry, now a TV star in Canada, taught him how to excel defensively... Rangers still laughed at for trading him to Boston in 1976 for fading veteran Ken Hodge... Best one-on-one player in NHL... Has scored 768 points in 741 career games.

Year	Club	GP	G	A	Pts.
1974-75	New York R	47	22	18	40
1975-76	New York R	77	24	26	50
1976-77	Boston	72	20	22	42
1977-78	Boston	79	25	35	60
1978-79	Boston	71	38	48	86
1979-80	Boston	80	40	52	92
1980-81	Boston	80	44	59	103
1981-82	Boston	75	51	43	94
1982-83	Boston	80	49	47	96
1983-84	Boston	80	47	58	105
	Totals	741	360	408	768

RAY BOURQUE 23 5-11 200   Defenseman

Bruins' assistant GM Tom Johnson, a Hall of Fame defenseman, rates Bourque as best defenseman in NHL...Can do it all but is primarily an offensive defenseman who often operates like a forward...Has blazing shot from blue line or slot that goalies fear...Won Calder Trophy in 1980 as Rookie of Year...Born Dec. 28, 1960, in Montreal...Big and strong...Powerful rusher...Play in defensive zone has improved each year...Likes to move from blue line to top of faceoff circles and unload heavy slap shot...Led Boston with +51 record, 340 shots, had career highs in goals, assists, points in 1983-84...First-Team All-Star.

Year	Club	GP	G	A	Pts.
1979-80	Boston	80	17	48	65
1980-81	Boston	67	27	29	56
1981-82	Boston	65	17	49	66
1982-83	Boston	65	22	51	73
1983-84	Boston	78	31	65	96
	Totals	355	114	242	356

MIKE O'CONNELL 28 5-9 180   Defenseman

Has terrific ability when making rapid transition from offense to defense or defense to offense in fast-flowing game...Hard worker who blocks many shots...Good at breaking up opponents' plays in defensive zone and sending Bruins on the attack...Born Nov. 25, 1955, in Chicago...Son of former Cleveland Browns' quarterback Tommy O'Connell...Raised in Boston and starred in sports at Archbishop Walsh High School.

Year	Club	GP	G	A	Pts.
1977-78	Chicago	6	1	1	2
1978-79	Chicago	48	4	22	26
1979-80	Chicago	78	8	22	30
1980-81	Chi-Buf.	82	15	38	53
1981-82	Boston	80	5	34	39
1982-83	Boston	80	14	39	53
1983-84	Boston	75	18	42	60
	Totals	449	65	198	263

PETE PEETERS 27 6-0 175   Goaltender

Needs to prove he can win in playoffs as well as during regular season to establish himself among NHL's best goalies...Has career record of 144-64-25 and is 69-27-11 with Bruins but has subpar 20-19 playoff mark...Moody disposition convinced Flyers to trade him...Has learned rudeness and sullen ways are not admirable qualities...Born Aug. 1, 1957, in Edmonton...Has

textbook style in net... Makes difficult saves look easy... Won
Vezina Trophy in 1982-83 with brilliant 40-11-9 record and 2.36
average... Was 29-16-2 last season, second to Edmonton's Grant
Fuhr in goalie wins.

Year	Club	GP	GA	SO	Avg.
1978-79	Philadelphia	5	16	0	3.43
1979-80	Philadelphia	40	108	1	2.73
1980-81	Philadelphia	40	115	2	2.96
1981-82	Philadelphia	44	160	0	3.71
1982-83	Boston	62	142	8	2.36
1983-84	Boston	50	151	0	3.16
	Totals	241	692	11	2.95

MIKE MILBURY 32 6-1 202   Defenseman

Dedicated team-first player... Fierce competitor... Few defensemen hit as hard as he does... Attended Colgate University on
football scholarship... Often body-checks with impact of a middle
linebacker... "He always plays hard," says Harry Sinden... Born
June 17, 1952, in Brighton, Mass.... An old-school defensive
defenseman... Ten-year veteran whose 1,202 career penalty minutes reflect his robust style of play.

Year	Club	GP	G	A	Pts.
1975-76	Boston	3	0	0	0
1976-77	Boston	77	6	18	24
1977-78	Boston	80	8	30	38
1978-79	Boston	74	1	34	35
1979-80	Boston	72	10	13	23
1980-81	Boston	77	0	18	18
1981-82	Boston	51	2	10	12
1982-83	Boston	78	9	15	24
1983-84	Boston	74	2	17	19
	Totals	586	38	155	193

DAVE SILK 26 5-11 190   Forward

Rangers never gave him the chance he deserved... They demoted
him to minor leagues and traded him to Bruins, who also assigned
him to minor leagues... Proved he belongs in NHL when recalled
from minors last season... Scored 30 points in 35 games... Used
at center on line with Rick Middleton... Not a great skater but a
vigorous worker and checker who makes things happen... Born
Jan. 1, 1958, in Scituate, Mass.... Capable of playing all three
forward positions... Cousin of teammate Mike Milbury...
Grandson of Hal Janvrin, who played major-league baseball from
1911-1922... Starred at Boston University... Assisted on two

goals when 1980 U.S. Olympic team upset Russia, 4-3, enroute to gold medal.

Year	Club	GP	G	A	Pts.
1979–80	New York R	2	0	0	0
1980–81	New York R	59	14	12	26
1981–82	New York R	64	15	20	35
1982–83	New York R	16	1	1	2
1983–84	Boston	35	13	17	30
	Totals	176	43	50	93

TERRY O'REILLY 33 6-1 205   **Forward**

Plagued by injuries last two seasons...Not quite the dominant force he has been but still the heart and soul of Bruins' aggressive style of play...Wears captain's letter C...Loved by Boston Garden fans...Worked hard to upgrade skill level and now is in 16th NHL season...Born June 7, 1951, in Niagara Falls, Ont....Never fails to give his best...Inspires teammates with feisty, rugged play...Needs nine goals to reach 200 for career...Has 1,927 career penalty minutes...Has waged profusion of classic fights with respected fighters such as Clark Gillies and Garry Howatt.

Year	Club	GP	G	A	Pts.
1971-72	Boston	1	1	0	1
1972-73	Boston	72	5	22	27
1973-74	Boston	76	11	24	35
1974-75	Boston	68	15	20	35
1975-76	Boston	80	23	27	50
1976-77	Boston	79	14	41	55
1977-78	Boston	77	29	61	90
1978-79	Boston	80	26	51	77
1979-80	Boston	71	19	42	61
1980-81	Boston	77	8	35	43
1981-82	Boston	70	22	30	52
1982-83	Boston	19	6	14	20
1983-84	Boston	58	12	18	30
	Totals	828	191	385	576

KEITH CROWDER 25 6-0 180   **Forward**

Like the Sutters and Hunters, forms another NHL brother combination with teammate Bruce Crowder...Right wing who can score, check and hit hard...Not fancy or flashy...Patrols his wing efficiently...Plays grinding game, likes to muck for puck in corners...Born Jan. 6, 1959, in Windsor, Ont....He and brother Bruce are Bruins' first brother combination since Bill and Max Quackenbush in 1950-51...Has amassed 100 or more penalty minutes in four NHL seasons.

Year	Club	GP	G	A	Pts.
1978-79	Birmingham (WHA) ..	5	1	0	1
1980-81	Boston	47	13	12	25
1981-82	Boston	71	23	21	44
1982-83	Boston	74	35	39	74
1983-84	Boston	63	24	28	52
	NHL Totals	255	95	100	195
	WHA Totals	5	1	0	1

KEN LINSEMAN 26 5-10 175   Forward

After ordinary 1983-84 season (18 goals, 67 points), he had an outstanding playoff with 10 goals as center in Oilers' fourth line...But now he's a Bruin, traded for forward Mike Krushelnyski...Very quick skater, good playmaker, strong penalty-killer...Joined team in August, 1982, from Philadelphia Flyers in three-way deal that involved Hartford Whalers...Doesn't like nickname "The Rat" although he has a rodent tattooed on his ankle...Born Aug. 11, 1958, in Kingston, Ont. ...Played junior hockey in his hometown, then signed with Birmingham in WHA in 1977...Flyers purchased him from Birmingham in 1978 and he had 79 and 92 points in two best Philly seasons.

Year	Club	GP	G	A	Pts.
1977-78	Birmingham (WHA) ..	71	38	38	76
1978-79	Philadelphia	30	5	20	25
1979-80	Philadelphia	80	22	57	79
1980-81	Philadelphia	51	17	30	47
1981-82	Philadelphia	79	24	68	92
1982-83	Edmonton..........	72	33	42	75
1983-84	Edmonton..........	72	18	49	67
	NHL Totals	384	119	266	385
	WHA Totals	71	38	38	76

GORD KLUZAK 20 6-4 220   Defenseman

Bruins were second-guessed for selecting him as No. 1 draft choice in 1982 over scoring star Brian Bellows...Struggled at first but is developing into solid all-around defenseman...Bruins are bringing him along slowly...Big things expected from big man in 1984-85...Born March 4, 1964, in Climax, Sask....Good passer...Size makes opposing forwards nervous...Could use size to greater advantage and do more body-checking . . . Has good mobility for big fellow and has been used at forward.

Year	Club	GP	G	A	Pts.
1982–83	Boston	70	1	6	7
1983–84	Boston	80	10	27	37
	Totals	150	11	33	44

COACH GERRY CHEEVERS: Gives outward impression of being as relaxed and unflustered behind Bruins' bench as coach as he was as their goaltender for many years . . . Has maintained winning tradition in Boston with 179-102-29 coaching record in four seasons . . . Uses his players well . . . They respect his knowledge of game . . . Treats his players like men, not kids . . . Born Dec. 7, 1940, in St. Catherines, Ont. . . . Starred in goal when Big Bad Bruins with Phil Esposito and Bobby Orr dominated NHL and won Stanley Cups in 1970 and 1972 . . . Played his best games under intense playoff pressure . . . Had 2.69 goals-against average in playoffs . . . Retired as goalie after playing in NHL from 1962 to 1980 with 230-94-74 record . . . Has sharp sense of humor . . . Nicknamed "Cheesy" during playing days . . . Operates successful Gerald M. Cheevers Stables . . . As successful in thoroughbred horse racing as he's been in hockey.

GREATEST ROOKIE

Who else but No. 4 . . . Bobby Orr?

Considered by many veteran hockey observers to have been the greatest player in NHL history, Orr burst upon the NHL scene in 1966, a shy, 18-year-old rookie with a boyish face and a blond crewcut.

Pro scouts had been following him since he was 14. He was a sensation starting with his first NHL game. He won the Calder

Trophy in 1966-67 as Rookie of the Year and launched a gloriously successful career.

Few players could dominate a game by themselves as Orr could. He had stickhandling moves seldom seen before, specializing in end-to-end rushes. He revolutionized modern hockey as an offensive defenseman who could score more goals and points than most forwards.

"Bobby was amazing . . . there will never be another one like him," said former Bruins' teammate Phil Esposito.

Orr did things no defenseman before him had done by leading the NHL in scoring. He scored 100 or more points five times. He won the Norris Trophy a record eight times as the NHL's most outstanding defenseman. He scored more goals and points in his career than any other defenseman. He still holds the season scoring record for defensemen; 46 goals, 102 assists, 139 points.

Sadly, Orr's great career lasted only nine full seasons. He was forced into premature retirement because his fragile, surgically repaired knees gave out on him. Orr left the Bruins, signed as a free agent with Chicago, but played for the Black Hawks for only two seasons before forced to hang up his skates at the end of 1978-79. His damaged knees limited him to only 36 games in his last three NHL seasons.

The Bruins gave him a night at Boston Garden and retired uniform No. 4. Elected to the Hockey Hall of Fame in 1979, Orr, now 36, lives in the New England area with his wife and family. A successful businessman, he's no longer directly involved with the NHL.

ALL-TIME BRUIN LEADERS

GOALS: Phil Esposito, 76, 1970-71
ASSISTS: Bobby Orr, 102, 1970-71
POINTS: Phil Esposito, 152, 1970-71
SHUTOUTS: Hal Winkler, 15, 1927-28

BUFFALO SABRES

TEAM DIRECTORY: Chairman: Seymour H. Knox III; Pres.: Northrup R. Knox; GM-Coach: Scotty Bowman; Dir. Pub. Rel.: Gerry Helper. Home ice: Memorial Auditorium (16,433; 196′ × 85′). Colors: Blue, white and gold. Training camp: Lake Placid and Buffalo, N.Y.

Dave Andreychuk was Sabres' second-leading scorer.

SCOUTING REPORT

OFFENSE: Like the Bruins, the Sabres count upon three or four players to provide most of the scoring. They, too, could use greater scoring from other players.

Veteran Gilbert Perreault, Dave Andreychuk, Mike Foligno and offensive defenseman Phil Housley produced 132 goals last season, 37 of them on power plays, 25 of them game-winners.

More scoring production from Real Cloutier, Lindy Ruff, Sean McKenna, Gilles Hamel, Paul Cyr and Ric Seiling would provide the scoring balance the Sabres need. Rookies John Tucker and 6-5 Adam Creighton, son of former NHL forward Dave Creighton, could be what GM-coach Scotty Bowman is looking for in 1984-85.

Buffalo ranked eighth in offense last season, fourth in the NHL, but flopped in the playoffs. Led by the play of defensive forward Craig Ramsay, Buffalo finished third in penalty-killing. The power play must improve; it was a poor 11th last season.

DEFENSE: Good goaltending and few mistakes by a steady corps of defensemen enabled the Sabres to have the second-best defensive record in the NHL last season.

Rookie Tom Barrasso had a sensational first season in the NHL, sharing the goaltending with veteran Bob Sauve. Mike Ramsey emerged as one of the league's best defensemen. Hard-hitting Larry Playfair, Bill Hajt and Hannu Virta play vital roles as defensemen. Housley is the Sabres' best all-around defenseman.

OUTLOOK: With Bowman in command, you know the Sabres will be somewhere near the top this season. They are working on a streak of 10 consecutive winning records.

SABRE PROFILES

GILBERT PERREAULT 33 6-0 205   Forward
Almost as much a part of Buffalo legend as Niagara Falls or the old Buffalo-head nickel . . . Sole surviving original 1970 expansion Sabre . . . Still a gracefully effective, scoring, playmaking center with deceptive one-on-one moves . . . Has led Sabres' scoring 10 times in 14 seasons . . . Needs 48 goals to reach 500 for career . . . Born Nov. 13, 1950, in Victoriaville, Que. . . . Better all-around player than he was early in career . . . As respected by peers

SABRE ROSTER

No.	Player	Pos.	Ht.	Wt.	Born	1983-84	G	A	Pts.	PIM
25	Dave Andreychuk	C	6-3	205	9-29-63/Hamilton, Ont.	Buffalo	38	42	80	42
8	Real Cloutier	RW	5-10	185	7-30-56/St. Emile, Que.	Buffalo	24	36	60	25
	Adam Creighton	C	6-5	202	6-2-65/Burlington, Ont.	Buffalo	2	2	4	4
						Ottawa	42	49	91	79
	Randy Cunneyworth	C	6-0	177	5-10-61/Etobichoke, Ont.	Rochester	18	17	35	85
18	Paul Cyr	LW	5-11	185	10-31-63/Pt. Alberoni, B.C.	Buffalo	16	27	43	52
25	Mal Davis	LW	5-11	180	10-10-56/Lockeport, N.S.	Buffalo	2	1	3	4
						Rochester	55	48	103	53
	Jeff Eatough	RW	5-9	168	6-2-63/Toronto, Ont.	Rochester	1	5	6	5
31	Dave Fenyves	D	5-11	188	4-29-60/Dunnville, Ont.	Buffalo	0	4	4	9
						Rochester	3	16	19	55
	Ron Fischer	D	6-2	195	4-12-59/Merritt, B.C.	Rochester	10	32	42	94
17	Mike Foligno	RW	6-2	195	1-29-59/Sudbury, Ont.	Buffalo	32	31	63	151
24	Bill Hajt	D	6-3	204	11-18-51/Borden, Sask.	Buffalo	3	24	27	32
9	Gilles Hamel	RW	6-0	183	12-15-57/Asbestos, Que.	Buffalo	21	23	44	37
66	Phil Housley	D	5-10	180	3-9-64/St. Paul, Minn.	Buffalo	31	46	77	33
	Val James	LW-D	6-2	203	2-14-57/Ocala, Fla.	Rochester	1	2	3	122
44	Jerry Korab	D	6-3	218	9-15-48/Sault Ste. Marie, Ont.	Buffalo	2	9	11	82
						Rochester	0	4	4	2
	Normand Lacombe	RW	5-11	190	10-18-64/—	Rochester	10	16	26	45
15	Yvon Lambert	LW	6-2	200	5-20-50/Drummondville, Que.	Rochester	27	43	70	14
12	Sean McKenna	C	6-0	186	3-17-62/Asbestos, Que.	Buffalo	20	10	30	45
14	Mike Moller	RW	6-0	189	6-16-62/Red Deer, Alta.	Buffalo	5	11	16	27
26	Steve Patrick	RW	6-4	206	2-4-61/Winnipeg, Man.	Buffalo	1	4	5	6
						Rochester	8	14	22	33
11	Gil Perreault	C	6-0	205	11-13-50/Victoriaville, Que.	Buffalo	31	59	90	32
20	Brent Peterson	C	6-0	190	2-15-58/Calgary, Alta.	Buffalo	9	12	21	52
27	Larry Playfair	D	6-4	225	6-23-58/Fort St. James, B.C.	Buffalo	5	11	16	209
10	Craig Ramsay	RW	5-10	175	3-17-51/Toronto, Ont.	Buffalo	9	17	26	17
5	Mike Ramsey	D	6-3	195	12-3-60/Minneapolis, Minn.	Buffalo	9	22	31	82
4	Mark Renaud	D	5-11	180	2-21-59/Windsor, Ont.	Buffalo	1	3	4	6
						Rochester	9	33	42	48
	Geordie Robertson	C	6-0	163	8-1-59/Victoria, B.C.	Rochester	37	54	91	103
22	Lindy Ruff	LW-D	6-2	190	2-17-60/Warburg, Alta.	Buffalo	14	31	45	101
16	Ric Seiling	RW	6-1	178	12-15-57/Elmira, Ont.	Buffalo	13	22	35	42
	Kai Suikkanen	LW	6-2	207	6-29-59/Finland	Rochester	7	10	17	2
	John Tucker	C	6-0	184	9-29-64/Windsor, Ont.	Buffalo	12	4	16	4
						Kitchener	40	60	100	25
21	Claude Verret	C	5-10	164	4-20-63/Lachine, Que.	Buffalo	2	5	7	2
						Rochester	39	51	90	4
3	Hannu Virta	D	6-0	176	3-22-63/Finland	Buffalo	6	30	36	12
19	Jim Wiemer	LW	6-4	197	1-9-61/Sudbury, Ont.	Buffalo	5	15	20	48
						Rochester	4	11	15	11

No.	Player	Pos.	Ht.	Wt.	Born		GP	GA	SO	Avg.
30	Tom Barrasso	G	6-3	195	3-31-65/Boston, Mass.	Buffalo	42	117	2	2.84
1	Jacques Cloutier	G	5-7	155	1-3-60/Noranda, Que.	Rochester	51	172	1	3.63
	Phil Myre	G	6-1	185	11-1-48/St. A. deBellevue, Que.	Rochester	33	104	4	3.46
28	Bob Sauve	G	5-8	165	6-17-55/Ste. Genevieve, Que.	Buffalo	40	138	0	3.49

as he is by fans...Highest scorer in Sabres' history...No. 1 draft choice in 1970...Finished last season with +19 record, 18.8 shooting percentage, seven game-winning goals.

Year	Club	GP	G	A	Pts.
1970-71	Buffalo	78	38	34	72
1971-72	Buffalo	76	26	48	74
1972-73	Buffalo	78	28	60	88
1973-74	Buffalo	55	18	33	51
1974-75	Buffalo	68	39	57	96
1975-76	Buffalo	80	44	69	113
1976-77	Buffalo	80	39	56	95
1977-78	Buffalo	79	41	48	89
1978-79	Buffalo	79	27	58	85
1979-80	Buffalo	80	40	66	106
1980-81	Buffalo	56	20	39	59
1981-82	Buffalo	62	31	42	73
1982-83	Buffalo	77	30	46	76
1983-84	Buffalo	73	31	59	90
	Totals.............	1021	452	715	1167

DAVE ANDREYCHUK 21 6-3 205   Forward

Establishing himself as rising young star as power forward-center...A tribute to GM-coach Scotty Bowman's ability to acquire and develop outstanding young players...Has clever moves and speed for a big man...Defenders find him difficult to check or neutralize in offensive zone because of size, strength and skating balance...Born Sept. 29, 1963, in Hamilton, Ont....Adept at scoring from close range and using size to screen goalies or out-muscle opponents in front of net or in corners...Scored 38 goals, 80 points, seven game-winning goals, scoring on 21.3 percent of shots last season.

Year	Club	GP	G	A	Pts.
1982–83	Buffalo	43	14	23	37
1983–84	Buffalo	78	38	42	80
	Totals.............	121	52	65	117

MIKE FOLIGNO 25 6-2 195   Forward

Can play it anyway you want...Tough and willing to fight...Rock-hard worker along boards or in corners...Capable of scoring frequent goals...Sabres made smart move to get him in six-player trade with Detroit in 1981...Willing to check as well as attack...Born Jan. 29, 1959, in Sudbury, Ont....Right wing who was Detroit's No. 1 draft pick in 1979...Has averaged 130 penalty minutes a season in NHL career.

Year	Club	GP	G	A	Pts.
1979-80	Detroit	80	36	35	71
1980-81	Detroit	80	28	35	63
1981-82	Det-Buf.	82	33	44	77
1982-83	Buffalo	66	22	25	47
1983-84	Buffalo	70	32	31	63
	Totals	378	151	170	321

MIKE RAMSEY 23 6-3 195   **Defenseman**

Outstanding all-around defenseman but doesn't always get credit he deserves because he prefers to play a defensive defenseman's role...American-born athlete chosen first in 1979 draft by Sabres...Played college hockey at University of Minnesota under Ranger coach Herb Brooks...Played for Brooks' 1980 "Miracle on Ice" gold-medal Olympians at Lake Placid...Born Dec. 3, 1960, in Minneapolis...Seldom caught out of position or beaten one-on-one in defensive zone...Knows how to find forwards for rush-forming breakout passes....Outstanding shot-blocking defenseman who once blocked nine shots in game against Rangers.

Year	Club	GP	G	A	Pts.
1979-80	Buffalo	13	1	6	7
1980-81	Buffalo	72	3	14	17
1981-82	Buffalo	80	7	23	30
1982-83	Buffalo	77	8	30	38
1983-84	Buffalo	72	9	22	31
	Totals	314	28	95	123

TOM BARRASSO 19 6-3 195   **Goaltender**

Skated out of high school into NHL stardom...Won job as NHL goalie at 18 and had remarkable rookie season...Compiled goaltending record of 26-12-3, finished second in NHL with 2.84 goals-against average, fifth in wins, third in save percentage..."He played with the poise and maturity of a veteran," says former Sabres' assistant coach and NHL star Red Berenson..."I knew I could play in the NHL but it went much better for me than I imagined it would," says confident, young star who was born May 31, 1965, in Boston....Allowed only 49 goals in 46 games at Massachusetts' Acton-Boxboro High School...Fifth pick in 1983 draft...Shunned chance to play for U.S. Olympic team so he could play in NHL..."The kid reminds me of Ken Dryden," says former coach Fred Shero...Won Calder Trophy as NHL Rookie of the Year and Vezina Trophy as league's most valuable goaltender.

Year	Club	GP	GA	SO	Avg.
1983–84	Buffalo	42	117	2	2.84

BOB SAUVE 29 5-8 165   Goaltender

Veteran shared goaltending with rookie Barrasso...Proven quality NHL goalie with 117-91-40 career record...Seldom gives up so-called bad goals...Buffalo's No. 1 draft pick in 1975...Had back-to-back shutouts of Montreal in 1983 playoffs...Born June 17, 1955, in Ste. Genevieve, Que....Shared Vezina Trophy in 1979-80 with Don Edwards, led NHL with 2.36 average...Has lightening-fast reflexes...Skilled at stopping flurries of shots ...Sabres reacquired him from Detroit.

Year	Club	GP	GA	SO	Avg.
1976-77	Buffalo	4	11	0	3.59
1977-78	Buffalo	11	20	0	2.50
1978-79	Buffalo	29	100	0	3.73
1979-80	Buffalo	32	74	4	2.36
1980-81	Buffalo	35	111	2	3.17
1981-82	Buf-Det	55	200	0	3.84
1982-83	Buffalo	54	179	1	3.45
1983-84	Buffalo	40	138	0	3.49
	Totals	260	833	7	3.36

PHIL HOUSLEY 20 5-10 180   Defenseman

Like Barrasso, another of the increasing number of young Americans achieving star status in NHL...Moved from Minnesota's South St. Paul High School into NHL in 1982-83...Rangers' Herb Brooks predicts superstardom for sandy-haired defenseman...Outstanding skater with quick acceleration who likes to rush puck up ice...Good passer and pass-receiver while on the move...Born March 9, 1964, in St. Paul, Minn....Sabres sometimes use him at center because of his offensive skills...Needs to sharpen puckhandling in defensive zone to reduce giveaways...Occasionally gambles too much on offense...Led Sabres with 234 shots . . . Scored on 13.2 percent of shots, high mark for a defenseman.

Year	Club	GP	G	A	Pts.
1982-83	Buffalo	77	19	47	66
1983-84	Buffalo	75	31	46	77
	Totals	152	50	93	143

CRAIG RAMSAY 33 5-10 175   Forward

One of hockey's most durable, dependable players . . . Did not miss playing in a game for Sabres for almost 10 years from 1974 to 1983 . . . Broken bone in foot finally ended his consecutive-game playing streak at 776, second to Garry Unger's NHL record of playing in 914 consecutive games . . . One of hockey's best defensive forwards . . . Annually a candidate for Frank Selke Trophy as NHL's best defensive forward . . . Born March 17, 1951, in Toronto, Ont. . . . Plays hard but clean style . . . Played entire 1973-74 season without incurring a penalty . . . Twenty-seven career shorthanded goals indicate he's a gifted penalty-killer . . . Needs nine games to reach 1,000 for NHL career . . . Smart player who will make a good coach.

Year	Club	GP	G	A	Pts.
1971-72	Buffalo	57	6	10	16
1972-73	Buffalo	76	11	17	28
1973-74	Buffalo	78	20	26	46
1974-75	Buffalo	80	26	38	64
1975-76	Buffalo	80	22	49	71
1976-77	Buffalo	80	20	41	61
1977-78	Buffalo	80	28	43	71
1978-79	Buffalo	80	26	31	57
1979-80	Buffalo	80	21	39	60
1980-81	Buffalo	80	24	35	59
1981-82	Buffalo	80	16	35	51
1982-83	Buffalo	64	11	18	29
1983-84	Buffalo	76	9	17	26
	Totals	991	240	399	639

RIC SEILING 26 6-1 178   Forward

Unsung hero who does unnoticed things well that lead to victories . . . Two-way right wing who excels in both ends of ice . . . Steady but unspectacular . . . Skilled penalty-killer and checker . . . Did not have good scoring production last season and capable of scoring more than he has...Born Dec. 15, 1957, in Elmira, Ont....Brother of former Ranger defenseman Rod Seiling...As a kid, used to visit older brother in Ranger dressing room...Works in offseason with family-owned harness racing business in Ontario.

Year	Club	GP	G	A	Pts.
1977-78	Buffalo	80	19	19	38
1978-79	Buffalo	78	20	22	42
1979-80	Buffalo	80	25	35	60
1980-81	Buffalo	74	30	27	57
1981-82	Buffalo	57	22	25	47
1982-83	Buffalo	75	19	22	41
1983-84	Buffalo	78	13	22	35
	Totals	522	148	172	320

LARRY PLAYFAIR 26 6-4 225   Defenseman

Opposing forwards never enjoy playing against big, bruising defenseman...Specializes in handing out bumps and bruises with robust, jarring bodychecks...Rivals tread lightly when entering his area of ice with or without puck..."He's one of the toughest hitters in the league," says Devils' Bob MacMillan...Born June 23, 1958, in Fort St. James, British Columbia...Occasionally becomes carried away with overly reckless physical play...Has led Sabres in penalty minutes last five seasons.

Year	Club	GP	G	A	Pts.
1978–79	Buffalo	26	0	3	3
1979–80	Buffalo	79	2	10	12
1980–81	Buffalo	75	3	9	12
1981–82	Buffalo	77	6	10	16
1982–83	Buffalo	79	4	13	17
1983–84	Buffalo	76	5	11	16
	Totals	412	20	56	76

COACH SCOTTY BOWMAN: Most powerful GM-coach active in hockey...Never has had losing record in NHL coaching career starting in 1967-68 with expansion St. Louis Blues...His teams have finished first 10 times...Coached Montreal to five Stanley Cup championships...Needs only 11 more regular-season coaching wins to become coach with most wins in NHL history...Has magnificent record of 680-274-193...Dick Irvin compiled best NHL coaching record (690-521-

226) from 1930 to 1955 with Toronto, Chicago, Montreal . . . His 111-69 playoff coaching record is all-time best in NHL . . . With 791 coaching wins in seasonal and playoff competition, has moved head of Irvin (790) in combined career coaching wins . . . Born Sept. 18, 1933, in Montreal . . . Shrewd general manager in acquiring good draft choices and making trades . . . "He's the best around . . . You just can't beat Scotty when it comes to changing lines," says Tom McVie . . . Stern, demanding coach . . . Not always liked by his players but always respected.

GREATEST ROOKIE

Gilbert Perreault was only 19, a shy French-Canadian who spoke little English, when Buffalo selected him as the first player chosen in the 1970 expansion-year draft.

He won the Calder Trophy as Rookie of the Year in 1970-71 and now, almost 15 years later, still is playing outstanding hockey for the Sabres.

Perreault speaks English with far greater skill than when he entered the NHL, but little else has changed. The tall, graceful center remains a gifted skater, stickhandler, playmaker and goal-scorer.

He is the Sabres' captain, Buffalo's all-time leading scorer, perhaps the city's best known professional athlete.

ALL-TIME SABRE LEADERS

GOALS: Danny Gare, 56, 1979-80
ASSISTS: Gil Perreault, 69, 1975-76
POINTS: Gil Perreault, 113, 1975-76
SHUTOUTS: Don Edwards, 5, 1977-78

HARTFORD WHALERS

TEAM DIRECTORY: Managing Gen. Partner: Howard Baldwin; Pres.-GM: Emile Francis; Dir. Pub. Rel.: Phil Langan; Coach: Jack Evans. Home ice: Hartford Civic Center (14,817; 200' × 85'). Colors: Green, blue and white. Training camp: Hartford, Ct.

SCOUTING REPORT

OFFENSE: Not nearly enough of it. The Whalers still have problems moving the puck from their end zone, through neutral ice and into the attacking zone. They have some decent shooters but the passing and playmaking is not always there. Too many unfinished scoring chances hurt the Whalers.

Hartford's offense was a poor 17th last season. Surprisingly, the power play ranked fifth. If coach Jack (Tex) Evans' Whalers played as well at even strength as they do with a manpower advantage, they might have challenged Montreal for fourth place and a playoff position in 1983-84.

As rookie, Sylvain Turgeon made 40 goals, 32 assists.

Mark Johnson (35 goals, 87 points); Ron Francis (23 goals, 83 points), and rookie Sylvain Turgeon (40 goals, 72 points) are Hartford's leading scorers. Bob Crawford (36 goals) had a fine season. Francis is capable of scoring close to 40 goals. Ray Neufeld (27 goals, 69 points) could do better.

DEFENSE: Not nearly enough of it, either. The Whalers lack a dominant defenseman who can make the big plays and the defense caves in under forechecking pressure and commits numerous giveaways.

GM Emile Francis (no relation to Ron Francis) would like to acquire a Denis Potvin-type defenseman but it's not easy to do.

Former Ranger Scot Kleinendorst should add something to the defense. So should rookie Sylvain Cote, the Whalers' No. 1 selection in the 1984 draft. Other prominent defensemen are Risto Siltanen, Joel Quenneville, Chris Kotsopoulos, Richie Dunn and Marty Howe. Ed Hospodar became a free agent when he and the Whalers couldn't come to terms.

Goalie Greg Millen needs more defensive support from his teammates as much as he needs a capable No. 2 goalie to provide occasional relief.

OUTLOOK: Showing signs of improvement under Emile Francis' expert direction but not enough to escape from last place and gain a playoff position in 1984-85.

WHALER PROFILES

MARK JOHNSON 27 5-9 165   Forward
Gained respect throughout NHL after having his best all-around season in 1983-84 . . . Led Whalers in scoring . . . Leadership qualities led to his selection as Hartford captain . . . Offsets lack of size with quick reactions and clever moves . . . Born Sept. 22, 1957, in Madison, Wis . . . . Has developed into multiskilled center . . . Smooth-passing playmaker . . . A star with 1980 gold-medal U.S. Olympic team . . . Son of Calgary coach Bob Johnson . . . Played for father at University of Wisconsin.

Year	Club	GP	G	A	Pts.
1979-80	Pittsburgh	17	3	5	8
1980-81	Pittsburgh	73	10	23	33
1981-82	Pitt-Minn	56	12	13	25
1982-83	Hartford	73	31	38	69
1983-84	Hartford	79	35	52	87
	Totals	298	91	131	222

WHALER ROSTER

No.	Player	Pos.	Ht.	Wt.	Born	1983-84	G	A	Pts.	PIM
34	Reid Bailey	D	6-2	200	5-28-56/Toronto, Ont.	Hartford	0	0	0	25
						St.C-Bing.	2	19	21	168
31	Dan Bourbonnais	LW	5-11	180	3-6-62/Winnipeg, Man.	Hartford	0	16	16	0
						Binghamton	16	32	48	40
	Jack Brownschidle	D	6-1	180	10-2-55/Buffalo, N.Y.	St. L.-Hart.	3	9	12	29
	Sylvain Cote	D	6-0	175	1-19-66/Quebec City, Que.	Quebec (QHL)	15	50	65	89
25	Bobby Crawford	RW	5-11	177	4-6-59/Belleville, Ont.	Hartford	36	25	61	32
18	Mike Crombeen	RW	5-11	192	7-16-57/Sarnia, Ont.	Hartford	1	4	5	25
26	Tony Currie	C-RW	5-11	166	12-12-57/Sydney, N.S.	Van.-Hart.	15	19	34	6
						Fredericton	6	11	17	16
	Kevin Dineen	LW	5-10	176	10-28-63/Quebec City, Que.	Can. Olymp.	–	–	–	–
4	Richie Dunn	D	6-0	192	5-12-57/Boston, Mass.	Hartford	5	20	25	30
15	Normand Dupont	LW	5-10	185	2-5-57/St. Michel, Que.	Hartford	7	15	22	12
						Binghamton	15	24	39	6
	Ray Ferraro	C	5-10	165	8-23-64/Trail, B.C.	Brandon	108	84	192	84
10	Ron Francis	C	5-11	175	3-1-63/Sault Ste. Marie, Ont.	Hartford	23	60	83	46
33	Mark Fusco	D	5-9	180	3-12-61/Woburn, Mass.	Hartford	0	4	4	2
	Mike Hoffman	LW	5-11	186	2-26-63/Cambridge, Ont.	Binghamton	11	13	24	92
27	Marty Howe	D	6-1	195	2-18-54/Detroit, Mich.	Hartford	0	11	11	34
	Randy Gilhen	LW	5-11	188	1-13-63/Winnipeg, Man.	Binghamton	8	12	20	72
	Dave Jensen	D	6-0	175	8-19-65/Newton, Mass.	U.S. Olymp.	–	–	–	–
12	Mark Johnson	C	5-9	165	9-22-57/Madison, Wis.	Hartford	35	52	87	27
	Scot Kleinendorst	D	6-3	205	1-16-60/Grand Rapids, Minn.	Rangers	0	2	2	35
						Tulsa	4	5	9	4
24	Chris Kotsopoulos	D	6-3	215	11-27-58/Toronto, Ont.	Hartford	5	13	18	118
5	Pierre Lacroix	D	5-11	185	4-11-59/Quebec City, Que.	Hartford	Injured—Did not play			
11	Paul Lawless	LW	5-11	181	7-2-64/Scarborough, Ont.	Hartford	0	3	3	0
						Windsor	31	49	80	26
	Brent Loney	D	6-0½	165	5-25-64/Cornwall, Ont.	Cornwall	24	38	62	56
	Paul MacDermid	RW	6-1	209	4-14-63/Chesley, Ont.	Hartford	0	1	1	0
						Binghamton	31	30	61	130
14	Greg Malone	C	6-0	190	3-8-56/Fredericton, N.B.	Hartford	17	37	54	56
32	Mike McDougal	RW	6-2	206	4-30-58/Port Huron, Mich.	Binghamton	11	14	25	56
17	Ray Neufeld	RW	6-3	215	4-13-59/St. Boniface, Man.	Hartford	27	42	69	97
6	Mark Paterson	D	6-0	195	2-22-64/Nepean, Ont.	Hartford	2	0	2	4
						Ottawa	8	16	24	114
38	Randy Pierce	RW	6-0	180	11-23-57/Arnprior, Ont.	Hartford	6	3	9	9
						Binghamton	21	24	45	41
3	Joel Quenneville	D	6-1	195	9-15-58/Windsor, Ont.	Hartford	5	8	13	95
32	Torrie Robertson	LW	5-11	184	8-2-61/Victoria, B.C.	Hartford	7	14	21	198
	Brad Shaw	D	5-10	169	4-28-64/Kitchener, Ont.	Ottawa	11	71	82	75
8	Risto Siltanen	D	5-9	180	10-31-58/Finland	Hartford	15	38	53	34
	Stu Smith	D	6-1	185	3-17-60/Toronto, Ont.	Binghamton	3	22	25	95
7	Steve Stoyanovich	LW	6-2	205	5-2-57/London, Ont.	Hartford	3	5	8	11
						Binghamton	11	8	19	0
15	Dave Tippett	C	5-10	175	8-25-61/Moosomin, Sask.	Hartford	4	2	6	2
16	Sylvain Turgeon	C	6-1	190	1-17-65/Noranda, Que.	Hartford	40	32	72	56
28	Ross Yates	C	5-11	170	6-18-59/Montreal, Que.	Binghamton	35	73	108	82
34	Mike Zuke	C	6-0	180	4-16-54/Sault Ste. Marie, Ont.	Hartford	6	23	29	36

							GP	GA	SO	Avg.
	Rollie Boutin	G	5-9	179	11-6-57/Westlock, Alta.	Binghamton	45	188	3	4.30
	Paul Fricker	G	6-0	175	10-20-60/Toronto, Ont.	Binghamton	30	149	0	5.16
30	Greg Millen	G	5-9	175	6-25-57/Toronto, Ont.	Hartford	60	221	2	3.70
1	Ed Staniowski	G	5-9	170	7-7-55/Moose Jaw, Sask.	Hartford	19	82	0	4.56

RON FRANCIS 21 5-11 175   **Forward**

Has ability to become one of best centers in NHL...Just needs to gain more experience and maturity...Has collected 241 points in first 210 NHL games...Impresses fans and rivals with energetic style of play...Born March 1, 1963, in Sault Ste. Marie, Ont....Gifted playmaking center...Whalers believe he has potential to score more goals.

Year	Club	GP	G	A	Pts.
1981-82	Hartford	59	25	43	68
1982-83	Hartford	79	31	59	90
1983-84	Hartford	72	23	60	83
	Totals	210	79	162	241

SYLVAIN TURGEON 19 6-1 190   **Forward**

Crafy GM Emile Francis made smart move choosing husky left wing as Whalers' first draft choice in 1983...Had outstanding rookie season...Led NHL rookies with 40 goals, 237 shots on goal...Produced 18 goals on power plays...Born Jan. 17, 1965, in Noranda, Que....Scouts started following him as 11-year-old youth-league player...Has good moves through traffic to net ...Deadeye shooter from blue line, faceoff circles or slot...Can only get better.

Year	Club	GP	G	A	Pts.
1983–84	Hartford	76	40	32	72

GREG MILLEN 27 5-9 175   **Goaltender**

Doesn't get recognition he deserves because he's played for losing teams in NHL...Rival shooters rate him highly as quality goalie...Accustomed to facing barrage of shots for defensively weak Whalers...Had best goals-against average in four years last season...Born June 25, 1957, in Toronto...Occasionally has habit of making difficult saves but surrendering goals on routine shots...Musically talented athlete who stays loose in net by rocking back and forth in crease to arena organist's tunes...Signed by Hartford as Pittsburgh free agent...Hard work doesn't faze him . . . One of hockey's best skaters among goalies . . . Has career record of 103-154-45.

Year	Club	GP	GA	SO	Avg.
1978-79	Pittsburgh	28	86	2	3.37
1979-80	Pittsburgh	44	157	2	3.64
1980-81	Pittsburgh	63	258	0	4.16
1981-82	Hartford	55	229	0	4.29
1982-83	Hartford	60	282	1	4.81
	Totals	250	1012	5	4.17

RAY NEUFELD 25 6-3 215   Forward

Came into his own last season with 27-goal, 69-point performance . . . Played in all 80 games for second consecutive season . . . Scored five winning goals . . . Right wing who often plays best games against strongest opponents . . . Born April 15, 1959, in St. Boniface, Manitoba . . . Tough, rugged forward who likes bump and grind style of play . . . Skilled at winning battles for pucks in corners, along boards, in front of net . . . Good at converting rebounds into goals.

Year	Club	GP	G	A	Pts.
1979-80	Hartford	8	1	0	1
1980-81	Hartford	52	5	10	15
1981-82	Hartford	19	4	3	7
1982-83	Hartford	80	26	31	57
1983-84	Hartford	80	27	42	69
	Totals	239	63	86	149

RISTO SILTANEN 25 5-9 180   Defenseman

Stocky offensive defenseman . . . Likes to rush puck . . . Speed makes him hard to check . . . Outstanding shot from blue line helped produce 12 power-play goals last season . . . Often leaves defense position to move toward net and operate like a forward . . . Born Oct. 31, 1958, in Manta, Finland . . . Makes his best moves with puck in neutral zone . . . Former member of Edmonton Oilers.

Year	Club	GP	G	A	Pts.
1978-79	Edmonton (WHA)	20	3	4	7
1979-80	Edmonton	64	6	29	35
1980-81	Edmonton	79	17	36	53
1981-82	Edmonton	63	15	48	63
1982-83	Hartford	74	5	25	30
1983-84	Hartford	75	15	38	53
	NHL Totals	355	58	176	234
	WHA Totals	20	3	4	7

CHRIS KOTSOPOULOS 25 6-3 215   Defenseman

Looks and acts mean on and off ice...Takes losses hard...Often sits in chair outside dressing room and broods after Whalers' lose...Still feels slighted over never being drafted by NHL team...Made it to big leagues the hard way as free agent...Born Nov. 27, 1958, in Toronto...Had 24 penalty minutes in first NHL game for Rangers against Flyers...Fell into disfavor with Ranger coach Herb Brooks and was dealt to Hartford...Has a mean streak in him and delivers smashing body checks...Not fast but can unleash hard, accurate slap shot...Had respectable minus-2 record last season...Weightlifter and drag-racing addict.

Year	Club	GP	G	A	Pts.
1980-81	New York R	54	4	12	16
1981-82	Hartford	68	13	20	33
1982-83	Hartford	68	6	24	30
1983-84	Hartford	72	5	13	18
	Totals	262	28	69	97

BOB CRAWFORD 25 5-11 177   Forward

Emile Francis reacquired him in waiver draft after leaving St. Louis to become Whalers' team president and GM...Move paid off...Scored 36 goals in first full NHL season in 1983-84 ...Compiled minus-1 record for weak defensive team...Played for Hartford coach Jack (Tex) Evans in Central League, scoring 54 goals, 99 points in 1981-82...Born April 6, 1959, in Belleville, Ont....Right wing who excels as skater and penalty-killer...Scored goals on 20.1 percent of his shots in first season with Whalers.

Year	Club	GP	G	A	Pts.
1980-81	Colorado	15	1	3	4
1982-83	Detroit	1	0	0	0
1983-84	Hartford	80	36	25	61
	Totals	96	37	28	65

MIKE ZUKE 30 6-0 180   Forward

One of NHL's best role-playing forwards...Emile Francis took him in waiver draft because he admired his play in St. Louis ...Defensive center who checks and kills penalties effectively...Born April 16, 1954, in Sault Ste. Marie, Ont. ...Outstanding faceoff man...Often used in crucial situations or assigned to check opposition's best center... Won't let team down in pressure spots... Was All-America collegian at Michigan Tech.

Year	Club	GP	G	A	Pts.
1976-77	Indianapolis (WHA)...	15	3	4	7
1977-78	Edmonton (WHA)....	71	23	34	57
1978-79	St Louis............	34	9	17	26
1979-80	St Louis............	69	22	42	64
1980-81	St Louis............	74	24	44	68
1981-82	St Louis............	76	13	40	53
1982-83	St Louis............	43	8	16	24
1983-84	Hartford............	75	6	23	29
	NHL Totals.........	371	82	182	264
	WHA Totals........	86	26	38	64

JOEL QUENNEVILLE 26 6-1 195   Defenseman

"Q Man"... A defensive defenseman... Scored only 13 points, took only 67 shots, in 80 games last season... Steady and dependable... May have been Whalers' best defenseman in 1983-84... Started NHL career with Toronto... Born Sept. 15, 1958, in Windsor, Ont.... Traded from Toronto to Colorado Rockies in 1979 with Lanny McDonald for Pat Hickey and Wilf Paiement... Played one season with New Jersey Devils... Devils traded him June 21, 1983, to Calgary to get Mel Bridgman and Phil Russell... Fifteen days later Calgary traded him to Hartford... Happy to get away from Devils' doldrums.

Year	Club	GP	G	A	Pts.
1978-79	Toronto	61	2	9	11
1979-80	Tor-Col	67	6	11	17
1980-81	Colorado	71	10	24	34
1981-82	Colorado	64	5	10	15
1982-83	New Jersey	74	5	12	17
1983-84	Hartford...........	80	5	8	13
	Totals.............	417	33	74	107

COACH JACK EVANS: Everyone calls him "Tex"... Returned to NHL coaching ranks last season... Whalers showed some signs of life under his guidance... Played pro hockey for 24 years... A rock-hard defenseman for Rangers from 1948 to 1958... Also played for Black Hawks for five seasons... "He was a good defenseman and very tough," says former teammate Fred Shero... Born April 21, 1928, in Garnant, South

Wales... Tall, strong, stoic, soft-spoken man... Favors defensive style of play... Successful Central League coach who won two championships and had 230-143-23 record in five seasons with Salt Lake City... Played hockey with Hartford president and GM Emile Francis... Coached weak California and Cleveland teams in NHL from 1975 to 1978 and had 74-129-37 record ... Including 28-42-10 record in first season with Whalers, has NHL career coaching record of 102-171-47.

GREATEST ROOKIE

Emile (The Cat) Francis is like the E. F. Hutton TV commercial.

When he speaks, people listen.

One of hockey's most experienced and respected hockey executives, the Hartford Whalers' energetic team president and general manager predicted that the player he had chosen first in the 1983 draft had superstar potential.

"Wait 'til you see Sylvain Turgeon shoot the puck," said Francis.

The Cat was correct. Turgeon was awesome last season. He scored 40 goals, 18 on power plays. He's the most dominant rookie the Whalers have had since entering the NHL in 1979-80.

"He has a great shot," New Jersey Devils' veteran goalie Glenn (Chico) Resch said of the husky rookie.

ALL-TIME WHALER LEADERS

GOALS: Blaine Stoughton, 56, 1979-80
ASSISTS: Mark Howe, 65, 1978-79
          Mike Rogers, 65, 1980-81
POINTS: Mark Howe, 107, 1978-79
SHUTOUTS: Al Smith, 3, 1972-73
          Louis Levasseur, 3, 1977-78

MONTREAL CANADIENS

TEAM DIRECTORY: Pres.: Ron Corey; GM: Serge Savard; Dir. Player Personnel: Claude Ruel; Dir. Publ. Rel.: Claude Mouton; Coach: Jacques Lemaire. Home ice: Montreal Forum (16,074; 200′ × 85′). Training camp: Montreal.

SCOUTING REPORT

OFFENSE: If only declining veterans Guy Lafleur and Steve Shutt could score goals the way they once did.

The Flying Frenchmen don't move with the speed they once did, don't score goals as they used to. The proud team with the rich heritage of success ranked a dreadful 18th in offense last season, scoring only 286 goals.

High-flying Bob Gainey and Guy Carbonneau are on the attack.

Bobby Smith started with a flourish but faded fast in his first season following his trade by Minnesota. Lafleur showed some signs of regaining his old scoring touch. Shutt had a dreadful regular season but came to life in the playoffs. Ryan Walter has not lived up to expectations since Montreal acquired him from Washington.

Three bright spots among the forewards are Lucien Deblois, traded from Winnipeg; Guy Carbonneau and Mats Naslund. Bob Gainey and Mario Tremblay are hard workers, diligent checkers but don't produce many goals. The Canadiens' power play was a disaster last season; it was 20th in the 21-team league. In the glory of yesteryear, no team matched the Canadiens' power play.

DEFENSE: A lot better than the offense with still-strong Larry Robinson, big Craig Ludwig, Jean Hamel, Rick Green and new-comer Chris Chelios, who performed well in last season's playoffs.

GM Serge Savard and new coach Jacques Lemaire will open this season with rookie Steve Penney as No. 1 goalie. Up from the minor leagues, Penney was sensational in last season's playoff conquests of Boston and Quebec. Unless it was a fluke, the Canadiens have a bright young goaltender for the future.

Rick Wamsley was traded to St. Louis in June and Richard Sevigny, who played out his option, signed with Quebec. For giving up Wamsley, the Canadiens acquired St. Louis' first-round draft choice, center Shayne Corson.

Montreal, ranked seventh in defense last season, may have come up with another outstanding prospect in the 1984 draft: Petr Svoboda, a 6-1, 162-pound, 18-year-old defenseman who defected from Czechoslovakia. He's been a star in European hockey.

OUTLOOK: The Canadiens aren't what they used to be. The team which has won a record 22 Stanley Cups had its first losing record since 1951 last season. Lemaire appears to have relighted the torch with his coaching. He has the Canadiens playing a tough, physical style instead of their old finesse game. Considering how well they functioned in the 1984 playoffs, don't sell them short this season.

CANADIEN PROFILES

GUY LAFLEUR 33 6-1 175   Forward
"The Flower"... Not in full bloom and a trifle faded in recent years... Emergence of Wayne Gretzky and Mike Bossy has pushed him into shadows... The best there was from 1974 to 1980... Six 100-point seasons... Goal totals of 60, 56, 53, 52, 50... Annual

CANADIEN ROSTER

No.	Player	Pos.	Ht.	Wt.	Born	1983-84	G	A	Pts.	PIM
	Danny Bonar	C	5-9	175	9-23-56/Deloraine, Man.	NH-Nova Scotia	23	37	60	102
21	Guy Carbonneau	C	5-11	177	3-18-60/Sept Isles, Que.	Montreal	24	30	54	75
2	Kent Carlson	D	6-3	200	1-11-62/Concord, N.H.	Montreal	3	7	10	73
29	John Chabot	C	6-2	190	5-18-62/Summerside, P.E.I.	Montreal	18	25	43	13
24	Chris Chelios	D	6-1	190	1-25-62/Chicago, Ill.	Montreal	0	2	2	12
	Shayne Corson	C	6-0	175	8-13-66/Barrie, Ont.	Brantford	25	46	71	165
	Lucien DeBlois	RW	5-11	200	6-21-57/Joliette, Que.	Winnipeg	34	45	79	50
23	Bob Gainey	LW	6-1	200	12-13-53/Peterborough, Ont.	Montreal	17	22	39	41
5	Rick Green	D	6-3	202	2-20-56/Belleville, Ont.	Montreal	0	1	1	7
28	Jean Hamel	D	5-11	182	6-6-52/Asbestos, Que.	Montreal	1	12	13	92
	Alain Heroux	C	6-2	190	5-20-64/Terrebonne, Que.	Nova Scotia	1	1	2	2
20	Mark Hunter	RW	6-0	194	11-12-62/Petrolia, Ont.	Montreal	6	4	10	42
	Bill Kitchen	D	6-1	198	7-16-60/Schoneberg, Ont.	Nova Scotia	4	20	24	193
10	Guy Lafleur	RW	6-1	175	9-20-50/Thurso, Que.	Montreal	30	40	70	19
17	Craig Ludwig	D	6-3	215	3-15-61/Rinelander, Wis.	Montreal	7	18	25	52
	Mike McPhee	C	6-2	205	2-14-60/Sydney, N.S.	Montreal	5	2	7	41
						Nova Scotia	22	33	55	101
6	Pierre Mondou	RW-C	5-10	185	11-27-55/Sorel, Que.	Montreal	15	22	37	8
26	Mats Naslund	RW	5-7	155	10-31-59/Sweden	Montreal	29	35	64	4
3	Ric Nattress	D	6-2	208	5-25-62/Hamilton, Ont.	Montreal	0	12	12	15
	John Newberry	C	6-1	185	4-8-62/Port Alberni, B.C.	Nova Scotia	25	37	62	116
30	Chris Nilan	RW	6-0	200	2-9-58/Boston, Mass.	Montreal	16	10	26	338
19	Larry Robinson	D	6-3	218	6-2-51/Winchester, Ont.	Montreal	9	34	43	39
18	Bill Root	D	6-0	197	9-6-59/Toronto, Ont.	Montreal	4	13	17	45
22	Steve Shutt	LW	5-11	185	7-1-52/Toronto, Ont.	Montreal	14	23	37	29
15	Bobby Smith	C	6-4	210	2-12-58/North Sydney, N.S.	Minn.-Mont.	29	43	72	71
	Petr Svoboda	D	6-0	167	1-19-66/Czechoslovakia	Czech Jr.	–	–	–	–
14	Mario Tremblay	RW	6-0	185	9-2-56/Montreal, Que.	Montreal	14	25	39	112
8	Alfie Turcotte	C	5-9	170	1-15-65/Gary, Ind.	Montreal	7	7	14	10
						Portland	22	41	63	39
11	Ryan Walter	C	6-0	195	4-23-58/New Westminster, B.C.	Montreal	20	29	49	83

							GP	GA	SO	Avg.
	Mark Holden	G	5-10	165	6-12-57/Weymouth, Mass.	Montreal	1	4	0	4.62
						Nova Scotia	47	153	0	3.35
	Greg Moffett	G	5-11	175	4-1-59/Bath, Me.	Nova Scotia	10	35	0	4.26
37	Steve Penney	G	6-1	190	2-2-61/Ste. Foy, Que.	Montreal	4	19	0	4.75
						Nova Scotia	27	92	0	3.51

All-Star at right wing... Born Sept. 20, 1951, in Thurso, Que.... "I know I can still play but I need more ice time," he says... Scored 500th career goal Dec. 20, 1983, in Meadowlands Arena against Devil goalie Glenn Resch... Needs 29 goals to pass legendary Maurice (Rocket) Richard as Canadiens' leading career goal-scorer... Montreal Forum fans still idolize him despite reduced scoring... Has more points and assists than any player in Montreal history... Hasn't scored a goal in last three seasons in play-offs... Has burned foes for 138 power-play goals, 93 game-winning goals in 13 seasons.

Year	Club	GP	G	A	Pts.
1971-72	Montreal	73	29	35	64
1972-73	Montreal	70	28	27	55
1973-74	Montreal	73	21	35	56
1974-75	Montreal	70	53	66	119
1975-76	Montreal	80	56	69	125
1976-77	Montreal	80	56	80	136
1977-78	Montreal	78	60	72	132
1978-79	Montreal	80	52	77	129
1979-80	Montreal	74	50	75	125
1980-81	Montreal	51	27	43	70
1981-82	Montreal	66	27	57	84
1982-83	Montreal	68	27	49	76
1983-84	Montreal	80	30	40	70
	Totals	943	516	725	1241

BOBBY SMITH 26 6-4 210   Forward

North Stars' first draft pick of 1978 fell into disfavor with management and fans... Traded to Montreal last season for Keith Acton and Mark Napier... Produced 63 points in 70 games with Montreal... Born Feb. 12, 1958, in North Sydney, Nova Scotia... Rookie of Year in 1978 with Minnesota... Had 114-point season in 1981-82... Has never quite lived up to expectations... Critics say he's too passive... Failed to distinguish himself in last season's playoffs.

Year	Club	GP	G	A	Pts.
1978-79	Minnesota	80	30	44	74
1979-80	Minnesota	61	27	56	83
1980-81	Minnesota	78	29	64	93
1981-82	Minnesota	80	43	71	114
1982-83	Minnesota	77	24	53	77
1983-84	Minn-Mont	80	29	43	72
	Totals	456	182	331	513

MATS NASLUND 25 5-7 155   Forward

First European player to make it big with Canadiens...One of three shortest players in NHL last season...Moves like ghost through and around defenders because of slick, quick speed and elusiveness...Give him a small piece of open ice and he's gone...Born Oct. 31, 1959, in Timra, Sweden...Seems to bounce off body checks thrown by bigger opponents...Has been tagged with only 14 penalty minutes in two seasons...Big favorite of fans in Montreal...Had outstanding 8-8-16 playoff scoring numbers last season.

Year	Club	GP	G	A	Pts.
1982-83	Montreal	74	26	45	71
1983-84	Montreal	77	29	35	64
	Totals	151	55	80	135

LARRY ROBINSON 33 6-3 218   Defenseman

Terrific all-around defenseman whose skills have eroded slightly in recent years...Silenced critics by playing magnificently in last season's playoff conquests of Bruins and Quebec...MVP in 1978 playoffs...Five-time All-Star...Won Norris Trophy in 1977 and 1980 as hockey's premier defenseman...Born June 2, 1951, in Winchester, Ont....Outstanding team leader who still gets job done well at both ends of rink...Seldom fails to clear puck or connect on passes to forwards...Closing in on 500 career assists...A farmer in offseason.

Year	Club	GP	G	A	Pts.
1972-73	Montreal	36	2	4	6
1973-74	Montreal	78	6	20	26
1974-75	Montreal	80	14	47	61
1975-76	Montreal	80	10	30	40
1976-77	Montreal	77	19	66	85
1977-78	Montreal	80	13	52	65
1978-79	Montreal	67	16	45	61
1979-80	Montreal	72	14	61	75
1980-81	Montreal	65	12	38	50
1981-82	Montreal	71	12	47	59
1982-83	Montreal	71	14	49	63
1983-84	Montreal	74	9	34	43
	Totals	851	141	493	634

GUY CARBONNEAU 24 5-11 177   Forward

Keep your eyes on him this season... Started climb to stardom in playoffs last season... Stopped Boston's Barry Pederson and Quebec's Peter Stastny with tight checking in Montreal playoff wins... Dominated Bryan Trottier in playoffs... Born March 18, 1960, in Sept-Isles, Que.... "I get as much satisfaction winning faceoffs and playing good defensive hockey as I do in scoring a goal," he says... Scrappy center not afraid to go down and block a shot... Outstanding at winning faceoffs... Deft scoring touch around net... Has 12 shorthanded goals as penalty-killer in two seasons.

Year	Club	GP	G	A	Pts.
1980–81	Montreal	2	0	1	1
1982–83	Montreal	77	18	29	47
1983–84	Montreal	78	24	30	54
	Totals	157	42	60	102

RYAN WALTER 26 6-0 195   Forward

Arrived in Montreal after controversial trade with Washington in which Canadiens gave up defensemen Rod Langway and Brian Engblom Sept. 9, 1983... Still a good addition for Montreal... Capable of developing into top-grade forward... Washington's first draft choice in 1978... Born April 23, 1958, in New Westminster, B.C.... Smooth skater with high skill level but needs to bear down harder... Plays center or left wing... Last season's statistics disappointing... Coach Jacques Lemaire convinced he'll do better this year.

Year	Club	GP	G	A	Pts.
1978-79	Washington	69	28	28	56
1979-80	Washington	80	24	42	66
1980-81	Washington	80	24	44	68
1981-82	Washington	78	38	49	87
1982-83	Montreal	80	29	46	75
1983-84	Montreal	73	20	29	49
	Totals	460	163	238	401

STEVE PENNEY 23 6-1 190   Goaltender

Last season's big playoff story... Unlikely hero of wins over Bruins and Quebec... Nearly led Canadiens to upset of Islanders... Unheralded 10th-round draft pick in 1980 who labored in minor leagues until called up late in season when Rick Wamsley and Richard Sevigny failed to do job in goal...Born Feb. 2, 1961, in Ste.-Foy, Que....Was 0-4 with 4.75 average and 19 goals-against in regular season...Stopped 240 of 255 shots, had two shutouts and 1.49 average in first 10 playoff games...Finished playoffs with 2.20 average and 9-6 record...Coaching by Hall-of-Fame goalie Jacques Plante helped rise to fame...Relies on lightning-fast reflexes...Made sensational saves throughout playoffs.

Year	Club	GP	GA	SO	Avg.
1983–84	Montreal	4	19	0	4.75

STEVE SHUTT 32 5-11 185   Forward

Like Guy Lafleur, his star has fallen...Former All-Star left wing and 60-goal, 105-point scorer...Scored 400th career goal same day Lafleur scored his 500th goal...Still has fast-breaking moves up left wing...Born July 1, 1952, in Toronto...Made up for his poorest season with seven goals in 11 playoff games...Has scored 49 game-winning goals in a distinguished career... Reporters respect him because he tells it as it is in interviews ...Friendly, likeable chap...Big fan of "Rush," the Canadian rock group.

Year	Club	GP	G	A	Pts.
1972-73	Montreal	50	8	8	16
1973-74	Montreal	70	15	20	35
1974-75	Montreal	77	30	35	65
1975-76	Montreal	80	45	34	79
1976-77	Montreal	80	60	45	105
1977-78	Montreal	80	49	37	86
1978-79	Montreal	72	37	40	77
1979-80	Montreal	77	47	42	89
1980-81	Montreal	77	35	38	73
1981-82	Montreal	57	31	24	55
1982-83	Montreal	78	35	22	57
1983-84	Montreal	63	14	23	37
	Totals	861	406	368	774

BOB GAINEY 30 6-1 200   Forward

Every team would love to have a player like Gainey...Smart, mature veteran and captain...Plays for his team instead of personal glory . . . One of hockey's best defensive forwards and hardest workers . . . Ideal role model for impressionable young fans and athletes . . . Born Dec. 13, 1953, in Peterborough, Ont. . . . Four-time winner of Selke Trophy as NHL's best defensive forward . . . Former playoff MVP . . . "As a pro athlete myself, I admire Bob Gainey's philosophy about sports, the way he works so hard for his team," says New York Giants' star punter Dave Jennings, an ardent hockey follower . . . Twenty-nine more goals and he'll reach 200 for his career.

Year	Club	GP	G	A	Pts.
1973-74	Montreal	66	3	7	10
1974-75	Montreal	80	17	20	37
1975-76	Montreal	78	15	13	28
1976-77	Montreal	80	14	19	33
1977-78	Montreal	66	15	16	31
1978-79	Montreal	79	20	18	38
1979-80	Montreal	64	14	19	33
1980-81	Montreal	78	23	24	47
1981-82	Montreal	79	21	24	45
1982-83	Montreal	80	12	18	30
1983-84	Montreal	77	17	22	39
	Totals	827	171	200	371

LUCIEN DEBLOIS 27 5-11 200   Forward

Front-line NHL winger traded by the Jets in June for Perry Turnbull, had best season of six-year NHL career in 1983-84 when he had 34 goals and 79 points . . . Had scored 25 and 27 goals in first two Jet seasons . . . Good skater and defensive player who does heavy penalty-killing load . . . Joined Jets from Colorado in complicated compensation deal for Ivan Hlinka, the Czech forward who was drafted by the Jets but signed by Vancouver . . . Born June 21, 1957, in Sorel, Quebec . . . Had two 56-goal seasons with Sorel juniors . . . First-round draft pick of New York Rangers in 1977 when John Ferguson, now Jet GM, ran that team . . . Spent two seasons in New York, then was traded to Colorado.

Year	Club	GP	G	A	Pts.
1977-78	New York R	71	22	8	30
1978-79	New York R	62	11	17	28
1979-80	NYR-Col	76	27	20	47
1980-81	Colorado	74	26	16	42
1981-82	Winnipeg	65	25	27	52
1982-83	Winnipeg	79	27	27	54
1983-84	Winnipeg	80	34	45	79
	Totals	507	172	160	332

CRAIG LUDWIG 23 6-3 215   **Defenseman**

Big, tall, strong blond defenseman...Moves with the authority of Lurch from the old Addams Family TV series...Developing into solid defenseman...Doesn't try to play an overly offensive style...Stays back and concentrates on being what he is: a defender...Born March 15, 1961, in Reinlander, Wis....Gained All-America recognition as college player at University of North Dakota...Seldom gets caught up ice or out of position to allow rivals to attack on two-on-one rush...Protects his area well...Skilled at disrupting opponents' play patterns...Has shot-blocking ability...Good at taking opposing forwards out of the play.

Year	Club	GP	G	A	Pts.
1982–83	Montreal	80	0	25	25
1983–84	Montreal	80	7	18	25
	Totals	160	7	43	50

COACH JACQUES LEMAIRE: One of the best all-around centers in Montreal history became coach Feb. 24, 1984, when Bob Berry was fired...Placed emphasis on aggressive, defensive style of play ...Struggling Canadiens won Lemaire's first game as coach, 7-4, against Rangers en route to three-game winning streak...Gave younger players a chance to play...Players responded to his coaching better than they did to the unpopular Berry...Member of eight Stanley Cup championship teams from 1967 through 1979 with Canadiens...Scored 366 goals, 835 points in 12 NHL seasons...Born Sept. 7, 1945, in LaSalle, Que....Had 7-10 record in 17 games as Montreal coach...Lemaire's Canadiens scored playoff upsets of Boston and Quebec...Came close to eliminating defending champion Islanders...Lemaire went to Switzerland to coach after retirement as player...Coached at Plattsburgh State College briefly...Coached Longueil Chevaliers to 37-29-5 record in Quebec Junior League before joining Montreal as assistant coach last season.

GREATEST ROOKIE

The Montreal Canadiens have won more championships and had more outstanding players than any team in NHL history. But the rookie performance of one man stands out above all others.

Few players achieved what goaltender Ken Dryden did in his rookie season of 1970-71.

A scholarly graduate of Cornell University and an All-American, he joined the Canadiens for six games. He won them all, surrendering only nine goals, an average of 1.65 goals-per-game. The tall, gentlemanly goalie carried Montreal on his back to a playoff upset of Boston and eventually to the Stanley Cup. His play in 20 playoff games was sensational. He was voted playoff MVP.

An NHL player is classified as rookie so long as he has not played more than 25 regular-season games. So Dryden still was a rookie in 1971-72. He played so well he won the Calder Trophy as Rookie of the Year . . . one year after he had won the Stanley Cup and been chosen playoff MVP.

Dryden sat out one season to return to law school. He then rejoined the Canadiens and was an All-Star goalie. He retired prematurely after only eight NHL seasons to enter the practice of law, author a best-selling book about hockey, and now is in the service of his native Canada in government work.

Dryden helped Montreal win six Stanley Cup championships. His marvelous career goaltending record showed a 258-57-74 record, 46 shutouts, a 2.24 goals-against average in regular-season play. In playoff competion, he was 80-32. He was elected in 1983 to the Hockey Hall of Fame.

ALL-TIME CANADIEN LEADERS

GOALS: Steve Shutt, 60, 1976-77
           Guy Lafleur, 60, 1977-78
ASSISTS: Pete Mahovlich, 82, 1974-75
POINTS: Guy Lafleur, 136, 1976-77
SHUTOUTS: George Hainsworth, 22, 1928-29

NEW JERSEY DEVILS

TEAM DIRECTORY: Owner John McMullen; VP-Operations/GM: Max McNab; Dir. Player Personnel: Marshall Johnston; Dir. Pub. Rel.: Larry Brooks; Coach: Doug Carpenter. Home ice: Byrne Meadowlands Arena (19,023; 200′ × 85′). Colors: White, red and green.

SCOUTING REPORT

OFFENSE: Seldom in modern hockey has a team's offense been so feeble and embarrassing as the Devils' in 1983-84. It can't help but be better this season because it can't get any worse. Or can it?

How bad was it? So bad that Wayne Gretzky scored almost as

Glenn Resch enters 12th year with one to go for 200th win.

many points (205) as the entire Devils' team scored goals (231).

The Devils were the lowest-scoring team in the NHL. Their power play also was last in the NHL. So bad, in fact, that some fans yelled, "don't take the penalty," when an opposing player headed for the penalty box to create a powerless Devils' power play. Many veteran hockey-watchers have not seen a power play so bad as the Devils in the last 10 or 15 years.

Mel Bridgman scored only 23 goals, 38 assists, 61 points—and still led the "Mighty Meadowlands Scoring Machine" in goals, assists and points.

Bridgman had a dreadful first half of the season, a strong second half. Tim Higgins, acquired Jan. 12, 1984, when the Devils traded Jeff Larmer to Chicago, gave New Jersey some much-needed offense. Young forwards Pat Verbeek and Czech Jan Ludvig showed considerable promise but Don Lever, Bob MacMillan (traded to Chicago for defenseman Don Dietrich and forward Rich Preston), Aaron Broten and Paul Gagne were major disappointments. If there was an unsung hero among the forwards, it was Dave Cameron, a hard worker who played his best at both ends of the ice.

For most of the season, watching the Devils was like watching hockey in slow-motion. The Devils had little significant speed.

Kirk Muller may change things this season. He was the second player chosen in the entry draft. Other new faces to watch: John MacLean, Rocky Trottier and Al Stewart.

DEFENSE: Average at best but significantly better than the offense. New Jersey was a poor 17th in defense, 16th in penalty-killing. Young Joe Cirella provided some excitement as a defenseman. Veteran Dave Lewis and Bob Lorimer, slow but steady, had good and bad moments. Veteran Phil Russell, Bob Hoffmeyer and Murray Brumwell were reasonably effective. Young defense prospects such as Ken Daneyko, Bruce Driver, Shawn Evans and West German's Ullrich Heimer and Dietrich may crack the lineup.

With Glenn (Chico) Resch and Ron Low, goaltending is the Devils' strongest position. Resch, 36, and Low, 34, are up in years and there's no bright young goalie waiting in the wings.

OUTLOOK: The Devils have earned the reputation as the sorriest franchise in the NHL. They have failed to come close to a winning record in their 10 NHL seasons, two in Kansas City, six in Denver, the last two in New Jersey. They have averaged only 17 wins a season. Winning 20 games this season would be a "Miracle at the Meadowlands."

Worse yet, New Jersey management continues to make the same mistakes made in Kansas City and Denver. The franchise

DEVIL ROSTER

No.	Player	Pos.	Ht.	Wt.	Born	1983-84	G	A	Pts.	PIM
18	Mel Bridgman	C	6-0	190	4-28-55/Trenton, B.C.	New Jersey	23	38	61	121
24	Aaron Broten	C	5-10	168	11-14-60/Roseau, Minn.	New Jersey	13	23	36	36
25	Murray Brumwell	D	6-1	190	3-31-60/Calgary, Alta.	New Jersey	7	13	20	14
						Maine	4	25	29	16
10	Dave Cameron	C	6-0	185	7-29-58/Charlottetown, P.E.I.	New Jersey	9	12	21	85
14	Rich Chernomaz	RW	5-9	175	9-1-63/Selkirk, Man.	New Jersey	2	1	3	2
						Maine	17	29	46	39
2	Joe Cirella	D	6-3	210	5-9-63/Hamilton, Ont.	New Jersey	11	33	44	137
3	Ken Daneyko	D	6-0	193	4-16-64/Windsor, Ont.	Kamloops	6	28	34	52
						New Jersey	1	4	5	17
	Don Dietrich	D	6-1	195	4-5-61/Deloraine, Man.	Chicago	0	5	5	0
						Springfield	14	21	35	14
	Bruce Driver	D	6-0	185	4-29-62/Toronto, Ont.	New Jersey	0	2	2	0
						Maine	2	6	8	15
	Shawn Evans	D	6-2	193	9-7-65/Kingston, Ont.	Peterborough	21	88	109	116
27	Larry Floyd	C	5-8	177	5-1-61/Peterborough, Ont.	New Jersey	1	3	4	7
						Maine	37	49	86	40
17	Paul Gagne	LW	5-10	178	2-6-62/Iroquois Falls, Ont.	New Jersey	14	18	32	33
	Allan Hepple	D	5-9	203	8-16-63/England	New Jersey	0	0	0	7
						Maine	4	23	27	117
	Ulrich Heimer	D	6-1	190	9-21-62/West Germany	Germany	23	23	46	–
20	Tim Higgins	RW	6-0	190	2-7-58/Ottawa, Ont.	Chi.-N.J.	19	14	33	48
21	Bob Hoffmeyer	D	6-0	182	7-27-55/Dodsland, Sask.	New Jersey	4	12	16	61
						Maine	3	1	4	27
26	Mike Kitchen	d	5-10	185	2-1-56/Newmarket, Ont.	New Jersey	1	4	5	24
9	Don Lever	LW	5-11	175	11-14-52/S. Porcupine, Ont.	New Jersey	14	19	33	44
25	Dave Lewis	D	6-2	205	7-3-53/Kindersley, Sask.	New Jersey	2	5	7	63
4	Bob Lorimer	D	6-0	190	8-25-53/Toronto, Ont.	New Jersey	2	10	12	62
29	Jan Ludvig	RW	5-10	180	9-17-61/Czechoslovakia	New Jersey	22	32	54	70
15	John MacLean	RW	6-0	193	11-20-64/Oshawa, Ont.	New Jersey	1	0	1	10
						Oshawa	23	36	59	58
20	Hector Marini	RW	6-1	204	1-27-57/Timmins, Ont.	New Jersey	2	2	4	47
						Maine	6	5	11	23
14	Kevin Maxwell	C	5-9	165	3-30-60/Edmonton, Alta.	New Jersey	0	3	3	2
						Maine	21	27	48	59
28	Gary McAdam	RW	5-11	175	12-31-55/Smith Falls, Ont.	Wash.-N.J.	10	11	21	27
						Maine	3	4	7	18
16	Rick Meagher	RW	5-10	175	11-4-53/Belleville, Ont.	New Jersey	14	14	28	16
						Maine	6	4	10	2
32	Glen Merkosky	C	5-10	175	8-4-60/Edmonton, Alta.	New Jersey	1	0	1	0
						Maine	28	28	56	56
	Kirk Muller	C	6-0	190	2-8-66/Kingston, Ont.	Guelph	31	63	94	27
21	Grant Mulvey	RW	6-3	202	9-17-56/Sudbury, Ont.	New Jersey	1	2	3	19
						Maine	6	8	14	49
	Rob Palmer	D	5-11	190	9-10-56/Sarnia, Ont.	New Jersey	0	5	5	10
						Maine	5	10	15	10
	Rich Preston	RW	6-0	185	5-22-52/Regina, Sask.	Chicago	10	18	28	50
5	Phil Russell	D	6-2	200	7-21-52/Edmonton, Alta.	New Jersey	9	22	31	96
	M.F. Schurman	D	6-3	205	7-18-57/Summerdale, P.E.I.	Maine	5	15	20	40
22	Doug Sulliman	LW	5-9	195	8-29-59/Glace Bay, N.S.	Hartford	6	12	18	20
	Rocky Trottier	C	5-11	185	4-11-64/Climax, Sask.	New Jersey	1	1	2	0
						Medicine Hat	34	50	84	41
19	Yvon Vautour	RW	6-0	200	9-10-56/St. John's, N.B.	New Jersey	3	4	7	78
						Maine	8	12	20	117
12	Pat Verbeek	C	5-9	190	5-24-64/Sarnia, Ont.	New Jersey	20	27	47	158

No.	Player	Pos.	Ht.	Wt.	Born		GP	GA	SO	Avg.
	Steve Baker	G	6-3	200	5-6-57/Boston, Mass.	Bing.-Maine	19	76	0	4.19
30	Ron Low	G	6-1	205	6-21-50/Birtle, Man.	New Jersey	44	161	0	4.36
	Shawn MacKenzie	G	5-7	155	8-22-62/Bedford, N.S.	Maine	34	113	0	3.48
1	Glenn Resch	G	5-9	165	7-10-48/Moose Jaw, Sask.	New Jersey	51	184	1	4.18

has had 12 coaches in 10 years, three in one year.

Veteran coach Tom McVie turned the Devils into a hard-working competitive force in the final 60 games of last season. He deserved to be retained as coach but, instead, Doug Carpenter, who never has coached in the NHL, was hired after being fired as a Toronto minor-league coach. Little does he know what he's getting into. Devils' management must decide upon a sensible building plan, stick to it despite mounting losses, stop changing coaches every season.

Gretzky called the Devils a "Mickey Mouse Operation on Ice" last season. The Devils are so much of a no-name team that, except for the popular Resch, anthem singer Rona Klinghofer gets more cheers than the Devils.

Slight improvement, perhaps, but another long season seems in store for the Devils.

DEVIL PROFILES

MEL BRIDGMAN 29 6-0 190   Forward
Started slowly and finished fast in first season with weak Devils...Compiled 18-34-52 scoring figures in last 51 games...Led low-scoring Devils in points...Named captain Jan. 9, 1984, by then-new coach Tom McVie, replacing Don Lever, and responded by providing team leadership...Rugged competitor with fierce pride...A player who hates to lose and had a lot to hate last season...Ten-year veteran started NHL career with Flyers...Devils acquired him in smart trade by former GM-coach Bill MacMillan with Calgary, getting Bridgman and Phil Russell for Steve Tambellini and Joel Quenneville...Born April 28, 1955, in Trenton, Ont....Outstanding faceoff center who won 53.5 percent of his draws...Set up 29 goals with faceoff wins...Blocked 12 shots...Led Devils with 10 winning-tying points.

Year	Club	GP	G	A	Pts.
1975-76	Philadelphia	80	23	27	50
1976-77	Philadelphia	70	19	38	57
1977-78	Philadelphia	76	16	32	48
1978-79	Philadelphia	76	24	35	59
1979-80	Philadelphia	74	16	31	47
1980-81	Philadelphia	77	14	37	51
1981-82	Phil-Calg	72	33	54	87
1982-83	Calgary	79	19	31	50
1983-84	New Jersey	79	23	38	61
	Totals	683	187	323	510

JAN LUDVIG 24 5-10 180   Forward

Known to teammates as "Loodie"... Slick and quick with natural
goal-scoring skills... Finesse player who also can play a physical
game... Defected from native Czechoslovakia to come to North
America to start hockey career... Increased goals from seven to
22, points from 17 to 54 in second NHL season... Has speed and
nifty moves... Can launch dangerous shots from blue line, slot
or faceoff circles... Born Sept. 17, 1961, in Liberec, Czechoslovakia... New Jersey's second-leading scorer... Led team with
176 shots... Plays left or right wing.

Year	Club	GP	G	A	Pts.
1982–83	New Jersey	51	7	10	17
1983–84	New Jersey	74	22	32	54
	Totals............	125	29	42	71

PAT VERBEEK 20 5-9 190   Forward

A Bobby Clarke clone... Plays hard every shift, every
game... Delighted fans in Meadowlands Arena with jarring body
checks and darting, hitting, buzzsaw style of play... Teammates
call him "Patty" or "Beeker"... A pig farmer in offseason... Had
impressive rookie season at center... Won 52.3 percent of faceoffs... Born May 24, 1964, in Sarnia, Ont.... Needs to become
more consistent scorer... Drew 30 penalties... Most penalized
Devil with 158 minutes... Assessed seven penalties for fighting.

Year	Club	GP	G	A	Pts.
1982–83	New Jersey	6	3	2	5
1983–84	New Jersey	79	20	27	47
	Totals............	85	23	29	52

JOE CIRELLA 21 6-3 210   Defenseman

Another bright young prospect to provide glimmer of hope for
one of the NHL's worst teams... "Joey has all the tools to develop
into a fine all-around defenseman for a long, successful career,"
says last season's coach, Tom McVie... Born May 9, 1963, in
Hamilton, Ont.... Has powerful slap shot from blue line and
moves puck skillfully with passes or by handling it himself

...Needs to improve positional play in defensive zone... Scored 11 goals, assisted on 33, led Devils' weak power play with six goals, 16 assists... Had eight shots strike goalposts instead of entering net... Must cut down giveaways... Played right defense in tandem with veteran Phil Russell.

Year	Club	GP	G	A	Pts.
1981–82	Colorado	65	7	12	19
1982–83	New Jersey	2	0	1	1
1983–84	New Jersey	79	11	33	44
	Totals.............	146	18	46	64

GLENN RESCH 36 5-9 165   Goaltender

"Chico"... The one and only... Bright, cheerful, friendly despite playing goal for so weak a team... One of sports' best interviews... Hears more cheers from fans than any of no-name Devils' players... Next win will be the 200th of his 11-season NHL goaltending career (199-170-75)... "Chico may be the best goalie in the league," says Philadelphia's Bobby Clarke.... Trouble is his 9-31-3 record for lowly Devils doesn't reflect how well he played... Born July 10, 1948, in Moose Jaw, Sask.... U.S. citizen now lives in Emily, Minn.... Master of making the seemingly impossible save because of quick reflexes... Collector of sports memorabilia... Never at a loss for words... Loves people and they love him... Has stopped eight of nine penalty shots in NHL career.

Year	Club	GP	GA	SO	Avg.
1973-74	New York I.........	2	6	0	3.00
1974-75	New York I.........	25	59	3	2.47
1975-76	New York I.........	44	88	7	2.07
1976-77	New York I.........	46	103	4	2.28
1977-78	New York I.........	45	112	3	2.55
1978-79	New York I.........	43	106	2	2.50
1979-80	New York I.........	45	132	3	3.04
1980-81	NYI-Col	40	121	3	3.20
1981-82	Colorado	61	230	0	4.03
1982-83	New Jersey	65	242	0	3.98
1983-84	New Jersey	51	184	1	4.18
	Totals.............	467	1383	26	3.12

RON LOW 34 6-1 205   Goaltender

Ten-year veteran of mostly losing teams... May have had his best NHL season in 1983-84... Played so well for losing team he gained equal status and shared goaltending with Glenn Resch... "It's the best I've ever seen him play," said former Flyers' all-star goalie Bernie Parent...Improved his concentration, shot anticipation and footwork under Tom McVie's coaching...Born June 21, 1950, in Birtle, Manitoba...Has played for six teams since starting NHL career...Good-natured guy...Works on farm in offseason...Enters 1984-85 with 96-192-34 career record.

Year	Club	GP	GA	SO	Avg.
1972–73	Toronto	42	152	1	3.89
1974–75	Washington	48	235	1	5.45
1975–76	Washington	43	208	0	5.45
1976–77	Washington	54	188	0	3.87
1977–78	Detroit	32	102	1	3.37
1979–80	Que–Edm	26	88	0	3.57
1980–81	Edmonton	24	93	0	4.43
1981–82	Edmonton	29	100	0	3.86
1982–83	Edm–NJ	14	51	0	4.30
1983–84	New Jersey	44	161	0	4.36
	Totals	356	1378	3	4.32

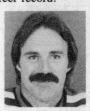

TIM HIGGINS 26 6-0 190 Forward

Devils were criticized for trading 21-year-old prospect Jeff Larmer to Chicago in Jan. 12, 1984, deal for Higgins...It looks as though they made a wonderful move..."It was pure hell for me in Chicago," says Higgins, who fell into disfavor with coach Orval Tessier and was benched...Big power forward scored 18 goals, 28 points in 37 games for Devils...Led Devils with three game-winning goals and scored on 25 percent of his shots...Born Feb. 7, 1958, in Ottawa, Ont....Worked well in tandem on line with Mel Bridgman...Showed terrific moves and quickness for a big man...Chicago's No. 1 draft choice in 1978...Needs three goals to reach 100 for NHL career.

Year	Club	GP	G	A	Pts.
1978–79	Chicago	36	7	16	23
1979–80	Chicago	74	13	12	25
1980–81	Chicago	78	24	35	59
1981–82	Chicago	74	20	30	50
1982–83	Chicago	64	14	9	23
1983–84	Chi–NJ	69	19	14	33
	Totals	395	97	116	213

PHIL RUSSELL 32 6-2 200 Defenseman

Starts 14th NHL season...Classy, sharp-witted old-pro type ...Never an all-star but always a consistently good defenseman since entering NHL in 1972 as Chicago's No. 1 draft choice...Devils traded with Calgary for him...Born July 21, 1952, in Edmonton, Alberta...Plays right or left defense

...Operates more in a defensive posture now than in his earlier years when he played an offensive role...Had some giveaway problems last season...Has 1,853 career penalty minutes...Drawing close to his 100th career goal...Smart business mind...Has seat on Chicago Board of Trade...Roots for Cubs...Blocked 51 shots last season, one less than team leader Bob Lorimer.

Year	Club	GP	G	A	Pts.
1972-73	Chicago	76	6	19	25
1973-74	Chicago	75	10	25	35
1974-75	Chicago	80	5	24	29
1975-76	Chicago	74	9	29	38
1976-77	Chicago	76	9	36	45
1977-78	Chicago	57	6	20	26
1978-79	Chi-Atl	79	9	29	38
1979-80	Atlanta	80	5	31	36
1980-81	Calgary	80	6	23	29
1981-82	Calgary	71	4	25	29
1982-83	Calgary	78	13	18	31
1983-84	New Jersey	76	9	22	31
	Totals	902	91	301	392

DAVE LEWIS 31 6-2 205   Defenseman

Acquired by Devils Oct. 3, 1983, in three-team trade, moving from Los Angeles to Minnesota to New Jersey in exchange for Brent Ashton...Unselfish team-first player...Played while hurt numerous times last season...Strictly a defensive defenseman who makes jokes about his weak shot and infrequent goals...Born July 3, 1953, in Kindersley, Sask....Did some outstanding body-checking in second half of last season...Blocked 30 shots...Worked well on defense in tandem with former Islander teammate Bob Lorimer...Played high school football with Islanders' Bob Bourne.

Year	Club	GP	G	A	Pts.
1973-74	New York I	66	2	15	17
1974-75	New York I	78	5	14	19
1975-76	New York I	73	0	19	19
1976-77	New York I	79	4	24	28
1977-78	New York I	77	3	11	14
1978-79	New York I	79	5	18	23
1979-80	NYI-LA	73	6	17	23
1980-81	Los Angeles	67	1	12	13
1981-82	Los Angeles	64	1	13	14
1982-83	Los Angeles	79	2	10	12
1983-84	New Jersey	66	2	5	7
	Totals	801	31	158	189

Czech Jan Ludvig soared in point production in second year.

COACH DOUG CARPENTER: Light a candle and say a prayer... He needs all the help he can get as coach of dreadfully weak Devils... Became Devils' third coach in less than one year, 12th coach in 10 years, on May 31... Given only one-year contract, which provides little job security... Devils' management picked his assistant coach, 1984 U.S. Olympic coach Lou Vairo, who is being groomed to become head coach... Born July 1, 1942, in Cornwall, Ont.... Faces toughest coaching job in league with no NHL experience whatsoever... Played in Eastern League from 1966 to 1973... Coached Flint of IHL from 1973–1977... Coached Cornwall Royals to

junior hockey Memorial Cup in 1980...Replaced veteran Tom McVie as Devils' coach after 159-135-26 record in four years of minor-league coaching with New Brunswick, St. Catharines and Cincinnati..."He's a good, competent coach," says Hartford GM Emile Francis.

GREATEST ROOKIE

Unfortunately for the franchise now based in the New Jersey Meadowlands Sports Complex, the greatest rookie it has had plays for the team across the Hudson River in Madison Square Garden.

Think what the former Kansas City Scouts-Colorado Rockies franchise could have been if it had not traded defenseman Barry Beck to the Rangers Nov. 2, 1979.

"We were all in state of shock when it happened," said Mike Kitchen, a New Jersey Devils' defenseman who was with the team in Colorado when it traded Beck. "Barry was the franchise," said Kitchen.

Built like a football player, Beck set an NHL record for rookie defensemen by scoring 22 goals for the Rockies in 1977-78. He was the No. 2 choice in the 1977 draft.

Since traded to the Rangers, Beck has become one of the NHL's most respected defensemen and team leaders. The struggling Devils, who never have come close to a winning record, are still paying heavily for trading Beck.

ALL-TIME DEVIL LEADERS

GOALS: Wilf Paiement, 41, 1976-77
ASSISTS: Wilf Paiement, 56, 1977-78
POINTS: Wilf Paiement, 87, 1977-78
SHUTOUTS: Doug Favell, 1, 1977-78
                Bill Oleschuk, 1, 1978-79
                Bill McKenzie, 1, 1979-80
                Glenn Resch, 1, 1983-84

NEW YORK ISLANDERS

TEAM DIRECTORY: Chairman of the Board: John Pickett; Pres.-GM: Bill Torrey; Dir. Pub. Rel.: Les Wagner; Coach: Al Arbour. Home ice: Nassau Coliseum (15,861; 200′ × 85′). Colors: White, blue and orange. Training camp: Hicksville, N.Y.

SCOUTING REPORT

OFFENSE: It starts with Mike Bossy, the best pure shooter-scorer in the NHL. It continues with scorer-playmaker Bryan Trottier. Add to it the names of Greg Gilbert, brothers Brent and Duane Sutter, old hands Clark Gillies and Bob Nystrom, as well as speedy Bob Bourne and John Tonelli.

And now there are two bright young faces among the forwards:

Duane Sutter hooks Oiler Dave Lumley in Cup playoffs.

slick, quick Pat LaFontaine and husky Pat Flatley, rookies from the 1984 Olympics in Sarajevo, who made a good impression with the Islanders late last season.

There's also defenseman Denis Potvin, whose passing, shooting and playmaking makes the Islanders' offense go.

The team from Long Island last season ranked No. 3 in the NHL in offense but its power play shorted out too frequently and the goal-scoring fell off noticeably in the playoffs. The Islanders must do better offensively in 1984-85, especially on power plays. They may need a bit more speed and finesse up front.

DEFENSE: Potvin is the bell-cow and catalyst, a defender willing to sacrifice himself as a shot-blocker. But, overall, the Islanders' backline lacks speed and mobility. Defensive defenseman Ken Morrow has been slowed by knee injuries. Body-checking, shot-blocking specialist Dave Langevin also has been slowed by injuries. Tomas Jonsson and Stefan Persson are skilled two-way defensemen. Two promising young defensemen are Paul Boutilier and Gord Dineen.

The Islanders are strong and three-deep in goal. Bill Smith has the best playoff goaltending record in NHL history. Roland Melanson, No. 2 goalie, could be No. 1 for most teams. Young Kelly Hrudey is being groomed for the future. GM Bill Torrey was trying to trade a goalie, probably Melanson, after the 1983-84 season.

OUTLOOK: The drive for a record-tying five straight Stanley Cup championships was stopped short of the mark by Edmonton last season. But make no mistake about it. The Islanders are NOT in a state of decline. They look good enough again to lead the Patrick Division and seek revenge from Edmonton in the playoffs.

ISLANDER PROFILES

MIKE BOSSY 27 6-0 185   **Forward**
Best natural goal-scorer in hockey . . . Has scored remarkable 416 goals, 811 points in only 533 NHL games . . . "The Boss" . . . Has spoken out against overly violent play in hockey . . . Averages 59 goals, 116 points a season . . . All-Star right wing . . . First player to score 50 or more goals in first seven years in NHL . . . Born Jan. 22, 1957, in Montreal . . . Amazingly accurate shooter with quickly released shot . . . Once scored 21 goals in a game in youth

ISLANDER ROSTER

No.	Player	Pos.	Ht.	Wt.	Born	1983-84	G	A	Pts.	PIM
22	Mike Bossy	RW	6-0	185	1-22-57/Montreal, Que.	Islanders	51	67	118	8
14	Bob Bourne	C-RW	6-3	205	6-11-54/Netherhill, Sask.	Islanders	22	34	56	75
4	Paul Boutilier	D	6-0	190	5-3-63/Sydney, N.S.	Islanders	0	11	11	36
						Indianapolis	6	17	23	56
25	Bill Carroll	RW	5-10	180	1-19-59/Toronto, Ont.	Islanders	5	2	7	12
	Kevin Devine	LW	5-8	170	12-9-54/Toronto, Ont.	Indianapolis	23	30	53	201
2	Gord Dineen	D	5-11	180	9-21-62/Toronto, Ont.	Islanders	1	11	12	32
						Indianapolis	4	13	17	63
	Gerald Diduck	D	6-2	195	4-6-65/Edmonton, Alta.	Lethbridge	10	24	34	133
8	Pat Flatley	RW		205	10-3-63/Toronto, Ont.	Islanders	2	7	9	6
17	Greg Gilbert	LW	6-1	195	1-22-62/Mississauga, Ont.	Islanders	31	35	66	59
9	Clark Gillies	LW	6-3	215	4-7-54/Moose Jaw, Sask.	Islanders	12	16	28	85
91	Butch Goring	C	5-9	166	10-22-49/St. Boniface, Man.	Islanders	22	24	46	8
20	Mats Hallin	LW	6-2	202	3-19-58/Sweden	Islanders	2	5	7	27
	Ron Handy	LW	5-10	174	1-15-63/Toronto, Ont.	Indianapolis	29	46	75	40
6	Tomas Jonsson	D	5-10	176	4-12-60/Sweden	Islanders	11	36	47	54
28	Anders Kallur	RW	5-10	190	7-6-52/Sweden	Islanders	9	14	23	24
	Roger Kortko	C	5-10	182	2-1-63/Hofford, Sask.	Indianapolis	16	27	43	48
16	Pat LaFontaine	C	5-9	170	2-22-65/St. Louis, Mo.	Islanders	13	6	19	6
24	Gordie Lane	D	6-1	185	3-31-53/Brandon, Man.	Islanders	0	3	3	70
26	Dave Langevin	D	6-2	215	5-15-54/St. Paul, Minn.	Islanders	3	16	19	53
	Red Laurence	C	5-9	173	6-27-57/Galt, Ont.	Indianapolis	41	37	78	42
	Tim Lockridge	D	6-0	215	1-18-59/Barrie, Ont.	Indianapolis	2	16	18	95
	Garth McGuigan	C	6-0	191	2-16-56/Charlottetown, P.E.I.	Islanders	0	1	1	0
						Indianapolis	25	41	66	109
9	Ken Morrow	D	6-4	205	10-17-56/Davison, Mich.	Islanders	3	11	14	46
23	Bob Nystrom	RW	6-1	200	10-10-52/Sweden	Islanders	15	29	44	80
7	Stefan Persson	D	6-1	190	12-22-54/Sweden	Islanders	9	24	33	65
5	Denis Potvin	D	6-0	202	10-29-53/Ottawa, Ont.	Islanders	22	63	85	87
	Darcy Regier	D	5-11	191	11-27-56/Swift Current, Sask.	Islanders	0	1	1	0
						Indianapolis	4	12	16	112
	Dave Simpson	C	6-0	187	3-3-62/London, Ont.	Indianapolis	24	43	67	26
	Vern Smith	D	6-1	195	5-30-64/Lethbridge, Alta.	New Westminster	13	44	57	94
11	Brent Sutter	C	5-11	175	6-11-62/Viking, Alta.	Islanders	34	15	49	69
12	Duane Sutter	RW	6-1	189	3-6-60/Viking, Alta.	Islanders	17	23	40	94
27	John Tonelli	LW	6-1	198	3-23-57/Hamilton, Ont.	Islanders	27	40	67	66
19	Bryan Trottier	C	5-11	195	7-17-56/Val Marie, Sask.	Islanders	40	71	111	59
	Monte Trottier	C	5-8	160	8-25-61/Val Marie, Sask.	Indianapolis	18	23	41	135

No.	Player	Pos.	Ht.	Wt.	Born	1983-84	GP	GA	SO	Avg.
30	Kelly Hrudey	G	5-10	182	1-13-61/Edmonton, Alta.	Islanders	12	28	0	3.14
						Indianapolis	6	21	0	3.41
	Roland Melanson	G	5-10	178	6-28-60/Moncton, N.B.	Islanders	37	110	0	3.27
1	Billy Smith	G	5-10	185	12-12-50/Perth, Ont.	Islanders	42	130	2	3.42

hockey...Fourteen teams made mistake of not selecting him in 1977 draft...Edmonton stopped him cold in Stanley Cup final victory.

Year	Club	GP	G	A	Pts.
1977-78	New York I.........	73	53	38	91
1978-79	New York I.........	80	69	57	126
1979-80	New York I.........	75	51	41	92
1980-81	New York I.........	79	68	51	119
1981-82	New York I.........	80	64	83	147
1982-83	New York I.........	79	60	58	118
1983-84	New York I.........	67	51	67	118
	Totals.............	533	416	395	811

BRYAN TROTTIER 28 5-11 195　　　　Forward

Considered best all-around center in NHL...Dynamic checker and hitter...Outstanding playmaker and scorer...With retirement of Flyers' Bobby Clarke, undisputed faceoff-winning king in NHL...Has amassed 960 points in 688 games...Had lofty +70 record last season...Born July 17, 1956, in Val Marie, Sask....Can jar opponents with devastating body checks...Didn't play up to par in last season's playoffs...Surprisingly, lost magic touch at winning faceoffs.

Year	Club	GP	G	A	Pts.
1975-76	New York I.........	80	32	63	95
1976-77	New York I.........	76	30	42	72
1977-78	New York I.........	77	46	77	123
1978-79	New York I.........	76	47	87	134
1979-80	New York I.........	78	42	62	104
1980-81	New York I.........	73	31	72	103
1981-82	New York I.........	80	50	79	129
1982-83	New York I.........	80	34	55	89
1983-84	New York I.........	68	40	71	111
	Totals.............	688	352	608	960

DENIS POTVIN 30 6-0 202　　　　Defenseman

Poised veteran plays with ice water in veins...An All-Star and former winner of Norris Trophy as league's best defenseman ...Plays best games under pressure...Overcame personal problems in last two seasons...Born Oct. 29, 1953, in Ottawa, Ont....Has outstanding all-around skill, offensively and defensively...Deadly shooter from blue line or slot...Blocked 21 shots in first 11 playoff games last season...Has a chance to surpass Bobby Orr's scoring records for defensemen of 270 career goals, 915 career points...Has more assists than any player in playoff history.

Year	Club	GP	G	A	Pts.
1973-74	New York I.........	77	17	37	54
1974-75	New York I.........	79	21	55	76
1975-76	New York I.........	78	31	67	98
1976-77	New York I.........	80	25	55	80
1977-78	New York I.........	80	30	64	94
1978-79	New York I.........	73	31	70	101
1979-80	New York I.........	31	8	33	41
1980-81	New York I.........	74	20	56	76
1981-82	New York I.........	60	24	37	61
1982-83	New York I.........	69	12	54	66
1983-84	New York I.........	78	22	63	85
	Totals.............	779	241	591	832

BILL SMITH 33 5-10 185   Goaltender

"Battling Billy"..."Best money goalie in hockey," says former coach Don Cherry..."The Islanders would never have won four Stanley Cups without him," says former All-Star goalie Eddie Giacomin...Broke Ken Dryden's Stanley Cup playoff goaltending record last season...Has 85-33 record in playoffs...Dryden was 80-34...Only goalie to score goal in NHL game when credited with goal Nov. 28, 1979, against Colorado...Feisty and outspoken...Uses stick to drive rivals away from his goalcrease...Has ability to pretend he's been fouled by opponents by taking dives to fool referees...Born Dec. 12, 1950, in Perth, Ont....Career record is 233-162-88...Most penalized goalie with 350 minutes during career.

Year	Club	GP	GA	SO	Avg.
1971-72	Los Angeles........	5	23	0	4.60
1972-73	New York I.........	37	147	0	4.16
1973-74	New York I.........	46	134	0	3.07
1974-75	New York I.........	58	156	3	2.78
1975-76	New York I.........	39	98	3	2.61
1976-77	New York I.........	36	87	2	2.50
1977-78	New York I.........	38	95	2	2.65
1978-79	New York I.........	40	108	1	2.87
1979-80	New York I.........	38	104	2	2.95
1980-81	New York I.........	41	129	2	3.28
1981-82	New York I.........	46	133	0	2.97
1982-83	New York I.........	41	112	1	2.87
1983-84	New York I.........	42	130	2	3.42
	Totals.............	507	1456	18	3.02

JOHN TONELLI 27 6-1 198   Forward

Symbol of what Islanders are all about... "He plays hard, battles every minute," coach Al Arbour says of husky, intense left wing... Sometimes plays at so high an intensity level he leaves ice totally exhausted after a game... One of the best hitters, forecheckers, grinders and cornermen in NHL... Born March 23, 1957, in Hamilton, Ont.... Saved Islanders from 1982 playoff elimination by Pittsburgh with two goals in gallant comeback victory... Epitomizes Islander-style hockey.

Year	Club	GP	G	A	Pts.
1975-76	Houston (WHA)	79	17	14	31
1976-77	Houston (WHA)	80	24	31	55
1977-78	Houston (WHA)	65	23	41	64
1978-79	New York I	73	17	39	56
1979-80	New York I	77	14	30	44
1980-81	New York I	70	20	32	52
1981-82	New York I	80	35	58	93
1982-83	New York I	76	31	40	71
1983-84	New York I	73	27	40	67
	NHL Totals	449	144	239	383
	WHA Totals	224	64	86	150

GREG GILBERT 22 6-1 195   Forward

Newcomer who moved into lineup... Looks as if he'll stay quite a while... "He does everything well," says teammate Bryan Trottier... Fit in well as left wing on line with Trottier and Mike Bossy... Red-haired athlete with fierce competitive pride... Good scorer... Always seems to concentrate on defensive job as backchecker... Born Jan. 22, 1962, in Mississaugua, Ont.... Proved to be accurate shooter-scorer in first full NHL season.

Year	Club	GP	G	A	Pts.
1981–82	New York I	1	1	0	1
1982–83	New York I	45	8	11	19
1983–84	New York I	79	31	35	66
	Totals	125	40	46	86

STEFAN PERSSON 29 6-1 190   Defenseman

Efficient all-around defenseman... Seldom makes giveaways or errant passes... Checks his man well... Difficult to beat one-on-one... Knows how to elude forecheckers and get puck out of defensive zone to forwards...Born Dec. 22, 1954, in Umea, Sweden...Starred in Sweden before joining Islanders... Playmaking defenseman who excels on specialty teams of power play and penalty-killing units...Has 279 assists in seven seasons.

Year	Club	GP	G	A	Pts.
1977-78	New York I.........	66	6	50	56
1978-79	New York I.........	78	10	56	66
1979-80	New York I.........	73	4	35	39
1980-81	New York I.........	80	9	52	61
1981-82	New York I.........	70	6	37	43
1982-83	New York I.........	70	4	25	29
1983-84	New York I.........	75	9	24	33
	Totals............	512	48	279	327

PAT LaFONTAINE 19 5-10 175   Forward

The rich get richer...Talent-laden Islanders' GM Bill Torrey outsmarted several teams to draft outstanding American-born center in 1983...Deceptively fast-moving forward has potential to become a star...Joined Islanders late last season after playing for unsuccessful U.S. Olympic team...Scored 13 goals, 19 points in first 15 NHL games...Scored on a remarkable 37.1 percent of his shots...Born Feb. 22, 1965, in St. Louis...Raised in Michigan...Scored a sensational 175 goals, 324 points in 79 games in 1981–82 playing in strong Detroit midget league ...Showed an American can go to Canada and become a junior hockey star...Named Canada's top junior player after scoring 104 goals, 130 assists, 234 points with Verdun of Quebec Junior League in 1982–83..."Patty does everything so quickly," says teammate Bryan Trottier..."He can be another Denis Savard," said Edmonton's Mark Messier, comparing LaFontaine to Chicago's swift center.

Year	Club	GP	G	A	Pts.
1983–84	New York I.........	15	13	6	19

PAT FLATLEY 21 6-1 195   Forward

Like Pat LaFontaine, he's another bright young prospect who will help keep Islanders a dominant team...Moved from Canadian

Olympic team to Islanders late last season... Quickly proved he's ready for big-time hockey... Fits into Islanders' system as hard-charging, hard-working strong right wing... Plays a physical game... Not a great scorer but capable of 30 goals a season... Born Oct. 3, 1963, in Toronto.... Starred for two seasons at University of Wisconsin... Islanders chose him 21st in 1983 draft... Uses size well in corners, along boards... "He'll be around a long time," says veteran teammate Bob Bourne.

Year	Club	GP	G	A	Pts.
1983-84	New York I.........	16	2	7	9

BRENT SUTTER 22 5-11 175　　　　　　　　Forward

One of NHL's six Sutter brothers... Teammate of brother Duane... Had outstanding playoff in 1983-84... Was terrific at winning faceoffs... Enjoyed his best season with 34 goals... Good defensive center who backchecks effectively and plays hard at both ends of ice... Born June 11, 1962, in Viking, Alberta... "He's a big reason why they beat us," Montreal's Larry Robinson said of Islanders' playoff win... Scored vital and spectacular shorthanded goal in Islanders' comeback victory... Willing to fight... Older brother Duane nicknamed "Dog"... Brent known as "Pup" to teammates.

Year	Club	GP	G	A	Pts.
1980–81	New York I.........	3	2	2	4
1981–82	New York I.........	43	21	22	43
1982–83	New York I.........	80	21	19	40
1983–84	New York I.........	69	34	15	49
	Totals.............	195	78	58	136

BOB BOURNE 30 6-3 205　　　　　　　　　Forward

Islanders missed his speed in losing Stanley Cup final to swift-skating Edmonton... Sidelined with ankle injury during most of playoffs... Has exceptional skating speed... Always a threat to make solo fast-break rush from one end of ice to the other... Born

June 21, 1954, in Netherhill, Sask. . . . Can play all three forward positions . . . Excels as penalty-killer . . . Good forechecker and backchecker . . . Likeable team player . . . Played minor-league baseball for Houston Astros . . . Has winning touch when taking faceoffs . . . Normally plays wing . . . Needs 10 points for career total of 500.

Year	Club	GP	G	A	Pts.
1974-75	New York I	77	16	23	39
1975-76	New York I	14	2	3	5
1976-77	New York I	75	16	19	35
1977-78	New York I	80	30	33	63
1978-79	New York I	80	30	31	61
1979-80	New York I	73	15	25	40
1980-81	New York I	78	35	41	76
1981-82	New York I	76	27	26	53
1982-83	New York I	77	20	42	62
1983-84	New York I	78	22	34	56
	Totals	708	213	277	490

CLARK GILLIES 30 6-3 215   Forward

Made up for disappointing regular season with 12 goals in play-offs . . . Bounced back after serious knee injury in 1982-83 . . . Has size and strength and uses it to best advantage . . . Effective positioning himself in front of net to screen goalie . . . Doesn't wear helmet . . . Has knack for scoring goals on close backhand shots . . . Doesn't look for trouble but can fight as well as any man in hockey if he has to . . . Once knocked out Rangers' Ed Hospodar with a punch . . . Born April 7, 1954, in Moose Jaw, Sask. . . . "Clarkie never gives up," says teammate Butch Goring . . . Played minor-league baseball for Houston Astros . . . Once impressed Mets as a power hitter when he took informal batting practice at Shea Stadium.

Year	Club	GP	G	A	Pts.
1974-75	New York I	80	25	22	47
1975-76	New York I	80	34	27	61
1976-77	New York I	70	33	22	55
1977-78	New York I	80	35	50	85
1978-79	New York I	75	35	56	91
1979-80	New York I	73	19	35	54
1980-81	New York I	80	33	45	78
1981-82	New York I	79	38	39	77
1982-83	New York I	70	21	20	41
1983-84	New York I	76	12	16	28
	Totals	763	285	332	617

Determined Denis Potvin has most assists in playoff history.

COACH AL ARBOUR: Radar... He and Hal Laycoe are only  men who wore glasses when they played in NHL... Arbour and GM Bill Torrey built weak expansion Islanders into dynasty in less than 10 years in NHL... Four-year reign as Stanley Cup champions ended with loss to Edmonton in last season's Stanley Cup final... Low-key coach... Shuns personal glory... Believes in fundamentals of hard work, strong team defense... Never loses confidence in his players... Always appears outwardly calm but inwardly is intense competitor who hates to lose... Born Nov. 1, 1932, in Sudbury, Ont.... Knows how to utilize his players to best advantage... Lets players know when he's upset with their performance . . . Coaching record of 515-294-176 is among best in NHL history . . . Second to Buffalo's Scotty Bowman in playoff coaching wins with 109-60 record . . . Was shot-blocking defensive defenseman with Detroit, Toronto, Chicago and St. Louis . . . Played for Stanley Cup championship teams in Detroit (1954); Chicago (1961), and Toronto (1964) . . . Islanders' coach for 11 years . . . Coached St. Louis for three years . . . "A great coach," says Bill MacMillan, former Islander player and assistant coach under Arbour.

GREATEST ROOKIE

In their sudden rise to power since entering the NHL as an expansion team in 1972-73, the four-time Stanley Cup champion New York Islanders have had a profusion of outstanding rookies.

Mike Bossy is one. Bryan Trottier is another. But the best was Denis Potvin.

As one of the most highly sought junior players in Canada, the poised, mature, 20-year-old Potvin was the first player selected in the 1973 amateur draft.

On a bright, sunny afternoon in June, 1973, in Montreal, he sat on a bed in his hotel room at an informal news conference and said his goal was to eventually become one of hockey's best defensemen. He said he hoped it wouldn't take him too long but mentioned that playing in the NHL were a couple of defensemen named Orr and Park.

Potvin rose to prominence even faster than the Islanders. He was Rookie of the Year in 1973-74 and was chosen to play in the All-Star game in Chicago. Soon he became an All-Star, considered in a class with Bobby Orr and Brad Park. Now an 11-season veteran of 30, he is considered by many as hockey's best all-around defenseman. Three times he has been voted winner of the Norris Trophy as the most outstanding defenseman in the NHL. He is the Islanders' catalyst and captain.

ALL-TIME ISLANDER LEADERS

GOALS: Mike Bossy, 69, 1978-79
ASSISTS: Bryan Trottier, 87, 1978-79
POINTS: Mike Bossy, 147, 1981-82
SHUTOUTS: Glenn Resch, 7, 1975-76

NEW YORK RANGERS

TEAM DIRECTORY: Pres.: John H. Krumpe; VP-GM: Craig Patrick; Bus. Mgr.-Dir. Pub. Rel.: Vince Casey; Coach: Herb Brooks. Home ice: Madison Square Garden (17,500; 200′ × 85′). Colors: Blue, red and white. Training camp: Rye, N.Y.

SCOUTING REPORT

OFFENSE: For all the weaving, criss-crossing and fancy moves in Herb Brooks' European-style motion offense, the Rangers still don't score enough goals.

They ranked ninth in offense last season and in nearly upsetting the Islanders in the opening playoff round abandoned their fast-

Popular Don Maloney has Ranger record for shorthanded goals.

breaking motion attack for a more conventional straight-ahead method.

The goal-scorers are there in Pierre Larouche, Mark Pavelich, Anders Hedberg and Don Maloney. Also in super-fast offensive-defenseman Reijo (Rexi) Ruotsalainen. He often operates like a fourth forward and may be moved to the front line this season. Other prominent forwards are Mike Allison, Peter Sundstrom, Mark Osborne, newcomer Bob Brooke, Larry Patey and Mike Rogers.

In truth, the Rangers still lack the big-game, game-breaking forward.

DEFENSE: One of the best and biggest groups in the NHL. The Rangers are overloaded with defensemen: Barry Beck, Ruotsalainen, veterans Ron Greschner, Dave Maloney, Tom Laidlaw and Willie Huber. They have an outstanding young prospect with star potential: rookie James Patrick. Rugged Steve Richmond and Grant Ledyard are other young defensemen to watch.

Red-haired Glen Hanlon had many magnificent moments in goal last season and should be No. 1 again this season. The Rangers are high on two young goalies, John Vanbiesbrouck and Ron Scott. Steve Weeks appears to be odd man out.

OUTLOOK: What can you say about an organization which has not won a championship since 1940? That's when the Rangers won their last Stanley Cup. Only baseball's Chicago Cubs are in the Rangers' class as non-champions. The Cubs last won the World Series in 1945.

The Rangers have made strides under the coaching of Herb Brooks and managing of Craig Patrick. They have skating speed and talent but somehow always find a way to lose in the playoffs. Some critics claim it's because of the Rangers' losing syndrome. With a little luck and no major injuries, they could give the Islanders a run for first place this season. Maybe.

RANGER PROFILES

PIERRE LAROUCHE 28 5-11 175   **Forward**
Another smart move by Ranger GM Craig Patrick... Rangers didn't have to spend a cent or give up a player to acquire him from Hartford as free agent before last season... Had sensational season as goal-scorer... Fell two goals short of tying Vic Hadfield's 1972 Ranger record of 50 goals... Born Nov. 16, 1955,

RANGER ROSTER

No.	Player	Pos.	Ht.	Wt.	Born	1983-84	G	A	Pts.	PIM
14	Mike Allison	C	6-0	200	3-28-61/St. Francis, Ont.	Rangers	8	12	20	64
21	Mike Backman	RW	5-10	175	1-2-53/Halifax, N.S.	Rangers	0	1	1	8
						Tulsa	12	28	40	103
5	Barry Beck	D	6-3	215	6-3-57/Vancouver, B.C.	Rangers	9	27	36	132
18	Mike Blaisdell	RW	6-1	195	1-18-60/Regina, Sask.	Rangers	5	6	11	31
						Tulsa	10	8	18	23
13	Bob Brooke	LW	6-2	207	12-18-60/Melrose, Mass.	Rangers	1	2	3	4
24	Gary Burns	C	6-1	190	1-5-55/Cambridge, Mass.	Tulsa	28	30	58	95
	Terry Carkner	D	6-3	197	3-7-66/Winchester, Ont.	Peterborough	4	21	25	91
	Cam Connor	LW	6-2	200	8-1-54/Winnipeg, Man.	Tulsa	18	32	50	218
	Gary DeGrio	LW/RW	5-11	180	2-16-60/Duluth, Minn.	Tulsa	10	19	29	24
20	Jan Erixon	LW	6-0	190	7-8-62/Sweden	Rangers	5	25	30	16
22	Nick Fotiu	LW	6-2	210	5-25-52/Staten Is., N.Y.	Rangers	7	6	13	115
8	Robbie Ftorek	C	5-8	160	1-2-52/Needham, Mass.	Rangers	3	2	5	22
						Tulsa	11	11	22	10
	Dave Gagner	C	5-10	182	12-11-64/Chatham, Ont.	Brantford	7	13	20	4
4	Ron Greschner	D	6-2	205	12-22-54/Goodsoil, Sask.	Rangers	12	44	56	117
	Randy Heath	LW	5-8	162	11-11-64/Vancouver, B.C.	Portland	44	46	90	107
15	Anders Hedberg	RW	5-11	175	2-25-51/Sweden	Rangers	32	35	67	16
27	Willie Huber	D	6-5	228	1-15-58/West Germany	Rangers	9	14	23	80
23	Chris Kontos	C	6-1	196	12-10-63/Toronto, Ont.	Rangers	0	1	1	8
						Tulsa	5	13	18	8
2	Tom Laidlaw	D	6-2	215	4-15-58/Brampton, Ont.	Rangers	3	15	18	62
10	Pierre Larouche	C	5-11	175	11-16-55/Taschereau, Que.	Rangers	48	33	81	22
	Grant Ledyard	D	6-2	190	11-19-61/Winnipeg	Tulsa	9	17	26	71
	Jim Malone	C	6-1	190	2-20-62/Chatham, Ont.	Tulsa	16	11	27	58
26	Dave Maloney	D	6-1	195	7-31-56/Kitchener, Ont.	Rangers	7	26	33	168
12	Don Maloney	LW	6-1	190	9-5-58/Lindsay, Ont.	Rangers	24	42	66	62
37	George McPhee	LW	5-9	170	7-2-58/Guelph, Ont.	Rangers	1	1	2	11
						Tulsa	20	28	48	133
	Mark Morrison	C	5-9	155	3-11-63/Delta, B.C.	Rangers	0	0	0	0
						Tulsa	4	4	8	2
	Graeme Nicolson	D	6-0	188	1-13-58/North Bay, Ont.	Tulsa	7	24	31	61
19	Mark Osborne	LW	6-1	185	8-13-61/Toronto, Ont.	Rangers	23	28	51	88
6	Larry Patey	C	6-1	185	2-17-53/Toronto, Ont.	St.L.-NYR	1	3	4	12
3	James Patrick	D	6-1	190	6-14-63/Winnipeg, Man.	Rangers	1	7	8	2
16	Mark Pavelich	C	5-8	165	2-28-58/Eveleth, Minn.	Rangers	29	53	82	96
41	Steve Richmond	D	6-1	205	12-11-59/Chicago, Ill.	Tulsa	1	17	18	114
						Rangers	2	5	7	110
27	Mike Rogers	C	5-9	175	10-24-54/Calgary, Alta.	Rangers	23	38	61	46
29	Reijo Ruotsalainen	D	5-8	165	4-1-60/Finland	Rangers	20	39	59	117
	Tomas Sandstrom	RW	6-1	179	9-4-64/Sweden	Swedish Nats.	–	–	–	–
21	Blaine Stoughton	RW	5-10	185	3-13-53/Gilbert Plains, Man.	Hart.-NYR	28	16	44	8
25	Peter Sundstrom	LW	6-0	180	12-14-61/Sweden	Rangers	22	22	44	24
	Vesa Salo	D	6-3	180	4-17-65/Finland	Finnish Nats.	–	–	–	–

							GP	GA	SO	Avg.
1	Glen Hanlon	G	5-11	180	2-20-57/Brandon, Man.	Rangers	50	166	1	3.51
35	Ron Scott	G	5-8	155	7-21-60/Guelph, Ont.	Tulsa	29	109	0	3.81
						Rangers	9	29	0	3.59
33	John Vanbiesbrouck	G	5-7	165	9-4-63/Detroit, Mich.	Tulsa	37	124	3	3.46
						Rangers	3	10	0	3.33
31	Steve Weeks	G	5-11	165	6-30-58/Scarborough, Ont.	Rangers	26	90	0	3.97
						Tulsa	3	7	0	2.33

in Taschereau, Que.... Overcame reputation as troublemaker and floater with diligent work ethic for coach Herb Brooks... Wore out his welcome despite 50-goal seasons with Pittsburgh and Montreal because of bad attitude... Became instant hero with demanding Madison Square Garden fans... Media loved his cooperative attitude and sense of humor... May not be a good defensive player but can create excitement and score goals.

Year	Club	GP	G	A	Pts.
1974-75	Pittsburgh	79	31	37	68
1975-76	Pittsburgh	76	53	58	111
1976-77	Pittsburgh	65	29	34	63
1977-78	Pitt-Mont	64	23	37	60
1978-79	Montreal	36	9	13	22
1979-80	Montreal	73	50	41	91
1980-81	Montreal	61	25	28	53
1981-82	Mont-Hart	67	34	37	71
1982-83	Hartford	38	18	22	40
1983-84	New York R	77	48	33	81
	Totals	636	320	340	660

MARK PAVELICH 26 5-8 165   Forward

"The Fishin' Magician"... Next to playing hockey, he loves fishing and field and stream best of all !.. Led Rangers in scoring last season... Has scored 233 points in 234 games in three NHL seasons... Small in size but has a big heart... Tough, durable center whose quick reactions enable him to elude bigger defenders... Born Feb. 28, 1958, in Eveleth, Minn.... Considered too small to play in NHL by most scouts... Rangers glad they took a chance and signed him as free agent... All-America at University of Minnesota-Duluth... Starred for gold-medal winning 1980 U.S. Olympic team... Has one of best backhand shots in NHL.

Year	Club	GP	G	A	Pts.
1981-82	New York R	79	33	43	76
1982-83	New York R	78	37	38	75
1983-84	New York R	77	29	53	82
	Totals	234	99	134	233

DON MALONEY 26 6-1 190   Forward

One of hockey's best cornermen and hardest workers... Dynamic forechecker... Favorite of Ranger fans... Younger brother of Ranger veteran defenseman Dave Maloney... Born Sept. 5, 1958, in Lindsay, Ont. . . . Friendly left wing always willing to chat with fans and reporters . . . Tied Mark Osborne for team lead with five winning goals last season . . . Set Ranger records in 1980-81 with nine game-winning goals, five shorthanded goals . . . Holds Ranger record of 14 career shorthanded goals . . . Effective scorer close to net . . . Scored goal on his first shift of first NHL game Feb. 14, 1979, added an assist on second shift.

Year	Club	GP	G	A	Pts.
1978-79	New York R	28	9	17	26
1979-80	New York R	79	25	48	73
1980-81	New York R	61	29	23	52
1981-82	New York R	54	22	36	58
1982-83	New York R	78	29	40	69
1983-84	New York R	79	24	42	66
	Totals.............	379	138	206	344

ANDERS HEDBERG 33 5-11 175   Forward

Has never scored in NHL as he did in WHA . . . Recognized as one of hockey's most dependable right wings . . . Impressive skater, scorer, playmaker . . . Always keeps himself in top physical condition and works hard . . . Born Feb. 25, 1951, in Ornskoldsvik, Sweden . . . Plays with poise and does his best under pressure in important games . . . Had +18 record last season . . . Career almost ended by knee surgery in 1981 . . . Scored only penalty shot goal in Ranger playoff history in St. Louis against goalie Mike Liut in 1981 . . . Has one of best wrist shots in hockey.

Year	Club	GP	G	A	Pts.
1974-75	Winnipeg (WHA).....	65	53	47	100
1975-76	Winnipeg (WHA).....	76	50	55	105
1976-77	Winnipeg (WHA).....	68	70	61	131
1977-78	Winnipeg (WHA).....	77	63	59	122
1978-79	New York R	80	33	45	78
1979-80	New York R	80	32	39	71
1980-81	New York R	80	30	40	70
1981-82	New York R	4	0	1	1
1982-83	New York R	78	25	34	59
1983-84	New York R	79	32	35	67
	NHL Totals.........	401	152	194	346
	WHA Totals	286	236	222	458

BARRY BECK 27 6-3 215   Defenseman

"Bubba" . . . Built like football tight end and hits like a linebacker . . . "He's a dominating force every time he's on the ice," says Buffalo GM-coach Scotty Bowman . . . Best known for neutralizing opposing forwards with smashing body checks...Has powerful, accurate shot from blue line but usually concentrates on defense more than offense...Born June 3, 1957, in Vancouver, B.C....Ranger captain...Forceful team leader...Trade in 1979 from Colorado Rockies to Rangers contributed to collapse of NHL franchise in Denver...Should score 100th career goal this season...Works with underprivileged kids in New York City.

Year	Club	GP	G	A	Pts.
1977-78	Colorado	75	22	38	60
1978-79	Colorado	63	14	28	42
1979-80	Col-NYR............	71	15	50	65
1980-81	New York R	75	11	23	34
1981-82	New York R	60	9	29	38
1982-83	New York R	66	12	22	34
1983-84	New York R	72	9	27	36
	Totals.............	482	92	217	309

REIJO RUOTSALAINEN 24 5-8 165   Defenseman

"Rexi"...Also known as "Ratso" or "Double R" to teammates...Last name pronounced Roots-Sa-Lay-Nen..."He's a perfect example of what a skater should be," says power-skating expert Laura Stamm...Born April 1, 1960, in Oulu, Finland...Exceptionally fast, elusive skater...Coach Herb Brooks calls him best skater in NHL...Lack of size hampers his defensive play...Offensively he resembles a fourth forward...Has learned to put his hard, quick shots on net instead of protective glass behind net...Set Ranger record for defensemen last season with 287 shots on goal.

Year	Club	GP	G	A	Pts.
1981-82	New York R	78	18	38	56
1982-83	New York R	77	16	53	69
1983-84	New York R	74	20	39	59
	Totals.............	229	54	130	184

GLEN HANLON 27 5-11 180   Goaltender

Rose from zero to hero in eyes of Ranger fans in one year...Fans booed his shaky goaltending when he joined Rangers Jan. 4, 1983, from St. Louis in trade for defenseman Andre Dore...Jeers changed to cheers..."Hanlon was red-hot," says last season's Devils' coach, Tom McVie...Born Feb. 20, 1957, in Brandon, Manitoba...Made many sensational, seemingly impossible saves...His 28-

14-4 record was among best in NHL... Has quick reflexes, agile footwork, uncanny sense of anticipation for location of oncoming shots... Career goaltending record is 83-99-27.

Year	Club	GP	GA	SO	Avg.
1977-78	Vancouver	4	9	0	2.70
1978-79	Vancouver	31	94	3	3.10
1979-80	Vancouver	57	193	0	3.47
1980-81	Vancouver	17	59	1	4.44
1981-82	Van-StL	30	114	1	4.06
1982-83	StL-NYR	35	117	0	3.81
1983-84	New York R	50	166	1	3.51
	Totals............	224	750	6	3.60

RON GRESCHNER 29 6-2 205   Defenseman

Made successful comeback from nagging back ailment which limited him to 39 games in two previous seasons... Not so mobile as he once was but still can make opponents look foolish with Bobby Orr-type stickhandling moves... Senior Ranger in length of service... Played first NHL game Nov. 3, 1974... Born Dec. 22, 1954, in Good Soil, Saskatchewan... Can play on forward line as well as defense... Has scored more career points than any Ranger defenseman... Excellent one-on-one moves... Fifty points from scoring 500th career point... Married fashion model Carol Alt last season.

Year	Club	GP	G	A	Pts.
1974–75	New York R	70	8	37	45
1975–76	New York R	77	6	21	27
1976–77	New York R	80	11	36	47
1977–78	New York R	78	24	48	72
1978–79	New York R	60	17	36	53
1979–80	New York R	76	21	37	58
1980–81	New York R	74	27	41	68
1981–82	New York R	29	5	11	16
1982–83	New York R	10	3	5	8
1983–84	New York R	77	12	44	56
	Totals............	631	134	316	450

NICK FOTIU 32 6-2 210   Forward

Not the most skilled player in Ranger history but one of the most popular... Madison Square Garden fans love his hard-charging, robust style of play... First native New Yorker to play for Rangers... Used to watch Rangers play in old Madison Square Garden... Boyhood dream was to play in NHL... Didn't start skating or play hockey until he was 15 . . . Spent formative hockey years in New York Metropolitan Junior Association . . . Born May 25, 1952, in Staten Island, N.Y. . . . Heritage is Greek-Italian . . . Won Police Athletic League boxing title as a kid . . . Has worked hard to improve skills . . . Name pronounced Fo-Tee-You . . . Played well in limited role last season . . . Tosses pucks to fans in stands before games . . . Has 1,102 career penalty minutes . . . Formed Nick Fotiu Youth Foundation.

Year	Club	GP	G	A	Pts.
1974-75	New England (WHA) ..	61	2	2	4
1975-76	New England (WHA) ..	49	3	2	5
1976-77	New York R	70	4	8	12
1977-78	New York R	59	2	7	9
1978-79	New York R	71	3	5	8
1979-80	Hartford	74	10	8	18
1980-81	Hart-NYR	69	9	9	18
1981-82	New York R	70	8	10	18
1982-83	New York R	72	8	13	21
1983-84	New York R	40	7	6	13
	NHL Totals	525	51	66	117
	WHA Totals	110	5	4	9

MIKE ROGERS 29 5-9 175   Forward

Didn't have outstanding 1983-84 season after three straight 100-point seasons . . . Finished with poor minus 24 record . . . Quick, clever playmaking center . . . Usually wins more faceoffs than he loses and is accurate passer . . . Born Oct. 24, 1954, in Calgary, Alberta . . . Good backhand shooter . . . Set Ranger record with 65 assists in 1981-82 following trade from Hartford . . . Teammates call him "Bucky" . . . Set Ranger record by scoring in 16 consecutive games in 1982 . . . Former WHA star . . . Constant breakaway threat . . . Has 15 shorthanded goals in career.

Year	Club	GP	G	A	Pts.
1974-75	Edmonton (WHA)	78	35	48	83
1975-76	Edm-NE (WHA)	80	30	29	59
1976-77	New England (WHA) ..	78	25	57	82
1977-78	New England (WHA) ..	80	28	43	71
1978-79	New England (WHA) ..	80	27	45	72
1979-80	Hartford	80	44	61	105
1980-81	Hartford	80	40	65	105
1981-82	New York R	80	38	65	103
1982-83	New York R	71	29	47	76
1983-84	New York R	78	23	38	61
	NHL Totals	389	174	276	450
	WHA Totals	396	145	222	367

Healthy again, Ron Greschner is in reach of 500th point.

COACH HERB BROOKS: Has outlasted previous seven coaches  for Ranger team which has not won Stanley Cup since 1940 and has history of firing coaches... Intense, perfectionist coach... An innovator always seeking new and better ways to do things... Favors skating game with strong European influence... Glib, sharp-witted man with sense of humor and occasional flashes of temper... Does commercials and is highly-sought motivational speaker... Born Aug. 5, 1937, in St. Paul, Minn.... Successful college coach at University of Minnesota... Coached Gophers to three NCAA championships and 175-100-20 record in seven seasons... Gained world-wide fame as coach of 1980 U.S. Olympic team which stunned Russians en route to Miracle on Ice at Lake Placid... Played for University of Minnesota...Last player cut from 1960 U.S. Olympic team...Stickler for discipline and good physical conditioning among his players...Would make an ideal gung-ho Marine Corps officer...Has 166-91-33 record in three seasons as Rangers' coach...Rumors persist he'll eventually end up coaching Minnesota North Stars.

GREATEST ROOKIE

When Ranger fans talk about outstanding rookies, the first name usually mentioned is Brad Park, who joined the team as a chubby 20-year-old in 1968.

He spent his first eight seasons in the NHL with the Rangers. If not for Bobby Orr, he would have been considered the best all-around defenseman in the league. He was an All-Star, breaking every scoring record by a Ranger defenseman. He played in the Big Apple with Ranger stars such as Jean Ratelle, Rod Gilbert, Vic Hadfield and Eddie Giacomin.

Park was dealt a stunning, personal blow Nov. 7, 1975. He was part of one of hockey's biggest trades. The Rangers traded Park, Jean Ratelle and Joe Zanussi to the arch-rival Bruins in exchange for Phil Esposito and Carol Vadnais.

He starred for eight seasons with Boston and became a hero there. But constant knee injuries and surgery reduced his mobility. He redesigned his style of play, shifted from the role of offensive to defensive defenseman.

Park left the Bruins and signed as a free agent with Detroit Aug. 9, 1983. He's 36 now, father of five children, still a gifted athlete and valuable defenseman. He broke one of Orr's profusion of scoring records for defensemen last season when he collected his 646th career assist.

ALL-TIME RANGER LEADERS

GOALS: Vic Hadfield, 50, 1971-72
ASSISTS: Mike Rogers, 65, 1981-82
POINTS: Jean Ratelle, 109, 1971-72
SHUTOUTS: John Roach, 13, 1928-29

PHILADELPHIA FLYERS

TEAM DIRECTORY: Chairman Exec. Comm.: Edward Snider; Chairman Board: Joseph Scott; Pres.: Jay Snider; Exec. VP: Keith Allen; GM: Bobby Clarke; Dir. Scouting-Asst. GM: Gary Darling; Dir. Press Rel.: Rodger Gottlieb; Coach: Mike Keenan. Home ice: The Spectrum (17,147; 200′ × 85′). Colors: Orange and white. Training camps: Voorhees, N.J., and Philadelphia.

SCOUTING REPORT

OFFENSE: The biggest thing the Flyers are missing this season is Bobby Clarke, a man for all seasons, the heart and soul of the Flyers, their captain and leader, outstanding playmaking and checking center and faceoff winner supreme.

Flyers count on Brian Propp to come through with key goals.

Say goodbye, Bobby Clarke, player. Say hello, Bob Clarke, Flyers' new general manager.

Clarke retired as a player after last season and one of his best scorers, Bill Barber, may miss this season and be forced to retire because of reconstructive knee surgery.

But the offense still looks good. Power forward Tim Kerr (54 goals, 93 points) emerged last season as a dominating scorer. Brian Propp (39 goals, 92 points) again came through. Rookie Dave Poulin (31 goals, 76 points) gave the Flyers the speed they need at center. Brothers Ron and Rich Sutter, Ilkka Sinisalo and veteran Darryl Sittler are capable of putting scoring points on the board.

Philadelphia set a team record of 350 goals last season and led NHL teams in shots-on-goal. But the specialty teams (power play and penalty killing) must improve this season. The Flyers were a poor 17th in the NHL on power plays, a poor 13th in penalty-killing.

DEFENSE: Mark Howe is coming off a subpar season and should regain his two-way form as a defenseman in 1984-85. The remainder of the defense isn't great but isn't bad: Thomas Eriksson, Doug Crossman, Miroslav Dvorak, Brad Marsh, Brad McCrimmon and Glen Cochrane. Essentially, the Flyers lack speed and mobility behind the blue line and encounter occasional lapses when they give the puck away under fore-checking pressure.

Goalie Bob Froese isn't Bernie Parent but he's better than some people think and is the best the Flyers have. Pelle Lindbergh hasn't come close to developing into the All-Star goalie the Flyers said he would be.

OUTLOOK: Philadelphia has had 12 consecutive winning seasons. With a new general manager, Clarke, and a new coach, Mike Keenan, who really knows what to expect? The Flyers should be able to compete with the Islanders, Rangers and Washington for first place in the Patrick Division.

FLYER PROFILES

BRIAN PROPP 25 5-10 190   **Forward**
Don't sell him short when ranking the best left wings in hockey . . . Fierce, feisty competitor has averaged 37 goals in first five NHL seasons . . . Has knack for scoring important goals . . . Produced 12 winning goals in 1982-83 . . . Led Flyers with 301 shots on goal last season and had impressive +49 rec-

FLYER ROSTER

No.	Player	Pos.	Ht.	Wt.	Born	1983-84	G	A	Pts.	PIM
19	Ray Allison	RW	5-9	178	3-4-59/Cranbrook, B.C.	Philadelphia	8	13	21	47
7	Bill Barber	LW	6-0	195	7-11-52/North Bay, Ont.	Philadelphia	22	32	54	36
5	Frank Bathe	D	6-1	190	9-27-54/Oshawa, Ont.	Maine	1	0	1	2
	Dave Brown	RW	6-5	205	10-12-62/Saskatoon, Sask.	Philadelphia	1	5	6	98
						Springfield	17	14	31	150
18	Lindsay Carson	C	6-2	190	11-21-60/Oxbow, Sask.	Philadelphia	1	3	4	10
						Springfield	2	4	6	5
29	Glen Cochrane	D	6-2	189	1-29-58/Cranbrook, B.C.	Philadelphia	7	16	23	225
3	Doug Crossman	D	6-2zzz	180	6-13-60/Peterborough, Ont.	Philadelphia	7	28	35	63
9	Miroslav Dvorak	D	5-10	198	10-11-51/Czechoslovakia	Philadelphia	4	27	31	27
6	Tom Eriksson	D	6-2	182	10-16-59/Sweden	Philadelphia	11	33	44	37
25	Paul Evans	C	5-9	180	5-2-54/Toronto, Ont.	Maine	23	36	59	65
22	Ross Fitzpatrick	LW	6-0	195	10-7-60/Penticton, B.C.	Philadelphia	4	2	6	0
						Springfield	33	30	63	28
	Paul Guay	RW	6-0	193	9-2-63/N. Smithfield, R.I.	Philadelphia	2	6	8	14
11	Len Hachborn	C	5-10	175	9-9-61/Brantford, Ont.	Philadelphia	11	21	32	4
						Springfield	18	42	60	15
24	Randy Holt	D	5-11	184	1-15-53/Pembroke, Ont.	Philadelphia	0	0	0	74
2	Mark Howe	D-RW	5-11	188	5-28-55/Detroit, Mich.	Philadelphia	19	34	53	44
12	Tim Kerr	C	6-3	225	1-5-60/Windsor, Ont.	Philadelphia	54	39	93	29
8	Brad Marsh	D	6-3	220	3-31-58/London, Ont.	Philadelphia	3	14	17	83
10	Brad MacCrimmon	D	5-10	186	3-29-59/Dodsland, Sask.	Philadelphia	0	24	24	76
13	Dave Michayluk	RW	5-11	182	5-18-62/Wakaw, Sask.	Springfield	18	44	62	37
20	Dave Poulin	C-LF	5-11	180	12-17-58/Timmons, Ont.	Philadelphia	31	45	76	47
26	Brian Propp	LW	5-10	190	2-15-59/Lanigan, Sask.	Philadelphia	39	53	92	37
23	Ilkka Sinisalo	LW	6-1	190	7-10-58/Finland	Philadelphia	29	17	46	29
27	Darryl Sittler	C	6-0	190	9-18-50/Kitchener, Ont.	Philadelphia	27	36	63	38
	Steve Smith	D	5-10½	210	4-4-63/Trenton, Ont.	Springfield	4	25	29	77
15	Rich Sutter	RW	5-11	175	12-2-63/Viking, Alta.	Pitt.-Phil.	16	12	28	93
						Baltimore	0	1	1	0
14	Ron Sutter	C	5-11	175	12-2-63/Viking, Alta.	Philadelphia	19	32	51	101
28	Darryl Stanley	D	6-2	200	12-2-62/Winnipeg, Man.	Philadelphia	1	4	5	71
						Springfield	4	10	14	122
	Rick Tocchet	RW	6-0	195	4-9-64/Scarborough, Ont.	Sault Ste. Marie	44	64	108	209
	Steve Tsujiura	C	5-5	165	2-28-62/Coaldale, Alta.	Springfield	24	56	80	27

No.	Player	Pos.	Ht.	Wt.	Born	1983-84	GP	GA	SO	Avg.
35	Bob Froese	G	5-11	180	6-30-58/St. Catharine's, Ont.	Philadelphia	48	150	2	3.14
	Gil Hudon	G	6-2	190	2-12-62/Lemon Park, Sask.	Springfield	27	101	0	4.34
	Darren Jensen	G	5-8	158	---/Cresta, B.C.	Fort Wayne	–	–	–	2.92
31	Pelle Lindbergh	G	5-9	160	3-24-59/Sweden	Philadelphia	36	135	1	4.05
						Springfield	4	12	0	3.00
	Sam St. Laurent	G	5-10	184	2-16-59/Arrida, Que.	Maine	38	145	0	4.03

ord...Needs 17 goals to reach 200 for career...Born Feb. 15, 1959, in Lanigan, Sask....Has accurate shot from blue line, slot or in close to net...Good forechecker...Beats opponents to loose pucks...Broke into NHL with 5-5-10 scoring spree in first six games...A one-man offense in 1982-83 game against Hartford with 13 shots, eight in one period.

Year	Club	GP	G	A	Pts.
1979-80	Philadelphia	80	34	41	75
1980-81	Philadelphia	79	26	40	66
1981-82	Philadelphia	80	44	47	91
1982-83	Philadelphia	80	40	42	82
1983-84	Philadelphia	79	39	53	92
	Totals	398	183	223	406

DAVE POULIN 25 5-11 180   Forward

Who says undrafted free agents can't overcome odds and make it in NHL?...Flyers' former GM Keith Allen made wise move signing Poulin as 1983 free agent...Had outstanding rookie year last season and excelled as defender as well on offense...Fast-skating center with good moves toward net...Effective penalty-killer who scored three shorthanded goals...Born Dec. 17, 1958, in Timmons, Ont....Played in Sweden after college career at Notre Dame...Scored goals on first two shots in NHL debut.

Year	Club	GP	G	A	Pts.
1982–83	Philadelphia	2	2	0	2
1983–84	Philadelphia	73	31	45	76
	Totals	75	33	45	78

DARRYL SITTLER 34 6-0 190   Forward

Controversial Maple Leafs' owner Harold Ballard angered Toronto fans by trading Sittler to Flyers...As classy as a person as he is as an athlete...Holds most career scoring records for Maple Leafs...Not fast but can do it all because of keen hockey instincts...Born Sept. 18, 1950, in Kitchener, Ont....Needs 27 goals to become 500-goal career scorer...A center who can score goals as well as set them up with passes...Scored record six goals, four assists Feb. 7, 1976, against Boston while wearing

Maple Leafs' blue and white . . . Scored five goals April 22, 1976, against Flyers in playoffs . . . Enters 15th NHL season.

Year	Club	GP	G	A	Pts.
1970-71	Toronto	49	10	8	18
1971-72	Toronto	74	15	17	32
1972-73	Toronto	78	29	48	77
1973-74	Toronto	78	38	46	84
1974-75	Toronto	72	36	44	80
1975-76	Toronto	79	41	59	100
1976-77	Toronto	73	38	52	90
1977-78	Toronto	80	45	72	117
1978-79	Toronto	70	36	51	87
1979-80	Toronto	73	40	57	97
1980-81	Toronto	80	43	53	96
1981-82	Tor-Phil	73	32	38	70
1982-83	Philadelphia	80	43	40	83
1983-84	Philadelphia	76	27	36	63
	Totals	1035	473	621	1094

TIM KERR 24 6-3 225   Forward

"Probably the best power forward in the league," says Tom McVie, last season's Devils' coach and veteran of more than 30 years in hockey . . . Hampered by assorted injuries in recent seasons . . . Went from injury plagued 11-goal, 19-point scorer in 1982-83 to 54 goals, 93 points last season . . . Born Jan. 5, 1960, in Windsor, Ont. . . . Size and strength make him a tower of power around the net . . . Big center who barges into enemy ice with impact of tank . . . Developing into a good faceoff man . . . Flyers signed him as free agent.

Year	Club	GP	G	A	Pts.
1980–81	Philadelphia	68	22	23	45
1981–82	Philadelphia	61	21	30	51
1982–83	Philadelphia	24	11	8	19
1983–84	Philadelphia	79	54	39	93
	Totals	232	108	100	208

BILL BARBER 32 6-0 195   Forward

At crossroads of brilliant career . . . Underwent career-jeopardizing reconstructive knee surgery after last season . . . May have to sit out 1984-85 but hasn't given up hope of continuing his career . . . "He's been one of the best left wings in the game for a long time," said former teammate Bobby Clarke, Flyers' new general manager . . . Born July 11, 1952, in North Bay, Ont. . . . Has

scored 420 career goals in 903 games since joining Flyers as No.
1 draft choice in 1972 . . . Outstanding all-around forward and epit-
ome of good team player . . . Scored 50 goals, 112 points in 1975-
76 . . . Played on two Flyers' Stanley Cup teams.

Year	Club	GP	G	A	Pts.
1972-73	Philadelphia	69	30	34	64
1973-74	Philadelphia	75	34	35	69
1974-75	Philadelphia	79	34	37	71
1975-76	Philadelphia	80	50	62	112
1976-77	Philadelphia	73	20	35	55
1977-78	Philadelphia	80	41	31	72
1978-79	Philadelphia	79	34	46	80
1979-80	Philadelphia	79	40	32	72
1980-81	Philadelphia	80	43	42	85
1981-82	Philadelphia	80	45	44	89
1982-83	Philadelphia	66	27	33	60
1983-84	Philadelphia	63	22	32	54
	Totals	903	420	463	883

BOB FROESE 26 5-11 180   Goaltender

Few goalies have started off so well as he did as rookie in
1982-83 . . . Compiled 12-0-1 record in first 13 games . . . While
Flyers have been waiting for Pelle Lindbergh to reach his potential,
Froese has quietly done steady job in nets . . . Another free agent
who has paid big to Flyers . . . Born June 30, 1958, in St. Catharines, Ont. . . . Nicknamed "Frosty" . . . Relieves stress of goaltending with sense of humor . . . Drafted by St. Louis . . . Plays
standup style in crease and covers angles well . . . Had impressive
28-13-7 record last season . . . Career goaltending record is impressive 45-17-9 for first two NHL seasons.

Year	Club	GP	GA	SO	Avg.
1982-83	Philadelphia	24	59	4	2.52
1983-84	Philadelphia	48	150	2	3.14
	Totals	72	209	6	2.94

MARK HOWE 29 5-11 188   Defenseman

Carrying on tradition of hockey legend father Gordie Howe
. . . Defenseman with good ability on offense and defense
. . . Flyers acquired him from Hartford in 1982 trade . . . Used to
earn money as kid sweeping stands at old Detroit Olympia when
father starred for Red Wings . . . He and brother Marty played with

famous father in WHA...Born May 28, 1955, in Detroit
...Made U.S. National Junior Team at 14, played for 1972 U.S.
Olympic team at 16...Excellent playmaker and shooter as power-
play pointman...Has ability to play left wing...Had subpar season in 1983-84.

Year	Club	GP	G	A	Pts.
1973-74	Houston (WHA)	76	38	41	79
1974-75	Houston (WHA)	74	36	40	76
1975-76	Houston (WHA)	72	39	37	76
1976-77	Houston (WHA)	57	23	52	75
1977-78	New England (WHA)	70	30	61	91
1978-79	New England (WHA)	77	42	65	107
1979-80	Hartford	74	24	56	80
1980-81	Hartford	63	19	46	65
1981-82	Hartford	76	8	45	53
1982-83	Philadelphia	76	20	47	67
1983-84	Philadelphia	71	19	34	53
	NHL Totals	360	90	228	318
	WHA Totals	426	208	296	504

ILKKA SINISALO 26 6-1 190   Forward

Finally learning how to effectively cope with physical play in
North America after making transition from European finesse
game...Eludes checks and moves through traffic well...Adapting
to taking a hit as well as giving one...Has accurate, quickly
released wrist shot...Born July 10, 1958, in Valeakoski, Finland...Skates well laterally and accepts or makes passes neatly
on the move...Sneaky quick...Plays either right or left wing...Gets
in position well for high-percentage shots...Scored first NHL
goal Oct. 11, 1982, on penalty shot against Pittsburgh goalie Paul
Harrison...Twenty-nine goals last season represent his best season since entering NHL.

Year	Club	GP	G	A	Pts.
1981-82	Philadelphia	66	15	22	37
1982-83	Philadelphia	61	21	29	50
1983-84	Philadelphia	73	29	17	46
	Totals	200	65	68	133

RON SUTTER 20 5-11 175   Forward

Member of hockey's famous family...Brothers Duane and Brent
play for Islanders; brother Darryl is with Chicago; brother Brian
is with St. Louis, twin brother Rich is a Flyer teammate...Out
of the mold of the Sutter brothers: hard hitter, hard worker, te-

nacious competitor...Some scouts believe Ron eventually may become best of six Sutter brothers...Born Dec. 2, 1963, in Viking, Alberta...A center who can create offense and play defense...Scored 19 goals in rookie season, three of them game-winners, three shorthanded...With retirement of Bobby Clarke, Flyers expect big things from Ron this season.

Year	Club	GP	G	A	Pts.
1982–83	Philadelphia	10	1	1	2
1983–84	Philadelphia	79	19	32	51
	Totals............	89	20	33	53

BRAD MARSH 26 6-3 220   Defenseman

Will never win a footrace for fast skating but plays a steady, stay-back style of defense...Fearless shot-blocker who will hurl body in front of pucks to prevent them from reaching goal...Can dish out crunching body checks and tie up opposing forwards with size, strength and stamina...Born March 31, 1958, in London, Ont....Knows his role and limitations well and gets the best from his ability...Not easily fooled one-on-one and knows how and when to play the man, not the puck...Was Calgary Flames' captain...Flyers gave up Mel Bridgman to get him.

Year	Club	GP	G	A	Pts.
1978–79	Atlanta	80	0	19	19
1979–80	Atlanta	80	2	9	11
1980–81	Calgary............	80	1	12	13
1981–82	Calg–Phil	83	2	23	25
1982–83	Philadelphia	68	2	11	13
1983–84	Philadelphia	77	3	14	17
	Totals............	468	10	88	98

COACH MIKE KEENAN: Steps into demanding job with no NHL background...Personal choice new Flyers' GM Bob Clarke...Named successor to Bob McCammon May 24, 1984, nine days after Clarke retired as player to become GM...Philadelphia now has youngest high command in NHL...Keenan is 34, Clarke 35, assistant coach Ted Sator, 33, team president Jay Snider, 26...Born Oct. 21, 1949, in Toronto...Coached

Univerisity of Toronto to Canadian collegiate championship last season... Washington defenseman Larry Murphy played for Keenan-coached 1979-80 Peterborough Petes, who won Ontario Junior Hockey League title with 47-20-1 record... Easily recognized by spiffy mustache... Compiled 115-98-26 record from 1980 to 1983 as GM-coach of American League Rochester Americans, who won AHL playoff title in 1982-83... Coached Canadian Junior National team in 1979-80... Played for championship Roanoke (Va.) Rebels of Southern League in 1973-74... Scored 25 goals, 59 points in 58 games, named playoff MVP... Was candidate for job as New Jersey Devils' coach... Played hockey at St Lawrence U. and University of Toronto.

GREATEST ROOKIE

An era began Oct. 11, 1969, when a slightly built, pale-complexioned, 20-year-old with blue eyes played in his first NHL game for the Flyers. He had the innocent face of a choir boy and short, neatly combed curly blond hair but already bore the mark of a hockey warrior: a toothless smile and a set of false teeth.

An era ended April 7, 1984, in the Philadelphia Spectrum when a 34-year-old veteran played his final game. He sat solemnly in the dressing room after The Flyers had been eliminated from the playoffs, 5-1, by Washington. He still had a trace of youth in a face nicked by stick cuts. He looked weary and emotionally drained and his more fashionably long hair was matted to his head with the sweat of hard, honest work.

A new era began May 15, 1984, when Bobby Clarke retired as a player after 15 glorious seasons to take on a new challenge— as general manager—for the team he served so well for so long.

"Bobby Clarke is the greatest competitor I've ever seen in hockey," said a former coach, Fred Shero. "With the way he works, he'll become as good a general manager as he was a player."

No. 16 was as courageous as he was skilled. He was a diabetic throughout his long career. Scouts said he lacked the size, strength and endurance to play in the NHL. The Flyers gambled. They selected him as the 17th player chosen in the 1969 draft.

He did not win the Calder Trophy as Rookie of the Year in 1969-70 (it went to Chicago's Tony Esposito). He played in 76 games (15 goals, 31 assists), but he quickly established himself as a never-say-die, team-first player who gave full effort each time he was on the ice. Critics said he played with a mean streak. They were correct. But he was always respected for his magnificent all-around play, offensively and defensively, and for his inspirational team leadership.

He helped bring two Stanley Cups to Philadelphia. His effort transcended mere statistics but for the record he completed his career with 358 goals, 852 assists, 1,210 points and 1,453 penalty minutes in 1,144 games.

ALL-TIME FLYER LEADERS

GOALS: Reggie Leach, 61, 1975-76
ASSISTS: Bobby Clarke, 89, 1974-75, 1975-76
POINTS: Bobby Clarke, 119, 1975-76
SHUTOUTS: Bernie Parent, 12, 1973-74, 1974-75

Ron Sutter may fill void left by Bobby Clarke's retirement.

PITTSBURGH PENGUINS

TEAM DIRECTORY: Owner: Edward DeBartolo; GM: Eddie Johnston; Dir. Player Personnel: Ken Schinkel; Dir. Media Relations: Terry Schiffhauer; Coach: Bob Berry. Home ice: Civic Arena (16,033; 200' × 85'). Colors: Black and gold. Training camp: Pittsburgh and Erie, Pa.

SCOUTING REPORT

OFFENSE: The name is spelled M-A-R-I-O L-E-M-I-E-U-X. If he's as good in the NHL as he was in Canadian junior hockey, the wobbly Penguins may finally straighten up and parade right.

Pittsburgh made Lemieux, a 6-4, 200-pound center, No. 1 player chosen in the June 9, 1984, draft in Montreal. He scored a record 133 goals, 149 assists, 282 points in 70 Quebec Junior League games last season. GM Ed Johnston believes new coach Bob Berry may use the 18-year-old rookie on a line with Andy Brickley and veteran Rick Kehoe.

Offensively, the Penguins were a one-man team last season when they ranked 20th in goal-scoring. Center Mike Bullard scored 51 goals, 92 points. More scoring power is expected this season with the addition of Lemieux and the presence of Brickley, Mark Taylor, Ron Flockhart, Doug Shedden, Bob Errey and Kehoe. One of the Penguins' three first-round draft picks, center Roger Belanger, should help, too.

DEFENSE: Worst in the NHL last season and may not be much better in 1984-85. Few Pittsburgh forwards backcheck well, giving no help to their defensemen. Opponents often control the puck in Pittsburgh ice for prolonged attacks. Acquiring defenseman Moe Mantha from Winnipeg may help. First-round draft choice Doug Bodger should make the team. Marty McSorley, Kevin McCarthy, Bryan Maxwell, Greg Hotham and Greg Fox are other defensemen.

The goaltending of Denis Herron, Michel Dion, Roberto Romano and Vince Tremblay really wasn't so bad as it seemed last season. They simply received almost no support from teammates, were constantly under withering fire. Romano, a small rookie, showed flashes of brilliance in defeat. He and Herron may share the goaltending this season.

OUTLOOK: It can't get any worse than it's been the last two seasons, in which Pittsburgh twice has finished last and has won only 34 games. The franchise has been hurting financially with

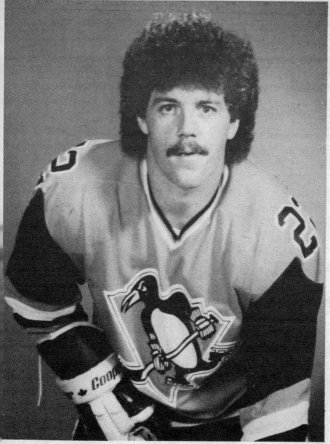

Penguins are hoping for more bullets to go with Mike Bullard.

only four winning records in 17 years in the NHL. The attendance average was only 6,000 last season and local fans saw Penguins win only seven of 40 games in the Civic Arena.

Lemieux should help improve attendance. Berry's coaching should be a plus. Johnston is doing a good job building for the future with quality young players. Injuries made it even worse last season. Pittsburgh has more talent than the Devils and should escape last place this season. Playoff tickets need not be printed for some time.

PENGUIN ROSTER

No.	Player	Pos.	Ht.	Wt.	Born	1983-84	G	A	Pts.	PIM
	Roger Belanger	C	6-0	188	12-1-65/Welland, Ont.	Kingston	44	46	90	66
	Doug Bodger	D	6-0	186	6-18-66/Chemainus, B.C.	Kamloops	21	77	98	90
2	Phil Bourque	D	6-0	179	6-8-62/Chelmsford, Mass.	Pittsburgh	0	1	1	2
						Baltimore	5	17	22	96
15	Pat Boutette	RW	5-8	175	3-1-52/Windsor, Ont.	Pittsburgh	14	26	40	142
23	Andy Brickley	LW	6-0	195	8-9-61/Melrose, Mass.	Pittsburgh	18	20	38	9
						Spring.-Balt.	1	10	11	4
22	Mike Bullard	C	5-11	185	3-10-61/Ottawa, Ont.	Pittsburgh	51	41	92	57
24	Ted Bulley	LW	6-1	192	3-25-55/Windsor, Ont.	Pittsburgh	3	2	5	12
						Baltimore	16	19	35	62
3	Todd Charlesworth	D	6-1	191	3-22-65/Ottawa, Ont.	Oshawa	11	35	46	54
31	Dean DeFazio	LW	5-11	185	4-16-63/Ottawa, Ont.	Pittsburgh	0	2	2	28
						Baltimore	18	13	31	114
10	Bob Errey	LW	5-10	183	9-21-64/Montreal, Que.	Pittsburgh	9	13	22	29
	Tony Feltrin	D	6-1	185	12-6-61/Nanaimo, B.C.	Salt Lake City	8	22	30	94
						Baltimore	0	0	0	2
9	Rob Flockhart	C	5-11	185	10-10-60/Smithers, B.C.	Phil.-Pitt.	27	21	48	44
2	Greg Fox	D	6-2	190	8-12-53/Port McNeill, B.C.	Chi.-Pitt.	2	10	12	97
20	Paul Gardner	C	6-0	193	3-5-56/Toronto, Ont.	Pittsburgh	0	5	5	6
						Baltimore	32	49	81	14
26	Steve Gatzos	RW	5-11	182	6-22-61/Toronto, Ont.	Pittsburgh	3	3	6	15
						Baltimore	14	19	33	43
	Jim Hamilton	RW	6-0	180	1-18-57/Barrie, Ont.	Pittsburgh	2	2	4	4
						Baltimore	34	45	79	54
19	Dave Hannan	C	5-10	173	11-26-61/Sudbury, Ont.	Pittsburgh	2	3	5	33
						Baltimore	18	24	42	98
6	Greg Hotham	D	5-11	185	3-9-56/London, Ont.	Pittsburgh	5	25	30	59
28	Tim Hrynewich	LW	5-11	187	10-2-63/Leamington, Ont.	Pittsburgh	4	5	9	34
						Baltimore	13	17	30	65
17	Rick Kehoe	RW	5-11	180	7-15-51/Windsor, Ont.	Pittsburgh	18	27	45	8
12	Mitch Lamoureaux	C	5-6	185	8-22-62/Ottawa, Ont.	Pittsburgh	1	1	2	6
						Baltimore	30	38	68	136
66	Mario Lemieux	C	6-4	200	10-5-65/Montreal, Que.	Laval	133	149	282	82
	Troy Loney	LW	6-3½	210	9-21-63/Bow Island, Alta.	Baltimore	18	13	31	147
	Darren Lowe	RW	5-10	185	10-13-60/Toronto, Ont.	Pittsburgh	1	2	3	0
	Moe Mantha	D	6-2	197	1-21-61/Lakewood, Ohio	Winnipeg	16	38	54	67
						Sherbrooke	1	1	2	10
5	Bryan Maxwell	D	6-2	198	9-7-55/North Bay, Ont.	Winn.-Pitt.	3	15	18	111
	Kevin McCarthy	D	5-11	195	7-14-57/Winnipeg, Man.	Van.-Pitt.	6	30	36	113
4	Marty McSorley	D	6-1	190	5-18-63/Hamilton, Ont.	Pittsburgh	2	7	9	224
	Ron Meighan	D	6-3	184	5-26-63/Montreal, Que.	Baltimore	4	16	20	36
22	Gary Rissling	LW	5-9	175	8-1-56/Saskatoon, Sask.	Pittsburgh	4	13	17	297
						Baltimore	12	13	25	47
18	Tom Roulston	C	6-1	185	11-20-57/Winnipeg, Man.	Edm.-Pitt.	16	24	40	24
11	Rocky Saganiuk	RW-C	5-8	185	12-15-57/Myrnam, Alta.	Pittsburgh	1	3	4	37
						Baltimore	1	1	2	0
19	Grant Sasser	C	5-10	185	2-13-64/Portland, Ore.	Portland	44	69	113	24
3	Norm Schmidt	D	5-11	190	1-24-63/Sault Ste. Marie, Ont.	Pittsburgh	6	12	18	12
						Baltimore	4	12	16	31
27	Rod Schutt	LW	5-10	185	10-13-56/Bancroft, Ont.	Pittsburgh	1	3	4	4
						Baltimore	15	19	34	48
14	Doug Shedden	C	6-0	184	4-26-61/Wallaceburg, Ont.	Pittsburgh	22	35	57	20
	Bobby Simpson	LW	6-0	190	11-17-56/Caughnawaga, Que.	Baltimore	16	16	32	36
16	Mark Taylor	C	5-11	185	1-26-58/Vancouver, B.C.	Phil.-Pitt.	24	21	45	24
	Tom Thornbury	D	5-11	175	3-17-63/Lindsay, Ont.	Pittsburgh	1	8	9	16
						Baltimore	17	46	63	64
	Tim Tookey	LW	5-11	180	8-29-60/Edmonton, Alta.	Pittsburgh	0	2	2	2
						Baltimore	16	28	44	25
3	Bennett Wolf	D	6-3	205	10-23-59/Kitchener, Ont.	Baltimore	3	13	16	349
	Warren Young	C	6-3	205	1-11-56/Weston, Ont.	Pittsburgh	1	7	8	19
						Baltimore	25	38	63	142

No.	Player	Pos.	Ht.	Wt.	Born		GP	GA	SO	Avg
29	Michel Dion	G	5-10	184	2-11-54/Granby, Que.	Pittsburgh	30	138	0	5.33
1	Denis Herron	G	5-11	165	6-18-52/Chambly, Que.	Pittsburgh	38	138	1	4.08
31	Roberto Romano	G	5-6	171	10-26-62/Montreal, Que.	Pittsburgh	18	78	1	4.59
						Baltimore	31	106	0	3.62
	Vince Tremblay	G	6-1	180	10-21-59/Quebec, Que.	Pittsburgh	4	24	0	6.00
						Baltimore	28	106	2	4.00

PENGUIN PROFILES

MIKE BULLARD 23 5-11 185   **Forward**
"The Bullet"..."He's by far our best player," says GM Ed Johnston...One-man offense for weak, wobbly last-place Penguins in 1983-84...Scored 51 goals, 41 assists, 92 points...Fifteen goals on power plays...Scored goals on 23.9 percent of 213 shots...Born March 10, 1961, in Ottawa, Ont....One of few No. 1 draft picks Penguins didn't give away...Moves skillfully to net...Needs to utilize his linemates more...Center who could improve playmaking...Suspended briefly last season by coach Lou Angotti for curfew violation with teammate Andy Brickley.

Year	Club	GP	G	A	Pts.
1980-81	Pittsburgh	15	1	2	3
1981-82	Pittsburgh	75	37	27	64
1982-83	Pittsburgh	57	22	22	44
1983-84	Pittsburgh	76	51	41	92
	Totals	223	111	92	203

PAT BOUTETTE 32 5-8 175   **Forward**
Hard-nosed competitor...Likes to hit...Not unwilling to menace opponent with stick...Always involved in play...Would prefer to forget last season when goal production dropped to 14...Finished with worst plus-minus record (minus 58) in NHL for weak defensive team...Born March 1, 1952, in Windsor, Ont....Makes things happen in offensive zone with scrappy, tenacious play...Had best years while playing on line in Hartford with Mike Rogers and Blaine Stoughton.

Year	Club	GP	G	A	Pts.
1975-76	Toronto	77	10	22	32
1976-77	Toronto	80	18	18	36
1977-78	Toronto	80	17	19	36
1978-79	Toronto	80	14	19	33
1979-80	Tor-Hart	79	13	35	48
1980-81	Hartford	80	28	52	80
1981-82	Pittsburgh	80	23	51	74
1982-83	Pittsburgh	80	27	29	56
1983-84	Pittsburgh	73	14	26	40
	Totals	709	164	271	435

DENIS HERRON 32 5-11 165   **Goaltender**
Deserves Purple Heart for wounds received in action while playing

for so many losing teams...On third tour of duty in Penguins' Igloo...Twelve-year veteran who endured many 50-shot games for weak Kansas City Scouts...Faced average of 32 shots a game last season...Had good save percentage of .884...Born June 18, 1952, in Chambly, Que....Won only eight of 34 decisions (8-24-2) last season...Had his moment of glory with Canadiens in 1982...Shared Vezina Trophy and led NHL goalies with 2.82 average...Better goalie than his 136-178-73 career record shows.

Year	Club	GP	GA	SO	Avg.
1972-73	Pittsburgh	18	55	2	3.41
1973-74	Pittsburgh	5	18	0	4.15
1974-75	Pitt-KC	25	91	0	3.93
1975-76	Kansas City	64	243	0	4.03
1976-77	Pittsburgh	34	94	1	2.94
1977-78	Pittsburgh	60	210	0	3.57
1978-79	Pittsburgh	56	180	0	3.37
1979-80	Montreal	34	80	0	2.51
1980-81	Montreal	25	67	1	3.50
1981-82	Montreal	27	68	3	2.64
1982-83	Pittsburgh	31	151	1	5.31
1983-84	Pittsburgh	38	138	1	4.08
	Totals	417	1395	9	3.60

MARK TAYLOR 26 5-11 185   Forward

Could blossom into stardom this season...Has all the tools to do it...Acquired from Flyers...Was 24-31-55 in 59 games with Pittsburgh...Plays center...Named College Player of Year in 1980 at University of North Dakota...Born Jan. 26, 1958, in Vancouver, B.C....Not overly swift but has nice moves...Hasn't reached full potential yet...Time is running out...Related to hockey legend Cyclone Taylor.

Year	Club	GP	G	A	Pts.
1981–82	Philadelphia	2	0	0	0
1982–83	Philadelphia	61	8	25	33
1983–84	Phil–Pitt	60	24	31	55
	Totals	123	32	56	88

RON FLOCKHART 23 5-11 185   Forward

"Flocky"...Flyers signed him as free agent...Came through with 33- and 29-goal seasons before dealt across state to Pittsburgh...Born Oct. 10, 1960, in Smithers, B.C....Smooth-skating center with above-average stick-handling skill...Needs to pass puck more often to linemates . . . One of better faceoff winners in NHL . . . Penguins counting heavily upon him to have productive season in 1984-85.

Year	Club	GP	G	A	Pts.
1980-81	Philadelphia	14	3	7	10
1981-82	Philadelphia	72	33	39	72
1982-83	Philadelphia	73	29	31	60
1983-84	Phil-Pitt	76	27	21	48
	Totals	235	92	98	190

RICK KEHOE 33 5-11 180   Forward

Respected veteran winger enters 14th NHL season . . . Injury-plagued 1983-84 made bad season even worse for dead-last Penguins . . . Scored 55 goals in 1980-81 . . . Twenty-nine goals from reaching 400 for career . . . Has always netted numerous power-play goals . . . Born July 15, 1951, in Windsor, Ont. . . . Expected to play 1,000th career game next season . . . Toronto's No. 1 draft selection in 1971 . . . Needs five goals to break Jean Pronovost's Pittsburgh career record of 316 goals . . . Clean player who has only 120 career penalty minutes . . . Former winner of Lady Byng Trophy for sportsmanship.

Year	Club	GP	G	A	Pts.
1971-72	Toronto	38	8	8	16
1972-73	Toronto	77	33	42	75
1973-74	Toronto	69	18	22	40
1974-75	Pittsburgh	76	32	31	63
1975-76	Pittsburgh	71	29	47	76
1976-77	Pittsburgh	80	30	27	57
1977-78	Pittsburgh	70	29	21	50
1978-79	Pittsburgh	57	27	18	45
1979-80	Pittsburgh	79	30	30	60
1980-81	Pittsburgh	80	55	33	88
1981-82	Pittsburgh	71	33	52	85
1982-83	Pittsburgh	75	29	36	65
1983-84	Pittsburgh	57	18	27	45
	Totals	900	371	394	765

ANDY BRICKLEY 23 6-0 195   Forward

Assistant Coach Mike Corrigan believes former All-America collegian will develop into fine left wing . . . Philadelphia draft choice who was dealt to Pittsburgh last season . . . Had impressive minus 7 record as rookie for defensively weak team . . . Born Aug. 9, 1961, in Melrose, Mass. . . . Starred at University of New Hampshire...Good defensive forward...Pro scouts rated him highly as college player...Flyers may regret dealing him to Pittsburgh.

Year	Club	GP	G	A	Pts.
1982–83	Philadelphia	3	1	1	2
1983–84	Pittsburgh	50	18	20	38
	Totals	53	19	21	40

KEVIN McCARTHY 27 5-11 195   Defenseman

Vancouver fans still upset with GM Harry Neale for trading McCarthy...Former Flyers' coach Fred Shero admires his style of play...Philadelphia's first draft pick in 1972...Traded from Vancouver to Penguins last season...Born July 14, 1957, in Winnipeg, Manitoba...Can't be labeled offensive or defensive defenseman...Can play both styles...Good team leader and passer...Has been used as forward.

Year	Club	GP	G	A	Pts.
1977-78	Philadelphia	62	2	15	17
1978-79	Phil-Van	23	1	2	3
1979-80	Vancouver	79	15	30	45
1980-81	Vancouver	80	16	37	53
1981-82	Vancouver	71	6	39	45
1982-83	Vancouver	74	12	28	40
1983-84	Van-Pitt	78	6	30	36
	Totals	467	58	181	239

MARIO LEMIEUX 18 6-4 200   Forward

Long-suffering Pittsburgh fans finally have something to become excited about...Lemieux generated as much excitement in junior hockey as NHL stars such as Bobby Orr, Wayne Gretzky and Mike Bossy...An 18-year-old scoring machine...Broke all existing Junior A scoring records in Canada last season for Laval Voisins...Scored remarkable 133 goals, 249 assists, 282 points in 70 games in Quebec Major Junior League...Had record 61-game scoring streak...Scored six goals, five assists in one game, despite being shadowed and double-teamed...Born Oct. 5, 1965, in Montreal..."An unbelievable goal-scorer," says Ed Johnston..."He has all the qualities to become a superstar," says Hall of Famer Jean Beliveau..."He's going to score lots of goals in our league," Wayne Gretzky said after watching Lemieux play ...Dominates games as Jimmy Brown did in football...

Outstanding puckhandler and passer...Not overly fast and has defensive flaws but has uncanny scoring ability...Penguins won rights to make first pick in draft and choose big, strong center by finishing in last place...Watch No. 66.

Year	Club	GP	G	A	Pts.
1981–82	Laval Voisins	70	33	66	96
1982–83	Laval Voisins	66	84	100	184
1983–84	Laval Voisins	70	133	149	282
	Totals.............	206	250	315	562

MARTY McSORLEY 21 6-1 190   Defenseman

Big and strong...Established himself in rookie season as one of best fighters in NHL...Waged classic standup slugfest in preseason game with Washington's Scott Stevens...Penguins signed him from Ontario Junior League as free agent...Born May 18, 1963, in Hamilton, Ont....Hits hard and finishes his checks...Still has a lot to learn about proper positional play...Penguins' fans like his style and toughness...Quick to retaliate when rivals try to intimidate smaller teammates...Spent 224 minutes in penalty box as rookie.

Year	Club	GP	G	A	Pts.
1983–84	Pittsburgh	72	2	7	9

COACH BOB BERRY: Never out of work for very long...Fired Feb. 24, 1984, as Montreal coach...Hired June 4, 1984, to replace Lou Angotti as coach of Pittsburgh, team with worst record in NHL last season...Failure to win in playoffs resulted in 1983 dismissal as Montreal coach and demotion to scout...Thirty-nine days later, rehired by Montreal...Born Nov. 29, 1943, in Montreal....Has reputation for being stern...Also for being successful...His Los Angeles teams were 107-94-39 in three years from 1978 to 1981 . . . Resigned as Kings' coach to coach Montreal . . . Guided Canadiens to 116-71-36 record from 1981 to 1984 . . . Career NHL coaching record is 223-165-44 but a poor 4-14 in playoffs . . . Reportedly rejected job as Devils' coach last May because New Jersey offers only one-year coaching contracts . . . Scored 159 goals as left wing for Los Angeles and Montreal from 1969 to 1977.

GREATEST ROOKIE

One of Pittsburgh's biggest reasons for failure in 17 NHL seasons is that it has unwisely traded away most of its No. 1 draft positions to try and buy short-term success with veteran players.

Thus, the Penguins have not been able to profit on a long-term basis from many outstanding rookies.

Pierre Larouche is the exception to the rule and, at least until the 1984-85 season, ranks as the best first-year player in Pittsburgh's unsuccessful history.

A slick, quick, colorful center, Larouche was the most dominant scorer in Canada's vast junior hockey program when the Penguins selected him in the 1974 draft. He orchestrated a fine rookie season in 1974-75; 31 goals, 37 assists, 68 points in 79 games. The next season he scored 53 goals.

The fast-skating Larouche, however, gained a reputation for being overly temperamental and difficult to coach, an allegedly undisciplined player on and off the ice. He was traded to Montreal and scored 50 goals, was dealt to Hartford, and last year to the Rangers. Older and wiser now, he's changed his attitude and personality and had an outstanding 48-goal season as a Ranger.

Larouche's reign as the Penguins' greatest rookie may not last beyond this season, if 18-year-old rookie star Mario Lemieux is as good as he's expected to be. The big, record-breaking center from Quebec junior hockey was made No. 1 choice in the June 9, 1984, draft by Pittsburgh.

ALL-TIME PENGUIN LEADERS

GOALS: Rick Kehoe, 55, 1980-81
ASSISTS: Syl Apps, 67, 1975-76
              Randy Carlyle, 67, 1980-81
POINTS: Pierre Larouche, 111, 1975-76
SHUTOUTS: Les Binkley, 6, 1967-68

QUEBEC NORDIQUES

TEAM DIRECTORY: Pres.: Marcel Aubut; GM: Maurice Filion; Dir. Pub. Rel.: Marius Fortier; Coach: Michel Bergeron. Home ice: Quebec Coliseum (15,153; 200′ × 85′). Training camp: Quebec City.

SCOUTING REPORT

OFFENSE: One of the most explosive teams and one of the most difficult for opponents to check. The Nordiques have speed and deception among their forwards and favor a European approach to hockey.

Left wing Michel Goulet (56 goals, 121 points) and center Peter Stastny (46 goals, 119 points) are two of the best forwards in the NHL. Brothers Anton and Marian Stastny, as well as veteran

Peter Stastny racked up 119 points, second to Michel Goulet.

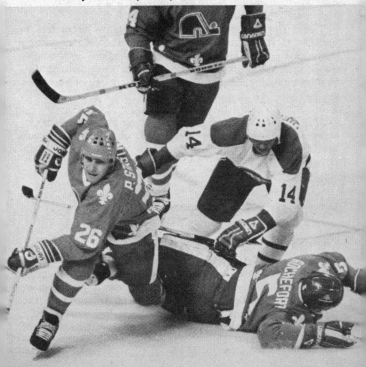

Wilf Paiement and Dale Hunter, provide scoring strength. Tony McKegney, a dedicated cornerman, added a new dimension last season after being acquired from Buffalo. The Nordiques believe he's capable of scoring 35 or 40 goals.

Quebec ranked second in offense last season but, despite its scoring power, finished a poor 10th in power-play efficiency.

DEFENSE: Until last season the Nordiques didn't seem to know the meaning of the word. They engaged in 8-6, 7-5 shootouts.

Coach Michel Bergeron placed greater emphasis on team defense last season. The forwards worked more effectively with the defensemen. They fore-checked and back-checked, played defense in neutral ice, made swifter transition from offense to defense.

The result: Quebec ranked fifth in defense, its best defensive record since entering the NHL in 1979-80, and had the fifth-best penalty-killing record in the NHL.

Mario Marois, once an erratic defenseman, has become a steady rearguard who makes few mistakes. The addition of Andre Dore from St. Louis helps. Normand Rochefort, Pat Price and Randy Moller are other mainstays behind the blue line.

Goalie Daniel Bouchard is a big reason why Quebec had the seventh-best record in the NHL last season. The veteran had what many believed to be his best season. For protection, the Nordiques signed veteran Richard Sevigny, a free agent who sat on the Montreal bench during the playoffs with the emergence of Steve Penney.

OUTLOOK: If the Nordiques can get their problem power play squared away and continue to play decent team defense, they could vault past Buffalo and threaten Boston for first place in the Adams Division.

NORDIQUE PROFILES

MICHEL GOULET 24 6-1 185   **Forward**
Most explosive left wing in NHL . . . Has put together back-to-back 56- and 57-goal seasons . . . Finished second in NHL in goals, third in points last season . . . Led Nordiques with 16 game-winning goals and +62 record . . . Establishes position near net and scores many of his goals from close range . . . Has fast-break speed to score on two-on-one or three-on-two rushes . . . Born April 21, 1960, in Perinbonqua, Que. . . . Long-striding skating style enables him to pull free from backcheckers and get extra step in one-on-

NORDIQUE ROSTER

No.	Player	Pos.	Ht.	Wt.	Born	1983-84	G	A	Pts.	PIM
17	Bo Berglund	RW	5-10	175	4-6-55/Sweden	Quebec	16	27	43	20
	Michel Bolduc	D	6-3	210	3-13-61/Ange Gardien, Que.	Fredericton	2	15	17	96
19	Alain Cote	LW	5-10	203	5-3-47/Matone, Que.	Quebec	19	24	43	41
28	Gord Donnelly	D	6-2	195	4-5-62/Montreal, Que.	Quebec	0	5	5	60
						Fredericton	2	3	5	146
2	Andre Dore	D	6-2	200	2-11-58/Montreal, Que.	St.L.-Quebec	4	28	32	83
23	Paul Gillis	C	5-11	191	12-31-63/Toronto, Ont.	Quebec	8	9	17	59
						Frdericton	7	8	15	47
16	Michel Goulet	LW	6-1	185	4-21-60/Peribonqua, Que.	Quebec	56	65	121	76
32	Dale Hunter	C	5-9	190	7-31-60/Petrolia, Ont.	Quebec	24	55	79	232
19	Rick Lapointe	D	6-2	200	8-2-55/Victoria, B.C.	Quebec	2	10	12	12
						Fredericton	8	22	30	79
22	Mario Marois	D	5-11	190	12-15-57/Ancienne Lorette, Que.	Quebec	13	36	49	151
9	Tony McKegney	LW	6-1	198	2-15-58/Montreal, Que.	Quebec	24	27	51	23
10	Jim Mann	RW	6-0	200	4-17-59/Montreal, Que.	Winn.-Que.	1	2	3	96
						Sherbrooke	6	3	9	94
21	Randy Moller	D	6-2	205	8-23-63/Calgary, Alta.	Quebec	4	14	18	147
27	Wilf Paiement	RW	6-1	210	10-16-55/Earlton, Ont.	Quebec	39	37	76	121
7	Pat Price	D	6-2	200	3-24-55/Nelson, B.C.	Quebec	3	25	28	188
5	Normand Rochefort	D	6-1	200	1-28-61/Three Rivers, Que.	Quebec	2	22	24	47
15	J.F. Sauve	C	5-6	175	1-23-60/St. Genevieve, Que.	Quebec	10	17	27	2
						Fredericton	19	31	50	23
11	Andre Savard	C	6-0	180	2-9-53/Temiskaming, Que.	Quebec	20	24	44	38
12	Louis Sleigher	RW	5-11	195	10-23-58/Nouvelle, Que.	Quebec	15	19	34	32
20	Anton Stastny	LW	6-0	185	8-5-59/Czechoslovakia	Quebec	25	37	62	14
18	Marian Stastny	RW	5-10	193	1-8-53/Czechoslovakia	Quebec	20	32	52	26
26	Peter Stastny	C	6-1	195	9-18-56/Czechoslovakia	Quebec	46	73	119	73
	Trevor Stienberg	RW	6-1	180	5-13-66/Moscow, Ont.	Guelph	33	18	51	104
	Christian Tanguay	C	5-10	190	8-4-62/Beauport, Que.	Milwaukee	41	50	91	
						Fredericton	2	0	2	0
	John Van Boxmeer	D	6-0	192	8-13-52/Petrolia, Ont.	Quebec	5	3	8	12
						Fredericton	10	34	44	48
2	Wally Weir	D	6-2	195	6-3-54/Verdun, Que.	Quebec	2	3	5	17
						Fredericton	6	17	23	45
25	Blake Wesley	D	6-1	200	7-10-59/Red Deer, Alta.	Quebec	2	8	10	75

No.	Player	Pos.	Ht.	Wt.	Born	1983-84	GP	GA	SO	Avg.
35	Danny Bouchard	G	6-0	190	12-12-50/Val D'Or, Que.	Quebec	57	180	1	3.20
	Mario Gosselin	G	5-8	160	6-15-63/Thetford Mines, Que.	Quebec	3	3	1	1.22
30	Clint Malarchuk	G	5-10	170	5-1-61/Edmonton, Alta.	Quebec	23	80	0	3.95
						Fredericton	11	40	0	3.62
33	Richard Sevigny	G	5-8	172	4--11-57/Montreal, Que.	Montreal	40	124	1	3.38

one duels with defensemen... Must be watched closely each shift on ice... Difficult to check.

Year	Club	GP	G	A	Pts.
1978-79	Birmingham (WHA) ..	78	28	30	58
1979-80	Quebec............	77	22	32	54
1980-81	Quebec............	76	32	39	71
1981-82	Quebec............	80	42	42	84
1982-83	Quebec............	80	57	48	105
1983-84	Quebec............	75	56	65	121
	NHL Totals.........	388	209	226	435
	WHA Totals	78	28	30	58

PETER STASTNY 28 6-1 195   Forward

World-class player who defected from Europe to North America and was followed by brothers Anton and Marian... Exceptional all-around performer always at his best in skating, free-wheeling game... A master of the art of bob-and-weave, criss-crossing, straight-ahead on lateral rushes with the puck... Born Sept. 18, 1956, in Bratislava, Czechoslovakia... Boyhood hero was former Chicago star and native Czech Stan Mikita... A center who excels at starting scoring plays with passes and finishing them off with shots and goals... Dynamite on power plays... Deadly driving from blue line to net... Has scored 491 points in 312 NHL career games but was neutralized in playoffs by Montreal.

Year	Club	GP	G	A	Pts.
1980-81	Quebec............	77	39	70	109
1981-82	Quebec............	80	46	93	139
1982-83	Quebec............	75	47	77	124
1983-84	Quebec............	80	46	73	119
	Totals.............	312	178	313	491

DALE HUNTER 24 5-9 190   Forward

One-third of family that is Eastern Canada's answer to Western Canada's hockey-playing Sutter brothers... Brothers Dave and Mark Hunter, respectively, play for Edmonton and Montreal... Stocky, compact, rock-hard center... Likes the rough going and plays a rugged, physical game... Often an instigator whose actions lead to fights or overly aggressive play... Born July 31, 1960, in Petrolia, Ont.... Plays with the tenacity of a bulldog . . . Good defensive forward . . . has been assessed 936 penalty minutes in four seasons with Nordiques.

Year	Club	GP	G	A	Pts.
1980-81	Quebec............	80	19	44	63
1981-82	Quebec............	80	22	50	72
1982-83	Quebec............	80	17	46	63
1983-84	Quebec............	77	24	55	79
	Totals.............	317	82	195	277

DANIEL BOUCHARD 33 6-0 190   Goaltender
Twelve-year veteran with career goaltending record of 262-205-107 . . . Intense, often moody athlete who seldom grants interviews or exchanges pleasantries with fans or teammates . . . Had fine 29-18-8 record last season in 57 games . . . When he's hot, he's hot, when he's not, he's not . . . Born Dec. 12, 1950, in Val D' Or, Que. . . . Active with Christian Athletes Federation . . . Originally property of Boston . . . Spent nine seasons with Atlanta-Calgary franchise . . . Keeps a low profile, hard to get to know . . . Gradually has shed reputation as a poor playoff goalie.

Year	Club	GP	GA	SO	Avg.
1972-73	Atlanta	34	100	2	3.09
1973-74	Atlanta	46	123	5	2.77
1974-75	Atlanta	40	111	3	2.77
1975-76	Atlanta	47	113	2	2.54
1976-77	Atlanta	42	139	1	3.51
1977-78	Atlanta	58	153	2	2.75
1978-79	Atlanta	64	201	4	3.33
1979-80	Atlanta	53	163	2	3.18
1980-81	Calg-Que	43	143	2	3.43
1981-82	Quebec............	60	230	1	3.86
1982-83	Quebec............	50	197	1	4.01
1983-84	Quebec............	57	180	1	3.20
	Totals.............	594	1853	25	3.22

MARIO MAROIS 26 5-11 190   Defenseman
Rangers gave up on him and so did Vancouver . . . Now he has the last laugh . . . Propensity for taking bad penalties and failure to display self-control partially caused trades by Rangers and Vancouver . . . "He's gained maturity and now he's a very fine defenseman, a team leader," says coach Michel Bergeron . . . Born Dec. 15, 1957, in Ancienne Lorette, Que. . . . Nordiques' captain . . . Hits hard and plays physical game but doesn't lose temper so easily . . . Has developed into good positional player . . . Last

season's statistics represent a career high for seven NHL seasons...had +51 record...Teaches at hockey school in Alaska in offseason...Has 911 career penalty minutes...Should reach 200 career points this season.

Year	Club	GP	G	A	Pts.
1977-78	New York R	8	1	1	2
1978-79	New York R	71	5	26	31
1979-80	New York R	79	8	23	31
1980-81	NYR-Van-Que	69	5	21	26
1981-82	Quebec	71	11	32	43
1982-83	Quebec	36	2	12	14
1983-84	Quebec	80	13	36	49
	Totals	414	45	151	196

WILF PAIEMENT 28 6-1 210   Forward

Still as aggressive and free with his stick as when he broke into NHL in 1974 as 18-year-old No. 1 draft selection of old Kansas City Scouts...One of hockey's steadiest right wings for 10 seasons...Also one of its meanest customers...Born Oct. 16, 1955, in Earlton, Ont....Learned to fight for everything he got as a kid because he was raised in a family of 16 children...Former star Phil Esposito hated playing against him because of his rough style of play...Brother Rosaire Paiement played in the NHL for Philadelphia.

Year	Club	GP	G	A	Pts.
1974-75	Kansas City	78	26	13	39
1975-76	Kansas City	57	21	22	43
1976-77	Colorado	78	41	40	81
1977-78	Colorado	80	31	56	87
1978-79	Colorado	65	24	36	60
1979-80	Col-Tor	75	30	44	74
1980-81	Toronto	77	40	57	97
1981-82	Tor-Que	77	25	46	71
1982-83	Quebec	80	26	38	64
1983-84	Quebec	80	39	37	76
	Totals	747	303	389	692

ANDRE DORE 26 6-2 200   Defenseman

Well-educated, well-spoken athlete developing into quality NHL defenseman...Rangers stunted his hockey growth by allowing him to languish in minor leagues...Played outstanding hockey when given a chance by Rangers in 1981-82...Rangers caught flak from fans for trading him to St. Louis Jan. 4, 1983, when he led them in plus-minus ratings but had to give him up to acquire goalie Glen Hanlon ... Nordiques have always wanted him, took him in trade last season with St. Louis ... Born Feb. 11, 1958, in Montreal, Que. ... Has plus record for NHL career ... Unspectacular but steady defenseman ... Plays one-on-one smartly ... Good passer and shot-blocker ... Give him an opening and he'll carry puck in deep to make plays or shoot ... Has studied business administration and marketing in college ... Twelve more points and he'll reach 100 for career.

Year	Club	GP	G	A	Pts.
1978-79	New York R	2	0	0	0
1979-80	New York R	2	0	0	0
1980-81	New York R	15	1	3	4
1981-82	New York R	56	4	16	20
1982-83	NYR-St L	77	5	27	32
1983-84	St L-Que	80	4	28	32
	Totals	232	14	74	88

ANTON STASTNY 25 6-0 185   Forward

Youngest of Quebec's three Stastny brothers ... Plays his best game when stationed at left wing on line with brothers Peter and Marian ... Outstanding skater and stick-handler in typical European fashion ... Makes a few mistakes with or without puck ... Born Aug. 5, 1959, in Bratislava, Czechoslovakia ... Especially effective when skating on power plays ... Skates fast, makes plays fast.

Year	Club	GP	G	A	Pts.
1980-81	Quebec	80	39	46	85
1981-82	Quebec	68	26	46	72
1982-83	Quebec	79	32	60	92
1983-84	Quebec	69	25	37	62
	Totals	296	122	189	311

TONY McKEGNEY 26 6-1 198   Forward

For some reason, Sabres' GM-coach Scotty Bowman was determined to unload him ... Nordiques are glad ... They needed a sizeable left wing capable of playing a defensive style to help them reduce their goals-against ... Quebec gave up Real (Buddy) Cloutier and No. 1 draft to acquire McKegney June 8, 1983 ... Born Feb. 15, 1958, in Montreal ... One of the few blacks playing in NHL ... Normal position is left wing but can play center or right wing, too ... Good checker in defensive zone ... Can go in corner, battle for puck and gain possession...May have untapped goal-scoring ability...Bright, pleasant athlete and good team player...Scored goal in first NHL game Oct. 12, 1978, against Islander goalie Bill Smith.

Year	Club	GP	G	A	Pts.
1978-79	Buffalo	52	8	14	22
1979-80	Buffalo	80	23	29	52
1980-81	Buffalo	80	37	32	69
1981-82	Buffalo	73	23	29	52
1982-83	Buffalo	78	36	37	73
1983-84	Quebec	75	24	27	51
	Totals	438	151	168	319

MARIAN STASTNY 31 5-10 193   Forward

Oldest of the Stastnys...Peter and Anton insist Marian is best hockey player in the family...Injuries in each of the last two seasons have limited his effectiveness and reduced his scoring totals...Born Jan. 8, 1953, in Bratislava, Czechoslovakia...Plays right wing and is most effective in free-flowing, skating game...Moves well through traffic to confuse opponents' checking patterns...Like brothers, a sharp passer, clever stickhandler and respected for his accurate shot from any angle or area inside the blue line.

Year	Club	GP	G	A	Pts.
1981-82	Quebec	74	35	54	89
1982-83	Quebec	60	36	43	79
1983-84	Quebec	68	20	32	52
	Totals	202	91	129	220

COACH MICHEL BERGERON: Earned respect for ability to get high-scoring Nordiques to improve defensive play last season...His tactics helped Quebec upset Buffalo in playoffs...Tough but fair coach who is respected by his players and rival coaches...Good tactician...Always alert and active on bench...Able to make strategical adjustments during games to help Quebec win...Born Nov. 11, 1946, in Chicoutimi, Que....

Seldom out-coached . . . Won three championships in six seasons coaching in Quebec Major Junior League . . . Can be opinionated and outspoken . . . Has sharp wit and sense of humor . . . Joined Nordiques in 1980-81 as assistant coach . . . NHL career coaching record is 138-122-54.

GREATEST ROOKIE

There's no doubt about the greatest rookie since Quebec entered the NHL in 1979.

His name: Peter Stastny.

The only question is: was he really a rookie when he skated into the NHL in 1980-81?

Technically, yes. He was playing in the NHL for the first time but was 24 and had starred in Czechoslovakian and international hockey before defecting to Canada. Under NHL rules, Stastny qualified as a rookie and was chosen winner of the Calder Trophy.

The Nordiques signed Stastny as a free agent Aug. 26, 1980, and he scored 39 goals, 109 points in his rookie season. His scoring points were an NHL rookie record.

Stastny has established himself as one of hockey's leading scorers. Brothers Anton and Marian also defected from Czechoslovakia and now are teammates.

ALL-TIME NORDIQUE LEADERS

GOALS: Real Cloutier, 75, 1978-79
ASSISTS: Peter Stastny, 93, 1981-82
POINTS: Marc Tardif, 154, 1977-78
SHUTOUTS: Richard Brodeur, 3, 1978-79
      Jim Corsi, 3, 1978-79

WASHINGTON CAPITALS

TEAM DIRECTORY: Chairman-Pres.: Abe Pollin; VP/GM: David Poile; Dir. Pub. Rel.: Lou Corletto; Coach: Bryan Murray. Home ice: Capital Centre (18,130; 200′ × 85′). Colors: Red, white and blue. Training camp: Washington, D.C.

SCOUTING REPORT

OFFENSE: Few teams in hockey have the offensive cohesion and ability to rapidly make the difficult transition from offense to

Defenseman Rod Langway again won the Norris Trophy.

defense and back to offense as do the Capitals. The forwards all have at least adequate speed, skate their playmaking routes effectively, are skilled passers and pass-receivers, work smoothly with their defensemen.

So why did Washington have so great a disparity in offense and defense?

Coach of the Year Bryan Murray would like to know.

The Capitals' offense ranked 12th and its power play 18th. Neither level is very good. Defensively, Washington was No. 1 in the NHL. So was its penalty-killing unit.

Mike Gartner is the Capitals' most dangerous shooter. Other forwards who specialize in scoring, checking and the team concept of play include Dave Christian, Bengt Gustafsson, Bob Carpenter, Alan Haworth, defensive star Doug Jarvis, Craig Laughlin, Bob Gould and Gaetan Duchesne.

DEFENSE: No. 1 in 1983-84. Also No. 1 in penalty-killing. But how do you figure this: Capitals allowed the fewest goals and fewest shots by opponents. And yet they surrendered 18 short-handed goals, most against any team in 1983-84.

As Mr. Spock might say, totally illogical.

Rod Langway won the Norris Trophy last season. He often logs 30 or more minutes of playing time a game, is a team leader, organizer of attack rushes with flawless passing, and a tower of strength in the defensive zone.

Scott Stevens is developing into the best young defenseman in the NHL. Larry Murphy, Darren Veitch, Timo Blomqvist and David Shand are other prominent backliners. Al Jensen and Pat Riggin provide outstanding goaltending.

OUTLOOK: Well-coached by Murray, well-managed by David Poile, the Capitals enjoyed their finest hour in 1983-84 since joining the NHL in 1974-75. They added a fine defense prospect, husky Kevin Hatcher, in the draft. They must upgrade their ability to finish their scoring plays and improve on the power play. With ample youth, they should be a force this season and in the future.

CAPITAL PROFILES

MIKE GARTNER 24 6-0 185   **Forward**
Sniper . . . Sharpshooter . . . Marksman . . . Whatever term you use, it describes him best . . . One of NHL's most accurate shooters . . . Can beat goalies with shots to all four corners of net . . . Has

CAPITAL ROSTER

No.	Player	Pos.	Ht.	Wt.	Born	1983-84	G	A	Pts.	PIM
19	Peter Andersson	D	6-2	200	—/Sweden	Washington	3	7	10	20
17	Timo Blomqvist	D	6-0	198	1-23-61/Finland	Washington	1	19	20	84
10	Bob Carpenter	C	6-0	190	7-13-63/Beverly, Mass.	Washington	28	40	68	51
3	Marc Chorney	D	6-0	200	11-8-59/Edmonton, Alta.	Pitt-LA	3	10	13	66
27	Dave Christian	D-C	5-11	175	5-12-59/Warroad, Minn.	Washington	29	52	81	28
12	Glen Currie	C	6-2	180	7-18-58/Montreal, Que.	Washington	12	24	36	20
14	Gaetan Duchesne	LW	5-11	195	7-11-62/Quebec City, Que.	Washington	17	19	36	29
24	Bryan Erickson	LW	5-9	170	—/—	Washington	12	17	29	16
						Hershey	16	12	28	11
	Dean Evason	C	5-9	172	8-22-64/Flin Flon, Man.	Kamloops	57	49	88	137
	Lou Franceschetti	LW	5-11	180	3-28-58/Toronto, Ont.	Hershey	26	34	60	130
11	Mike Gartner	RW	6-0	185	10-29-59/Ottawa, Ont.	Washington	40	45	85	90
16	Bengt Gustafsson	C	6-0	185	3-23-58/Sweden	Washington	32	43	75	16
23	Bob Gould	RW	5-11	195	9-2-57/Petrolia, Ont.	Washington	21	19	40	74
	Kevin Hatcher	D	6-3	183	9-9-66/Sterling Hgts., Mich.	North Bay	10	39	49	61
15	Alan Haworth	LW	5-10	188	9-11-60/Drummondville, Que.	Washington	24	31	55	52
25	Doug Jarvis	C	5-9	165	3-24-55/Peterborough, Ont.	Washington	13	29	42	12
5	Rod Langway	D	6-3	215	5-3-57/Taiwan	Washington	9	24	33	61
18	Craig Laughlin	RW	5-11	198	9-19-57/Toronto, Ont.	Washington	20	32	52	69
	Jm McGeough	C	5-9	170	4-13-63/Regina, Sask.	Hershey	40	36	76	108
8	Larry Murphy	D	6-1	210	3-8-61/Scarborough, Ont.	LA-Wash.	13	36	49	50
20	Gary Sampson	RW	6-0	190	8-24-59/International Falls, Minn.	Washington	1	1	2	6
26	Dave Shand	D	6-2	200	8-11-56/Cold Lake, Alta.	Washington	4	15	19	124
						Hershey	0	1	1	2
	Mike Siltala	LW	6-1	185	8-5-63/—	Hershey	15	17	32	29
3	Scott Stevens	D	6-0	200	4-1-64/Kitchener, Ont.	Washington	13	32	45	201
20	Greg Theberge	D	5-10	187	9-3-59/Peterborough, Ont.	Washington	1	2	3	4
						Hershey	3	27	30	25
28	Chris Valentine	RW	6-0	191	12-6-61/Belleville, Ont.	Washington	6	5	11	21
						Hershey	15	44	59	41
6	Darren Veitch	D	6-0	188	4-24-60/Saskatoon, Sask.	Washington	6	18	24	17
						Hershey	1	6	7	4

No.	Player	Pos.	Ht.	Wt.	Born		GP	GA	SO	Avg.
35	Al Jensen	G	5-10	180	11-27-58/Hamilton, Ont.	Washington	43	117	4	2.91
						Hershey	3	16	0	5.33
31	Bob Mason	G	6-1	180	4-22-61/International Falls, Minn.	Washington	2	3	0	1.50
						Hershey	5	26	0	5.53
1	Pat Riggin	G	5-9	163	5-26-59/Kincardine, Ont.	Washington	41	102	4	2.66
						Hershey	3	7	0	2.27

effective wrist, slap or snap shot from in close, slot or directly from pass in either faceoff circle...Born Oct. 29, 1959, in Ottawa, Ont....Has made red goal-light glow 197 times in five years with Capitals...Swift right wing needs 29 points to pass Dennis Maruk as Washington's leading career scorer...Has led Capitals in shots four straight years.

Year	Club	GP	G	A	Pts.
1979-80	Washington	77	36	32	68
1980-81	Washington	80	48	46	94
1981-82	Washington	80	35	45	80
1982-83	Washington	73	38	38	76
1983-84	Washington	80	40	45	85
	Totals.............	390	197	206	403

DAVE CHRISTIAN 25 5-11 175   Forward

Finished second in scoring to Mike Gartner...Had best scoring production of career in 1983-84...Scored five goals, nine points in eight playoff games...Winnipeg traded him to Washington June 8, 1983, for No. 1 draft position...Born May 12, 1959, in Warroad, Minn....Center who doesn't lose many faceoffs ...Skilled on power play and penalty-killing units...Played defense for championship U.S. Olympic team in 1980...Has good hockey bloodlines...Father Bill Christian and uncles Roger and Gordon are former Olympic players.

Year	Club	GP	G	A	Pts.
1979-80	Winnipeg	15	8	10	18
1980-81	Winnipeg	80	28	43	71
1981-82	Winnipeg	80	25	51	76
1982-83	Winnipeg	55	18	26	44
1983-84	Washington	80	29	52	81
	Totals.............	310	108	182	290

ROD LANGWAY 27 6-3 215   Defenseman

With apologies to Edmonton's Paul Coffey, most NHL players and coaches consider Langway hockey's premier defenseman ...Doesn't have Coffey's offensive power but is better all-around defenseman...Exceptional team leader...Won Norris Trophy in 1983 and 1984 as hockey's best defenseman...Has great endurance and logs vast amount of ice time...Born May 3, 1957, in Taiwan...Raised in Canada by Canadian-born parents...

Montreal blundered by trading him to Capitals in 1982... Seldom misses target when skimming breakout passes to forwards to launch attacks...Playmaking power-play pointman... Powerful shooter...Blocks many shots...All-Star first-team pick again.

Year	Club	GP	G	A	Pts.
1977-78	Birmingham (WHA) ..	52	3	18	21
1978-79	Montreal...........	45	3	4	7
1979-80	Montreal...........	77	7	29	36
1980-81	Montreal...........	80	11	34	45
1981-82	Montreal...........	66	5	34	39
1982-83	Washington	80	3	29	32
1983-84	Washington	80	9	24	33
	NHL Totals	428	38	154	192
	WHA Totals	52	3	18	21

SCOTT STEVENS 20 6-0 200   Defenseman
Pittsburgh GM Ed Johnston calls him best young defenseman in NHL...May also be one of the toughest...Has size, strength, desire...Finally learning to control hot temper and emotions and avoid needless fights and penalties...Born April 1, 1964, in Kitchener, Ont....Excels as bodychecker, shot-blocker, passer...Has cannon shot from blue line...Scored goal on first shot in first NHL game Oct. 6, 1982, as 18-year-old rookie against Rangers at Madison Square Garden... "He can beat you in a lot of ways," says assistant coach Terry Murray.

Year	Club	GP	G	A	Pts.
1982-83	Washington	77	9	16	25
1983-84	Washington	78	13	32	45
	Totals.............	155	22	48	70

BENGT GUSTAFSSON 26 6-0 185   Forward
His knee injury hurt Capitals' chances in last season's playoffs...Respected scorer who also excels defensively... "He has a great defensive mind for hockey," says Devils' GM Max McNab...Nicknamed "Gunner"...Born March 23, 1958, in Karlskoga, Sweden...May be Washington's best all-around forward...Fits in well at left wing, right wing or center...Like most Washington forwards, has fast-breaking speed and on-the-

fly pass-receiving, pass-making ability...Has a five-goal game to his credit...Willing backchecker.

Year	Club	GP	G	A	Pts.
1979-80	Washington	80	22	38	60
1980-81	Washington	72	21	34	55
1981-82	Washington	70	26	34	60
1982-83	Washington	67	22	42	64
1983-84	Washington	69	32	43	75
	Totals............	358	123	191	314

BOB CARPENTER 21 6-0 190   Forward

Became first American player selected as high as third in draft...Washington chose him as its first draft pick in 1981... Smooth skater who breaks well into openings for shots or passes...Went from Massachusetts' St. John's Prep directly into NHL...Works hard...Plays left wing or center...Born July 13, 1963, in Beverly, Mass....Has not yet reached full potential...Has ability to develop into 100-point scorer.

Year	Club	GP	G	A	Pts.
1981-82	Washington	80	32	35	67
1982-83	Washington	80	32	37	69
1983-84	Washington	80	28	40	68
	Totals............	240	92	112	204

CRAIG LAUGHLIN 27 5-11 198   Forward

Gained recognition for superb playoff in 1984...Three of four goals were game-winners...Scoring opportunist around net ...Forgotten man in Washington's trade for Montreal's Rod Langway...Played college hockey at Clarkson...Drafted in 1977 by Montreal...Plays all three forward positions...Born Sept. 19, 1957, in Toronto...Works hard, checks hard... Always a good interview...Knows the game and knows how to analyze it for reporters to relay to fans.

Year	Club	GP	G	A	Pts.
1981-82	Montreal...........	36	12	11	23
1982-83	Washington	75	17	27	44
1983-84	Washington	80	20	32	52
	Totals............	191	49	70	119

DOUG JARVIS 29 5-9 165   Forward

Enters season having played in 720 consecutive games... Ranks third in NHL history for playing consecutive games behind Garry Unger (914) and Sabres' Craig Ramsay (776)... Has not missed a game in nine years... One of hockey's best defensive forwards... Tireless, dedicated worker... Played with four Montreal Stanley Cup championship teams before included in Rod Langway trade which helped Washington and hurt Montreal ... Born March 24, 1955, in Peterborough, Ont.... Quick, darting forechecker and penalty-killer... Intense, serious athlete... Beat Islanders' faceoff ace Bryan Trottier consistently in 1984 playoff series.

Year	Club	GP	G	A	Pts.
1975–76	Montreal	80	5	30	35
1976–77	Montreal	80	16	22	38
1977–78	Montreal	80	11	28	39
1978–79	Montreal	80	10	13	23
1979–80	Montreal	80	13	11	24
1980–81	Montreal	80	16	22	38
1981–82	Montreal	80	20	28	48
1982–83	Washington	80	8	22	30
1983–84	Washington	80	13	29	42
	Totals	720	112	205	317

AL JENSEN 26 5-10 180   Goaltender

Took time but finally reached NHL and established himself as top-grade goalie... Shared league lead for best team goals-against average with goaltending partner Pat Riggin... Uses minimum of moves and motion to make difficult saves look easy... Has nimble catching glove... Born Nov. 27, 1958, in Hamilton, Ont.... Drafted by Detroit in 1978... Missed part of second half of last season because of back injury sustained when lifting weights on Super Bowl Sunday... His 2.91 average was third best in NHL last season... A 25-13-3 record increased his career mark to 55-34-13.

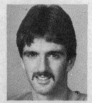

Year	Club	GP	GA	SO	Avg.
1980-81	Detroit	1	7	0	7.00
1981-82	Washington	26	81	0	3.81
1982-83	Washington	40	135	1	3.44
1983-84	Washington	43	117	4	2.91
	Totals	110	340	5	3.35

PAT RIGGIN 25 5-9 163   Goaltender

Came through when most needed last season...Started season with 0-8-1 record...Sent to minor leagues...Summoned to Washington when Al Jensen injured his back...Took over in net and went on 21-6-1 roll for second half of season..."He did the job for us when we really needed it," says Capitals' David Poile...Led NHL with 2.66 goals-against average...Tied for league lead with Jensen in shutouts (4)...Born May 26, 1959, in Kincardine, Ont....Goalie with quick reflexes...Specializes in diving, tumbling, acrobatic saves...Has quick reactions to make point-blank saves on rebounds...Finally established himself as quality NHL goalie...Has NHL career record of 88-67-28...Son of former Detroit goalie Dennis Riggin.

Year	Club	GP	GA	SO	Avg.
1978-79	Birmingham (WHA) ..	46	158	1	3.78
1979-80	Atlanta	25	73	2	3.20
1980-81	Calgary.	42	154	0	3.83
1981-82	Calgary.	52	207	2	4.23
1982-83	Washington	38	121	0	3.36
1983-84	Washington	41	102	4	2.66
	NHL Totals	198	657	8	3.53
	WHA Totals	46	158	1	3.78

COACH BRYAN MURRAY: Did outstanding job behind bench

in Capitals' best season since entering NHL in 1974-75...Out-coached Bob McCammon in Washington's playoff conquest of Flyers last season...Demands the best from his players...Won Jack Adams Award as NHL Coach of the Year in 1982-83...Does much of his own team's advance scouting of opponents...Brother Terry Murray is assistant coach and right-hand man...Born Dec. 5, 1942, in Shawville, Que....Paid his dues before reaching NHL...Drove a truck...Worked in family-owned hotel...Was successful junior coach in Regina of Western League...Produced good teams as coach of Hershey in American League...Former player, coach, athletic director and physical education teacher at McGill University...Not afraid to speak out on issues...Noted referee-needler from bench...Has NHL coaching record of 112-80-34 in three seasons with Washington.

GREATEST ROOKIE

David Poile, Washington's successful young general manager, placed a telephone call to a New York sportswriter during the 1982-83 season.

Being new in the NHL, Poile wanted to know the best way to see that young players are given proper recognition. He expressed concern that rookie defenseman Scott Stevens might be overlooked by some factions of the hockey media.

He was told not to worry. Already the word was out that Stevens, then only 18, was recognized as a most promising rookie.

"The best young defenseman to come into the league that I've seen in a long while," Pittsburgh GM Ed Johnston said of Stevens.

Stevens, big, strong, agile and aggressive, was named to the Professional Hockey Writers Association All-Rookie team in 1982-83.

He improved greatly last season, helping the Capitals enjoy their best season since joining the NHL in 1974-75. A versatile defenseman, he's been the most prominent rookie the Capitals have had, playing with drive and gusto in his first two NHL seasons.

ALL-TIME CAPITAL LEADERS

GOALS: Dennis Maruk, 60, 1981-82
ASSISTS: Dennis Maruk, 76, 1981-82
POINTS: Dennis Maruk, 136, 1981-82
SHUTOUTS: Al Jensen, 4, 1983-84
        Pat Riggin, 4, 1983-84

Sniper Mike Gartner was the Capitals' leading scorer.

CALGARY FLAMES

TEAM DIRECTORY: Pres.-GM: Cliff Fletcher; Asst. to Pres.: Al Coates; Asst. GM: Al MacNeil; Dir. Pub. Rel.: Rick Skaggs; Coach; Bob Johnson. Home ice: Olympic Saddledome (16,764; 200' × 85'). Colors: Red, white and gold. Training camp: Calgary.

SCOUTING REPORT

OFFENSE: The Flames have high hopes that a total team approach which carried them to seven games in the Smythe Division final with the Edmonton Oilers is the style of hockey that will see them climb to within shouting distance of the Oilers this season.

Coach Bob Johnson likes players who can work both ways and play with a little belligerence, too. The eight rookies who were in the team's line-up at the end of the season give Badger Bob upgraded talent and flexibility.

For the Flames to have sufficient attack to be competitive over the long haul with the awesome Oiler offense, several young players must come through. Forwards Dan Quinn (52 points in 54 games) and Carey Wilson from the Canadian Olympic team are key men in the Flame future attack, as is defenseman Allan MacInnis, who had 45 points in 51 games, 14 playoff points and owns one of the game's most devastating shots.

The team had a record four 30-goal scorers last season in Ed Beers, Lanny McDonald, Kent Nilsson and Swedish rookie Hakan Loob, an All-Rookie selection. McDonald was plagued by injuries and his goal production fell from 66 to 33.

Mike Eaves, Doug Risebrough, Jim Peplinski, Richard Kromm and Steve Bozek are industrious grinders, good foot soldiers any team can use.

If defenseman Paul Reinhart is healthy for the entire season after missing 51 games in 1983-84, the Flame attack will be noticeably better. He produced 17 points in 11 playoff games and is such a good attacker that he often has worked as a forward.

DEFENSE: Goalie Rejean Lemelin was perhaps the NHL's most improved player last season and the key figure in the Flames' late surge to move above the .500 mark.

A splendid goalie for a half dozen seasons in Buffalo, Don Edwards had a miserable time in Calgary after a 1982 trade to the Flames. However, working with Hall-of-Fame goalie Glen Hall, Edwards finished 1983-84 strongly and will team with Lemelin to give the club first-class work in goal.

The defense needs a healthy Reinhart to do the job although youngsters Jamie Macoun, who made the All-Rookie team, and MacInnis have great promise. Steve Konroyd, Paul Baxter and Charles Bourgeois are defensive types who can be effective if paired with a puckhandler.

The Flames now have several large, abrasive forwards who can shut down the opposition's big shooters with muscle, a fact they demonstrated in several games against the Oilers.

OUTLOOK: Now that Johnson, one of the game's very best minds has had time to look around the NHL, get his bearings and

Lanny McDonald figured in near upset of Edmonton in playoffs.

FLAME ROSTER

No.	Player	Pos.	Ht.	Wt.	Born	1983-84	G	A	Pts.	PIM
4	Paul Baxter	D	5-11	200	10-25-55/Winnipeg, Man.	Calgary	7	20	27	182
27	Ed Beers	LW	6-2	205	10-12-59/Merritt, B.C.	Calgary	36	39	75	88
2	Charles Bourgeois	D	6-4	205	11-11-59/Moncton, N.B.	Calgary	1	3	4	35
						Colorado	12	32	44	133
26	Steve Bozek	C	5-11	186	11-26-60/Castlegar, B.C.	Calgary	10	10	20	16
	Jeff Brubaker	LW	6-2	210	2-24-58/Hagerstown, Md.	Calgary	0	0	0	19
						Colorado	16	19	35	218
	Bruce Eakin	C	5-10	180	9-28-62/Winnipeg, Man.	Calgary	2	1	3	4
						Colorado	33	69	102	18
7	Mike Eaves	C	5-10	178	6-10-56/Denver, Colo.	Calgary	14	36	50	20
20	Kari Eloranta	D	6-2	200	4-29-56/Finland	Calgary	5	34	39	44
18	Dave Hindmarch	LW	5-11	182	10-15-58/Vancouver, B.C.	Calgary	6	5	11	2
17	Jamie Hislop	RW	5-10	180	1-20-54/Sarnia, Ont.	Calgary	1	8	9	2
19	Tim Hunter	RW	6-1	186	9-10-60/Calgary, Alta.	Calgary	4	4	8	130
16	Jim Jackson	RW	5-8	200	—/—	Calgary	6	14	20	13
						Colorado	5	27	32	4
3	Steve Konroyd	D	6-1	195	2-10-61/Scarborough, Ont.	Calgary	1	13	14	97
22	Richard Kromm	LW	5-11	190	3-29-64/Trail, B.C.	Calgary	11	12	23	27
						Portland	10	4	14	13
	Mark Lamb	C	5-9	167	8-3-64/Swift Current, Sask.	Medicine Hat	59	77	136	30
12	Hakan Loob	LW	5-9	175	—/Sweden	Calgary	30	25	55	22
2	Allan MacInnis	D	6-1	185	7-11-63/Inverness, N.B.	Calgary	11	34	45	42
						Colorado	5	14	19	22
34	Jamie Macoun	D	6-2	200	—/—	Calgary	9	23	32	97
9	Lanny McDonald	RW	6-0	190	2-16-53/Hanna, Alta.	Colorado	33	33	66	64
25	Greg Meredith	RW	6-1	210	2-23-58/Toronto, Ont.	Colorado	23	20	43	39
14	Kent Nilsson	C	6-1	185	8-31-56/Sweden	Calgary	31	49	80	22
11	Colin Patterson	RW	6-2	195	—/—	Calgary	13	14	27	15
						Colorado	2	3	5	9
24	Jim Peplinski	RW	6-3	201	10-24-60/Renfrew, Ont.	Calgary	11	22	33	114
10	Dan Quinn	C	5-10	172	6-1-65/Ottawa, Ont.	Calgary	19	33	52	20
						Belleville	23	36	59	12
23	Paul Reinhart	D	5-11	215	1-8-60/Kitchener, Ont.	Calgary	6	15	21	10
28	Pat Ribble	D	6-4	210	4-26-54/Leamington, Ont.	Colorado	4	27	31	60
8	Doug Risebrough	C	5-11	180	1-29-54/Kitchener, Ont.	Calgary	23	28	51	161
	Gary Roberts	LW	6-2	185	5-23-66/Whitby, Ont.	Ottawa	27	30	57	144
	Mario Simioni	C	6-1	200	4-1-63/Toronto, Ont.	Colorado	16	21	37	35
21	Tony Stiles	D	6-0	200	8-12-59/Carstairs, Alta.	Calgary	2	7	9	20
						Colorado	3	18	21	24
15	Steve Tambellini	C	6-0	190	5-14-58/Trail, B.C.	Calgary	15	10	25	16
	Jeff Vaive	C	5-9	169	6-13-63/Ottawa, Ont.	Calgary	13	21	34	39
5	Mickey Volcan	D	6-0	190	3-3-62/Edmonton, Alta.	Calgary	1	4	5	18
						Colorado	8	9	17	20
	Carey Wilson	C	6-2	205	5-19-62/Winnipeg, Man.	Calgary	2	5	7	2

No.	Player	Pos.	Ht.	Wt.	Born	Team	GP	GA	SO	Avg.
	Tim Bernhardt	G	5-9	159	4-19-58/Sarnia, Ont.	St. Catharine's	42	154	0	3.69
	Mark D'Amour	G	5-9	185	4-29-61/Sudbury, Ont.	Colorado	36	131	0	4.10
1	Don Edwards	G	5-9	160	9-28-55/Hamilton, Ont.	Calgary	41	157	0	4.09
31	Rejean Lemelin	G	5-11	160	11-19-54/Sherbrooke, Que.	Calgary	51	150	0	3.50
35	Mike Vernon	G	5-9	160	2-24-63/Calgary, Alta.	Calgary	1	4	0	21.82
						Colorado	46	148	1	3.35

add the type of players he wants to the roster, the Flames should be on their way up.

The club doesn't have overpowering amounts of great talent but it does have sufficient ability to be a tough out. The players now seem to be believers in Johnson's approach. Obviously, they did what they were told against the Oilers and came very close to a major upset.

However, until the kids learn the ropes, the health of Reinhart and McDonald is very important. The Flames need these quality players to carry a large part of the ropes. The team also hopes center Nilsson can be healthy and devoted for an entire season.

FLAME PROFILES

REJEAN LEMELIN 29 5-11 160   **Goaltender**

Had finest season in nine-year pro career in 1983-84 . . . Played in 51 games, had the most wins (21) in career, 3.50 average and recorded longest undefeated streak of any NHL goalie, 19 games (12 wins, seven ties) . . . Was a finalist for both Masterton and Vezina trophies. . . . Named the club's Most Valuable Player . . . Born Nov. 19, 1954, in Sherbrooke, Que. . . . Spent several seasons in Philadelphia Flyers' chain but saw no NHL action . . . Flames, then in Atlanta, signed him as a free agent in 1978 but he didn't become NHL regular until 1980-81 . . . Good stand-up goalie who plays angles strongly . . . Played a big role in Flames' strong second half and had good playoff showing. . . . Proves that many goalies need much time to develop into competent big-leaguers.

Year	Club	GP	GA	SO	Avg.
1978–79	Atlanta	18	55	0	3.32
1979–80	Atlanta	3	15	0	6.00
1980–81	Calgary	29	88	2	3.24
1981–82	Calgary	34	135	0	4.34
1982–83	Calgary	39	133	0	3.61
1983–84	Calgary	51	150	0	3.50
	Totals	174	576	2	3.67

PAUL REINHART 24 5-11 215   **Defenseman**

Missed 51 games in 1983-84 with a back injury that placed his career in jeopardy . . . Disc problem was corrected by injections of serum made from papaya juice base . . . Returned to line-up for last two weeks of schedule, then was Flames' leading scorer in playoffs with 17 points in 11 games . . . Strong, swift skater of versatility who can play both defense and center...Born Jan. 8, 1960, in Kitchener, Ont. ... Spent four strong junior seasons with Kitchener Rangers...Flames' first-round draft pick in 1979. ...Played well in international hockey as Team Canada member in 1981 Canada Cup and 1983 world tournaments...Flames are hopeful he can avoid injuries and be the All-Star defenseman around which club can be built.

Year	Club	GP	G	A	Pts.
1979-80	Atlanta	79	9	38	47
1980-81	Calgary	74	18	49	67
1981-82	Calgary	62	13	48	61
1982-83	Calgary	78	17	58	75
1983-84	Calgary	27	6	15	21
	Totals	320	63	208	271

MIKE EAVES 28 5-10 178   Forward

Acquired by Flames from Minnesota in summer of 1983 in exchange for Steve Christoff and a draft pick...Had best NHL season with 14 goals and 36 assists while pivoting team's best line with wingers Ed Beers and Hakan Loob...Played college hockey at University of Wisconsin for Flame coach Bob Johnson...Flames wanted his speed, smarts and defensive ability...Born June 10, 1956, in Denver....Grew up in Canada, where he played minor and junior hockey...Was captain of Wisconsin Badgers, where he set scoring records...Rookie award winner in Central League in 1978-79...Made North Stars the next season and was solid player there for four seasons...Leading scorer for Team USA in 1981 Canada Cup tournament.

Year	Club	GP	G	A	Pts.
1978-79	Minnesota	3	0	0	0
1979-80	Minnesota	56	18	28	46
1980-81	Minnesota	48	10	24	34
1981-82	Minnesota	25	11	10	21
1982-83	Minnesota	75	16	16	32
1983-84	Calgary	61	14	36	50
	Totals	268	69	114	183

PAUL BAXTER 29 5-11 200   Defenseman

Led the Flames with 182 minutes in penalties in his first season with team...That total represents almost a reformation for rugged backliner who had 851 minutes in three seasons with Pittsburgh Penguins, including 409 PIM in 1981-82...Has ability to get under the skin of opponents, as indicated when several players earned suspensions for actions in trying to attack him when he

was with the Pens...Tough type who won't give an inch, is also
a master needler...Born Oct. 25, 1955, in Winnipeg...Played
junior hockey with Winnipeg Cubs, then logged time in WHA
with Cleveland and Quebec....Penguins, who had claimed him
in the 1975 draft, reclaimed him from Quebec prior to 1979 expansion draft...Was reclaimed by Quebec in draft for one season,
then signed by Pens as free agent...Flames signed him as a free
agent in 1983.

Year	Club	GP	G	A	Pts.
1974-75	Cleveland (WHA)	5	0	0	0
1975-76	Cleveland (WHA)	67	3	7	10
1976-77	Quebec (WHA)	66	6	17	23
1977-78	Quebec (WHA)	76	6	29	35
1978-79	Quebec (WHA)	76	10	36	46
1979-80	Quebec............	61	7	13	20
1980-81	Pittsburgh	51	5	14	19
1981-82	Pittsburgh	76	9	34	43
1982-83	Pittsburgh	75	11	21	32
1983-84	Calgary............	74	7	20	27
	NHL Totals	337	39	102	141
	WHA Totals	290	25	89	114

DOUG RISEBROUGH 30 5-11 180   Forward

Banner season in good career of solid two-way player...Played
in 77 games, the most in one season in seven years, and scored
a career high 23 goals...Worked with wingers Richard Kromm
and Colin Patterson on defensive line that did a big job against
Edmonton's Wayne Gretzky in playoff series...Flames were able
to land him from Montreal in a 1982 trade for two draft picks
because Canadiens figured persistent injuries placed his career in
jeopardy...Born Jan. 29, 1954, in Guelph, Ont....Played junior
hockey with Kitchener Rangers, claimed in first round of 1974
draft by Canadiens...Member of four Stanley Cup champs in
Montreal...Has outstanding leadership qualities...Shares Flames'
captaincy with Lanny McDonald.

Year	Club	GP	G	A	Pts.
1974-75	Montreal...........	64	15	32	47
1975-76	Montreal...........	80	16	28	44
1976-77	Montreal...........	78	22	38	60
1977-78	Montreal...........	72	18	23	41
1978-79	Montreal...........	48	10	15	25
1979-80	Montreal...........	44	8	10	18
1980-81	Montreal...........	48	13	21	34
1981-82	Montreal...........	59	15	18	33
1982-83	Calgary............	71	21	37	58
1983-84	Calgary............	77	23	28	51
	Totals............	641	161	250	411

LANNY McDONALD 30 6-0 190   **Forward**

After superb 1982-83 season when he scored 66 goals, injuries cut him down to 33 scores last season... Moved into select 400-goal club and now has 418.... Had superb playoff series in near upset of Edmonton, scoring 13 points in seven games... Strong all-around player who owns one of the best shots in NHL and is among best at delivering open-ice body checks... Born Feb. 16, 1953, in Hanna, Alta.... Great junior with Medicine Hat Tigers... First-round draft pick in 1973... Very popular player in Toronto but was traded to Colorado Rockies in controversial 1979 deal for Wilf Paiement... Flames got him from Rockies early in 1981-82 for Bob MacMillan and Don Lever... Deeply involved in projects to aid mentally retarded children, including Special Olympics.

Year	Club	GP	G	A	Pts.
1973-74	Toronto	70	14	16	30
1974-75	Toronto	64	17	27	44
1975-76	Toronto	75	37	56	93
1976-77	Toronto	80	46	44	90
1977-78	Toronto	74	47	40	87
1978-79	Toronto	79	43	42	85
1979-80	Tor-Col	81	40	35	75
1980-81	Colorado	80	35	46	81
1981-82	Col-Calg	71	40	42	82
1982-83	Calgary	80	66	32	98
1983-84	Calgary	65	33	33	66
	Totals	819	418	413	831

CHARLES BOURGEOIS 24 6-4 205   **Defenseman**

His 1983-84 season had two distinct parts to it.... Until mid-February, he was with Colorado in Central League, where he was named to the CHL All-Star team... Then was summoned to Flames, where he had strong finish and an excellent playoffs.... His third and most extensive try at an NHL job and Flames are confident he's there to stay... Born on Nov. 11, 1959, in Moncton, N.B. ... Played college hockey with University of Moncton Blue Eagles... Signed as a free agent by Flames in 1981.... His size and aggressiveness make him a tough defensive-type backliner.

Year	Club	GP	G	A	Pts.
1981-82	Calgary	54	2	13	15
1982-83	Calgary	15	2	3	5
1983-84	Calgary	17	1	3	4
	Totals	86	5	19	24

EDDY BEERS 24 6-2 205   Forward

Big, strong youngster who burst into prominence in 1983-84 when he led Flames in goals with 36 and was second high scorer with 75 points.... Had scored 11 goals in 41 games in 1982-83 in first NHL whirl... That season was shortened by a serious concussion... Born Oct. 12, 1959, in Merritt, B.C.... Had fine college career at University of Denver, where he achieved a rare feat with 50 goals in 42 games in 1981-82... Flames signed him as a free agent and with size, speed, strength and skill, he has the potential to be an All-Star on left wing... Excellent on power play, leading Flames with 16 goals.

Year	Club	GP	G	A	Pts.
1981–82	Calgary	5	1	1	2
1982–83	Calgary	41	11	15	26
1983–84	Calgary	73	36	39	75
	Totals	119	48	55	103

KENT NILSSON 28 6-1 185   Forward

Broken leg suffered in last week of season kept him out of playoffs... Missed 13 games early because of injuries but finished as team's leading scorer with 80 points and had a club-record nine shorthanded goals... Perplexing player of superb talent who always seems capable of more... Born Aug. 31, 1956, in Nynashamn, Sweden... Had two 100-point seasons with Winnipeg Jets in WHA... Reclaimed by Flames in 1979 expansion draft... Had best NHL season in 1980-81 when he established Flame scoring record with 131 points... Exceptional skater and stickhandler, owner of a devastating shot... Excellent athlete who's also good at tennis and soccer.

Year	Club	GP	G	A	Pts.
1977-78	Winnipeg (WHA)	80	42	65	107
1978-79	Winnipeg (WHA)	78	39	68	107
1979-80	Atlanta	80	40	53	93
1980-81	Calgary	80	49	82	131
1981-82	Calgary	41	26	29	55
1982-83	Calgary	80	46	58	104
1983-84	Calgary	67	31	49	80
	NHL Totals	348	192	271	463
	WHA Totals	158	81	133	214

JIM PEPLINSKI 24 6-3 201   Forward

After four NHL seasons, he seems to have settled into a niche as two-way grinder... When he scored 30 goals in 1981-82, he appeared to have high-scoring potential...But seasons of 15 and 11 goals showed that wasn't his strength...However, his defensive ability and hard-working approach will keep him employed...Not slick or fancy but he's strong in the corners and a good leader who sticks up for mates...Born in Renfrew, Ont., on Oct. 24, 1960...Good junior with Toronto Marlboros...Fifth-round draft pick by Flames in 1979...Witty and gregarious, he's a favorite interview of NHL media people.

Year	Club	GP	G	A	Pts.
1980-81	Calgary............	80	13	25	38
1981-82	Calgary............	74	30	37	67
1982-83	Calgary............	80	15	26	41
1983-84	Calgary............	74	11	22	33
	Totals.............	308	69	110	179

COACH BOB JOHNSON: Steady transition in Flames' roster had eight rookies worked into line-up by play-offs...Johnson's shrewd preparation of team saw Flames extend Edmonton to seventh game in Smythe Division final..."Our future outlook has been improved by a large amount," Johnson said. "We have size, speed and aggressiveness that we didn't have before."... Born March 4, 1931, in Minneapolis... Coached high school hockey in Warroad, Minn., then Colorado College for four years...In 1967, was named coach of University of Wisconsin Badgers, where in 15 seasons he built a 367-75-23 record and won three NCAA titles...Badger Bob coached U.S. national and Olympic team five times and handled Team USA in 1981 and 1984 Canada Cup tournaments...Joined Flames in 1982 and admitted to big adjustment, especially in lack of workout time...Son Mark was a member of 1980 U.S. Olympic champs, now with Hartford Whalers...Few NHL hockey people can match his enthusiasm.

GREATEST ROOKIE

Since they entered the NHL in 1972 in Atlanta, the Flames have had two players who won the Calder Memorial Trophy, awarded to the best first-year player in the league—Eric Vail in 1974-75 and Willi Plett in 1976-77—plus a few more who had excellent debut campaigns.

The unusual part of the Vail and Plett careers that started so strongly is that their first years probably were the best seasons in their careers.

Vail was a second-round pick by the Flames in the 1973 entry draft from Sudbury juniors. He did play 23 games with the team in 1973-74, not enough to lose his rookie status in 1974-75 when he scored 39 goals and 21 assists in 72 games to win the Calder award. Vail never matched that goal total, although he did have seasons of 32 and 35 scores.

Plett was a fourth-round draft pick of the Flames in 1975 and after a season in the minors, he joined the Flames early in 1976-77. He scored 33 goals and was named top rookie. He did score 38 goals in 1980-81, the Flames' first season in Calgary. But he never lived up to the promise of that good rookie campaign and was traded to Minnesota in 1982.

ALL-TIME FLAME LEADERS

GOALS: Lanny McDonald, 66, 1982-83
ASSISTS: Kent Nilsson, 82, 1980-81
POINTS: Kent Nilsson, 131, 1980-81
SHUTOUTS: Dan Bouchard, 5, 1973-74
                         Phil Myre, 5, 1974-75

CHICAGO BLACK HAWKS

TEAM DIRECTORY: Pres.: William W. Wirtz; VP: Arthur M. Wirtz Jr.; VP: Tommy Ivan; GM: Bob Pulford; Dir. Pub. Rel.: Jim DeMaria; Coach: Orval Tessier. Home ice: Chicago Stadium (17,300; 188′ × 85′). Colors: Red, black and white. Training camp: Chicago.

Doug Wilson hopes to return to pre-injury form.

SCOUTING REPORT

OFFENSE: At times in 1983-84, the Black Hawks had as many as eight players out of their line-up with injuries and the more than 300 man-games they lost was too big a handicap for just about any team to overcome. The result was a decline of 36 points.

The Hawks' offensive production dipped by 61 goals and 50 of those lost goals belonged to winger Al Secord, one of the NHL's premier players, who missed 66 games because of severely pulled stomach muscles.

In 1982-83, he had scored 54 goals working the left flank on a line with center Denis Savard and right winger Steve Larmer. Last season, he managed only four goals and his linemates both sagged without him. Secord not only is a splendid scorer but also one of the league's toughest performers. His presence does much for his mates' outlook.

If all hands can stay sound for a big part of 1984-85, the Hawks have the material to regain their position in the upper echelon. Larmer, Savard, Secord, Tom Lysiak, Darryl Sutter and Bob MacMillan (from Devils) are established big-league shooters.

Bill Gardner (27 goals) was the team's defensive center who showed that he was capable of a solid offensive contribution. Tom McMurchy and Ken Yaremchuk are two youngsters with big potential.

Doug Wilson, Bob Murray, Keith Brown and Behn Wilson give the attack plenty of skill on the backline.

The Hawks have the potential to score plenty of goals—if they can steer clear of the injury list.

DEFENSE: While the Hawks' attack sagged last season, the defense did, too, a combination that spells trouble. The team surrendered 43 more goals than in the previous campaign.

However, goalie Murray Bannerman moved front and center in the Hawk net and Tony Esposito, the man who held that post for the past 15 years, was relegated to the No. 3 spot, mostly in the press box. Bob Janecyk was backup for most games.

Bannerman, who had a good 3.38 average, probably will play in 65 games this season and goal is one spot about which the Hawks have few worries.

The blueline gang (the two Wilsons, Murray, Dave Feamster, Keith Brown) is plenty adequate to do the job. However, the big problem was that the Hawks got away from the total defense Tessier had stressed in his successful first term.

Tessier must get his crew back on his wavelength and devoted to excellence when the Hawks don't have the puck.

BLACK HAWK ROSTER

No.	Player	Pos.	Ht.	Wt.	Born	1983-84	G	A	Pts.	PIM
2	Randy Boyd	D	5-11	195	1-23-62/Coniston, Ont.	Pitt.-Chi.	0	5	5	22
						Balt.-Spring.	8	24	32	69
4	Keith Brown	D	6-1	192	5-6-60/Cornerbrook, Nfld.	Chicago	10	25	35	94
	Bruce Cassidy	D	5-11	176	5-20-65/Ottawa, Ont.	Chicago	0	0	0	0
						Ottawa	27	68	95	58
11	Denis Cyr	RW	5-11	180	2-4-61/Montreal, Que.	Chicago	12	13	25	19
						Springfield	4	13	17	11
25	Jerome Dupont	D	6-3	190	2-21-62/Ottawa, Ont.	Chicago	2	2	4	116
						Springfield	2	3	5	65
3	Dave Feamster	D	5-11	180	9-10-58/Detroit, Mich.	Chicago	6	7	13	42
8	Curt Fraser	LW	6-0	190	1-12-58/Winnipeg, Man.	Chicago	5	12	17	26
14	Bill Gardner	C	5-10	170	3-19-60/Toronto, Ont.	Chicago	27	21	48	12
10	Jeff Larmer	RW	5-10	172	10-10-62/Peterborough, Ont.	N.J.-Chi.	15	26	41	28
28	Steve Larmer	RW	5-10	185	6-16-61/Peterborough, Ont.	Chicago	35	40	75	34
29	Steve Ludzik	C	5-11	170	4-3-61/Toronto, Ont.	Chicago	9	20	29	73
12	Tom Lysiak	C	6-1	196	4-22-53/High Prairie, Alta.	Chicago	17	30	47	35
	Bob MacMillan	C-LW	5-11	185	12-3-52/Charlottetown, P.E.I.	New Jersey	17	23	40	23
17	Peter Marsh	RW	6-1	180	12-21-56/Halifax, N.S.	Chicago	4	6	10	44
						Springfield	8	13	21	32
33	Tom McMurchy	LW	5-9	165	12-2-63/New Westminster, B.C.	Chicago	3	1	4	42
						Springfield	16	14	30	54
6	Bob Murray	D	5-10	185	11-26-54/Kingston, Ont.	Chicago	11	37	48	78
19	Troy Murray	C	5-11	180	7-31-62/Edmonton, Alta.	Chicago	15	15	30	45
5	Jack O'Callahan	D	6-1	185	7-24-57/Charleston, Mass.	Chicago	4	13	17	67
	Ed Olczyk	LW-C	6-1	195	8-16-66/Palos Heights, Ill.	U.S. Olymp.	21	47	68	36
26	Rick Paterson	C	5-9	187	2-10-58/Kingston, Ont.	Chicago	7	6	13	41
	Wayne Presley	RW	5-11	172	3-23-65/Taylor, Mich.	Kitchener	63	76	139	156
18	Denis Savard	C	5-10	167	2-4-61/Pt. Gatineau, Que.	Chicago	37	57	94	71
14	Al Secord	LW	6-1	205	3-3-58/Sudbury, Ont.	Chicago	4	4	8	7
	Brian Shaw	RW	6-0	180	5-20-62/Edmonton, Alta.	Springfield	2	2	4	2
27	Darryl Sutter	C	5-11	175	8-19-58/Viking, Alta.	Chicago	20	20	40	44
23	Behn Wilson	D	6-3	210	12-19-58/Kingston, Ont.	Chicago	10	22	32	143
24	Doug Wilson	D	6-1	187	7-5-57/Ottawa, Ont.	Chicago	13	45	58	64
7	Ken Yaremchuk	C	5-11	185	1-1-64/Edmonton, Alta.	Chicago	6	7	13	19

No.	Player	Pos.	Ht.	Wt.	Born		GP	GA	SO	Avg
30	Murray Bannerman	G	5-11	184	4-27-57/Ft. Frances, Ont.	Chicago	56	188	2	3.3
	Jim Ralph	G	5-11	162	5-13-62/Sault Ste. Marie, Ont.	Spring.-Balt.	34	129	0	4.0
	Warren Skorodenski	G	5-9	165	3-22-60/Winnipeg, Man.	Spring.-Sher.	33	155	0	5.1

OUTLOOK: The talent is there for a solid club if the Hawks can avoid last season's massive injury list and become believers again in the Tessier approach, something they didn't appear to do last season.

The roster contains some good talent but not enough to survive anything but consistent, two-way effort.

BLACK HAWK PROFILES

MURRAY BANNERMAN 27 5-11 184   **Goaltender**
After sharing goaltending chores with Tony Esposito for two seasons, he took over No. 1 job in 1983-84.... Worked in 56 games for team that struggled much of season and had fine 3.38 average...Paid lengthy dues to become front-line goalie...Excellent technique, stand-up style and good catching hand...Born April 27, 1957, in Fort Francis, Ont....Played junior hockey with Victoria Cougars....Fifth-round pick of Vancouver Canucks in 1977 entry draft...Spent one season in Canuck chain, then was traded to the Hawks for Pit Martin in 1978...Served solid two-season apprenticeship with New Brunswick in American League...Cracked Hawk line-up in 1980 as Esposito's backup and saw workload increase from 15 to 29 to 41 to 56 games.

Year	Club	GP	GA	SO	Avg.
1977-78	Vancouver	1	0	0	0.00
1980-81	Chicago	15	62	0	4.30
1981-82	Chicago	29	116	1	4.17
1982-83	Chicago	41	127	4	3.10
1983-84	Chicago	56	188	2	3.38
	Totals	142	493	7	3.54

KEITH BROWN 24 6-1 192   **Defenseman**
After two seasons in which he missed much time with injuries, playing 33 and 50 games, he had healthy 74-game term in 1983-84...Was one of the team's solid workers in downhill season, producing 35 points, a sound total for basically a defensive backliner...Strong and aggressive, handles the puck well...Born May 6, 1960, in Cornerbrook, Newfoundland...Played junior hockey with Portland Winterhawks...Hawks' first-round entry draft choice in 1979...Became an NHL regular in 1979-80 season at 19....Had good first two years, then knee injuries chopped

him down for two seasons. . . . Won the NHL players' arm wrestling championship one year.

Year	Club	GP	G	A	Pts.
1979–80	Chicago	76	2	18	20
1980–81	Chicago	80	9	34	43
1981–82	Chicago	33	4	20	24
1982–83	Chicago	50	4	27	31
1983–84	Chicago	74	10	25	35
	Totals	313	29	124	153

DOUG WILSON 27 6-1 187   Defenseman

His 1983-84 season ended in early March when he was struck by a puck and suffered a slight fracture of the skull . . . Returned for playoffs but was far below top form . . . High-quality defenseman with complete skills, excellent attacker with devastating shot, strong defensively. . . . Won Norris Trophy and earned first All-Star team berth in 1981-82 . . . Worked hard on defense early in career, then slowly expanded his participation in the attack . . . Born July 5, 1957, in Ottawa . . . Played junior hockey with Ottawa 67s . . . First-round selection in 1977 entry draft . . . Suffers from hyperglycemia and must watch diet closely . . . Brother of former Canadien and King Murray Wilson.

Year	Club	GP	G	A	Pts.
1977-78	Chicago	77	14	20	34
1978-79	Chicago	56	5	21	26
1979-80	Chicago	73	12	49	61
1980-81	Chicago	76	12	39	51
1981-82	Chicago	76	39	46	85
1982-83	Chicago	74	18	51	69
1983-84	Chicago	66	13	45	58
	Totals	498	113	271	384

BOB MURRAY 29 5-10 185   Defenseman

Solid, reliable backliner who was one of the few Hawk regulars who had a plus figure in 1983-84 . . . Good defensively and a fine rusher, who had 48 points last season . . . Missed much of 1981-82 with serious knee injury but has played 79 and 78 games in the past two seasons . . . Born in Kingston, Ont., on Nov. 26, 1954 . . . Played junior hockey for Cornwall Royals, where the coach was Orval Tessier, now Hawk mentor . . . Third-round draft pick of Hawks in 1974 . . . Spent one season in minors, became a

Hawk regular in 1975-76 . . . Made steady progress to become good NHL defenseman.

Year	Club	GP	G	A	Pts.
1975-76	Chicago	64	1	2	3
1976-77	Chicago	77	10	11	21
1977-78	Chicago	70	14	17	31
1978-79	Chicago	79	19	32	51
1979-80	Chicago	74	16	34	50
1980-81	Chicago	77	13	47	60
1981-82	Chicago	45	8	22	30
1982-83	Chicago	79	7	32	39
1983-84	Chicago	78	11	37	48
	Totals	643	99	234	333

DENIS SAVARD 23 5-10 167   Forward

Quick, exciting center who can fire up Chicago Stadium fans in the way Bobby Hull once did . . . After seasons of 119 and 120 points, he "sagged" to 94 last season . . . Absence of left winger Al Secord for most of season is a big reason for that decline . . . Has ability to execute all his moves at top speed . . . Few NHL players can match his acceleration . . . Born Feb. 4, 1961, in Pt. Gatineau, Quebec . . . Excellent junior with Montreal team, scoring 181 points in final season . . . Hawks' first-round entry draft pick in 1980 . . . Canadiens have been criticized strongly for picking Doug Wickenheiser and bypassing Savard.

Year	Club	GP	G	A	Pts.
1980-81	Chicago	76	28	47	75
1981-82	Chicago	80	32	87	119
1982-83	Chicago	78	35	85	120
1983-84	Chicago	75	37	57	94
	Totals	309	132	276	408

TOM LYSIAK 31 6-1 196   Forward

Stormy season in good career of solid center . . . Suspended for 20 games after he dumped linesman Ron Foyt . . . Took NHL to court to earn right to appeal suspension but NHL board refused to change ban . . . Had 47 points in 54 games he did play . . . Skilled in all areas of the game, perfect No. 2 pivot behind Savard . . . Often covers the opposition's top center . . . Born in High Prairie, Alta., on April 22, 1953 . . . Big junior star with Medicine Hat Tigers . . . First-round draft choice of Atlanta Flames in 1973 . . . Sent to Chicago in big eight-player trade in 1979 . . . Was tabbed a can't-miss superstar as a junior but became good player instead...Lives on a farm in rural Georgia in offseason.

Year	Club	GP	G	A	Pts.
1973-74	Atlanta	77	19	45	64
1974-75	Atlanta	77	25	52	77
1975-76	Atlanta	80	31	51	82
1976-77	Atlanta	79	30	51	81
1977-78	Atlanta	80	27	42	69
1978-79	Atl-Chi	66	23	45	68
1979-80	Chicago	77	26	43	69
1980-81	Chicago	72	21	55	76
1981-82	Chicago	71	32	50	82
1982-83	Chicago	61	23	38	61
1983-84	Chicago	54	17	30	47
	Totals	794	274	502	776

STEVE LARMER 23 5-10 185   Forward

Has big-league career off to a fine start with two good seasons...Was the NHL's best rookie in 1982-83 when he had 43 goals and 90 points...Followed that with 35 goals and 75 points in second season as both he and center Denis Savard missed winger Al Secord on big line...Good all-round player, the result of finishing his junior eligibility and playing season in AHL...Born in Peterborough, Ont., on June 16, 1961...Scored 45 and 55 goals in junior hockey with Niagara Falls Flyers...Key member of New Brunswick Hawks, AHL champs in 1981-82, coached by Orval Tessier....Was reunited with younger (by a year) brother Jeff when Hawks obtained him from New Jersey Devils last season.

Year	Club	GP	G	A	Pts.
1980-81	Chicago	4	0	1	1
1981-82	Chicago	3	0	0	0
1982-83	Chicago	80	43	47	90
1983-84	Chicago	80	35	40	75
	Totals	167	78	88	166

DARRYL SUTTER 26 5-11 175   Forward

Black Hawk captain for the past two seasons...One of six Sutter brothers in NHL...Missed 21 games in 1983-84 after he was hit in the face by shot from teammate Doug Wilson....Scored 20 goals, 40 points in shortened season...Family traits very evident as he's not a gifted natural player but effort makes him a good one...Born Aug. 19, 1958, in Viking, Alta....Played junior ockey with Lethbridge Broncos . . . Claimed by the Hawks on the 1th round of the 1978 draft . . . Spent a season in Japan, then was op AHL rookie in 1979-80 . . . One of only three NHL rookies to core 40 goals (Richard Martin, Mike Bossy are the others).

Year	Club	GP	G	A	Pts.
1979-80	Chicago	8	2	0	2
1980-81	Chicago	76	40	22	62
1981-82	Chicago	40	23	12	35
1982-83	Chicago	80	31	30	61
1983-84	Chicago	59	20	20	40
	Totals	263	116	84	200

AL SECORD 26 6-1 205 Forward

Hawks were the most-injured NHL team last season and the big absence was the 66 games missed by Secord because of pulled stomach muscles . . . Had scored 54 goals in 1982-83 when he was a team leader and worked well on line with Denis Savard and Steve Larmer . . . Whole team sagged without him . . . Born March 3, 1958, in Sudbury, Ont. . . . Played junior hockey with Sudbury Wolves . . . First-round draft choice of Boston Bruins in 1978 . . . Was traded to Hawks in 1980 for defenseman Mike O'Connell . . . One of the NHL's toughest players, an awesome fist-fighter who has dabbled in amateur boxing . . . Worked hard to improve hockey skills . . . Best season was 23 goals until he hit for 44 in 1981-82.

Year	Club	GP	G	A	Pts.
1978-79	Boston	71	16	7	23
1979-80	Boston	77	23	16	39
1980-81	Bos-Chi	59	13	12	25
1981-82	Chicago	80	44	31	75
1982-83	Chicago	80	54	32	86
1983-84	Chicago	14	4	4	8
	Totals	381	154	102	256

BILL GARDNER 24 5-10 170 Forward

His defensive ability earned him an NHL job . . . But he has steadily matured into solid offensive player, too, scoring 27 goals and 48 points last season . . . Defensive work stayed at a high level, too, as he was one of the team's few plus players . . . Born in Toronto on March 19, 1960 . . . Spent three seasons in junior hockey with Peterborough Petes . . . Hawks' third-round choice in 1979 entry draft . . . Had a good season in minor-league hockey in 1980-81, earned a job with the Hawks at training camp . . . Good skater

and solid puckhandler . . . The perfect "third" center behind Savard
and Lysiak.

Year	Club	GP	G	A	Pts
1980–81	Chicago	1	0	0	0
1981–82	Chicago	69	8	15	23
1982–83	Chicago	77	15	25	40
1983–84	Chicago	79	27	21	48
	Totals	226	50	61	111

BOB MacMILLAN 32 5-11 185   Forward

Bachelor "Bobby Mac" . . . Was heartthrob of Devils' young fe
male fans . . . Came in swap with Black Hawks' for Don Dietrich
and Rich Preston . . . Didn't have the season he wanted to have in
1983-84 but did explode for two three-goal hat tricks within six
game span . . . Ten-year veteran who can play right wing, left wing
or center . . . Best season was 1978-79 when he scored 37 goals,
108 points for Atlanta Flames . . . Born Sept. 3, 1952, in Char
lottetown, Prince Edward Island . . . Started NHL career with Ranger
in 1972 . . . Excels as penalty-killer . . . Younger brother of forme
Devils' GM-coach Bill MacMillan.

Year	Club	GP	G	A	Pts
1972-73	Minnesota (WHA)	75	13	27	40
1973-74	Minnesota (WHA)	78	14	34	48
1974-75	New York R	22	1	2	3
1975-76	St Louis	80	20	32	52
1976-77	St Louis	80	19	39	58
1977-78	StL-Atl	80	38	33	71
1978-79	Atlanta	79	37	71	108
1979-80	Atlanta	77	22	39	61
1980-81	Calgary	77	28	35	63
1981-82	Calg-Col	80	22	39	61
1982-83	New Jersey	71	19	29	48
1983-84	New Jersey	71	17	23	40
	NHL Totals	717	223	342	565
	WHA Totals	153	27	61	88

ALL-TIME BLACK HAWK LEADERS

GOALS: Bobby Hull, 58, 1968-69
ASSISTS: Denis Savard, 87, 1981-82
POINTS: Denis Savard, 121, 1982-83
SHUTOUTS: Tony Esposito, 15, 1969-70

COACH ORVAL TESSIER: Followed the pattern of what happened to many winners of the NHL Coach-of-the-Year award... Collected that honor in first NHL season, 1982-83, when he guided Hawks to a 32-point improvement to 104 points... In 1983-84, team declined by 36 points and was in danger of missing the playoffs... His abrasive approach had some critics among the players... Big factor in slump was fact that team lost more than 300 man-games to injuries... A winner at all levels of the game... Coached New Brunswick Hawks to American League crown in 1981-82... Had great success in junior hockey with Quebec Remparts, Chicoutimi Saugeens, Cornwall Royals and Kitchener Rangers... Won Canadian junior crowns in Cornwall and Kitchener... Born June 3, 1933, in Cornwall, Ont. ... Played junior hockey with Kitchener Greenshirts and Barrie Flyers... Played only 50 NHL games with Montreal and Boston but was a big scorer during 15-year minor-league career, including four 50-goal seasons... Lack of skating speed kept him out of the NHL.

GREATEST ROOKIE

In their long history as an NHL franchise, the Black Hawks have had many players who produced excellent rookie seasons. Six Hawks have won the Calder Trophy as the best freshman—Mike Karakas (1935-36), Cully Dahlstrom (1937-38); Ed Litzenberger (1954-55); Bill (Red) Hay (1959-60), Tony Esposito (1969-70) and Steve Larmer (1982-83).

However, undoubtedly the greatest first season for any Hawk player and one of the greatest of any rookie was delivered by goalie Esposito.

The Hawks secured Esposito from Montreal Canadiens in the 1969 intra-league draft. He had played 19 games with 2.42 average in the 1968-69 season but the Canadiens had several good young goalies and didn't protect Tony O.

As a rookie with the Hawks, Esposito played 63 games, had a glittering 2.17 average, recorded 15 shutouts and won the Calder and Vezina (leading goalie) trophies.

That was the start of a splendid career in which Esposito was the busiest NHL goaltender, the way he wanted it.

DETROIT RED WINGS

TEAM DIRECTORY: Owner: Michael Illich; GM: Jim Devellano; Dir. Pub. Rel.: Bill Jamieson; Coach and Asst. GM: Nick Polano. Home ice: Joe Louis Arena (19,275; 200′ × 85′). Training camp: Port Huron, Mich.

SCOUTING REPORT

OFFENSE: With a combination of good youngsters and recycled veterans, the Wings improved their attack by 35 goals last season, from 263 to 298, and a vastly improved power play was a big factor.

In 1982-83, the Wings had only 37 goals with a man advantage while they scored 82 last season. It's more than a coincidence that the "old man" (defenseman Brad Park) and "the kid" (rookie Steve Yzerman) were added to the unit.

Yzerman's brilliant season, when he scored 39 goals, 87 points, was the big boost the Wings needed. Now they have a superb, young, offensive center around whom they can construct their attack. They also have a dandy in John Ogrodnick (42 goals in 64 games).

Ron Duguay, the former Ranger glamor boy, did a big job in his first Detroit campaign with 33 goals and old Ivan Boldirev forgot that he is supposed to be at the end of the line and had his best NHL season with 83 points.

Lane Lambert (20 goals), Kelly Kisio, Murray Craven and some energetic defensive types, led by Dwight Foster and Danny Gare, give the team a solid forward arrangement.

What the Wings really need is a defenseman to help Reed Larson on the attack. Park was a fine addition and more than two-thirds of his 58 points were on the power play.

When Jim Devellano took over as Wing general manager in 1982, he said that he had to land some vets to buy time until the club rounded up some good young prospects. Jimmy D has done a good job at both tasks.

DEFENSE: To reach the first plateau—a .500 season—on the climb to respectability, the Wings must move their goals-for total above 300 and their goals-against below that number. Last season, they improved by 21 scores defensively but still surrendered 323.

The Wings will continue to employ a three-goalie arrangement, although young Greg Stefan appears set as the main man. He had a 3.51 average in 50 games. He'll share the net with veteran Eddie Mio and another youngster, Corrado Micalef.

Steve Yzerman made the NHL's All-Rookie team.

The Wings' big problem is that they don't have a top-flight young defenseman. That's why they signed Park, a gimpy-wheeled old warhorse, who had a big year but has a limited future. Reed Larson had a good season and John Barrett, Greg Smith, Colin Campbell and Randy Ladouceur are solid but not spectacular backliners.

OUTLOOK: The Wings' gain to a playoff spot was important but it was a modest upgrading, considering that beating out Toronto Maple Leafs was all it took in the weak Norris Division.

RED WING ROSTER

No.	Player	Pos.	Ht.	Wt.	Born	1983-84	G	A	Pts.	PIM
	Pierre Aubry	C	5-10	170	4-15-60/Cape de la Madeline, Que.	Que.-Det.	5	2	7	25
						Fredericton	4	5	9	4
3	John Barrett	D	6-1	208	7-1-58/Ottawa, Ont.	Detroit	2	8	10	70
19	Ivan Boldirev	C	6-0	190	8-15-49/Yugoslavia	Detroit	35	48	83	20
	Shawn Burr	C	6-1	180	7-1-66/Sarnia, Ont.	Kitchener	41	44	85	50
5	Colin Campbell	D	5-9	190	1-28-53/London, Ont.	Detroit	3	4	7	108
	Murray Craven	C	6-1	170	7-20-64/Medicine Hat, Alta.	Detroit	0	4	4	6
						Medicine Hat	38	56	94	53
10	Ron Duguay	RW-C	6-2	210	7-6-57/Sudbury, Ont.	Detroit	33	47	80	34
11	Blake Dunlop	C	5-11	175	4-4-53/Hamilton, Ont.	St. L.-Det.	7	24	31	24
20	Dwight Foster	C-RW	5-10	175	4-2-57/Toronto, Ont.	Detroit	9	12	21	50
	Jody Gage	RW-LW	5-11	182	11-29-59/Toronto, Ont.	Detroit	0	0	0	0
						Adirondack	40	32	72	32
	Gerard Gallant	RW	5-11	164	9-2-63/Summerside, P.E.I.	Adirondack	31	33	64	195
18	Danny Gare	RW	5-9	175	5-14-54/Nelson, B.C.	Detroit	13	13	26	147
24	Brian Johnson	RW-C	6-1	185	4-1-60/Montreal, Que.	Detroit	0	0	0	5
						Adirondack	4	27	31	233
17	Ed Johnstone	RW	5-9	165	3-2-54/Brandon, Man.	Detroit	12	11	23	54
22	Greg Joly	D	6-1	182	5-30-54/Calgary, Alta.	Adirondack	10	33	43	133
16	Kelly Kisio	RW	5-9	170	9-18-59/Peace River, Alta.	Detroit	23	37	60	34
29	Randy Ladouceur	D	6-2	220	6-30-60/Brockville, Ont.	Detroit	3	17	20	50
						Adirondack	3	5	8	12
14	Lane Lambert	RW	5-11	173	11-18-64/Melfort, Sask.	Detroit	20	15	35	115
28	Reed Larson	D	6-0	195	7-30-56/Minneapolis, Minn.	Detroit	23	39	62	122
21	Claude Loiselle	C	5-11	171	5-29-63/Ottawa, Ont.	Detroit	4	6	10	32
						Adirondack	13	16	29	59
23	Rick MacLeish	C	5-11	185	1-3-50/Lindsay, Ont.	Phil.-Det.	10	22	32	0
33	Bob Manno	D	6-0	185	10-31-56/Niagara Falls, Ont.	Detroit	9	13	22	60
						Adirondack	5	11	16	18
	Rob McClanahan	RW	5-10	180	1-9-58/St. Paul, Minn.	Rangers	6	8	14	21
						Tulsa	4	10	14	10
26	Barry Melrose	D	6-2	205	2-15-56/Kelvington, Sask.	Detroit	0	1	1	24
						Adirondack	2	1	3	37
8	Ted Nolan	RW	6-0	185	4-7-58/Sault Ste. Marie, Ont.	Detroit	1	2	3	25
						Adirondack	10	16	26	76
25	John Ogrodnick	RW	6-0	190	6-20-59/Ottawa, Ont.	Detroit	42	36	78	14
22	Brad Park	D	6-0	200	7-6-48/Toronto, Ont.	Detroit	5	53	58	85
7	Joe Paterson	LW-C	6-1	208	6-25-60/Calgary, Alta.	Detroit	2	5	7	148
						Adirondack	10	15	25	43
	Andre St. Laurent	C	5-10	168	2-16-53/Rouyn, Que.	Pitt.-Det.	3	3	6	30
						Adirondack	26	43	69	129
	Brad Smith	C	6-1	195	4-13-58/Windsor, Ont.	Detroit	2	1	3	36
						Adirondack	15	29	44	128
	Derek Smith	C	5-10	177	7-31-54/Quebec, Que.	Adirondack	16	29	45	10
5	Greg Smith	D	6-0	190	7-8-55/Ponoka, Alta.	Detroit	3	20	23	108
	Larry Trader	D	6-1	197	7-7-63/Barry Bay, Ont.	Adirondack	13	28	41	89
15	Paul Woods	C	5-10	172	4-12-55/Milton, Ont.	Detroit	2	5	7	18
19	Steve Yzerman	C	5-11	177	5-9-65/Cranbrook, B.C.	Detroit	39	48	87	33

No.	Player	Pos.	Ht.	Wt.	Born	1983-84	GP	GA	SO	Avg.
35	Ken Holland	G	5-8	160	11-10-55/Vernon, B.C.	Detroit	3	10	0	4.10
						Adirondack	42	154	0	3.70
41	Ed Mio	G	5-10	180	1-31-54/Windsor, Ont.	Detroit	24	95	1	4.40
						Adirondack	4	11	0	2.64
31	Corrado Micalef	G	5-8	175	4-20-61/Montreal, Que.	Detroit	14	52	0	3.86
						Adirondack	29	132	0	4.48
30	Greg Stefan	G	5-11	178	2-11-61/Brantford, Ont.	Detroit	50	152	2	3.51

However, the strong work by some good young players is a good sign for the future. Time is needed to round up a few more kids of promise, especially on defense.

The team's slight recovery has started Detroit back to the top among hockey towns. Joe Louis Arena will be jammed all the time if the improvement continues.

RED WING PROFILES

GREG STEFAN 23 5-11 178   **Goaltender**
Promising young goalie who made big strides forward in third pro season . . . Played in 50 games for the Wings and had 3.51 average plus a good 19-22-2 won-lost-tied record . . . Had a 2.29 mark in three playoff games . . . Very competitive, combative type . . . Has had 49 penalty minutes in past two seasons . . . Born in Brantford, Ont., on Feb. 11, 1961 . . . Was a teammate of another Brantford native, Wayne Gretzky, in boys' hockey . . . Played junior hockey with Oshawa Generals. . . . Wings' fifth-round choice in 1981 entry draft . . . Spent most of rookie pro season in minors. . . . Played 35 games with the Wings in 1982-83.

Year	Club	GP	GA	SO	Avg.
1981–82	Detroit	2	10	0	5.00
1982–83	Detroit	35	139	0	4.52
1983–84	Detroit	50	152	2	3.51
	Totals	87	301	2	3.96

REED LARSON 28 6-0 195   **Defenseman**
Eight-year veteran had one of his finest seasons in 1983-84 . . . Played some solid defense and had 23 goals, 62 points . . . Excellent skater and a poll of NHL coaches named him as the player with the hardest shot . . . Likes to shoot and was among NHL leaders with 262 shots on goal . . . Last season was his fifth consecutive 20-goal year and the third in a row in which he played all 80 games . . . Born July 30, 1956, in Minneapolis . . . Claimed on the second round in the 1976 entry draft from U. of Minnesota . . . Had 14-game tryout with NHL team at end of 1976-77 season after college suspension over fighting incident . . . Once said he was

frustrated over team's also-ran status but now is happy and relaxed with improving club.

Year	Club	GP	G	A	Pts.
1976-77	Detroit	14	0	1	1
1977-78	Detroit	75	19	41	60
1978-79	Detroit	79	18	49	67
1979-80	Detroit	80	22	44	66
1980-81	Detroit	78	27	31	58
1981-82	Detroit	80	21	39	60
1982-83	Detroit	80	22	52	74
1983-84	Detroit	78	23	39	62
	Totals	564	152	296	448

BRAD PARK 36 6-0 200   Defenseman

Biggest surprise of 1983 was signing of veteran defenseman by the Wings as free agent from Boston Bruins... Felt he could still play but that Bruins planned to ease him out of active duty... Played a large role in Wings' earning of a playoff spot... Despite gimpy knees, he played in all 80 games, producing 58 points and making the team's power play a positive factor... Won Masterson Trophy as player exemplifying sportsmanship, perseverance and dedication... Born in Toronto on July 6, 1948... Junior star with Toronto Marlboros... Claimed by New York Rangers in 1966 draft... Had eight good seasons with Rangers, then was traded to Bruins in 1975, where he continued great career... Passed the 1,000-game mark and became career leader in assists (653) among defensemen last season.

Year	Club	GP	G	A	Pts.
1968-69	New York R	54	3	23	26
1969-70	New York R	60	11	26	37
1970-71	New York R	68	7	37	44
1971-72	New York R	75	24	49	73
1972-73	New York R	52	10	43	53
1973-74	New York R	78	25	57	82
1974-75	New York R	65	13	44	57
1975-76	NYR-Bos	56	18	41	59
1976-77	Boston	77	12	55	67
1977-78	Boston	80	22	57	79
1978-79	Boston	40	7	32	39
1979-80	Boston	32	5	16	21
1980-81	Boston	78	14	52	66
1981-82	Boston	75	14	42	56
1982-83	Boston	76	10	26	36
1983-84	Detroit	80	5	53	58
	Totals	1046	200	653	853

JOHN BARRETT 26 6-0 208   Defenseman

Old-style defensive defenseman...One of the few remaining
practitioners of the art of the open-ice, stand-up body check with
shoulder and hip...Enjoys a good slam as much as most players
like to score a goal...Has produced only 50 points in 282 NHL
games but is very solid in own zone...Born in Ottawa, Ont., on
July 1, 1958...Younger brother of Fred Barrett, who had a long
career with Minnesota...Played junior hockey with Windsor Spit-
fires....Tenth-round draft pick in 1978...Served a three-season
apprenticeship in Kalamazoo and Adirondack...Very active
member of NHL Players' Association.

Year	Club	GP	G	A	Pts.
1980-81	Detroit	56	3	10	13
1981-82	Detroit	69	1	12	13
1982-83	Detroit	79	4	10	14
1983-84	Detroit	78	2	8	10
	Totals	282	10	40	50

STEVE YZERMAN 19 5-11 177   Forward

A large part of the team's future...Had superb rookie season in
1983-84 at 18 with 39 goals, 87 points, and did everything with
flair and style...Had six points in four playoff games...Good
skater, gifted natural scorer and playmaker...Played the point
on the much-improved power play...Born May 9, 1965, in Cran-
brook, B.C....Had 91 points in 56 games with Peterborough
juniors in 1982-83...Wings' first-round choice, fourth overall,
in 1983 entry draft...From opening day of training camp, there
was no doubt that he would be a regular...Did a big job on line
with wingers John Ogrodnick and Ron Duguay.

Year	Club	GP	G	A	Pts.
1983-84	Detroit	80	39	48	87

KELLY KISIO 25 5-9 170   Forward

Free-agent signee who returned from year in Switzerland to have
a big season for the Wings in 1983-84...Scored 23 goals, 60

points and led the team with a plus-16... Smart, smooth center, a fine playmaker and a good defensive worker... Born Sept. 18, 1959, in Peace River, Alta.... Despite two good seasons with Calgary Wrangler juniors, in which he had 263 points, he wasn't claimed in 1979 entry draft... Wings signed him as a free agent... Had big year on loan to Dallas of Central League in 1981-82 (62 goals, 29 playoff points), where coach was Dan Belisle, now Wing assistant... Spent 1982-83 season in Davos, Switzerland, then joined Wings for last 15 games.

Year	Club	GP	G	A	Pts.
1982–83	Detroit	15	4	3	7
1983–84	Detroit	70	23	37	60
	Totals	85	27	40	67

RON DUGUAY 27 6-2 210   Forward

Tagged as a playboy who appeared in gossip columns more than on sports pages during days with New York Rangers... Traded to Wings in June, 1983, delivered splendid two-way season... Had 33 goals, 80 points and did big penalty-killing job... Excellent skater with choppy stride, good on faceoffs, although he played wing much of last season... Born at Sudbury, Ont., on July 6, 1957... Good junior with Sudbury Wolves... First-round draft pick by Rangers in 1978... Scored 151 goals in six Ranger seasons... Disagreement with Ranger coach Herb Brooks plus decline from 40 to 19 goals in 1982-83 led to trade... Worked well with rookie Steve Yzerman... Has worked as a model, is part owner of a New York restaurant.

Year	Club	GP	G	A	Pts.
1977-78	New York R	71	20	20	40
1978-79	New York R	79	27	36	63
1979-80	New York R	73	28	22	50
1980-81	New York R	50	17	21	38
1981-82	New York R	72	40	36	76
1982-83	New York R	72	19	25	44
1983-84	Detroit	80	33	47	80
	Totals	497	184	207	391

DANNY GARE 30 5-9 175   Forward

Made a major change in his approach.... After seven seasons as a big goal scorer, he anchored Wings' defensive line in 1983-84, often shutting down the opposition's big gunners... Has scored

319 goals in career, including seasons of 50 and 56 with Buffalo... Came to the Wings from Buffalo in 1981 deal involving six players... Born in Nelson, B.C. on May 14, 1954... Fine junior with Calgary Centennials... Sabres' second-round draft pick in 1974... Scored 31 goals in rookie season and never looked back... Has had large problems with back injuries in career although clear for past two seasons... Has scored three playoff overtime goals.

Year	Club	GP	G	A	Pts.
1974-75	Buffalo	78	31	31	62
1975-76	Buffalo	79	50	23	73
1976-77	Buffalo	35	11	15	26
1977-78	Buffalo	69	39	38	77
1978-79	Buffalo	71	27	40	67
1979-80	Buffalo	76	56	33	89
1980-81	Buffalo	73	46	39	85
1981-82	Buf-Det.	59	20	24	44
1982-83	Detroit	79	26	35	61
1983-84	Detroit	63	13	13	26
	Totals	682	319	291	610

JOHN OGRODNICK 25 6-0 190   Forward

Excellent big-league left winger who was headed for All-Star team and 50-goal season when he broke his wrist and missed last 16 games... Had 42 goals and 78 points in 64 games... Big, hard-striding winger with a good shot who likes physical style... Born in Ottawa on June 20, 1959... Played junior hockey with New Westminster Bruins, scoring 59 and 48 goals in last two seasons... However, for some strange reason, was a fourth-round draft pick in 1979... Earned Wing job in second pro season... A key figure in the team's future... Minnesota GM Lou Nanne offered all 12 1984 draft picks for Ogrodnick.

Year	Club	GP	G	A	Pts.
1979-80	Detroit	41	8	24	32
1980-81	Detroit	80	35	35	70
1981-82	Detroit	80	28	26	54
1982-83	Detroit	80	41	44	85
1983-84	Detroit	64	42	36	78
	Totals	345	164	165	329

IVAN BOLDIREV 35 6-0 190   Forward

Solid veteran who appeared to be a stopgap for Wings but had his best NHL season in long career with 83 points, including 35 goals... A center much of his career, shifted to the wing last

season...Helped upgrade team's power play...Easy skater, good
puckhandler, smart playmaker...Wings got him from Vancouver
Canucks late in 1982-83 season for forward Mark Kirton...Born
Aug. 15, 1949, in Zranjanin, Yugoslavia...Parents migrated
to Canada when he was an infant...Played junior hockey with
Oshawa Generals...Drafted by Boston in 1969...Wings are his
sixth NHL team...Longest stay was in Chicago, where he had
five good seasons.

Year	Club	GP	G	A	Pts.
1970-71	Boston	2	0	0	0
1971-72	Bos-Cal	68	16	25	41
1972-73	California	56	11	23	34
1973-74	California	78	25	31	56
1974-75	Chicago	80	24	43	67
1975-76	Chicago	78	28	34	62
1976-77	Chicago	80	24	38	62
1977-78	Chicago	80	35	45	80
1978-79	Chi-Atl	79	35	43	78
1979-80	Atl-Van	79	32	35	67
1980-81	Vancouver	72	26	33	59
1981-82	Vancouver	78	33	40	73
1982-83	Van-Det	72	18	37	55
1983-84	Detroit	75	35	48	83
	Totals	977	342	475	817

COACH NICK POLANO: Hard work and patience paid off

when team's steady improvement led to 1983-
84 playoff spot...Patience is a Polano vir-
tue—he had 15-season playing career and five
years of coaching in minor leagues before land-
ing NHL job...Has both head-coach and as-
sistant-GM jobs in Detroit, supplying him with
a full look at the organization...Born in Sudbury, Ont., on March 25, 1941...Played jun-
ior hockey with Hamilton...Was a defenseman for 15 seasons
with three American League and two Central League clubs...Had
brief stint with Philadelphia Blazers in World Hockey Association...Was both GM and coach of Erie Blades in Eastern League
for five years...Won three EHL championships...Was assistant
coach with Buffalo Sabres in 1981-82 season...Wings hired him
from there as head man...Likes disciplined, close-checking hockey.

GREATEST ROOKIE

An interesting note on the Wings' rookies is that the last three members of the team to win the Calder Trophy as top freshman were goaltenders and those excellent debut seasons launched superb careers. They share the Wing greatest rookie honors.

Back in 1950-51, Terry Sawchuk, considered by many as the best goalie ever to play the game, worked all 70 games for Detroit club and had an astounding 1.98 goals-against average and 11 shutouts.

Then in 1955-56, Glenn Hall, the man who brought the inverted "Y" style of playing goal to the NHL, arrived. He played all 70 games, had a 2.11 average and 12 shutouts. Later, he was traded to Chicago when the Wings reacquired Sawchuk from Boston.

In 1964-65, Roger Crozier, a little squirt with a consistently upset stomach, joined the team and had a 2.42 average in 70 games.

The rookie season of another Wing deserves mention. In 1946-47, a somewhat shy 18-year-old made a modest debut with a 7-15-22 point total in 58 games. Lad's name was Gordie Howe.

ALL-TIME RED WING LEADERS

GOALS: Mickey Redmond, 52, 1972-73
ASSISTS: Marcel Dionne, 74, 1974-75
POINTS: Marcel Dionne, 121, 1974-75
SHUTOUTS: Terry Sawchuk, 12, 1951-52, 1954-55
Glenn Hall, 12, 1955-56

EDMONTON OILERS

TEAM DIRECTORY: Owner: Peter Pocklington; Pres.-GM-Coach: Glen Sather; Dir. Player Personnel: Barry Fraser; Dir. Pub. Rel.: Bill Tuele. Home ice: Northlands Coliseum (17,498; 200' × 85'). Colors: Royal blue, orange and white. Training camp: Edmonton.

SCOUTING REPORT

OFFENSE: Scoring goals is a skill the Oilers have possessed in abundance from the time they entered the NHL in 1979. Of course, having center Wayne Gretzky, the most prolific gunner the league has owned, is a big start in that direction.

In 1981-82, the Oilers became the first team to score more than 400 goals when they hit for 417 and they've pushed that mark upward to 424 and 446 in the next two seasons. However, in the 1983-84 campaign, the goal-happy kids discovered that it's possible to score plenty while playing sound defense and the result was the team's first Stanley Cup championship.

In full attacking flight, the Oilers are simply magnificent to watch. Even their slow skaters are quick and their checking line is a threat to score. Puck control is a big part of their defense—the old "tough to score against us if we have the puck" theory—and they do it beautifully to the joy of the spectators.

Gretzky (87 goals, 205 points) leads the assault but he's only one of four 100-point men on the team. Defenseman Paul Coffey (126 points), Jari Kurri (52, 113) and Mark Messier (37, 101) are the others. Glenn Anderson missed the century by one point but he had 54 goals.

Willy Lindstrom, Pat Hughes, Dave Hunter and Kevin MacClelland are good two-way forwards and the defensemen all handle and move the puck well.

Center Ken Linesman is gone, swapped for Boston forward Mike Krushelnyski (45 points), who missed 14 Bruin games due to shoulder injury.

The attack is mighty and the men who make it go are young. Another good Finn, left winger Raimo Summanen, likely will be added this season.

DEFENSE: The Oilers didn't improve defensively by learning to hang back in their own zone and prevent the opposition from scoring. Instead, to handle New York Islanders, who had swept them out of the 1983 final in four games, the Oilers used their speed to force play in the attacking zone and cause the Isles to bog down.

The Cup says it all for Wayne Gretzky and the Oilers.

OILER ROSTER

No.	Player	Pos.	Ht.	Wt.	Born	1983-84	G	A	Pts.	PIM
9	Glenn Anderson	RW	5-11	180	10-2-60/Vancouver, B.C.	Edmonton	54	44	99	65
	Jeff Beukeboom	D	6-4	208	3-28-65/Ajax, Ont.	Sault Ste. Marie	6	30	36	178
18	Ken Berry	LW	5-9	165	6-21-60/New Westminster, B.C.	Edmonton	2	3	5	10
						Moncton	18	20	38	75
	Todd Bidner	LW	6-2	205	7-5-61/Petrolia, Ont.	Moncton	17	16	33	75
6	Rick Chartraw	D-RW	6-2	215	7-13-54/Venezuela	Tulsa	1	4	5	25
						NYR-Edm.	2	6	8	25
7	Paul Coffey	D	6-0	200	6-1-61/Weston, Ont.	Edmonton	40	86	126	104
15	Pat Conacher	C	5-8	185	5-1-59/Edmonton, Alta.	Edmonton	2	8	10	31
						Moncton	7	16	23	30
14	Ray Cote	C	5-11	160	5-31-61/Pincher Creek, Alta.	Edmonton	0	0	0	2
						Moncton	26	36	62	99
	Dale Derkatch	C	5-5	131	10-17-54/Preeceville, Sask.	Regina	72	87	159	92
2	Lee Fogolin	D	6-0	204	2-7-55/Chicago, Ill.	Edmonton	5	16	21	125
	Tom Gorence	RW	6-0	180	3-11-57/St. Paul, Minn.	Edmonton	1	1	2	0
						Moncton	13	14	27	17
8	Steve Graves	LW	6-0	180	4-7-64/Ottawa, Ont.	Sault Ste. Marie	41	48	89	47
						Edmonton	0	0	0	0
21	Randy Gregg	D	6-4	210	2-19-56/Edmonton, Alta.	Edmonton	13	27	40	56
99	Wayne Gretzky	C	6-0	170	1-26-61/Brantford, Ont.	Edmonton	87	118	205	39
23	Marc Habscheid	C	5-11	169	3-1-63/Swift Current, Sask.	Edmonton	1	0	1	6
						Moncton	19	37	56	32
22	Charlie Huddy	D	6-0	197	6-2-59/Oshawa, Ont.	Edmonton	8	34	42	43
16	Pat Hughes	RW	6-1	180	3-25-55/Toronto, Ont.	Edmonton	27	28	55	61
12	Dave Hunter	LW	5-11	195	1-1-58/Petrolia, Ont.	Edmonton	22	26	48	90
29	Don Jackson	D	6-2	210	9-2-56/Minneapolis, Minn.	Edmonton	8	12	20	120
	Mike Krushelnyski	LW-C	6-2	200	4-27-60/Montreal	Boston	25	20	45	55
17	Jari Kurri	LW	6-0	185	5-18-60/Finland	Edmonton	52	61	113	14
11	Willy Lindstrom	RW	6-0	180	5-5-51/Sweden	Edmonton	22	16	38	38
13	Ken Linseman	C	5-9	168	8-11-58/Kingston, Ont.	Edmonton	18	49	67	119
4	Kevin Lowe	D	6-2	191	4-15-59/Lachute, Que.	Edmonton	4	42	46	59
20	Dave Lumley	C	6-1	185	9-1-54/Toronto, Ont.	Edmonton	6	15	21	68
24	Kevin McClelland	RW	6-0	180	7-4-62/Oshawa, Ont.	Edmonton	10	24	34	189
						Baltimore	1	1	2	0
	Larry Melnyk	D	6-0	193	2-21-60/New Westminster, B.C.	Hersh.-Monct.	0	21	21	173
11	Mark Messier	LW	6-0	205	1-18-61/Edmonton, Alta.	Edmonton	37	64	101	165
	Paul Miller	C	5-10	170	8-21-59/Billerea, Mass.	Moncton	9	2	11	68
	Selmar Odelein	D	6-2	195	4-11-66/Quill Lake, Sask.	Regina	9	42	51	45
5	Jim Playfair	D	6-3	186	5-22-64/Vanderhoof, B.C.	Edmonton	1	1	2	2
						Port.-Calg. (WHL)	16	21	37	172
10	Jaroslav Pouzar	LW	5-11	196	1-23-51/Czechoslovakia	Edmonton	13	19	32	44
27	Dave Semenko	LW	6-3	215	7-12-57/Winnipeg, Man.	Edmonton	6	11	17	118
28	Todd Strueby	C	6-1	186	6-15-63/Lanigan, Sask.	Edmonton	0	1	1	2
						Moncton	17	25	42	38
	Raimo Summenen	RW	5-9	178	3-2-62/Finland	Edmonton	1	4	5	2

No.	Player	Pos.	Ht.	Wt.	Born		GP	GA	SO	Avg.
1	Grant Fuhr	G	5-10	185	9-28-62/Spruce Grove, Alta.	Edmonton	45	171	1	3.91
	Lindsay Middlebrook	G	5-7	170	9-7-55/Collingwood, Ont.	Montana	36	162	0	4.62
33	Andy Moog	G	5-9	165	2-18-60/Princeton, B.C.	Edmonton	38	139	1	3.77
	Mike Zanier	G	5-11	175	8-22-63/Trail, B.C.	Moncton	31	96	0	3.30

That speed and puck control is a good system but the Oilers also have improved at work in their own zone. They no longer are susceptible to heavy forechecking pressure.

Grant Fuhr has matured into a first-rate big-league goalie and when Andy Moog got the call in the last two games of the final, he did an excellent job. They're both young and that position should be well covered for the next decade.

The defense pairs—Coffey and Charlie Huddy, Lee Fogolin and Kevin Lowe, Randy Gregg and Don Jackson—are set for a few seasons unless Gregg makes an early exit from hockey to pursue his orthopedic surgeon ambitions.

The addition of MacLelland halfway through 1983-84 gave the Oilers a dimension they lacked—the big, strong, hard-checking center who can do a number on the opposition's big pivot.

OUTLOOK: Bright, bright bright! All the ingredients are there—with youth on their side—for the Oilers to have an extended hold in the throne room.

OILER PROFILES

GRANT FUHR 22 5-10 185   Goaltender

Added maturity to natural talent in 1983-84 and played a big role in Stanley Cup triumph... After an off season, he had 3.91 average in 45 games plus 30-10-4 won-lost-tied record... Sported 2.99 average in 16 playoff games until he missed last two wins of final over New York Islanders because of shoulder injury .. Very athletic and extremely quick, now has added stand-up, stand-my-ground technique... Has perhaps the best catching hand of all NHL goalies... Born on Sept. 28, 1962, in Spruce Grove, Alta.... Superb junior with Victoria Cougars... Oilers' first-round draft pick in 1981... Became first-stringer at 19... Had excellent rookie season (second All-Star team) in 1981-82 .. Offseason shoulder surgery and weight gain hampered him in second term and he did a stint in the minors in 1982-83.

Year	Club	GP	GA	SO	Avg.
1981–82	Edmonton..........	48	157	0	3.31
1982–83	Edmonton..........	32	129	0	4.29
1983–84	Edmonton..........	45	171	1	3.91
	Totals.............	125	457	1	3.77

PAUL COFFEY 23 6-0 200   Defensema

Exceptionally talented player who was runnerup to Wayne Gretzk for scoring title with 126 points, including 40 goals...Probabl the fastest skater in NHL with long, flowing stride...Excelle puckhandler and playmaker with a big shot...Is frequently cri icized for defensive shortcomings but that's so much bald ney...Has made big improvement in that area as he proved i '84 final...Born June 1, 1961, in Weston, Ont....First-roun draft choice from Kitchener Rangers in 1980...Staggered throug first half of rookie season until he started to rush the puck...Certai future All-Star who has a chance to erase Bobby Orr's scorin marks for defensemen.

Year	Club	GP	G	A	P
1980-81	Edmonton	74	9	23	
1981-82	Edmonton	80	29	60	
1982-83	Edmonton	80	29	67	
1983-84	Edmonton	80	40	86	1
	Totals	314	107	236	3

WAYNE GRETZKY 23 6-0 170   Forwar

Being captain of a Stanley Cup championship team means, at 2 he's done it all...Holder of 38 NHL scoring records...His 8 goals, 118 assists in 1983-84 raised five-season NHL totals to 35 goals, 558 assists for 914 points...Led playoff scorers with 1 22-35 total and now has 109 points in 52 Cup games...Score two goals in each of concluding two games of final against I landers...Has the highest profile, especially in the U.S., of an NHL player in history...Born Jan. 26, 1961, in Brantford, On ...Has earned reams of publicity since he was 10 years o age...Oilers bought him from Indianapolis team in WHA de back in 1978...Has won most top athlete honors in Canada an U.S....Demand for interviews is enormous but he handles it wi grace and humor.

Year	Club	GP	G	A	P
1978-79	Ind-Edm (WHA)	80	46	64	1
1979-80	Edmonton	79	51	86	1
1980-81	Edmonton	80	55	109	1
1981-82	Edmonton	80	92	120	2
1982-83	Edmonton	80	71	125	1
1983-84	Edmonton	74	87	118	2
	NHL Totals	393	356	558	9
	WHA Totals	80	46	64	

KEVIN LOWE 25 6-2 191 Defenseman

The Oilers' backbone... Solid, reliable worker who's a model of consistency.... Probably the club's best player game in, game out, in playoff march to Stanley Cup... Excellent defensively, teamed with veteran Lee Fogolin, good on penalty-killing unit and when opposition has big shooters on the ice... Improving on the attack as 46 points was career high... Mature, gregarious man who is one of the best interviews in the NHL on self, team and game... Born April 15, 1959, in Lachute, Quebec... Oilers' first-round pick in 1979 entry draft... Was strong attacker in junior hockey with Quebec Remparts but took defensive approach as a pro... One of the NHL's leading gourmets: excellent cook and knowledgeable about good restaurants.

Year	Club	GP	G	A	Pts.
1979-80	Edmonton	64	2	19	21
1980-81	Edmonton	79	10	24	34
1981-82	Edmonton	80	9	31	40
1982-83	Edmonton	80	6	34	40
1983-84	Edmonton	80	4	42	46
	Totals	383	31	150	181

RANDY GREGG 28 6-4 210 Defenseman

The Doc... Medical doctor who plans to become an orthopedic surgeon... Has set no schedule on how long he'll play hockey but admits to loving the game... An important addition for the Oilers late in 1981-82 because he added much-needed size and muscle, especially teamed on backline with Don Jackson... Improving offensively, he had 13 goals, 40 points last season, 10 points in playoffs... Born Feb. 19, 1956, in Edmonton... Was Canadian college all-star at U. of Alberta, where he studied medicine... Spent 1979-80 with Canadian Olympic team, then continued medical studies and played for Kokudo Bunnies in Japan... Signed as a free agent by the Oilers... His hair is the brightest red of any NHL carrot-top.

Year	Club	GP	G	A	Pts.
1982-83	Edmonton	80	6	22	28
1983-84	Edmonton	80	13	27	40
	Totals	160	19	49	68

CHARLIE HUDDY 25 6-0 197   Defenseman

A free agent who made good... When he wasn't claimed in the 1979 entry draft after solid junior career with Oshawa Generals, Oilers signed him as a free agent... After 2½ seasons in Central League with Houston and Wichita, he was called up by Oilers during injury emergency and made most of opportunity... Has solid offensive skills but, teamed with high-scoring Paul Coffey, he's taken on defensive role... Born June 2, 1959, in Oshawa, Ont.... Solid junior, surprise that he wasn't drafted... Strong, quick skater who's good at moving puck up ice... Was first winner of Emory Edge Award in 1982-83 as the NHL's leading plus player... Missed seven games of Cup march with shoulder injury... Was strong in late wins over the Islanders.

Year	Club	GP	G	A	Pts.
1980-81	Edmonton	12	2	5	7
1981-82	Edmonton	41	4	11	15
1982-83	Edmonton	76	20	37	57
1983-84	Edmonton	75	8	34	42
	Totals	204	34	87	121

JARI KURRI 24 6-0 185   Forward

Splendid winger who teams magnificently with Wayne Gretzky... Had excellent 1983-84, scoring 52 goals and 113 points during the season, then leading all playoff scorers with 14 goals... Superb skater with speed and agility, fine passer and owner of a devastating shot... Was an 1982-83 nominee as best defensive forward... Born May 18, 1960, in Helsinki, Finland... Spent three seasons with Jokerit team in Finnish First Division... Fourth-round pick in 1980 entry draft... Word was that he had signed new contract to stay in Finland and many teams passed on him... Oilers knew he was available and signed him... Scored 32 goals in each of first two NHL seasons, then 45 before hitting for the 52.

Year	Club	GP	G	A	Pts
1980-81	Edmonton	75	32	43	7
1981-82	Edmonton	71	32	54	8
1982-83	Edmonton	80	45	59	10
1983-84	Edmonton	64	52	61	11
	Totals	290	161	217	37

MARK MESSIER 23 6-0 205   Forward

Awesome! That's the only suitable word to describe his play in
1984 playoffs... All-Star left winger in 1981-82 and 1982-83, he
shifted to center late last season and won Conn Smythe Trophy
as playoff MVP... Had eight goals and 18 points in playoffs but
several goals were important ones... Outstanding skater with great
speed and acceleration... With size, agility, abrasive attitude and
big shot, he can be terrifying when on the prowl... Born Jan. 18,
1961, in Edmonton.... Father Doug was a minor-league defenseman, coached Oilers' New Brunswick farm team past two
years... Has been a pro for seven seasons because he jumped
from Tier Two junior to WHA in 1978... A third-round selection
by Oilers in 1979 entry draft... Needed two Oiler seasons to
overcome less-than-serious approach.

Year	Club	GP	G	A	Pts.
1978-79	Ind-Cin (WHA)	52	1	10	11
1979-80	Edmonton..........	75	12	21	33
1980-81	Edmonton..........	72	23	40	63
1981-82	Edmonton..........	78	50	38	88
1982-83	Edmonton..........	77	48	58	106
1983-84	Edmonton..........	73	37	64	101
	NHL Totals	375	170	221	391
	WHA Totals	52	1	10	11

GLENN ANDERSON 24 5-11 180   Forward

Another jet who helps make Oilers one of the fastest-ever NHL
teams... Ultra-quick skater who can execute all his moves at top
speed... Had 54 goals, 99 points in 1983-84, then was strong
playoff performer with 17 points... Tough and bellicose, he can
play both wings... Now has scored 170 goals in four NHL seasons... Has a laid-back, off-the-wall approach to life... Born
Oct. 2, 1960, in Vancouver... Excellent college player at U. of
Denver with 55 points in 40 games in 1978-79... Spent 1979-80
with Canadian Olympic team... Oilers' third-round draft pick in
1979... Has played on line with Mark Messier much of NHL
time.

Year	Club	GP	G	A	Pts.
1980-81	Edmonton..........	58	30	23	53
1981-82	Edmonton..........	80	38	67	105
1982-83	Edmonton..........	72	48	56	104
1983-84	Edmonton..........	80	54	45	99
	Totals.............	290	170	191	261

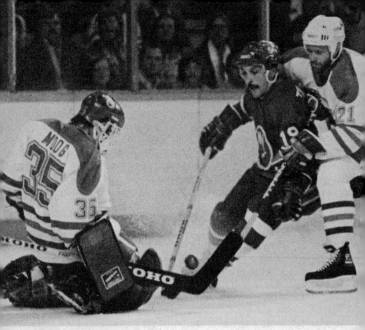

"Doc" Gregg administers to Bryan Trottier in Cup play.

COACH GLEN SATHER: Stuck to plan to build club with swift, young offensive players and it paid off with Stanley Cup in fifth NHL season ... Allowed players to mature offensively, then slowly inspired defensive improvement... Has the most wide-ranging responsibilities of any NHL executive with president, general manager and head coach titles in addition to being alternate governor to NHL board...  Can handle heavy load because he has good people around him and delegates authority well... Born Sept. 2, 1943, in High River, Alta.... Played junior hockey in Edmonton and nine seasons in NHL with six different teams... Defensive specialist who scored 80 goals in 648 games... Joined Oilers in WHA as a player in 1977 and moved into executive end of the game as assistant coach later that season... Close friend of owner Peter Pockling-ton... Made wise investments in real estate in resort town of Banff, Alta., where he operated a summer hockey school for many years.

GREATEST ROOKIE

When is a player in his first season in a league not a rookie? Well, when he's Wayne Gretzky and the season is 1979-80 in the National Hockey League.

Gretzky had joined Edmonton Oilers in the previous season when the Oilers were in the final year of the WHA. He was a legitimate pro hockey rookie that year when he produced 110 points at 17 years of age and added 30 points in 13 playoff games.

However, when the four survivors of the WHA (Edmonton, Hartford, Winnipeg, Quebec) joined the NHL in the 1979 merger, the NHL decreed that players with WHA experience would not be eligible for the Calder Trophy in the 1979-80 season. An unusual law considering that Quebec's Peter Stastny, a veteran of the Czechoslovakian national team and the Czech major league, won the Calder in 1980-81.

While Gretzky officially wasn't a "rookie", for our purposes here, he'll be called "the greatest first-year NHL player" the Oilers have had. In that 1979-80 season, he produced 137 points, the same total as Marcel Dionne of Los Angeles Kings. Dionne was named scoring champ because he had more goals than No. 99.

ALL-TIME OILER LEADERS

GOALS: Wayne Gretzky, 92, 1981-82
ASSISTS: Wayne Gretzky, 125, 1982-83
POINTS: Wayne Gretzky, 212, 1981-82
SHUTOUTS: Eddie Mio, 1, 1979-80
      Andy Moog, 1, 1982-83, 1983-84
      Grant Fuhr, 1, 1983-84

LOS ANGELES KINGS

TEAM DIRECTORY: Chairman: Dr. Jerry Buss; Pres.: Lou Baumeister; GM: Rogie Vachon; Dir. Pub. Rel.; Scott Carmichael; Coach: Pat Quinn. Home ice: The Forum (16,005; 200' × 85'). Colors: Royal blue and gold. Training camp: Victoria, B.C.

SCOUTING REPORT

OFFENSE: Usually when a team finishes as far down the ladder as the Kings (19th overall), lack of attack is a big reason. Of course, a lack of defense contributes, too. But in the Kings' case, scoring goals isn't the problem. Preventing them is.

The Kings scored 310 goals in 1983-84, more than 10 teams acquired, but many of those teams were far above L.A. because their defensive play was much better.

The Kings have some quality offensive forwards in Bernie Nicholls (41 goals), Charlie Simmer (44), Marcel Dionne (39) and Jimmy Fox (30). There are some useful support folks, too, in Brian MacLellan, Doug Smith, Anders Hakansson, J.P. Kelly and Terry Ruskowski.

Dave Taylor, one of the NHL's premier players, has had two miserable seasons because of a complicated broken wrist. He's a solid 45-goal man, who scored 20 in 63 games last season, if he's healthy.

Mike McEwen, Mark Hardy and Brian Engblom are defensemen who handle the puck and move it well enough to be assets.

However, if the Kings are to move up to playoff contention in the Smythe Division (it's not such a huge leap forward), their new coach, Pat Quinn, must switch the team's emphasis to solid defense. The Kings can score solidly but they can't produce enough goals to survive the huge leaks when they don't have the puck.

DEFENSE: Only the laughable Toronto Maple Leafs and Pittsburgh Penguins surrendered more goals than the Kings' 376 in 1983-84. Unless new GM Rogie Vachon makes a deal before camp opens, the team will start another season minus an important ingredient—a competent NHL goaltender.

The team used five men at that position in 1983-84—Marco Baron, Markus Mattsson, Mike Blake, Gary Laskoski and Mario Lessard—and not one had much success. Lessard is out of the picture now, his contract purchased by the team.

Blake and Laskoski are young enough to develop into solid goalies but undoubtedly the Kings' netminding future is in other directions.

Colorful Bernie Nicholls led the Kings in scoring.

In Hardy, McEwen, Engblom and Jay Wells, the Kings have the basis for some sort of a competent defense. However, they need much support from the forwards in front of them and the goalie behind them and that hasn't been there.

OUTLOOK: The Kings always have paid a high price for trading away all those first-round draft picks and it shows in their patchwork roster and the need to sign free-agent players to fill roster gaps, especially on defense.

The team is in a position now with key players in the "aging" category—such as Dionne and Simmer—so they need to make a long-term plan to rebuild and stick with it.

KING PROFILES

MARK HARDY 25 5-11 195   **Defenseman**
Strong skater, good puckhandler who has developed into competent big-league backliner...His 49 points in 1983-84 were a

KING ROSTER

No.	Player	Pos.	Ht.	Wt.	Born	1983-84	G	A	Pts.	PIM
4	Russ Anderson	D	6-3	210	2-12-55/Minneapolis, Minn.	Los Angeles	5	12	17	126
28	Fred Barrett	D	6-0	194	1-26-50/Ottawa, Ont.	Los Angeles	2	0	2	8
	Dave Chartier	C	5-9	172	2-15-64/St. Lamare, Man.	Saskatoon	9	21	30	136
12	Steve Christoff	LW-C	6-1	180	1-23-58/Richfield, Minn.	Los Angeles	8	7	15	13
16	Marcel Dionne	C	5-8	185	8-3-51/Drummondville, Que.	Los Angeles	39	53	92	28
5	Brian Engblom	D	6-2	200	1-27-55/Winnipeg, Man.	Wash.-LA	2	28	30	67
15	Darryl Evans	RW	5-8	176	1-12-61/Toronto, Ont.	Los Angeles	0	1	1	0
						New Haven	51	35	86	14
19	Jim Fox	RW	5-8	183	5-18-60/Coniston, Ont.	Los Angeles	30	42	72	26
	Dave Gans	C	5-11	179	6-6-64/Brantford, Ont.	Oshawa	56	76	132	89
	John Goodwin	C	6-0	170	9-25-61/Toronto, Ont.	N.S.-N. Haven	24	62	86	46
21	Anders Hakansson	RW	6-2	192	4-27-56/Sweden	Los Angeles	15	17	32	41
20	Mark Hardy	D	5-11	195	2-1-59/Switzerland	Los Angeles	8	41	49	122
15	Billy Harris	RW	6-2	194	1-29-52/Toronto, Ont.	Tor.-LA	9	14	23	20
						St. Catharine's	0	1	1	0
38	Mike Heidt	D	6-1	193	11-4-63/Calgary, Alta.	Los Angeles	0	1	1	7
						New Haven	4	20	24	49
12	Dean Hopkins	RW	6-1	210	6-6-59/Cobourg, Ont.	New Haven	35	47	82	162
26	Wes Jarvis	C	5-11	185	5-30-58/Toronto, Ont.	Los Angeles	9	13	22	36
22	Dean Jenkins	RW	6-0	190	11-21-59/Billerica, Mass. .	New Haven	24	26	50	131
7	John Paul Kelly	LW	6-0	215	11-15-59/Edmonton, Alta.	Los Angeles	7	14	21	73
6	Dean Kennedy	D	602	195	1-18-63/Reduer, Sask.	Los Angeles	1	5	6	50
						New Haven	1	7	8	23
14	Kevin Levallee	LW	5-8	180	9-16-61/Sudbury, Ont.	Los Angeles	3	3	6	2
						New Haven	29	23	52	25
27	Brian MacLellan	LW	6-3	212	10-27-58/Guelph, Ont.	Los Angeles	25	29	54	45
						New Haven	0	2	2	2
2	Mike McEwen	D	6-1	185	8-10-58/Hornepayne, Ont.	NYI-LA	10	26	36	20
						New Haven	3	7	10	26
	Carl Mokosak	LW	6-1	200	9-22-62/Ft. Saskatchewan, Sask.	New Haven	18	21	39	206
	Don Nachbaur	C	6-1	183	1-30-59/Kitimat, B.C.	New Haven	33	32	65	194
9	Bernie Nicholls	C	6-0	185	6-24-61/Haliburton, Ont.	Los Angeles	41	54	95	83
	Craig Redmond	D	5-10	190	9-22-65/Langley, B.C.	Can. Olymp.	9	10	19	38
10	Terry Ruskowski	C	5-9	170	12-31-54/Prince Edward, Sask.	Los Angeles	7	25	32	92
11	Charlie Simmer	LW	6-3	210	3-20-54/Terrace Bay, Ont.	Los Angeles	44	48	92	78
3	Doug Smith	C	5-11	180	5-17-63/Ottawa, Ont.	Los Angeles	16	20	36	28
14	Phil Sykes	LW	6-0	178	5-18-59/Dawson Creek, B.C.	Los Angeles	0	0	0	2
						New Haven	29	37	66	101
18	Dave Taylor	RW	6-0	190	12-4-55/Levack, Ont.	Los Angeles	20	49	69	91
24	Jay Wells	D	6-1	205	5-18-59/Paris, Ont.	Los Angeles	3	18	21	141

No.	Player	Pos.	Ht.	Wt.	Born		GP	GA	SO	Avg.
30	Mike Blake	G	6-1	184	4-6-56/Kitchener, Ont.	Los Angeles	29	118	0	4.33
						New Haven	16	64	0	4.44
	Darren Eliot	G	6-1	175	11-26-61/Hamilton, Ont.	Can. Olymp.	0	0	0	0
						New Haven	7	30	0	4.93
	Bob Janecyk	G	6-1	180	5-18-57/Chicago, Ill.	Chicago	8	28	0	4.08
						Springfield	30	94	0	3.39
29	Gary Laskowski	G	6-1	175	6-6-59/Ottawa, Ont.	Los Angeles	13	55	0	4.96
						New Haven	22	97	0	4.94

career high...Excellent shot from the point...Has improved considerably defensively in past couple of seasons...Born in Semaden, Switzerland, on Feb. 1, 1959...His father played hockey in Europe and his mother was a member of England's Olympic team in 1952, placing seventh in figure skating...Excellent junior defenseman with Montreal, named tops at position in Quebec league in 1977-78...Kings' second-round draft choice in 1979...Spent part of rookie pro season in minors but has been an NHL player ever since.

Year	Club	GP	G	A	Pts.
1979-80	Los Angeles	15	0	1	1
1980-81	Los Angeles	77	5	20	25
1981-82	Los Angeles	77	6	39	45
1982-83	Los Angeles	74	5	34	39
1983-84	Los Angeles	79	8	41	49
	Totals	322	24	135	159

BRIAN ENGBLOM 29 6-2 200   Defenseman

Excellent defensive rearguard who plays with intelligence and good technique...Joined the Kings early in 1983-84 with Ken Houston from Washington Caps in exchange for Larry Murphy...Very hard worker who moves the puck well...Had splendid five seasons with Montreal Canadiens, where he played on three Stanley Cup teams...Traded to the Caps in controversial 1982 deal involving six players...Born Jan. 27, 1955, in Winnipeg...Attended University of Wisconsin, where he was coached by Bob Johnson, now with Calgary...Spent two seasons in minors before joining Canadiens, who had drafted him in 1975...Member of Team Canada in 1981 Canada Cup tournament...Second team All-Star in 1981-82.

Year	Club	GP	G	A	Pts.
1977-78	Montreal	28	1	2	3
1978-79	Montreal	62	3	11	14
1979-80	Montreal	70	3	20	23
1980-81	Montreal	80	3	25	28
1981-82	Montreal	76	4	29	33
1982-83	Washington	73	5	22	27
1983-84	Wash-LA	80	2	28	30
	Totals	469	21	137	158

MARCEL DIONNE 33 5-8 185   Forward

Rates on any list of the truly great in NHL history...His 39 goals and 92 points in 1983-84 were below his accustomed 50 and 100 standards...However, he's fourth on the career list in goals (583) and points (1379) and seventh in assists (796) . . . At 33, he remains among the league's best and quickest skaters . . . Extremely dangerous in the attacking zone . . . Born Aug. 3, 1951, in Drummondville, Que. . . . Second player picked (by Detroit) in 1971 entry draft after Canadiens' Guy Lafleur . . . Was a productive Wing for four seasons, then moved to Los Angeles in 1975 as the first big-name player to change teams as a free agent . . . Has been outspoken (at times) critic of team's operation because Kings have improved overall very little . . . Was highest paid NHLer until Wayne Gretzky came along.

Year	Club	GP	G	A	Pts.
1971-72	Detroit	78	28	49	77
1972-73	Detroit	77	40	50	90
1973-74	Detroit	74	24	54	78
1974-75	Detroit	80	47	74	121
1975-76	Los Angeles	80	40	54	94
1976-77	Los Angeles	80	53	69	122
1977-78	Los Angeles	70	36	43	79
1978-79	Los Angeles	80	59	71	130
1979-80	Los Angeles	80	53	84	137
1980-81	Los Angeles	80	58	77	135
1981-82	Los Angeles	78	50	67	117
1982-83	Los Angeles	80	56	51	107
1983-84	Los Angeles	66	39	53	92
	Totals	1003	583	796	1379

DAVE TAYLOR 28 6-0 190   Forward

Complications from a broken wrist suffered early in 1982-83 have dogged this premier player for the past two seasons . . . Missed 34 games in 1982-83 and 17 last season, when he had 20 goals and 69 points in 63 matches . . . Was 100-point producer in two seasons before injury . . . Can do it all—skate, shoot, score, make plays and hit hard . . . Born Dec. 4, 1955, in Levack, Ont. . . . Attended Clarkson College, where he attained All-America status . . . Was 210th player picked in 1975 draft after sophomore season . . . By senior term he had added 30 pounds and set NCAA scoring mark . . . Has been at his best on a line with Simmer and Dionne.

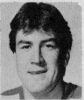

Year	Club	GP	G	A	Pts.
1977-78	Los Angeles	64	22	21	43
1978-79	Los Angeles	78	43	48	91
1979-80	Los Angeles	61	37	53	90
1980-81	Los Angeles	72	47	65	112
1981-82	Los Angeles	78	39	67	106
1982-83	Los Angeles	46	21	37	58
1983-84	Los Angeles	63	20	49	69
	Totals	462	229	340	569

CHARLIE SIMMER 30 6-3 210   Forward

Has rebounded strongly from severely broken leg suffered in March, 1981...Missed 30 games of the 1981-82 season due to slow recovery but scored 29 and 44 goals in past two seasons...Was first-team all-star left winger in two pre-injury seasons, scoring 56 goals in each...Not a fast skater but among smartest NHL players, using size and reach to best advantage...Born March 20, 1954, in Terrace Bay, Ont....Signed by Kings as a free agent in 1977...Spent five seasons between NHL and minors and was ready to give up on NHL career...Called up by Kings in 1978-79 and clicked immediately on line with Marcel Dionne and Dave Taylor.

Year	Club	GP	G	A	Pts.
1974-75	California	35	8	13	21
1975-76	California	21	1	1	2
1976-77	Cleveland	24	2	0	2
1977-78	Los Angeles	3	0	0	0
1978-79	Los Angeles	38	21	27	48
1979-80	Los Angeles	64	56	45	101
1980-81	Los Angeles	65	56	49	105
1981-82	Los Angeles	50	15	24	39
1982-83	Los Angeles	80	29	51	80
1983-84	Los Angeles	79	44	48	92
	Totals	459	232	258	490

JAY WELLS 25 6-1 205   Defenseman

Tough defensive type who doesn't produce many offensive points but does a good job in his team's zone...Strong and willing, is one of the best at moving foes from in front of the net...His 21 points in 1983-84 were the top output of career...Born in Paris, Ont., on May 18, 1959...Played junior hockey with Kingston Canadians, where he was Ontario league All-Star in 1978-79...Kings' first-round draft pick in 1979...Spent part of rookie pro season, 1979-80, in minors at Binghamton...Has missed parts of two seasons with knee and hand injuries.

Year	Club	GP	G	A	Pts.
1979-80	Los Angeles	43	0	0	0
1980-81	Los Angeles	72	5	13	18
1981-82	Los Angeles	60	1	8	9
1982-83	Los Angeles	69	3	12	15
1983-84	Los Angeles	69	3	18	21
	Totals	313	12	51	63

BERNIE NICHOLLS 23 6-0 185   Forward

Flamboyant, extroverted type who fits the Kings' show-business setting well . . . Team's leading scorer in 1983-84 with 95 points, including 41 goals . . . Quick skater for his size with a big shot . . . Has a "nose for the net" which makes him dangerous on the attack . . . Born in Haliburton, Ont., on June 24, 1961 . . . Was Kings' fourth-round pick in 1980 draft from Kingston Canadians . . . Returned to junior hockey for 1980-81 season and produced 152 points . . . Strong play at New Haven in AHL in 1981-82 earned call-up to Kings, where he notched 32 points in 22 games . . . Knee injury slowed his 1982-83 season but he rebounded last year . . . California beaches are a long way from small Ontario hometown, where his father is a trapper.

Year	Club	GP	G	A	Pts.
1981-82	Los Angeles	22	14	18	32
1982-83	Los Angeles	71	28	22	50
1983-84	Los Angeles	79	41	54	95
	Totals	172	83	94	177

RUSS ANDERSON 29 6-3 210   Defenseman

Signed for 1983-84 season by the Kings as a free agent from Hartford Whalers . . . Had solid but not spectacular season in California . . . Robust defensive type who likes to throw body checks . . . Spent 4½ seasons with Pittsburgh Penguins before going to Whalers in trade for Rick MacLeish . . . Born in Minneapolis on Feb. 12, 1955 . . . Played college hockey at U. of Minnesota . . . Penguins' second choice in 1975 draft . . . Missed 46 games in 1980-81 because of badly shattered finger . . . Wife Dorothy was Miss America in 1977.

Year	Club	GP	G	A	Pts.
1976-77	Pittsburgh	66	2	11	13
1977-78	Pittsburgh	74	2	16	18
1978-79	Pittsburgh	72	3	13	16
1979-80	Pittsburgh	76	5	22	27
1980-81	Pittsburgh	34	3	14	17
1981-82	Pitt-Hart	56	1	4	5
1982-83	Hartford	57	0	6	6
1983-84	Los Angeles	70	5	12	17
	Totals	505	21	98	119

JOHN PAUL KELLY 25 6-0 215   Forward

Roger Neilson, King coach for last third of 1983-84 season, called Kelly "the best body-checking forward in the NHL." . . . Hard-working grinder type who had only 21 points last season . . . A left winger, he often is assigned to check the NHL's best shooters who play the right side... Born in Edmonton on Nov. 15, 1959... Played four seasons of junior hockey with New Westminster Bruins... Member of Canadian championship team in 1977-78... Claimed by the Kings on third round of the 1979 draft... Played in all three pro leagues (NHL, AHL, CHL) in 1980-81... Twice passed up Kings' postseason bonus trips to Hawaii to help on parents' farm in Alberta.

Year	Club	GP	G	A	Pts.
1979–80	Los Angeles	40	2	5	7
1980–81	Los Angeles	19	3	6	9
1981–82	Los Angeles	70	12	11	23
1982–83	Los Angeles	65	16	15	31
1983–84	Los Angeles	72	7	14	21
	Totals	266	40	51	91

JIM FOX 24 5-8 183   Forward

Had the second 30-goal season of his four NHL campaigns in 1983-84... His 72 points were best total... Has all the offensive tools, small but very quick... Can play all three forward positions... Good on the power play because of ability to get open... Born May 18, 1960, in Coniston, Ont. ... Had fine junior career with Ottawa 67s, counting 396 points in three seasons... Won scoring title in good Ontario league with 166 points in 62 games in 1979-80... First-round draft pick, 10th overall, in 1980... Played for Canada in 1979 world junior championships in Helsinki.

Year	Club	GP	G	A	Pts.
1980-81	Los Angeles	71	18	25	43
1981-82	Los Angeles	77	30	38	68
1982-83	Los Angeles	77	28	40	68
1983-84	Los Angeles	80	30	42	72
	Totals	305	106	145	251

COACH PAT QUINN: Returned to NHL coaching ranks after a two-year absence during which he attended law school in Philadelphia... Kings look for him to supply disciplined approach and improve team's defensive record... After two years as head coach of Philadelphia Flyers, he was fired halfway through 1981-82 season... In his first full season as head coach, 1979-80, Flyers set record with 35-game unbeaten streak... Earned respect of players with well-organized, intellectual approach to the job... Born in Hamilton, Ont., on Jan. 29, 1943... Played junior hockey in Hamilton and Edmonton... Logged time in nine-season NHL career with Toronto, Vancouver and Atlanta (five seasons)... Joined Flyers in 1977 as assistant to Fred Shero ... Coached Maine Mariners, Flyers' farm team for 50 games in 1978-79, then was promoted to the NHL club... Earned bachelor's degree after attending nine different colleges during playing career... NHL's Coach of the Year in 1979-80.

GREATEST ROOKIE

Since entering the NHL in the 1967 expansion, the Kings have made first-round selections in the entry draft, the top source of talent, in only three seasons. Most of the first-round selections were traded away for stopgap veterans, a big reason why the team never has been a serious contender.

As a result, the Kings seldom have had top rookies in their line-up. In fact, the best first-year player they've owned, defenseman Larry Murphy in 1980-81, no longer is with the Kings. He was traded to Washington Capitals halfway through the 1983-84 season.

The Kings had claimed Murphy from the Peterborough juniors in the 1980 draft and he had an excellent freshman year. He counted 16 goals and 60 assists for 76 points, his assist and point totals the best ever by a King rookie at any position.

However, Murphy was unable to duplicate that effort and in the next two seasons he often was jeered loudly by the L.A. fans. His play, especially the defensive side of it, suffered badly and he was traded to the Caps for Brian Engblom and Ken Houston.

ALL-TIME KING LEADERS

GOALS: Marcel Dionne, 59, 1978-79
ASSISTS: Marcel Dionne, 84, 1979-80
POINTS: Marcel Dionne, 137, 1979-80
SHUTOUTS: Rogatien Vachon, 8, 1976-77

MINNESOTA NORTH STARS

TEAM DIRECTORY: Co-Chairmen: George Gund III and Gordon Gund; Pres.: John Karr; GM: Lou Nanne; Dir. Hockey Info.: Dick Dillman; Coach: Bill Mahoney. Home ice: Met Center (15,184; 200' × 85'). Colors: Green, white and gold. Training camp: Bloomington, Minn.

Brian Lawton showed promise as an 18-year-old rookie.

SCOUTING REPORT

OFFENSE: The North Stars seem to be a team having problems in finding a niche in which to fit, a style of hockey that suits their personnel to good advantage.

A few seasons ago, they were all-attack, a hard-driving offensive team that played a good puck control game and enough defense to get the job done. Then the men who run the team started to talk about improved defensive play and since then the Stars have yielded so many goals (344 last season) that not even their good attack (345 goals) could overcome it.

The club did shake the Chicago Black Hawks off their backs after losing twice in the playoffs to their rivals but they didn't have enough of anything to handle Edmonton in the conference final.

Now the Stars must try to build a solidly balanced team and the ingredients are there for the offensive side of it, at least. Neal Broten, Brian Bellows, Dino Ciccarelli, Tom McCarthy, Keith Acton, Mark Napier, Steve Payne and Dennis Maruk are all quality attackers.

Brian Lawton, the No. 1 draft pick in 1983, showed flashes of skill in his rookie season, about all that could be expected from an 18-year-old fresh from New England high-school hockey.

Brad Maxwell, Gordie Roberts, Curt Giles, Craig Levie and a healthy Craig Hartsburg all handle the puck from the backline better than they collectively play defense.

DEFENSE: Last season, the Stars often appeared to be a team without a total plan on how to prevent goals and frequent breakdowns in their own zone occurred when opponents forechecked strongly.

Of course, the absence of the team's best defenseman, Craig Hartsburg, for much of the season with knee problems, didn't help.

Don Beaupre's strong finish to the season and good work in the playoffs indicates that, at 23, he's set to be a consistent NHL goalie. He'll join veteran Gilles Meloche, who is consistent, on a good goaltending tandem.

The defense of Hartsburg (if sound), Giles, Maxwell, Roberts, Levie, Dan Mandich and Tom Hirsch should be NHL caliber. The Stars added veteran defenseman Harold Snepsts from Vancouver in June in exchange for forward Al McAdam.

OUTLOOK: The potential of the talent on the Stars' roster always seems to indicate better things than show on the result board.

NORTH STAR ROSTER

No.	Player	Pos.	Ht.	Wt.	Born	1983-84	G	A	Pts.	PIM
2	Keith Acton	C	5-8	170	4-15-58/Stouffville, Ont.	Mont.-Minn.	20	45	65	64
2	Brent Ashton	LW	6-1	210	5-18-60/Saskatoon, Sask.	Minnesota	7	10	17	54
3	Brian Bellows	RW	5-11	194	9-1-64/St. Catharine's, Ont.	Minnesota	41	42	83	14
	Scott Bjugstad	C	6-1	185	6-2-61/New Brighton, Minn.	Minnesota	0	0	0	0
						Salt Lake City	10	8	18	6
	Neal Broten	RW	5-9	160	11-24-59/Roseau, Minn.	Minnesota	28	61	89	43
	Dino Ciccarelli	C	5-10	181	2-8-60/Sarnia, Ont.	Minnesota	38	33	71	58
	George Ferguson	C	6-0	190	8-22-52/Trenton, Ont.	Minnesota	6	10	16	19
	Curt Giles	D	5-8	180	11-30-58/The Pas, Man.	Minnesota	6	22	28	59
	Craig Hartsburg	D	6-1	200	6-19-59/Stratford, Ont.	Minnesota	7	7	14	37
	Tom Hirsch	D	6-4	210	1-27-63/Minneapolis, Minn.	Minnesota	1	3	4	20
	Paul Holmgren	RW	6-3	210	12-2-55/St. Paul, Minn.	Phil.-Minn.	11	18	29	151
	Craig Homola	C	5-9	170	11-29-58/Eveleth, Minn.	Salt Lake City	29	27	56	37
	Dave H. Jensen	D	6-1	190	3-5-61/Minneapolis, Minn.	Salt Lake City	0	7	7	6
						Minnesota	0	1	1	0
	Brian Lawton	C	6-0	178	6-29-65/New Brunswick, N.J.	Minnesota	10	21	31	33
	Craig Levie	D	5-11	190	8-17-59/Calgary, Alta.	Minnesota	6	13	19	44
						Salt Lake City	8	20	28	101
	Don Mandich	D	6-3	205	6-12-60/Brantford, Ont.	Minnesota	2	7	9	77
						Salt Lake City	2	2	4	13
	Dennis Maruk	C	5-8	165	11-17-55/Toronto, Ont.	Minnesota	17	43	60	42
	Brad Maxwell	D	6-2	192	7-8-57/Brandon, Man.	Minnesota	19	54	73	225
	Tom McCarthy	LW	6-1	200	7-31-60/Toronto, Ont.	Minnesota	39	31	70	49
	Mark Napier	RW	5-10	185	1-28-57/Toronto, Ont.	Mont.-Minn.	16	30	46	17
	Steve Payne	LW	6-2	205	8-16-58/Toronto, Ont.	Minnesota	28	31	59	49
	Willi Plett	RW	6-3	205	6-7-55/Paraguay	Minnesota	15	23	38	316
	David Quinn	D	6-0	206	7-30-66/Cranston, R.I.	Kent School	12	20	32	--
	Dave Richter	D	6-5	220	4-8-60/Winnipeg, Man.	Minnesota	2	3	5	132
						Salt Lake City	1	4	5	39
	Gordie Roberts	D	6-0	195	10-2-57/Detroit, Mich.	Minnesota	8	45	53	132
	Harold Snepsts	D	6-3	215	10-24-54/Edmonton, Alta.	Vancouver	4	16	20	152
	Tim Trimper	LW	5-9	184	9-28-59/Windsor, Ont.	Salt Lake City	18	27	45	26

	Player	Pos.	Ht.	Wt.	Born		GP	GA	SO	Avg.
	Don Beaupre	G	5-8	150	9-19-61/Waterloo, Ont.	Salt Lake City	7	30	0	4.30
						Minnesota	33	123	0	4.12
	Jon Casey	G	5-9	155	8-29-62/Grand Rapids, Minn.	Minnesota	2	6	0	4.29
	Jim Craig	G	6-1	190	5-31-57/North Easton, Mass.	Minnesota	3	9	0	4.91
						Salt Lake City	27	108	1	4.23
	Gilles Meloche	G	5-9	180	7-12-50/Montreal, Que.	Minnesota	52	201	2	4.18
	Mike Sands	G	5-9	150	4-6-53/Sudbury, Ont.	Salt Lake City	23	93	0	4.87

Bellows, a player of fine character and leadership, despite his tender years, and old warhorse Paul Holmgren, if the medical staff can patch his battered body together, could combine to light a fire under the team.

NORTH STAR PROFILES

DON BEAUPRE 23 5-8 150   Goaltender

Up-and-down pro career of fine prospect leveled off late in 1983-84 season and playoffs... Worked in 13 of Stars' 16 Stanley Cup games with 3.07 average and was key man in advance to conference final... Made a socko NHL debut in 1980-81 at 19 when he had a 3.20 average in 44 games... Since then, he's logged three stints in minors trying to find consistency... Showed a mature stand-up style last season and appears ready for first string duty... Born Sept. 19, 1961, in Waterloo, Ont.... Excellent junior with Sudbury Wolves... Stars' second-round choice, 37th overall, in 1980 entry draft... Attended Stars' camp for 1980-81 season, expecting to be returned to junior level for another season... Strong exhibition game work earned him a share of the job with veteran Gilles Meloche.

Year	Club	GP	GA	SO	Avg
1980–81	Minnesota	44	138	0	3.2
1981–82	Minnesota	29	101	0	3.7
1982–83	Minnesota	36	120	0	3.5
1983–84	Minnesota	33	123	0	4.1
	Totals	142	482	0	3.6

CURT GILES 25 5-8 180   Defenseman

Solid backliner who has anchored Stars' defense for the past four seasons... Proves that there's a big difference between a small man and a weak one... He might be short—nickname is "Pengy," short for Penguin—but he's strong enough to move the biggest forwards from the front of the net... Smart puckhandler and passer... Born Nov. 30, 1958, in The Pas, Manitoba... Enrolled at U. of Minnesota-Duluth when he was 16... Earned All-America honors twice and degree in secondary education in next four years... Stars' fourth-round draft pick in 1978... Spent part

of rookie pro season, 1979-80, in minors but has been a Star
fixture ever since.

Year	Club	GP	G	A	Pts.
1979-80	Minnesota	37	2	7	9
1980-81	Minnesota	67	5	22	27
1981-82	Minnesota	74	3	12	15
1982-83	Minnesota	76	2	21	23
1983-84	Minnesota	70	6	22	28
	Totals.............	324	18	84	102

BRAD MAXWELL 27 6-2 192   Defenseman

Had perhaps his best NHL season in 1983-84 when he was thrust
into heavy workload by injury to Craig Hartsburg...Made
his best offensive output of seven-season NHL career with
73 points...Added another 13 points in playoffs...Strong,
quick skater who owns one of the best shots from the point in
league...Has worked hard to improve defensive play...Born in
Brandon, Manitoba, on July 8, 1957...Star junior with New
Westminster Bruins where he was defense partner of Rangers'
Barry Beck on 1978 Canadian junior champs...First-round pick
of Stars in 1977 draft...Except for one two-game stint in minors,
has been a North Star regular ever since...Among the best golfers
in NHL with a five-handicap.

Year	Club	GP	G	A	Pts.
1977-78	Minnesota	75	18	29	47
1978-79	Minnesota	70	9	28	37
1979-80	Minnesota	58	7	30	37
1980-81	Minnesota	27	3	13	16
1981-82	Minnesota	51	10	21	31
1982-83	Minnesota	77	11	28	39
1983-84	Minnesota	78	19	54	73
	Totals.............	436	77	203	280

GORDIE ROBERTS 27 6-0 195   Defenseman

Had excellent season in 1983-84 and was team's best playoff
player until back injury chopped him down in first game of conference final against Edmonton...Good all-around player who
handles and moves the puck well and is sound defensively...Is
entering 10th major-league season, surprising when age is considered...Joined New England Whalers in WHA in 1975-76 at
17...Born Oct. 2, 1957, in Detroit...Was named after Gordie
Howe...Played junior hockey in Victoria, B.C....Spent six seasons with Whalers in WHA and NHL...Was traded to Stars in

1980 for winger Mike Fidler...Older brother Doug played for Detroit and the Whalers.

Year	Club	GP	G	A	Pts.
1975-76	New England (WHA)	77	3	19	22
1976-77	New England (WHA)	77	13	33	46
1977-78	New England (WHA)	78	15	46	61
1978-79	New England (WHA)	79	11	46	57
1979-80	Hartford	80	8	28	36
1980-81	Hart-Minn.	77	8	42	50
1981-82	Minnesota	79	4	30	34
1982-83	Minnesota	80	3	41	44
1983-84	Minnesota	77	8	45	53
	NHL Totals	393	31	186	217
	WHA Totals	311	42	144	186

CRAIG HARTSBURG 25 6-1 200 Defenseman

North Stars surrendered 54 more goals last season than in 1982-83 and big reason for that was absence for 54 games of this All-Star candidate with knee problems...Complex surgery was required to reconstruct knee but full recovery expected...Skilled two-way player who was team captain...Strong on the attack, sound defensively...Point-per-game and high plus potential...Born June, 19, 1959, in Stratford, Ont. ...Father Bill played minor league pro hockey...Junior All-Star with Sault Ste. Marie Greyhounds...Turned pro early with Birmingham in WHA...First-round draft pick by Stars in 1979...Member of Team Canada in 1981 Canada Cup and All-Star in two world championships...Signed seven-year contract, longest ever granted by Stars, in 1982.

Year	Club	GP	G	A	Pts.
1978-79	Birmingham (WHA)	77	9	40	49
1979-80	Minnesota	79	14	30	44
1980-81	Minnesota	74	13	30	43
1981-82	Minnesota	76	17	60	77
1982-83	Minnesota	78	12	50	62
1983-84	Minnesota	26	7	7	14
	NHL Totals	333	63	177	240
	WHA Totals	77	9	40	49

KEITH ACTON 26 5-8 170 Forward

One of hockey's best little men...Was shocked by trade with Mark Napier from Montreal Canadiens to Stars for Bobby Smith early in 1983-84...However, he shook it off to play extremely well, counting 55 points in 62 games for Stars...Very quick skater who's a smart playmaker... Strong defensively and good on face-offs... Born April 15, 1958, in Stouffville, Ont.... Scored 249 points in two junior seasons with Peterborough Petes... Was fifth-round pick, 103rd overall, of Canadiens in 1978 draft... Had two good seasons in minors before earning NHL spot... Best season was 1981-82 when he had 36 goals and 88 assists... Had strong playoff for Stars with 11 points.

Year	Club	GP	G	A	Pts.
1979–80	Montreal	2	0	1	1
1980–81	Montreal	61	15	24	39
1981–82	Montreal	78	36	52	88
1982–83	Montreal	78	24	26	50
1983–84	Mont-Minn	71	20	45	65
	Totals	290	95	148	243

NEAL BROTEN 24 5-9 160   Forward

Started his NHL career in 1981-82 with 38 goals and 97 points and hasn't matched that performance in next two seasons... Had 28 goals and 89 points in 1983-84 campaign, with a plus-16... Slick, creative center who's one of the NHL's best puckhandlers and playmakers... Born in Roseau, Minn., on Nov. 29, 1959... Fine high-school player at Roseau High School... Great college career at U. of Minnesota, where he was an All-American and college Player of the Year in 1980-81... Strong member of the U.S. team that won a gold medal in 1980 Olympics... Joined Stars late in 1980-81 season and helped team advance to Stanley Cup final... Brother Aaron is a center with New Jersey Devils.

Year	Club	GP	G	A	Pts.
1980-81	Minnesota	3	2	0	2
1981-82	Minnesota	73	38	59	97
1982-83	Minnesota	79	32	45	77
1983-84	Minnesota	76	28	61	89
	Totals	231	100	165	265

BRIAN LAWTON 19 6-0 178   Center

Came to Minnesota as first U.S.-born player to be chosen first overall in NHL draft... Got into 58 games but was plagued by injuries and also the fact that the North Stars had four centers... Occasionally played wing... Had 10 goals, 21 assists... No question of his potential... Voted team Rookie of the

Year... Born June 29, 1965, in New Brunswick, N.J.... Led Mt. St. Charles High to Providence state championship and represented the U.S. in the world junior championships in Leningrad and in world "B" tournament in Tokyo... Father is a pressman on Providence newspaper.

Year	Club	GP	G	A	Pts.
1983-84	Minnesota	58	10	21	31

BRIAN BELLOWS 20 5-11 194   Forward

Heart and soul of the team at 20 years of age... Followed good rookie season (65 points) in 1982-83 with 41 goals, 83 points last year when he was named team captain... Much-publicized junior player and Stars traded two players to Boston Bruins to guarantee he would be available when they picked second in 1982 entry draft... Plays well on all 200 feet of ice... Tough and aggressive... Born Sept. 1, 1964, in St. Catharines, Ont.... Outstanding junior with Kitchener Rangers... Led team to Canadian junior title in 1982, with three goals and two assists in 5-2 win over Sherbrooke in decisive game... Strong power-play player with 29 goals in that situation in first two seasons.

Year	Club	GP	G	A	Pts.
1982-83	Minnesota	78	35	30	65
1983-84	Minnesota	78	41	42	83
	Totals.............	156	76	72	148

TOM McCARTHY 24 6-1 200   Defenseman

Injuries have been a curse on the career of this fine player... Missed 70 games with a variety of wounds in first three seasons ... Healthy for the first time in 1982-83, he played in all 80 games and had 76 points... Last season, had 39 goals and 70 points in 66 games when a broken arm ended season for him... Big, fast, strong winger who handles puck well and has a good scoring touch... Born in Toronto on July 31, 1960... Oshawa Generals picked him ahead of Wayne Gretzky in junior draft of 16-year-old players . . . Top junior with 141 points in 1978-79 . . . First-round draft choice in 1979 . . . If he can stay healthy, has 50-goal potential.

Year	Club	GP	G	A	Pts.
1979-80	Minnesota	68	16	20	36
1980-81	Minnesota	62	23	25	48
1981-82	Minnesota	40	12	30	42
1982-83	Minnesota	80	28	48	76
1983-84	Minnesota	66	39	31	70
	Totals	316	118	154	272

DINO CICCARELLI 24 5-10 181   Forward

One of several Stars who have tailed off in past two seasons after fast starts to careers . . . Scored 55 goals in 1981-82, first full NHL season, but has had 37 and 38 in two seasons since then . . . Has been outspoken critic of club's switch of emphasis to defense . . . Has uncanny ability to find openings and to appear where loose pucks are prevalent in the attacking zone . . . Owns very accurate, quickly-released shot . . . Born Feb. 8, 1960, in Sarnia, Ont. . . . High scorer with London Knights . . . Career was threatened by severely broken leg . . . Signed by Stars as a free agent when he was by-passed in the draft because of injury . . . Made a complete recovery and is big fan favorite in Minnesota.

Year	Club	GP	G	A	Pts.
1980-81	Minnesota	32	18	12	30
1981-82	Minnesota	76	55	52	107
1982-83	Minnesota	77	37	38	75
1983-84	Minnesota	79	38	33	71
	Totals	264	148	135	283

COACH BILL MAHONEY: First season at North Star helm was a stormy one as he attempted to inspire devotion to defense in an attack-oriented team . . . Two weeks into season, there was speculation about his replacement but team rallied to win Norris Division before losing to Edmonton in Campbell Conference final . . . Served 20-year apprenticeship at all levels of the game before earning first head-coaching job . . . Was head coach at McMaster University in Hamilton, Ont., for 16 years, winning three Canadian titles . . . Moved to the NHL in 1980-81 as assistant coach with Washington Capitals under head coach Gary Green . . . Coached Adirondack of AHL in 1982-83 . . . Born June 23, 1939, in Peterborough, Ont. . . . Was fine junior player with Peterborough Petes, where he was coached by Scotty Bowman . . . Has college degrees in history and physical education.

GREATEST ROOKIE

Several good, young players have made impressive NHL debuts with the North Stars but two rookie seasons stand out. One, by Bobby Smith in 1978-79, earned him the Calder Trophy as best rookie; the other, by Neal Broten in 1981-82, established all scoring records for a North Star freshman.

When the Stars were purchased by the Gund brothers in 1978 and merged with Cleveland Barons, the first plank in the construction of the new team was to claim Smith from the Ottawa 67s as the first player selected in that year's entry draft.

Smith had an excellent first season with 30 goals and 74 points to win the Calder. In the 1981-82 season, he set assist (71) and points (114) marks for the team but, early in 1983-84, he was traded to the Montreal Canadiens.

In 1981-82, fresh from the 1980 U.S. Olympic team victory and a big college season at U. of Minnesota, Broten had 38 goals and 59 assists for 97 points in his first full season with the Stars.

ALL-TIME NORTH STAR LEADERS

GOALS: Dino Ciccarelli, 55, 1981-82
ASSISTS: Bobby Smith, 71, 1981-82
POINTS: Bobby Smith, 114, 1981-82
SHUTOUTS: Cesare Maniago, 6, 1967-68

ST. LOUIS BLUES

TEAM DIRECTORY: Chairman-Pres.: Harry Ornest; VP-Dir. Player Personnel: Ronald Caron; Pub. Dir.: Susie Mathieu; Coach: Jacques Demers. Home ice: St. Louis Arena: (17,967; 200' × 85'). Colors: White, blue, gold and red. Training camp: Peoria, Ill.

SCOUTING REPORT

OFFENSE: The Blues had no first-round entry draft pick in 1982 and didn't participate at all in the 1983 draft because the franchise was at loggerheads with the league at the time. For the next couple of seasons, the team will pay the price of that lack of new talent,

Brian Sutter's 83 points were a career high.

208 THE COMPLETE HANDBOOK OF PRO HOCKEY

especially the offensive players to provide a selection for the team's attack.

That's why last season's development of rookie center Doug Gilmour, who had 53 points and improved steadily, was important. It gave the Blues at least one good quality young forward.

The team does have some high-grade offensive players in Bernie Federko (41 goals, 107 points), Joe Mullen (41 goals), Brian Sutter (32 goals) and Jorgen Pettersson, who slumped to 28 scores but has the potential to be a 40-goal-plus sniper.

Rob Ramage (60 points) supplies a good rusher from the blue line and there are several fairly young defensemen with offensive potential—Gilbert Delorme, Dave Pichette and Rik Wilson.

The 291 goals scored by the Blues last season simply weren't enough for a club that hopes to push to the .500 mark in 1984-85. To attain that mark, the Blues need all their shooters to produce at top level—and to cut down their goals-against figure considerably.

DEFENSE: Mike Liut didn't earn many All-Star votes but he was one of the best half-dozen goalies in the NHL in 1983-84, a major reason why the Blues climbed to second place in the Norris Division.

Liut was angered by claims that he had regained the form of 1980-81 when he was named the league's best goalie. He feels that his work merely reflected the overall team performance. However, through the season and the 1984 playoffs, the Blues won assorted games that could be attributed directly to their goalie's excellence.

Rick Heinz and Bunny Larocque are adequate backups but they'll see little action because Liut would play every game if possible.

Ramage, an improving player, anchors the defense, where several players need to show all their potential if the Blues are to have a .500 backline. Tim Bothwell (plus-22), Pichette, Delorme, Wilson, Dwight Schofield and Terry Johnson is a list with few All-Star candidates on it.

A lowering of a too-high goals-against average will key on another good season for Liut and a total team devotion to the reduction of goals.

OUTLOOK: Because the Norris Division is the NHL's weakest, the Blues can place highly if they can climb above .500. However, for a team that doesn't have a large amount of good, young talent, that makes upgrading their work a tough chore.

To be a break-even team, they need their veterans to all have good seasons while their scouting staff rounds up a few good kids.

BLUE ROSTER

No.	Player	Pos.	Ht.	Wt.	Born	1983-84	G	A	Pts.	PIM
12	Perry Anderson	LW	6-0	194	10-14-61/Barrie, Ont.	St. Louis	7	5	12	195
						Montana	7	3	10	34
10	Wayne Babych	RW	5-11	196	6-6-58/Edmonton, Alta.	St. Louis	13	29	42	52
	Dave Barr	C	6-1	185	11-30-60/Edmonton, Alta.	NYR-St. L.	0	0	0	2
						Tulsa	28	37	65	24
25	Tim Bothwell	D	6-3	190	5-6-55/Vancouver, B.C.	St. Louis	2	13	15	65
						Montana	0	3	3	0
20	Jack Carlson	C	6-3	200	8-23-54/Virginia, Minn.	St. Louis	6	8	14	95
17	Guy Chouinard	C	5-11	182	12-20-56/Quebec City, Que.	St. Louis	12	34	46	10
27	Gilbert Delorme	D	6-1	205	11-25-62/Boucherville, Que.	Mont.-St. L.	2	12	14	49
24	Bernie Federko	C	6-0	192	5-12-56/Foam Lake, Sask.	St. Louis	41	66	107	43
	Perry Ganchar	RW	5-9	180	10-28-63/Saskatoon, Sask.	Montana	23	22	45	77
18	Doug Gilmour	C	5-11	164	6-25-63/Kingston, Ont.	St. Louis	25	28	53	57
26	Terry Johnson	D	6-3	210	11-28-58/Calgary, Alta.	St. Louis	2	6	8	141
23	Alain Lemieux	C	6-0	185	5-29-61/Montreal, Que.	Montana	28	41	69	36
						St. Louis	4	5	9	6
						Springfield	11	14	25	18
	John Markell	LW	5-10	180	3-10-56/Cornwall, Ont.	Montana	44	40	84	61
7	Joe Mullen	RW	5-9	182	2-26-57/New York, N.Y.	St. Louis	41	44	85	19
28	Greg Paslawski	LW	5-11	185	8-25-61/Kindersley, Sask.	Mont.-St. L.	9	10	19	21
35	Jim Pavese	D	6-2	204	6-8-62/New York, N.Y.	St. Louis	0	1	1	19
						Montana	1	19	20	147
22	Jorgen Pettersson	LW	6-2	184	7-11-56/Sweden	St. Louis	28	34	62	29
29	Dave Pichette	D	6-3	190	2-4-60/Grand Falls, Nfld.	Que.-St. L.	2	18	20	18
						Fredericton	2	1	3	13
5	Rob Ramage	D	6-2	210	1-11-59/Byron, Ont.	St. Louis	15	45	60	121
15	Mark Reeds	RW	5-10	188	1-24-60/Burlington, Ont.	St. Louis	11	14	25	23
	Marty Ruff	D	6-1	205	5-19-63/Marburg, Alta.	Montana	0	0	0	2
21	Dwight Schofield	D	6-3	195	3-15-56/Waltham, Mass.	St. Louis	4	10	14	219
11	Brian Sutter	LW	5-11	181	10-7-56/Viking, Alta.	St. Louis	32	51	83	162
	Alain Vigneault	D	5-11	195	5-14-61/Quebec City, Que.	Montana	2	14	16	139
						Maine	0	1	1	46
14	Doug Wickenheiser	C	6-1	197	3-30-61/Regina, Sask.	Mont.-St. L.	12	26	38	25
34	Rik Wilson	D	6-0	180	6-17-62/Long Beach, Cal.	St. Louis	7	11	18	53
						Montana	0	3	3	2

No.	Player	Pos.	Ht.	Wt.	Born		GP	GA	SO	Avg.
31	Rick Heinz	G	5-10	165	5-30-55/Essex, Ont.	St. Louis	22	80	0	4.29
33	Michel Larocque	G	5-11	185	4-6-52/Hull, Que.	St. Louis	5	31	0	6.20
						Springfield	5	21	0	4.19
1	Mike Liut	G	6-2	192	1-7-56/Weston, Alta.	St. Louis	58	197	3	3.45
	Paul Skidmore	G	6-0	185	7-22-56/Smithtown, N.Y.	Montana	1	8	0	8.00
	Rick Wamsley	G	5-11	178	5-25-59/Simcoe, Ont.	Montreal	42	144	2	3.70

BLUE PROFILES

MIKE LIUT 28 6-2 192   Goaltender
Workhorse goalie who had superb 1983-84 with 3.45 average in 58 games plus sparkling 2.44 in 11 playoff games . . . Has played 315 games in five NHL seasons . . . Hints that he slumped after brilliant 1980-81 campaign when he was first-team All-Star and close runnerup to Wayne Gretzky as MVP aggravate him . . . Claims that a goalie is only as good as the team in front of him . . . Born Jan. 7, 1956, in Weston, Ont. . . . Was backup to Toronto's Mike Palmateer in Junior B hockey. . . . Attended Bowling Green University . . . Spent two seasons in WHA with Cincinnati . . . Blues, who had claimed him in 1976 draft, reclaimed him in 1979 expansion . . . Excellent interview because of candor and strong viewpoints.

Year	Club	GP	GA	SO	Avg.
1977-78	Cincinnati (WHA)	27	86	0	4.25
1978-79	Cincinnati (WHA)	54	184	3	3.47
1979-80	St Louis	64	194	2	3.18
1980-81	St Louis	61	199	1	3.34
1981-82	St Louis	64	250	2	4.06
1982-83	St Louis	68	235	1	3.72
1983-84	St Louis	58	197	3	3.55
	NHL Totals	315	1075	9	3.55
	WHA Totals	81	270	3	3.69

GILBERT DELORME 22 6-1 205   Defenseman
Big, strong youngster acquired in December, 1983, trade with Montreal along with forwards Greg Paslawski and Doug Wickenheiser for winger Perry Turnbull . . . Defensive type who was solid addition to Blues . . . Was especially strong in the playoffs . . . Good at clearing traffic from front of team's net . . . Born in Boucherville, Quebec, on Nov. 25, 1962 . . . Good junior with Chicoutimi Saugeens . . . First-round draft pick of Canadiens in 1981 . . . Had only five assists in 44 Blues' games but 217 points in two junior seasons indicates big potential as a rusher.

Year	Club	GP	G	A	Pts.
1981-82	Montreal	60	3	8	11
1982-83	Montreal	78	12	21	33
1983-84	Mont-St L	71	2	12	14
	Totals	209	17	41	58

ROB RAMAGE 25 6-2 210   **Defenseman**

Had an excellent season in 1983-84 as great potential started to show after some disappointing early seasons . . . Set club records for backliners with 45 assists and 60 points . . . Named to Wales Conference team for All-Star Game . . . Had best playoff with nine points in 11 games . . . Big, strong, good skater who is always among NHL leaders in shots on goal . . . Born Jan. 11, 1959, in Byron, Ont. . . . Junior All-Star with London Knights . . . All-Star in WHA with Birmingham Bulls in 1978-79 . . . Colorado Rockies made him first player selected in 1979 draft . . . Was solid worker with Rockies for three seasons but asked for a trade . . . Blues acquired him in 1982 for two first-round draft picks.

Year	Club	GP	G	A	Pts.
1978-79	Birmingham (WHA) ..	80	12	36	48
1979-80	Colorado	75	8	20	28
1980-81	Colorado	79	20	42	62
1981-82	Colorado	80	13	29	42
1982-83	St Louis	78	16	35	51
1983-84	St Louis	80	15	45	60
	NHL Totals	392	72	171	243
	WHA Totals	80	12	36	48

DAVE PICHETTE 24 6-3 190   **Defenseman**

Joined the Blues in February, 1984, from Quebec in exchange for Andre Dore . . . Tied a club record for defensemen with four assists in first game as a Blue . . . Finished the season with 20 points in 46 games . . . Had showed good potential in flashes in four years in Nordique chain, notably the 1982 playoffs . . . Blues liked his age, size and attitude . . . Born Feb. 4, 1960, in Grand Falls, Newfoundland . . . Played junior hockey with Quebec Remparts . . . Wasn't claimed in entry draft . . . Signed as a free agent with Quebec in 1979 . . . Split his Quebec days between NHL club and minors . . . Blues feel Pichette and Gilbert Delorme can be future anchors of defense.

Year	Club	GP	G	A	Pts.
1980-81	Quebec............	46	4	16	20
1981-82	Quebec............	67	7	30	37
1982-83	Quebec............	53	3	21	24
1983-84	Que–St L	46	2	18	20
	Totals.............	212	16	85	101

BERNIE FEDERKO 28 6-0 192   **Forward**

Consistently excellent player in very front ranks of NHL centers...Had career high 41 goals and 107 points in 1983-84...Has produced 576 points in six seasons...Smooth, effortless skater who is among hockey's best passers...Good on faceoffs and penalty-killing unit...Born May 12, 1956 at Foam Lake, Sask. ...Junior star with Saskatoon Blades who was Blues' first-round draft pick in 1976...Top rookie in Central League in 1976-77 although Blues called him up late that season...Teamed well with Brian Sutter and Joe Mullen on solid line that had 41 power-play goals...Passed Garry Unger as team's career scoring leader last season...Has scored 52 points in 43 playoff games.

Year	Club	GP	G	A	Pts.
1976-77	St Louis	31	14	9	23
1977-78	St Louis	72	17	24	41
1978-79	St Louis	74	31	64	95
1979-80	St Louis	79	38	56	94
1980-81	St Louis	78	31	73	104
1981-82	St Louis	74	30	62	92
1982-83	St Louis	75	24	60	84
1983-84	St Louis	79	41	66	107
	Totals	562	226	414	640

DOUG GILMOUR 21 5-11 164   Forward

Excellent rookie season important factor for Blues who had no 1983 entry-draft picks...Had only one assist in first 10 games but finished the season with 25 goals, 53 points...Team's top scorer in playoffs with 11 points...One of his goals was an overtime winner against Minnesota...Did a big job of penalty-killing and working against opposition's big shooters...Born June 25, 1963, in Kingston, Ont....Outstanding junior with Cornwall Royals with 331 points in three seasons...Was Ontario League's Most Valuable Player in 1982-83 with 170 points...Blues claimed him on fourth round of 1982 entry draft...Defensive ability earned him an NHL job, then offense followed quickly.

Year	Club	GP	G	A	Pts.
1983–84	St. Louis	80	25	28	43

WAYNE BABYCH 26 5-11 196   Forward

His 1980-81 point line, 54-42-96, stands out in his record like a misprint...Has scored only 48 goals in three seasons since his banner year but has settled into a niche as a two-way worker...A puzzling player who simply lost his scoring touch after 54-goal year...Has all the equipment, speed, size, big shot, aggressive approach to be a top star...Born June 6, 1958, in Edmonton...Excellent junior with Portland Winterhawks...First-round draft pick by Blues in 1978...Started career well with 26 and 27 goals in first two terms...Good enough baseball prospect to be offered contract in Montreal Expos' chain...He and defenseman brother Wayne of Winnipeg Jets married twin sisters in 1982.

Year	Club	GP	G	A	Pts.
1978-79	St Louis	67	27	36	63
1979-80	St Louis	59	26	35	61
1980-81	St Louis	78	54	42	96
1981-82	St Louis	51	19	25	44
1982-83	St Louis	71	16	23	39
1983-84	St Louis	70	13	29	42
	Totals	396	155	190	345

JOE MULLEN 27 5-9 182   Forward

His 41 goals in 1983-84 were the most ever scored in NHL season by U.S.-born player, breaking record of 38 set by Minnesota's Neal Broten...Fast skater, very strong despite short stature and has accurate, quickly-released shot...Scored 25 goals in 45 games in 1981-82 NHL debut...Born Feb. 26, 1957, in New York...Grew up in Manhattan where father was a maintenance man at Madison Square Garden...Played much street and roller hockey as a boy...Had 212 points in 111 games in four seasons at Boston College...Blues signed him as a free agent in 1979...Had 40- and 59-goal seasons in Central League with Salt Lake City.

Year	Club	GP	G	A	Pts.
1981-82	St. Louis	45	25	34	59
1982-83	St. Louis	49	17	30	47
1983-84	St Louis	80	41	44	85
	Totals	174	83	108	191

BRIAN SUTTER 27 5-11 181   Forward

NHL trailblazer for remarkable family from Viking, Alta., the first of six brothers now in league...Not especially talented but a splendid player who demonstrates what can be done through hard work and aggressiveness....His 32 goals in 1983-84 gave him two 40-goal- and three 30-goal seasons in his career...His 83 points are a career high...Voted the toughest player in the

league in a poll of coaches . . . Born Oct. 7, 1956, in Viking, Alta.
. . . Played junior hockey in Lethbridge . . . Blues' second-round
pick in 1976 draft . . . Had a hairline pelvis fracture last season but
missed only four games . . . Daughter Abigail, born in April, 1983,
is the first female born in the Sutter clan in three generations.

Year	Club	GP	G	A	Pts.
1976-77	St Louis	35	4	10	14
1977-78	St Louis	78	9	13	22
1978-79	St Louis	77	41	39	80
1979-80	St Louis	71	23	35	58
1980-81	St Louis	78	35	34	69
1981-82	St Louis	74	39	36	75
1982-83	St Louis	79	46	30	76
1983-84	St Louis	76	32	51	83
	Totals	568	229	248	477

JORGEN PETTERSSON 28 6-2 184   Forward

Dipped below 30-goal mark for the first time in his four NHL
seasons in 1983-84 when he scored 28. . . . Made up for it in the
playoffs with seven scores in 11 games . . . Scored all three goals,
including overtime winner in playoff game against Detroit . . . Had
37, 38 and 35 goals in his first three seasons with Blues . . . Signed
as a free agent from the Vastra Frolunda team in Swedish Elite
Division. . . . Born July 11, 1956, in Gothenberg, Sweden . . .
Played in top Swedish league at 16 and was on national team for
60 games . . . Excellent skater with long stride, fine stickhandler
who is good at beating opponents one-on-one.

Year	Club	GP	G	A	Pts.
1980-81	St Louis	62	37	36	73
1981-82	St Louis	77	38	31	69
1982-83	St Louis	74	35	38	73
1983-84	St Louis	77	28	34	62
	Totals	290	138	139	277

COACH JACQUES DEMERS:

Despite having no draft picks
and a thin farm system, he engineered a steady
improvement in Blues in 1983-84 . . . Club won
seven more games than in previous season and
extended Minnesota to overtime in the seventh
game of the division final . . . Honest, straight-
forward approach is appreciated by his players . . . Blues played a much more disciplined
game than in previous seasons . . . Born

Aug. 26, 1944, in Montreal...Good junior player until serious leg injury ended days on the ice at 17...Started coaching in 1967 with Outrement Junior B team and won the Quebec title at that level in three of four seasons...Logged considerable time in WHA as director of personnel and coach with Chicago Cougars and Indianapolis Racers, coach with Cincinnati, and coach with Quebec Nordiques in their last season in WHA and first in NHL...Coached Nordiques' farm team, Fredericton Express, for three years and was American League Coach of the Year in 1982-83.

GREATEST ROOKIE

No Blue ever has won the Calder Trophy as top NHL rookie and their good players have tended to mature into frontliners gradually, rather than making a big initial splash.

The club's records for first-year players are held by one man, winger Jorgen Pettersson, and he qualifies as the best freshman in the team's history.

Pettersson was 24 with several seasons in the Swedish Elite League when the Blues signed him as a free agent from the Vastra Frolunda team in his hometown of Gothenberg in 1980.

That season was the best in the Blues' history when the club had 107 points to finish second in the overall standings behind New York Islanders. Pettersson played a key role in that good term when he scored 37 goals and 36 assists for 73 points, all club standards for first-year players.

Honorable mention for Blues' rookie must go to goalie John Davidson, the Blues' first-round draft pick in 1973, who had a 3.08 average in 39 games in the 1973-74 season and center Doug Gilmour, who had 53 points in a fine debut last season.

ALL-TIME BLUE LEADERS

GOALS: Wayne Babych, 54, 1980-81
ASSISTS: Bernie Federko, 73, 1980-81
POINTS: Bernie Federko, 107, 1983-84
SHUTOUTS: Glenn Hall, 8, 1968-69

TORONTO MAPLE LEAFS

TEAM DIRECTORY: Pres.: Harold E. Ballard; Chairman: Paul McNamara; GM: Gerry McNamara; Dir. Pub.: Stan Obodiac; Coach: Dan Maloney. Home ice: Maple Leaf Gardens (16,307; 200′ × 85′). Colors: Blue and white. Training camp: Toronto.

SCOUTING REPORT

OFFENSE: The 1983-84 season was one of pure misery for the Maple Leafs, not exactly a new situation for a once-proud NHL team that has accomplished very little since the 1960s. A massive injury list—more than 330 man-games lost—was a contributing

Rick Vaive rolled up third straight 50-goal season.

factor in the team's slide to 18th overall out of the playoffs but, even healthy, the Leafs were not a team free of problems.

The material is there for a respectable attack but scoring goals isn't the Leaf problem. Only the Pittsburgh Penguins surrendered more goals than Leafs' 387.

Winger and team captain Rick Vaive, who had his third consecutive 50-goal season, is the big gunner around whom an attack can be constructed. Bill Derlago (40 goals), John Anderson (37) and Dan Daoust (74 points) plus three players who were injured much of last season—Peter Ihnacak, Walt Poddubny and Mirko Frycer—are experienced forwards.

Promising youngsters Russ Courtnall, Dan Hodgson, Jeff Jackson and defenseman Cam Plante, who set a Western junior-league scoring record, are all likely to get a long look.

Old Borje Salming and young Jim Benning are good offensive defensemen.

However, unless the Leafs find a way to chop down their disastrous goals-against total, all the attack they can muster won't be enough.

DEFENSE: New coach Dan Maloney has listed an improvement in the team's work in its own zone at the top of his priorities. Such an upgrading will be a long, tough struggle.

The Leafs used five goalies last season, casting aside veterans Mike Palmateer and Rick St. Croix, and taking a short look at junior Ken Wreggett and a long one at little Alan Bester, who was subjected to great cruelty—working behind the Leaf defense in 25 consecutive games.

Wreggett and Bester are promising kids but just that, kids. The Leafs can hardly go with two greenhorns as their net tandem and need a veteran to do the job.

Benning made a big gain as an NHL defenseman and Salming is still a solid player. However, the team needs Gary Nylund, who has missed big chunks of his first two big-league seasons, to be healthy and relaxed.

A big defensive problem is a pack of undisciplined forwards who show defensive know-how only in brief flashes. Maloney will have a tough chore to establish some consistency in that area.

OUTLOOK: An old, familiar story is that the Leafs are down but plan a rebuilding job to get the club on the move up. It's happened at least seven times in the past 13 seasons and, at best, the repeated new looks last for 1½ seasons.

Maloney was a hard-working, bellicose player, qualities he'll need in large quantities in his new job.

MAPLE LEAF ROSTER

No.	Player	Pos.	Ht.	Wt.	Born	1983-84	G	A	Pts.	PIM
34	Russ Adam	C	5-10	185	5-5-61/Windsor, Ont.	St. Catharine's	32	24	56	76
10	John Anderson	RW	5-11	189	3-28-57/Toronto, Ont.	Toronto	37	31	68	32
	Normand Aubin	C	6-0	185	7-26-60/St. Leonard, Que.	St. Catharine's	47	47	94	63
15	Jim Benning	D	6-0	185	4-29-63/Edmonton, Alta.	Toronto	12	39	51	66
11	Fred Boimstruck	D	6-0	191	1-14-62/Sudbury, Ont.	St. Catharine's	2	28	30	68
6	Bruce Boudreau	C	5-9	175	1-9-55/Toronto, Ont.	St. Catharine's	47	62	109	44
16	Rich Costello	RW	6-0	185	--/Natick, Mass.	Toronto	2	1	3	2
						St. Catharine's	0	0	0	12
	Russ Courtnall	C	5-9	163	1-2-65/Duncan, B.C.	Toronto	3	9	12	6
						Victoria	29	37	66	63
24	Dan Daoust	C	5-11	160	2-29-60/Montreal, Que.	Toronto	18	56	74	88
19	Bill Derlago	C	5-10	190	8-25-58/Birtle, Man.	Toronto	40	20	60	50
28	Dave Farrish	D	6-1	195	9-1-56/Lucknow, Ont.	Toronto	4	19	23	57
						St. Catharine's	0	2	2	6
14	Miroslav Frycer	C	6-0	196	9-17-59/Czechoslovakia	Toronto	10	16	26	55
9	Stewart Gavin	LW	6-0	180	3-15-60/Ottawa, Ont.	Toronto	10	22	32	90
11	Gaston Gingras	D	6-0	191	2-13-59/North Bay, Ont.	Toronto	7	20	27	16
	Ernie Godden	C	5-8	162	3-13-61/Windsor, Ont.	St. Catharine's	31	36	67	69
23	Pat Graham	LW	6-1	190	5-25-61/Toronto, Ont.	St. Catharine's	7	7	14	18
	Dan Hodgson	C	5-10	170	8-29-65/Ft. McMurray, Alta.	Prince Albert	62	119	181	65
33	Dave Hutchison	D	6-3	205	5-2-52/London, Ont.	Toronto	0	3	3	137
	Al Iafrate	D	6-3	190	3-21-66/Livonia, Mich.	Belleville	2	4	6	2
						U.S. Olymp.	4	17	21	28
18	Peter Ihnacek	C	6-0	190	5-3-57/Czechoslovakia	Toronto	10	13	23	24
20	Jim Korn	LW-D	6-3	210	7-28-57/Hopkins, Minn.	Toronto	12	14	26	257
34	Gary Leeman	LW	5-11½	175	2-19-64/Wilcox, Sask.	Toronto	4	8	12	31
25	Terry Martin	RW-LW	5-11	175	10-23-53/Barrie, Ont.	Toronto	15	10	25	51
4	Bob McGill	D	6-0	202	4-27-62/Edmonto, Alta.	Toronto	0	2	2	51
						St. Catharine's	1	15	16	217
32	Frank Nigro	RW	5-9	182	2-11-60/Richmond Hill, Ont.	Toronto	2	3	5	16
						St. Catharine's	17	24	41	16
	Lee Norwood	D	6-0	190	2-26-60/Oakland, Cal.	St. Catharine's	13	46	59	91
2	Gary Nylund	D	6-4	200	10-28-63/Surrey, B.C.	Toronto	2	14	16	103
	Fred Perlini	C	6-2	175	4-12-62/Sault Ste. Marie, Ont.	St. Catharine's	21	31	52	67
	Cam Plante	D	6-1	195	3-12-64/Brandon, Man.	Brandon	22	118	140	96
8	Walt Poddubny	C-LW	6-1	203	2-14-60/Thunder Bay, Ont.	Toronto	11	14	25	48
21	Borje Salming	D	6-1	185	4-17-51/Sweden	Toronto	5	38	43	92
7	Greg Terrion	C	5-11	190	5-2-60/Peterborough, Ont.	Toronto	15	24	39	36
	Steve Thomas	RW	5-10	180	7-15-63/Markham, Ont.	Toronto (OHL)	51	54	105	77
22	Rick Vaive	RW	6-1	190	5-14-59/Ottawa, Ont.	Toronto	52	41	93	114
	Gary Yaremchuk	C	6-0	183	8-15-61/Edmonton, Alta.	St. Catharine's	24	37	61	84

No.	Player	Pos.	Ht.	Wt.	Born		GP	GA	SO	Avg.
31	Alan Bester	G	5-7	152	3-26-63/Hamilton, Ont.	Toronto	32	134	0	4.35
						Brantford	23	71	1	3.35
	Bruce Dowie	G	5-8	155	12-9-62/Oakville, Ont.	Toronto	2	4	0	3.33
						St. Catharine's	9	41	0	6.00
29	Mike Palmateer	G	5-9	170	1-13-54/Toronto, Ont.	Toronto	34	149	0	4.88
	Bob Parent	G	5-9	175	2-19-58/Windsor, Ont.	St. Catharine's	18	73	0	4.87
	Nick Ricci	G	5-10	160	6-3-59/Niagara Falls, Ont.	St. Catharine's	15	47	0	4.72
1	Rick St. Croix	G	5-9	160	1-3-55/Kenora, Ont.	Toronto	20	80	0	5.11
						St. Catharine's	8	29	0	3.61
	Ken Wregget	G	6-1	185	3-25-64/Medley, Alta.	Toronto	3	14	0	5.09
						Lethbridge	53	161	0	3.16

MAPLE LEAF PROFILES

ALAN BESTER 21 5-7 152 Goaltender

Built more like a jockey than a big-league goalie... Summoned out of junior hockey for last half of 1983-84 season and placed in the cannon's mouth... Played in 22 consecutive games in one stretch and in most of them had more than 40 shots... Faced 32 shots in one period at Hartford... Toiled valiantly with positive attitude and had an 11-16-4 won-lost-tied mark, respectable considering chaos in front of him... Born March 26, 1963, in Hamilton, Ont.... Played junior hockey with Brantford Alexanders ... Leafs' fifth-round draft pick in 1983... Original plan was for him to complete junior eligibility but after he shared goaltending job with Canada's team in world junior championship with another Leaf prospect, Ken Wreggett, he was promoted to NHL team... Very quick, a good competitor.

Year	Club	GP	GA	SO	Avg.
1983–84	Toronto	32	134	0	4.35

GARY NYLUND 21 6-4 200 Defenseman

First two seasons of NHL career for very promising young backliner have been pure hell because of knee injuries.... Two serious operations reduced play to 63 games in that span and he wears a heavy brace now... Frustrating time for gung-ho lad who has spent more time in therapy than on the ice... Blue-chip prospect who was Leafs' first-round choice, third overall, in 1982 entry draft... Injured knee in exhibition game, had surgery and returned late in 1982-83 season... Played 16 games, reinjured knee forcing another operation and returned halfway through 1983-84... Born in Surrey, B.C., on Oct. 28, 1963.... Splendid junior with Portland Winter Hawks... Member of Canadian team that won world junior crown in 1981.

Year	Club	GP	G	A	Pts.
1982–83	Toronto	16	0	3	3
1983–84	Toronto	47	2	14	16
	Totals	63	2	17	19

BORJE SALMING 33 6-1 185   Defenseman

First European player to be a star in the NHL...Now in 12th season on the Leaf defense...Had heavy-duty season with weak club in 1983-84 but had 43 points...Finished with minus-34, worst of his career...Excellent athlete, agile skater, splendid passer...Has been an NHL All-Star six times in career...Born April 17, 1951, in Kiruna, Sweden...Played for Swedish national team and club champs Brynas...Signed with Leafs in 1973, made adjustment to NHL very quickly...Leading scorer among Leaf defensemen with 126 goals, 641 points...Has three years to go on long-term contract as highest paid player in club's history.

Year	Club	GP	G	A	Pts.
1973-74	Toronto	76	5	34	39
1974-75	Toronto	60	12	25	37
1975-76	Toronto	78	16	41	57
1976-77	Toronto	76	12	66	78
1977-78	Toronto	80	16	60	76
1978-79	Toronto	78	17	56	73
1979-80	Toronto	74	19	52	71
1980-81	Toronto	72	5	61	66
1981-82	Toronto	69	12	44	56
1982-83	Toronto	69	7	38	45
1983-84	Toronto	68	5	38	43
	Totals	800	126	515	641

JIM BENNING 21 6-0 185   Defenseman

One of the very few Leafs for whom 1983-84 season was a positive experience...After two seasons as struggling teenager, matured into solid NHL defenseman in third term...Showed offensive skills with 51 points and played sound defensive hockey...Leaf leader in plus-minus with smallest minus (3) on club with no plus players...Awkward looking but effective skater who's smart and creative with the puck...Born in Edmonton on April 29, 1963...Produced Western league record 139 points with Portland juniors in 1980-81...Leafs' first-round draft choice in 1980 ...Rushed into regular NHL duty with poor team at 17...First two terms were painful learning experiences.

Year	Club	GP	G	A	Pts.
1981–82	Toronto	74	7	24	31
1982–83	Toronto	74	5	17	22
1983–84	Toronto	79	12	39	51
	Totals	227	24	80	104

RICK VAIVE 25 6-1 190   Forward

Leafs' one legitimate NHL star...Has had three consecutive
50-goal seasons, scoring 157 goals in that stretch...Became first
Leaf in that category in 1981-82 when he scored 54 to break club
mark of 48, set in 1960-61 by Frank Mahovlich...Excellent skater
with long stride, can shoot the puck on the fly as well as any
player...Has learned to control temper tantrums of early seasons...Team captain and very popular athlete in Toronto...Born
in Ottawa on May 14, 1959...Played junior with Sherbrooke
Beavers, turned pro early with Birmingham in WHA...Vancouver
Canucks' first-round draft pick in 1979...Canucks gave up on
him quickly because they felt he had a bad attitude...Traded to
Leafs with Bill Derlago in 1980 for Tiger Williams and Jerry
Butler.

Year	Club	GP	G	A	Pts.
1978-79	Birmingham (WHA) ..	75	26	33	59
1979-80	Van-Tor	69	22	15	37
1980-81	Toronto	75	33	29	62
1981-82	Toronto	77	54	35	89
1982-83	Toronto	78	51	28	79
1983-84	Toronto	76	52	41	93
	NHL Totals	375	212	148	360
	WHA Totals	75	26	33	59

DAN DAOUST 24 5-11 160   Forward

The 1984-85 season is critical in career of live-wire little center...Joined Leafs in trade from Montreal Canadiens halfway
through 1982-83 season, produced 52 points in 52 games and was
key man in club's revival...Had 74 points last season but was a
minus player and suffered in general team malaise...Gung-ho
type who likes to hit, despite small stature...Born in Montreal
on Feb. 29, 1960...Played junior hockey with Cornwall Royals....Wasn't claimed in entry draft but signed with Canadiens
as a free agent...Had two good seasons in AHL but couldn't
crack Canadiens' line-up....Was center on 1982-83 rookie All-
Star team.

Year	Club	GP	G	A	Pts.
1982-83	Mont-Tor	52	18	34	52
1983-84	Toronto	78	18	56	74
	Totals.............	130	36	90	126

BILL DERLAGO 26 5-10 190   Forward

Rebounded from knee problems in 1982-83 to score career-high 40 goals last season...Moved back into role as team's top center...Slick, smooth pivot with all the offensive skills...Also a good penalty-killer....Had sagged to 13-24-37 point total in 1982-83 after 84 points in previous season...Teams well with Vaive...Born Aug. 25, 1958 in Birtle, Manitoba...Counted 96 and 89 goals in two standout junior seasons with Brandon Wheat Kings...Vancouver Canucks' first-round choice in 1978...Rookie season was wrecked by knee problems as he played only nine games...Became a Leaf in 1980 with Vaive in trade for Jerry Butler and Tiger Williams.

Year	Club	GP	G	A	Pts.
1978-79	Vancouver	9	4	4	8
1979-80	Van-Tor	77	16	27	43
1980-81	Toronto	80	35	39	74
1981-82	Toronto	75	34	50	84
1982-83	Toronto	58	13	24	37
1983-84	Toronto	79	40	20	60
	Totals	378	142	164	306

JOHN ANDERSON 27 5-11 189   Forward

Had most productive NHL season with 37 goals but for the second consecutive season, quality of play tailed off in last third of year...Has good speed, shot and is sound defensively, when he wants to be...Has played some of his best hockey on a line with Vaive and Derlago...Born in Toronto on March 28, 1957...Fine junior with Toronto Marlboros, scoring 57 goals in last season...First-round draft choice in 1977...Likes fast cars and boats...Has played well on two trips to Europe, 1977 world junior championships and 1983 world championships.

Year	Club	GP	G	A	Pts.
1977-78	Toronto	17	1	2	3
1978-79	Toronto	71	15	11	26
1979-80	Toronto	74	25	28	53
1980-81	Toronto	75	17	26	43
1981-82	Toronto	69	31	26	57
1982-83	Toronto	80	31	49	80
1983-84	Toronto	73	37	31	68
	Totals	459	157	173	330

GREG TERRION 24 5-11 190   Forward

Defensive specialist whose checking ability—plus a few goals— will keep him employed for many seasons...Had best offensive season with 15 goals and 39 points...Was near the top of Leafs' sorry plus-minus list...Assigned to cover the NHL's top centers and does good job...Has haltered Wayne Gretzky in a few games...Born May 2, 1960, in Peterborough, Ont....Played junior hockey with Brantford Alexanders, where he had 122 points in final season...Los Angeles' third-round pick in 1980 draft...Spent two seasons with Kings, then was traded to the Leafs for a fourth-round draft pick early in 1982-83 season... Hard-working player who gets the most out of his limited skills.

Year	Club	GP	G	A	Pts.
1980–81	Los Angeles	73	12	25	37
1981–82	Los Angeles	61	15	22	37
1982–83	Toronto	74	16	16	32
1983–84	Toronto	79	15	24	39
	Totals	287	58	87	145

PETER IHNACAK 27 6-0 190   Forward

Knee and shoulder injuries wrecked his 1983-84 season...Played in 47 games and had 23 points...Had excellent rookie season in 1982-83 when he set a Leaf record for first-year players with 66 points...Solid two-way center, strong skater and puckhandler who isn't bothered by tough NHL play...Born in Poprad, Czechoslovakia, on May 3, 1957...Spent four seasons with Sparta club in Prague, scoring 64 goals in 133 games in Czech First Division...Was a member of Czech national team for two years ...Defected to Canada at world championships in Finland in 1982...Leafs claimed him on the second round of entry draft.

Year	Club	GP	G	A	Pts.
1982-83	Toronto	80	28	38	66
1983-84	Toronto	47	10	13	23
	Totals	127	38	51	89

COACH DAN MALONEY: After two years as assistant coach to head man Mike Nykoluk, he was promoted to top job in May 1984, after Nykoluk was sacked...Was very aggressive, hard-working player and Leaf brass hopes that approach rubs off on sad-sack team...Two years as assistant were good experience as he did pregame preparation and, at various times, handled both defensemen and forwards...Born Sept. 24, 1950, in Barrie, Ont. . . . Played junior hockey with London Knights . . . Was claimed by Chicago on first round of 1970 draft . . . Was dealt to Los Angeles Kings in 1973, then went to Detroit in 1975 as part of compensation package when Kings signed Marcel Dionne as free agent . . . Joined Leafs in 1978 when Toronto team paid a high price for him. . . . Scored 27 goals in two best NHL seasons . . . Finished career with 192 goals, 451 points in 737 games . . . Toughness on the ice demonstrated by 1,489 penalty minutes in career.

GREATEST ROOKIE

Although the Maple Leafs have accomplished very little since the 1960s and have been shut out of the Calder Trophy competition since 1966, the club's long-ago tradition of great first-year players brings some splendid names to the foreground.

In 30 seasons from 1936 to 1966, eight Leaf players were named best rookie in the NHL—Syl Apps, Gaye Stewart, Gus Bodnar, Frank McCool, Frank Mahovlich, Dave Keon, Kent Douglas and Brit Selby.

To single out one of them as the greatest rookie in Leaf history is impossible. Apps finished second in scoring in 1936-37 with 45 points while Bodnar set a rookie scoring record in 1943-44 with 62 points that endured until the late 1960s.

Mahovlich won the Calder in 1957-58 to start his superb NHL career that included four Stanley Cup wins with the Leafs and two more with Montreal. Center Dave Keon, one of the greatest defensive players in NHL history, collected the freshman award in 1960-61 to start a brilliant 22-year career.

Two latter-day rookies in blue and white had big seasons in 1982-83. Forwards Walt Poddubny and Peter Ihnacak each scored 66 points to break Bodnar's club record for first-year players.

ALL-TIME MAPLE LEAF LEADERS

GOALS: Rick Vaive, 54, 1981-82
ASSISTS: Darryl Sittler, 72, 1977-78
POINTS: Darryl Sittler, 117, 1977-78
SHUTOUTS: Harry Lumley, 13, 1953-54

VANCOUVER CANUCKS

TEAM DIRECTORY: Chairman: Frank A. Griffiths; Asst. to Chairman: Arthur R. Griffiths; Sr. VP: Jake Milford; VP-GM: Harry Neale; Asst. GM: Jack Gordon; Dir. Player Personnel: Larry Popein; Dir. Pub. Rel.: Norm Jewison; Coach: Bill LaForge. Home ice: Pacific Coliseum (15,613; 200' × 85'). Colors: Black, red and yellow. Training camp: Duncan, B.C.

Patrik Sundstrom's 91 points are a Canuck record.

SCOUTING REPORT

OFFENSE: The Canucks are perched in a familiar spot heading into the new season. They appear to be on the verge of accomplishing some good things but if past history repeats itself, it won't happen that way.

Since they entered the NHL in 1970, the Canucks have looked to be on their way several times but have been above the .500 mark only three times in 14 seasons and made noise in only one playoff, 1982, when they advanced to the Stanley Cup final. The New York Islanders swept them out in four games and the expected upturn in the Canucks' fortunes didn't happen. They've been back in the mediocre category ever since.

This season's optimism is based on the presence of some good young players in the team's line-up, notably the chaps who set Canuck scoring marks last season—Patrik Sundstrom, 91 points, and Tony Tanti, 45 goals.

The team has some dandy veterans, too. Stan Smyl, Thomas Gradin, Darcy Rota and Tiger Williams are useful big-league forwards while Cam Neely and Moe Lemay are lads who could develop into good ones. And the Canucks have added Al McAdam in the deal that sent Harold Snepsts to Minnesota.

Rick Lanz, Doug Halward and Jiri Bubla are defensemen who carry the puck well and contribute to the attack.

New coach Bill LaForge has produced some fine two-way teams during his four years of Major Junior coaching experience. The Canucks' 306 goals last season indicate sufficient attack to do the job but LaForge's big challenge is convincing the forwards that they can score and check a little, too.

DEFENSE: Richard Brodeur's 4.02 goals-against average in 1983-84 was the worst of his four years with the Canucks, where he's been one of the best NHL goalies. He remains the No. 1 man with veteran John Garrett and young Frank Caprice, who played well in a brief stretch last season, as backup.

The defense could use some new blood. Veterans Halward and Bubla are okay but they aren't likely to get much better. Lanz has matured into a good one and the Canucks need such youngsters as Garth Butcher and Michel Petit to do the same if they're to move up the ladder.

LaForge likes hard-nosed, aggressive teams but he might have to alter that outlook somewhat in Vancouver or make wholesale changes in the team's roster. If the team is to compete with the

CANUCK ROSTER

No.	Player	Pos.	Ht.	Wt.	Born	1983-84	G	A	Pts.	PIM
15	Neil Belland	D	5-11	175	4-3-61/Parry Sound, Ont.	Vancouver	7	13	20	24
						Fredericton	3	15	18	2
29	Jiri Bubla	D	5-11	197	1-27-50/Czechoslavakia	Vancouver	6	33	39	43
5	Garth Butcher	D	6-0	195	10-8-63/Regina, Sask.	Vancouver	2	0	2	34
						Fredericton	4	13	17	43
28	Marc Crawford	LW	5-11	178	2-13-61/Belland, Ont.	Vancouver	0	1	1	9
						Fredericton	9	22	31	96
	J.J. Daigneault	D	5-11	180	10-12-65/Montreal, Que.	Can. Olymp.	3	14	17	40
						Longueuil	2	11	13	6
19	Ron Delorme	RW	6-2	185	9-3-55/Cochin, Sask.	Vancouver	2	2	4	68
10	Jere Gillis	LW	6-0	190	1-18-57/Bend, Ore.	Vancouver	9	13	22	7
						Fredericton	22	28	50	35
23	Thomas Gradin	C	5-11	172	2-18-56/Sweden	Vancouver	21	57	78	32
28	Taylor Hall	LW	5-11	188	2-20-64/Regina, Sask.	Vancouver	1	0	1	0
						Regina	63	79	142	42
2	Doug Halward	D	6-1	198	11-1-55/Toronto, Ont.	Vancouver	7	16	23	35
16	Mark Kirton	C	5-10	170	2-3-58/Toronto, Ont.	Vancouver	2	3	5	2
						Fredericton	8	10	18	8
10	J.M. Lanthier	D	6-2	195	3-27-63/Montreal, Que.	Fredericton	25	17	42	29
4	Rick Lanz	D	6-1	195	9-16-61/Czechoslavakia	Vancouver	18	39	57	45
10	Moe Lemay	C	5-11	172	2-18-62/Saskatoon, Sask.	Vancouver	12	18	30	38
						Fredericton	9	7	16	32
25	Doug Lidster	D	6-1	195	10-18-60/Kamloops, B.C.	Vancouver	0	0	0	0
7	Gary Lupul	C	5-8	175	4-4-59/Powell River, B.C.	Vancouver	17	27	44	51
20	Grant Martin	C	5-10	193	3-3-62/Smooth Rock Falls, Ont.	Vancouver	0	2	2	6
						Fredericton	36	24	60	46
25	Al MacAdam	LW	6-0	180	3-6-52/Charlottetown, P.E.I.	Minnesota	22	13	35	23
8	Peter McNab	C	6-3	203	5-8-52/Vancouver, B.C.	Bos.-Van.	15	22	37	20
	Gerry Minor	C	5-8	178	10-27-58/Regina, Sask.	Fredericton	16	42	58	85
	Dave Morrison	RW	6-0	186	6-12-62/Toronto, Ont.	NH-Fredericton	14	23	37	53
21	Cam Neely	RW	6-1	185	6-6-65/Maple Ridge, B.C.	Vancouver	16	15	31	57
3	Michel Petit	D	6-1	180	2-12-64/St. Maulo, Que.	Vancouver	6	9	15	53
18	Darcy Rota	LW	5-11	178	2-16-53/Vancouver, B.C.	Vancouver	28	20	48	73
	Andy Schliebener	D	6-0	190	8-16-62/Ottawa, Ont.	Vancouver	2	10	12	40
						Fredericton	1	6	7	27
12	Stan Smyl	RW	5-8	190	1-28-58/Glendon, Alta.	Vancouver	24	43	67	136
17	Patrik Sundstrom	C	6-0	198	12-14-61/Sweden	Vancouver	38	53	91	37
9	Tony Tanti	C	5-9	190	9-7-63/Toronto, Ont.	Vancouver	45	41	86	50
22	Tiger Williams	LW	5-11	188	2-3-54/Weyburn, Sask.	Vancouver	15	16	31	294

No.	Player	Pos.	Ht.	Wt.	Born		GP	GA	SO	Avg.
35	Richard Brodeur	G	5-7	185	9-15-52/Longueuil, Que.	Vancouver	36	141	1	4.02
30	Frank Caprice	G	5-9	147	5-2-62/Hamilton, Ont.	Vancouver	19	62	1	3.38
						Fredericton	18	49	2	2.70
1	Ken Ellacott	G	5-8	155	3-3-59/Paris, Ont.	Montana	41	208	1	5.11
31	John Garrett	G	5-8	175	6-17-51/Toronto, Ont.	Vancouver	29	113	0	4.10
	Wendell Young	G	5-8	178	8-1-63/Halifax, N.S.	Salt Lake City	20	80	0	4.39
						Fredericton	11	39	1	4.11

Edmonton Oilers, speed and attack must be important ingredients for it, not grind-it-out types.

OUTLOOK: Once again, the Canucks must look at .500 as just about the limit of their horizon. Sundstrom and Tanti are exciting offensive players who give the team some entertainment value. It will be interesting to see if LaForge allows them to ramble or tries to turn them into carbon copies of Tiger Williams.

The Canucks are the only team in the NHL to have their own plane, which eases their heavy travel schedule considerably. GM Harry Neale is one of the game's best original humorists, the producer of many memorable one-liners.

The team sure can fly and laugh. Now if it can just do as well on the ice.

CANUCK PROFILES

RICHARD BRODEUR 32 5-7 185   Goaltender
One of the great bargains in NHL history... His career was dead-ended in New York Islander organization in 1980 when Canucks acquired him as net insurance for exchange of fifth-round draft picks in 1981... Since then, he's been one of the NHL's best goalies... Played a big role in the Canucks' advancing to the Cup final in 1982... Born in Longeuil, Que., on Sept. 15, 1952... Was outstanding in Cornwall Royals' winning Canadian junior title in 1972... Spent seven seasons with Quebec Nordiques in WHA... Islanders reclaimed him before expansion draft in 1979 and he spent 1979-80 in minors... Nickname is "Kermit" but Canuck fans call him King Richard... Suffered perforated eardrum when hit by shot in 1982-83.

Year	Club	GP	GA	SO	Avg.
1972-73	Quebec (WHA)	24	102	0	4.75
1973-74	Quebec (WHA)	30	89	1	3.32
1974-75	Quebec (WHA)	51	188	0	3.84
1975-76	Quebec (WHA)	69	244	2	3.69
1976-77	Quebec (WHA)	53	167	2	3.45
1977-78	Quebec (WHA)	36	121	0	3.70
1978-79	Quebec (WHA)	42	126	3	3.11
1979-80	New York I.	2	6	0	4.50
1980-81	Vancouver	52	177	0	3.51
1981-82	Vancouver	52	168	2	3.35
1982-83	Vancouver	58	208	0	3.79
1983-84	Vancouver	36	141	1	4.02
	NHL Totals	200	700	3	3.65
	WHA Totals	305	1037	8	3.64

RICK LANZ 23 6-1 195   Defenseman

Has made steady progress in four NHL seasons... Had best offensive season in 1983-84 with 57 points... Good point man on power play because of puckhandling skill and excellent shot... Much improved defensively as he's learned to use size and reach to good advantage... Severe knee injury that cost him half of second NHL season was setback to development... Born Sept. 16, 1961, in Karlouyvary, Czechoslovakia... Lanz family was on holiday outside of country in 1968 when USSR sent troops into Czechoslovakia and they never returned, migrating to Canada... Good track and field athlete in high school... Played junior hockey with Oshawa Generals... Canucks' first-round draft pick in 1980.

Year	Club	GP	G	A	Pts.
1980-81	Vancouver	76	7	22	29
1981-82	Vancouver	39	3	11	14
1982-83	Vancouver	74	10	38	48
1983-84	Vancouver	79	18	39	57
	Totals.............	268	38	110	148

PATRIK SUNDSTROM 22 6-0 198   Forward

Superbly talented player who set Canuck point record with 91, including 38 goals, in 1983-84, his second season in NHL... Strong skater, good puckhandler, excellent touch around the net... His twin brother, Peter, had fine rookie season last year with New York Rangers... Born Dec. 14, 1961, in Skellefteaa, Sweden... As a teenager, played on Bjorkloven team in Swedish Elite Division... Played in 51 games for Swedish national team and was named top forward in 1981 world junior championships... Claimed by Canucks on the eighth round of the 1980 draft... Didn't migrate until 1982 when he had finished military duty... Had 23 goals, 46 points as NHL rookie in 1982-83.

Year	Club	GP	G	A	Pts.
1982-83	Vancouver	74	23	23	46
1983-84	Vancouver	78	38	53	91
	Totals.............	152	61	76	137

TONY TANTI 21 5-9 190   **Forward**
First deal by Harry Neale when he became Canuck GM in 1982 was a dandy . . . He sent winger Curt Fraser to Chicago in exchange for Tanti, who was in junior hockey at the time . . . Quick, strong winger had eight goals in 39 games for Canucks in 1982-83, then set team record with 45 scores in 1983-84 . . . Teamed well with Patrik Sundstrom . . . Has ability to get clear in goal area . . . Born Sept. 7, 1963, in Toronto . . . Scored 81 and 62 goals for Oshawa Generals . . . Hawks' first-round draft pick in 1981 . . . Worked in weight program to build up weight to 190 pounds . . . A good soccer player which undoubtedly helped balance and ability to work in traffic.

Year	Club	GP	G	A	Pts.
1982-83	Chi-Van	40	9	8	17
1983-84	Vancouver	79	45	41	86
	Totals	119	54	49	103

THOMAS GRADIN 28 5-11 172   **Forward**
The old smoothie . . . Few NHL players skate or handle the puck any better . . . His 78 points in 1983-84, his sixth NHL season, made him the Canucks' career leader with 445 points . . . Was drafted originally by Chicago in 1976 but chose to remain in Sweden, play for the AIK team in Stockholm and finish his schooling, a degree in physical education . . . Canucks acquired his rights in 1978 . . . Born Feb. 18, 1956, in Solleftea, Sweden . . . Played an important role in the Canucks' advance to the Cup final in 1982, counting 19 points in 17 playoff games . . . Superbly conditioned player who dislikes weight training . . . Has worked at outdoor jobs in offseason to build up strength, including a summer as a trash collector.

Year	Club	GP	G	A	Pts.
1978-79	Vancouver	76	20	31	51
1979-80	Vancouver	80	30	45	75
1980-81	Vancouver	79	21	48	69
1981-82	Vancouver	76	37	49	86
1982-83	Vancouver	80	32	54	86
1983-84	Vancouver	75	21	57	78
	Totals	466	161	284	445

STAN SMYL 26 5-8 190   **Forward**
Hard-working, aggressive player who slumped in 1983-84 after
setting team points record (88) in previous season... Slipped from
38 to 24 goals and had 67 points last year... Not a gifted natural
but, through great desire, became frontline winger... Team leader
who was named captain in 1982... Good open-ice bodychecker
who surprises foes with impact when he hits because he doesn't
look as big as he is... Born Jan. 28, 1958, in Glendon, Alta... Spent
four seasons of junior hockey with New Westminster Bruins and
is the only player to participate in four Canadian junior championships... Canucks' third-round pick in 1978 entry draft... Makes
things happen on the ice with abrasive approach.

Year	Club	GP	G	A	Pts.
1978-79	Vancouver	62	14	24	38
1979-80	Vancouver	77	31	47	78
1980-81	Vancouver	80	25	38	63
1981-82	Vancouver	80	34	44	78
1982-83	Vancouver	74	38	50	88
1983-84	Vancouver	80	24	43	67
	Totals	453	166	246	412

DARCY ROTA 31 5-11 178   **Forward**
After best season in lengthy career in 1982-83 when he scored a
club record 42 goals, had injury problems last year... In 59 games,
had 28 goals... Good skater with fine offensive skills... Has
always worked hard at defensive side of the game... Spent five
seasons with Chicago, parts of two in Atlanta and is in his sixth
year with Canucks... Has scored 256 NHL goals... Born in Vancouver on Feb. 16, 1953... Splendid junior with Edmonton Oil
Kings, scoring 167 goals in 199 games over three seasons... Chicago's first-round draft pick in 1973... Friendly, out-
going sort who is extremely popular among his peers and media.

Year	Club	GP	G	A	Pts.
1973-74	Chicago	74	21	12	33
1974-75	Chicago	78	22	22	44
1975-76	Chicago	79	20	17	37
1976-77	Chicago	76	24	22	46
1977-78	Chicago	78	17	20	37
1978-79	Chi-Atl	76	22	22	44
1979-80	Atl-Van	70	15	14	29
1980-81	Vancouver	80	25	31	56
1981-82	Vancouver	51	20	20	40
1982-83	Vancouver	73	42	39	81
1983-84	Vancouver	59	28	20	48
	Totals	794	256	239	495

DOUG HALWARD 28 6-1 198   Defenseman

Another good Canuck who is trying to rebound from injuries and subpar play in 1983-84... The 1982-83 season was his best in seven years when he scored 19 goals, 52 points, and excelled defensively... An assortment of injuries reduced him to 54 games last season and he had only 23 points... Born in Toronto on Nov. 1, 1955... Played junior hockey with Peterborough Petes... Boston Bruins' first-round draft pick in 1975... Was traded to L.A. Kings in 1978, then to the Canucks in 1981... Was strong for the team in 1982 advance to the final.

Year	Club	GP	G	A	Pts.
1975-76	Boston	22	1	5	6
1976-77	Boston	18	2	2	4
1977-78	Boston	25	0	2	2
1978-79	Los Angeles	27	1	5	6
1979-80	Los Angeles	63	11	45	56
1980-81	LA-Van	58	4	16	20
1981-82	Vancouver	37	4	13	17
1982-83	Vancouver	75	19	33	52
1983-84	Vancouver	54	7	16	23
	Totals	379	49	137	186

GARY LUPUL 25 5-8 175   Forward

Good defensive player and penalty-killer who has demonstrated some offensive skill with 18 and 17 goals in past two seasons... The 18 goals came in 40 games in 1982-83 and Canucks figured he had arrived as a scorer... However, last season, his main role was checking the opposition's best shooters... Born in Powell River, B.C., on April 4, 1959... Played junior hockey with Victoria Cougars... Had 53 goals and 107 points in final junior season but wasn't claimed in 1979 draft... Canucks signed him as a free agent... The 1983-84 season was the first one in which he logged no minor-league time.

Year	Club	GP	G	A	Pts.
1979–80	Vancouver	51	9	11	20
1980–81	Vancouver	7	0	2	2
1981–82	Vancouver	41	10	7	17
1982–83	Vancouver	40	18	10	28
1983–84	Vancouver	69	17	27	44
	Totals	208	54	57	111

DAVE WILLIAMS 30 5-11 188   Forward

The Tiger still roars... Hardboot veteran who has a wide lead as the most-penalized player in NHL history... His 294 minutes last season lifted career total to 2,994 minutes... Also rebounded to score 15 goals and 31 points... Has little natural ability but hard work has made him a useful winger... Does good defensive work against top right wingers... Born Feb. 3, 1954, in Weyburn, Sask.... Played junior hockey in Swift Current, where a linemate was Islanders' Bryan Trottier... Second-round choice in 1974 draft by Toronto... Very popular player with Maple Leafs... Traded to Canucks in 1980 with Jerry Butler for Rick Vaive and Bill Derlago... Has topped the 300-minute mark in penalties in four seasons.

Year	Club	GP	G	A	Pts.
1974–75	Toronto	42	10	19	29
1975–76	Toronto	78	21	19	40
1976–77	Toronto	77	18	25	43
1977–78	Toronto	78	19	31	50
1978–79	Toronto	77	19	20	39
1979–80	Tor–Van	78	30	23	53
1980–81	Vancouver	77	35	27	62
1981–82	Vancouver	77	17	21	38
1982–83	Vancouver	68	8	13	21
1983–84	Vancouver	67	15	16	31
	Totals	719	192	214	406

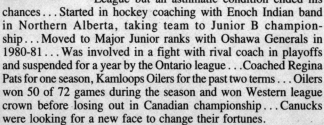

COACH BILL LAFORGE: Youngest coach in NHL at 33... Hired by Canucks after building a remarkable record (.636 winning percentage) with three different Major Junior teams... Canuck GM Harry Neale claims he liked LaForge's ability to motivate his teams... Born in Edmonton on Sept. 2, 1951... Promising football player who had two tryout offers in Canadian League but an asthmatic condition ended his chances... Started in hockey coaching with Enoch Indian band in Northern Alberta, taking team to Junior B championship... Moved to Major Junior ranks with Oshawa Generals in 1980-81... Was involved in a fight with rival coach in playoffs and suspended for a year by the Ontario league... Coached Regina Pats for one season, Kamloops Oilers for the past two terms... Oilers won 50 of 72 games during the season and won Western league crown before losing out in Canadian championship... Canucks were looking for a new face to change their fortunes.

234 THE COMPLETE HANDBOOK OF PRO HOCKEY

GREATEST ROOKIE

Maybe the heading on this section simply doesn't apply to the Canucks. They've never really had a rookie who qualifies for the adjective "great" to describe his freshman season. They've had some good rookies and a few who continued on to become good, maybe great, players, but the achievements of their first terms were less than great.

Thus, a list of the Canucks' "best" rookies would be more accurate, including several first-round draft picks who were supposed to become the cornerstones of the franchise but fell short.

The first good junior the Canucks owned was defenseman Dale Tallon, claimed in their first draft in 1970. Tallon had a 14-42-56 point total in his first season. His assist mark is a record for team rookies.

Dennis Ververgaert, the team's first pick in the 1973 draft, had 26 goals, a rookie record, and 57 points but never really lived up to what the team expected of him.

Thomas Gradin made a good debut in 1978-79 with 51 points and that was just the start of some good things. He's been among the Canucks' leading scorers ever since.

ALL-TIME CANUCK LEADERS

GOALS: Tony Tanti, 45, 1983-84
ASSISTS: Andre Boudrias, 62, 1974-75
POINTS: Patrik Sundstrom, 91, 1983-84
SHUTOUTS: Gary Smith, 6, 1974-75

WINNIPEG JETS

TEAM DIRECTORY: Chairman: Bob Graham; Pres.: Barry Shen-
karow; VP-GM: John Ferguson; Dir. Hockey/Media Inf.: Ralph
Carter; Dir. Player Personnel: Mike Doran; Coach: Barry Long.
Home ice: Winnipeg Arena (15,342; 200′ × 95′). Colors: Blue,
red and white. Training camp: Winnipeg.

SCOUTING REPORT

OFFENSE: There's absolutely nothing wrong with the Jets' attack that a little defense wouldn't cure.

The team scored 340 goals in 1983-84 and only five teams
topped that figure. But it surrendered 374 and only three teams
topped that numeral.

Dale Hawerchuk proves that the young shall inherit the ice.

Because they play in a division with the champion Edmonton Oilers, the masters of attack, to own a strong offense is not a bad idea. However, the Jets' problem is that their attack is not on a par with the Oilers'—no one's is—and they don't have the defense to compensate.

The offense is led by center Dale Hawerchuk (102 points), who recorded his second century in three seasons and is one of the premier young (21) players in the league. Laurie Boschman, a fine all-around center, would have been close to 100 points if a shoulder injury hadn't chopped him down for 19 games. He had 74 points.

Lucien DeBlois (34 goals) has gone to Montreal for Perry Turnbull, but Paul MacLean (40) had a productive season while Thomas Steen, Morris Lukowich (30 goals), Brian Mullen and two good youngsters, Andrew McBain and Scott Arniel, supply a deep, sound forward complement.

Addition of veteran Randy Carlyle, a point-a-game backliner when healthy, to the defense means that in he and David Babych, the Jets have two of the NHL's best power-play point men.

All the ingredients are there for a high-level attack.

DEFENSE: What coach Barry Long, a defensive defenseman through his 15-season pro career, must do is convince the Jets that while scoring is fun, preventing goals is what really wins.

The two parts of the game are very compatible. The Oilers proved that by maintaining their high-octane attack but playing a good puck control game and moving the puck quickly from their own zone, they could be a good defensive team.

The Jets have been very susceptible to foes who fore-check them strongly. Their defense—Babych, Robert Picard, Tim Watters, Wade Campbell and now Carlyle—handles the puck well but the team's forwards are not the best in the NHL at helping out on their home turf.

Building teams often allow their young players to establish their confidence offensively and when that's accomplished, request that they devote themselves to defense. The Jets are at the point where they must do that or remain a high-scoring but sub-.500 team.

OUTLOOK: There's a sizeable amount of first-rate material on the Jet roster, certainly enough for the club to do much better than it has for the past two seasons.

A team with the talent to score as many goals as the Jets do has the talent to prevent far more than this team has. Somebody must make them believe that theory or they'll lurch around where they've been.

JET ROSTER

No.	Player	Pos.	Ht.	Wt.	Born	1983-84	G	A	Pts.	PIM
11	Scott Arniel	LW	6-2	190	9-17-62/Kingston, Ont.	Winnipeg	21	35	56	68
44	Dave Babych	D	6-2	210	5-23-61/Edmonton, Alta.	Winnipeg	21	35	56	62
16	Laurie Boschman	C	6-0	185	6-4-60/Major, Sask.	Winnipeg	28	46	74	234
4	Wade Campbell	D	6-4	220	2-1-61/Peace River, Alta.	Winnipeg	7	14	21	147
	Randy Carlyle	D	5-10	200	4-19-56/Sudbury, Ont.	Pitt.-Winn.	3	26	29	84
5	Bobby Dollas	D	6-2	195	1-31-65/Montreal, Que.	Laval	–	–	–	–
14	Jordy Douglas	C	6-0	195	1-20-58/Winnipeg, Man.	Winnipeg	7	6	13	18
26	Murray Eaves	C	5-10	185	5-10-60/Calgary, Alta.	Sherbrooke	47	68	115	40
14	John Gibson	D	6-3	208	6-2-59/St. Catharine's, Ont.	Sherbrooke	4	11	15	174
10	Dale Hawerchuk	C	5-11	180	4-4-63/Toronto, Ont.	Winnipeg	37	65	102	73
6	Jim Kyte	D	6-3	205	3-21-64/Ottawa, Ont.	Winnipeg	1	2	3	55
12	Morris Lukowich	LW	5-9	172	6-1-56/Speers, Sask.	Winnipeg	30	25	55	71
22	Bengt Lundholm	C	6-0	172	8-4-55/Sweden	Winnipeg	5	14	19	20
15	Paul MacLean	RW	6-0	205	3-9-58/France	Winnipeg	40	31	71	155
20	Andrew McBain	RW	6-1	190	2-18-65/Toronto, Ont.	Winnipeg	11	19	30	37
19	Brian Mullen	LW	5-10	170	3-16-62/New York, N.Y.	Winnipeg	21	41	62	28
3	Robert Picard	D	6-2	211	5-25-57/Montreal, Que.	Mont.-Winn.	6	18	24	34
28	Jyrki Seppa	D	6-1	189	11-14-61/Finland	Sherbrooke	5	35	40	43
9	Doug Smail	LW	5-9	175	9-2-57/Moose Jaw, Sask.	Winnipeg	20	17	37	62
27	Don Spring	D	5-11	195	6-1-59/Venezuela	Winnipeg	0	4	4	4
						Sherbrooke	0	17	17	21
25	Thomas Steen	C	5-10	195	6-8-60/Sweden	Winnipeg	20	45	65	69
	Perry Turnbull	LW	6-2	200	3-9-59/Bentley, Alta.	St. L.-Mont.	20	15	35	140
7	Tim Watters	D	5-11	180	7-25-59/Kamloops, B.C.	Winnipeg	3	20	23	169
	Bill Whelton	D	6-1	180	8-28-59/Everett, Mass.	Sherbrooke	2	14	16	32
24	Ron Wilson	LW	5-9	168	5-13-56/Toronto, Ont.	Winnipeg	3	12	15	12
						Sherbrooke	10	30	40	16
17	Tim Young	C	6-1	192	2-22-55/Scarborough, Ont.	Winnipeg	15	19	34	25

No.	Player	Pos.	Ht.	Wt.	Born		GP	GA	SO	Avg.
29	Marc Behrand	G	6-1	185	1-11-61/Madison.Wis.	Winnipeg	6	32	0	5.47
1	Brian Hayward	G	5-10	175	6-25-60/Kingston, Ont.	Winnipeg	28	124	0	4.86
						Sherbrooke	15	69	0	5.30
30	Doug Soetaert	G	6-1	185	4-21-55/Edmonton, Alta.	Winnipeg	47	182	0	4.31
31	Mike Veisor	G	5-8	158	7-25-52/Toronto, Ont.	Hart.-Winn.	12	46	0	4.18
						Sherbrooke	5	24	0	5.56

JET PROFILES

DALE HAWERCHUK 21 5-11 180   Forward

Splendid young star who has had three fine seasons to start NHL
career... Had 37 goals and 102 points in 1983-84 to lift three-
season totals to 122 goals and 296 points... Quick, agile skater,
smart and creative with the puck, excellent shot and touch around
the net... Like many young players, his defensive play can be
better... Born in Toronto on April 4, 1963... Excellent junior
with Cornwall Royals... Led team to two consecutive Canadian
junior championships in 1980 and 1981... Top junior in Canada
in 1980-81 season when he had 81 goals and 102 assists... Jets'
first pick in 1981 draft... Teams well with winger Paul MacLean.

Year	Club	GP	G	A	Pts.
1981-82	Winnipeg	80	45	58	103
1982-83	Winnipeg	79	40	51	91
1983-84	Winnipeg	80	37	65	102
	Totals.............	239	122	174	296

LAURIE BOSCHMAN 24 6-0 185   Forward

After a stormy four-year start to his NHL career, had splendid
season with 28 goals and 74 points... Missed 19 games with
shoulder injury... Good offensive player and strong checker who
plays with bellicose approach (234 penalty minutes)... Not overly
fast but smart with the puck... Born June 4, 1960, in Major,
Sask. ... Fine junior with Brandon Wheat Kings... Maple Leafs'
first-round pick in 1979 had nothing but trouble in three Toronto
seasons... Had good rookie season in 1979-80 but second term
was ruined by mononucleosis and third, 1981-82, by owner Harold
Ballard's criticism of his personal beliefs... Was traded to Edmonton Oilers in March 1982, then to the Jets a year later.

Year	Club	GP	G	A	Pts.
1979-80	Toronto	80	16	32	48
1980-81	Toronto	53	14	19	33
1981-82	Tor-Edm...........	65	11	22	33
1982-83	Edm-Winn	74	11	17	28
1983-84	Winnipeg	61	28	46	74
	Totals.............	333	80	136	216

PAUL MacLEAN 26 6-0 205   **Forward**

Good all-around big-league player who has improved offensively
in three NHL seasons... Had best scoring campaign last year with
40 goals after counting 36 and 32 in first two years with
Jets... Combines strongly with center Hawerchuk... Doesn't have
great speed but shoots well and uses size and strength to good
advantage to get to net... Had 13 power-play goals and kills
penalities, too... Born March 9, 1958, in Grotenquin, France, as
father was stationed there with Canadian forces... Played junior
hockey in Hull, was claimed by St. Louis in 1978 draft... Spent
1979-80 with Canadian Olympic team... Played with Blues'
minor-league pro team in 1980-81, then was traded to Jets.

Year	Club	GP	G	A	Pts.
1980-81	St Louis	1	0	0	0
1981-82	Winnipeg	74	36	25	61
1982-83	Winnipeg	80	32	44	76
1983-84	Winnipeg	76	40	31	71
	Totals	231	108	100	208

RANDY CARLYLE 28 5-10 200   **Defenseman**

Acquired in trade from Pittsburgh for draft pick and defenseman
Moe Mantha during 1983-84 season... Had knee problems and
worked in only five games plus playoffs for Jets... Could be big
help to young team if he could regain form of 1980-81 season
when he was NHL's top defenseman, Norris Trophy winner and
first All-Star... Had 83 points that season and only 29 in 55 games
last term... Born April 19, 1956, in Sudbury, Ont.... Played
junior hockey with Sudbury Wolves... Second-round draft pick
by Toronto in 1976... Played parts of two seasons with Leafs,
then was traded with George Ferguson to Pens for Dave Burrows
in 1978... One of the best power-play point men in the
NHL... Handles the puck well and has excellent shot.

Year	Club	GP	G	A	Pts.
1976-77	Toronto	45	0	5	5
1977-78	Toronto	49	2	11	13
1978-79	Pittsburgh	70	13	34	47
1979-80	Pittsburgh	67	8	28	36
1980-81	Pittsburgh	76	16	67	83
1981-82	Pittsburgh	73	11	64	75
1982-83	Pittsburgh	61	15	41	56
1983-84	Pitt-Winn	55	3	26	29
	Totals	496	68	276	344

THOMAS STEEN 24 5-10 195　　　　　　　Forward

Has arrived as a competent NHL center who can play both ways...Had highest point total (65) of three seasons with Jets...Has all the Europeans' offensive skills, speed, puckhandling and passing, but is very strong defensively, a surprise because he learned the game on big Swedish ice surfaces...Born on June 8, 1960, in Tocksmark, Sweden...Played for Swedish national team in 1980 world junior championships and 1981 Canada Cup...Spent three seasons in Swedish Elite league with Leksands and Farjestads teams...Jets claimed him on the fifth round of 1979 draft.

Year	Club	GP	G	A	Pts.
1981-82	Winnipeg	73	15	29	44
1982-83	Winnipeg	75	26	33	59
1983-84	Winnipeg	78	20	45	65
	Totals	226	61	107	168

SCOTT ARNIEL 22 6-2 190　　　　　　　Forward

Big, strong, young player who has all the equipment to develop into excellent NHL worker...Counted 21 goals and 56 points last season...Handles the puck well because he's logged time at center but prefers to play the wing...At his most effective when he plays aggressively...Born in Kingston, Ont., on Sept. 17, 1962...Good junior with Cornwall Royals...Played on a line with Dale Hawerchuk on two Canadian championship teams...Was strong player for Canadian junior team in 1981 world championship victory...Called up to Jets for second half of 1981-82 season, missed much time with badly cut hand...Had 13 goals in first full NHL season, 1982-83.

Year	Club	GP	G	A	Pts.
1981–82	Winnipeg	17	1	8	9
1982–83	Winnipeg	75	13	5	18
1983–84	Winnipeg	80	21	35	56
	Totals	172	35	48	83

DAVID BABYCH 23 6-2 210　　　　　　Defenseman

Blue-chip prospect who has demonstrated top potential only in flashes . . . Has all the equipment—size, skating ability, puckhandling shot and aggressiveness—to be All-Star . . . Splendid on the power play, scoring 10 of his 18 goals that way last season . . . Born May 23, 1961, in Edmonton . . . Was regular in junior hockey with Portland Winter Hawks at 16 . . . Second player picked, behind Doug Wickenhieser, in 1980 draft . . . Has logged heavy load of ice time in first four seasons . . . He and brother Wayne, a forward with St. Louis, married twin sisters in 1982.

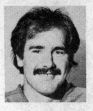

Year	Club	GP	G	A	Pts.
1980-81	Winnipeg	69	6	38	44
1981-82	Winnipeg	79	19	49	68
1982-83	Winnipeg	79	13	61	74
1983-84	Winnipeg	66	18	39	57
	Totals.	293	56	187	243

MORRIS LUKOWICH 28 5-9 172   Forward

Solid veteran who rebounded from off year in 1982-83 to score 30 goals last season . . . Has counted 163 goals in five NHL seasons . . . Quick skater with good shot . . . Abrasive approach despite small stature . . . Had best NHL season, 43 goals, in 1981-82 . . . Born June 1, 1956, in Speers, Sask. . . . Scored 142 points for Medicine Hat juniors in 1975-76 . . . Drafted by Pittsburgh in NHL draft in 1976 but chose to sign with Houston in WHA . . . Spent two seasons in Texas and when Aeros folded, contract was purchased by Winnipeg . . . Scored 65 goals for Jets in 1978-79, last WHA season, then was Jets' protected player for expansion draft . . . Deeply involved in several charities in Winnipeg.

Year	Club	GP	G	A	Pts.
1976-77	Houston (WHA)	62	27	18	45
1977-78	Houston (WHA)	80	40	35	75
1978-79	Houston (WHA)	80	65	34	99
1979-80	Winnipeg	78	35	39	74
1980-81	Winnipeg	80	33	34	67
1981-82	Winnipeg	77	43	49	92
1982-83	Winnipeg	69	22	21	43
1983-84	Winnipeg	80	30	25	55
	NHL Totals	384	166	168	331
	WHA Totals	222	132	87	219

DOUG SOETAERT 29 6-1 185   Goaltender

Veteran goalie who took over No. 1 job for Jets in 1983-84 . . . Had a 4.31 average in 47 games and an 18-15-7 won-lost-tied record... Stand-up style with good technique, owns strong catching hand... Had 19-19-6 record in 1982-83, not an easy feat with club below .500... Born in Edmonton on April 21, 1955.... Had four excellent seasons with Edmonton Oil King juniors... Claimed by New York Rangers on second round (30th overall) in 1975 entry draft... Divided six seasons between Rangers and American League farm teams at New Haven and Providence ... Jets acquired him for a third-round draft pick in 1981... Jets hope he'll be a late bloomer who can provide stable goaltending to young team.

Year	Club	GP	GA	SO	Avg.
1975-76	New York R	8	24	0	5.27
1976-77	New York R	12	28	1	2.95
1977-78	New York R	6	20	0	3.33
1978-79	New York R	17	57	0	3.80
1979-80	New York R	8	33	0	4.55
1980-81	New York R	39	152	0	3.93
1981-82	Winnipeg	39	155	2	4.31
1982-83	Winnipeg	44	174	0	4.12
1983-84	Winnipeg	47	182	0	4.31
	Totals	220	825	3	4.08

COACH BARRY LONG: Moved up from assistant coach post to head job when Tom Watt was sacked halfway through 1983-84 season... Guided team to playoff spot but Jets were swept in three games in first round by Edmonton... Has the same laid-back, easy-going approach to coaching as he did to playing... Had 15-year playing career—starting in minors in Chicago chain—with Los Angeles, Detroit and Jets in NHL,

Edmonton and Jets in WHA... Was a defensive defenseman although he did score 20 goals one season in WHA... Born in Brantford, Ont., on Jan. 3, 1949... Played junior hockey with Moose Jaw Canucks, sponsored by Black Hawks at the time... Was reclaimed by Detroit in 1979 expansion draft, then sold back to Jets by Wings a year later... Serious hand injury ended his career in 1981-82.

GREATEST ROOKIE

Because the Jets' history is split into two distinct periods—
their seven seasons in the old WHA and five in the NHL—rookies
from each era must be considered when rating the best first-year
players.

In the 1981 NHL draft, the Jets had first pick overall and
selected center Dale Hawerchuk, 18 at the time, from the Cornwall
Royals juniors. He had led the Royals to two consecutive Canadian
junior championships and the Jets liked both his hockey skill and
leadership qualities.

If anything, he was better than expected. Hawerchuk scored
45 goals and 103 points to win the Calder Trophy as the best NHL
rookie in 1981-82, a season in which the Jets made the biggest
one-year improvement, 48 points, of any team in NHL history.

The Jets were one of the classiest teams in the WHA and a big
reason for that was their stylish Swedish forwards, Anders Hedberg
and Ulf Nilsson, who teamed with Bobby Hull to form one of the
best-ever forward lines.

Their rookie season, 1974-75, was sensational. Hedberg scored
53 goals and had 100 points while Nilsson produced 120 points.

ALL-TIME JET LEADERS

GOALS: Bobby Hull, 77, 1974-75
ASSISTS: Ulf Nilsson, 94, 1974-75
POINTS: Bobby Hull, 142, 1974-75
SHUTOUTS: Joe Daley, 5, 1975-76

Quebec's Michel Goulet led NHL with 16 game-winning goals.

Official NHL Statistics

1983–84

FINAL STANDINGS

CLARENCE CAMPBELL CONFERENCE

NORRIS DIVISION

	GP	W	L	T	GF	GA	PTS	PCT
Minnesota........	80	39	31	10	345	344	88	.550
St. Louis.........	80	32	41	7	293	316	71	.444
Detroit	80	31	42	7	298	323	69	.431
Chicago	80	30	42	8	277	311	68	.425
Toronto	80	26	45	9	303	387	61	.381

SMYTHE DIVISION

	GP	W	L	T	GF	GA	PTS	PCT
Edmonton........	80	57	18	5	446	314	119	.744
Calgary	80	34	32	14	311	314	82	.513
Vancouver	80	32	39	9	306	328	73	.456
Winnipeg	80	31	38	11	340	374	73	.456
Los Angeles	80	23	44	13	309	376	59	.369

PRINCE OF WALES CONFERENCE

ADAMS DIVISION

	GP	W	L	T	GF	GA	PTS	PCT
Boston	80	49	25	6	336	261	104	.650
Buffalo	80	48	25	7	315	257	103	.644
Quebec	80	42	28	10	360	278	94	.588
Montreal.........	80	35	40	5	286	295	75	.469
Hartford	80	28	42	10	288	320	66	.413

PATRICK DIVISION

	GP	W	L	T	GF	GA	PTS	PCT
NY Islanders......	80	50	26	4	357	269	104	.650
Washington	80	48	27	5	308	226	101	.631
Philadelphia	80	44	26	10	350	290	98	.613
NY Rangers	80	42	29	9	314	304	93	.581
New Jersey	80	17	56	7	231	350	41	.256
Pittsburgh........	80	16	58	6	254	390	38	.238

STANLEY CUP: EDMONTON

INDIVIDUAL LEADERS

Goals: Wayne Gretzky, Edmonton, 87
Assists: Wayne Gretzky, Edmonton, 118
Points: Wayne Gretzky, Edmonton, 205
Penalty Minutes: Chris Nilan, Montreal, 338
Power-Play Goals: Wayne Gretzky, Edmonton, 20
Shorthanded Goals: Wayne Gretzky, Edmonton, 12
Game-Winning Goals: Michel Goulet, Quebec, 16
Three-or-More Goals Games: Wayne Gretzky, Edmonton, 8
Game-Tying Goals: Bill Gardner, Chicago, and Peter Stastny, Quebec, 4 each
Shutouts: Pat Riggin, Washington, and Al Jensen, Washington, 4 each
Goaltender Wins: Grant Fuhr, Edmonton, 30
Best Personal Goals-Against Average: Tom Barrasso, Buffalo, 2.84

INDIVIDUAL SCORING LEADERS

PLAYER	TEAM	GP	G	A	PTS	+/−	PIM	PP	SH	GW
Wayne Gretzky	Edmonton	74	87	118	205	76	39	20	12	11
Paul Coffey	Edmonton	80	40	86	126	52	104	14	1	4
Michel Goulet	Quebec	75	56	65	121	62	76	11	2	16
Peter Stastny	Quebec	80	46	73	119	22	73	11	0	4
Mike Bossy	NY Islanders	67	51	67	118	66	8	6	0	11
Barry Pederson	Boston	80	39	77	116	27	64	10	3	7
Jari Kurri	Edmonton	64	52	61	113	38	14	10	5	4
Bryan Trottier	NY Islanders	68	40	71	111	70	59	7	3	4
Bernie Federko	St. Louis	79	41	66	107	3−	43	14	0	4
Rick Middleton	Boston	80	47	58	105	26	14	16	4	6
Dale Hawerchuk	Winnipeg	80	37	65	102	14−	73	10	0	4
Mark Messier	Edmonton	73	37	64	101	40	165	7	4	7
Glenn Anderson	Edmonton	80	54	45	99	41	65	11	4	11
Ray Bourque	Boston	78	31	65	96	51	57	12	1	5
Bernie Nicholls	Los Angeles	78	41	54	95	21−	83	8	4	2
Denis Savard	Chicago	75	37	57	94	13−	71	12	0	5
Tim Kerr	Philadelphia	79	54	39	93	30	29	9	0	5
Rick Vaive	Toronto	76	52	41	93	14−	114	17	0	6
Mike Bullard	Pittsburgh	76	51	41	92	33−	57	15	0	0
Charlie Simmer	Los Angeles	79	44	48	92	7	78	13	1	4
Marcel Dionne	Los Angeles	66	39	53	92	8	28	13	0	2
Brian Propp	Philadelphia	79	39	53	92	49	37	11	1	4
Patrik Sundstrom	Vancouver	78	38	53	91	11−	37	7	0	7
Gilbert Perreault	Buffalo	73	31	59	90	19	32	8	2	7
Neal Broten	Minnesota	76	28	61	89	16	43	8	3	5
Steve Yzerman	Detroit	80	39	48	87	17−	33	13	0	2

PLAYERS BY TEAM

PLAYER	TEAM	GP	G	A	PTS	+/−	PIM	PP	SH	GW
Barry Pederson	Boston	80	39	77	116	27	64	10	3	7
Rick Middleton	Boston	80	47	58	105	26	14	16	4	6
Ray Bourque	Boston	78	31	65	96	51	57	12	1	5
Tom Fergus	Boston	69	25	36	61	8	12	6	0	3
Mike O'Connell	Boston	75	18	42	60	18	42	9	0	1
Keith Crowder	Boston	63	24	28	52	12	128	4	0	4
Mike Krushelnyski	Boston	66	25	20	45	9	55	3	2	1
Craig MacTavish	Boston	70	20	23	43	9	35	7	0	4
Gord Kluzak	Boston	80	10	27	37	9	135	5	0	3
Nevin Markwart	Boston	70	14	16	30	2	121	0	0	3
Dave Silk	Boston	35	13	17	30	11	64	5	0	1
Terry O'Reilly	Boston	58	12	18	30	9	124	2	0	2
Jim Nill	Vancouver	51	9	6	15	7−	78	0	0	0
	Boston	27	3	2	5	5−	81	0	0	0
	Total	78	12	8	20	12−	159	0	0	0
Bruce Crowder	Boston	74	6	14	20	1	44	0	0	0
Mike Milbury	Boston	74	2	17	19	2	159	0	0	0

Islander All-Star Mike Bossy posted 118 points.

PLAYER	TEAM	GP	G	A	PTS	+/−	PIM	PP	SH	GW
Guy LaPointe	Boston	45	2	16	18	3−	34	1	0	1
Mike Gillis	Boston	50	6	11	17	7−	35	0	0	1
Randy Hillier	Boston	69	3	12	15	5−	125	0	0	0
Steve Kasper	Boston	27	3	11	14	3	19	0	0	0
Luc DuFour	Boston	41	6	4	10	2	47	0	0	1
Dave Donnelly	Boston	16	3	4	7	13	2	0	0	0
Lyndon Byers	Boston	10	2	4	6	3	32	0	0	0
Doug Kostynski	Boston	9	3	1	4	2	2	0	0	0
Greg Johnston	Boston	15	2	1	3	3−	2	0	0	0
John Blum	Edmonton	4	0	1	1	0	2	0	0	0
	Boston	12	1	1	2	5	30	0	0	1
	Total	16	1	2	3	5	32	0	0	1
Brian Curran	Boston	16	1	1	2	0	57	0	0	0
Jim Schoenfeld	Boston	39	0	2	2	18	20	0	0	0
Dave Reid	Boston	8	1	0	1	1	2	0	0	0
Mike Moffat	Boston	4	0	0	0	0	0	0	0	0
Geoff Courtnall	Boston	5	0	0	0	1−	0	0	0	0
Doug Keans	Boston	33	0	0	0	0	2	0	0	0
Pete Peeters	Boston	50	0	0	0	0	36	0	0	0
Gilbert Perreault	Buffalo	73	31	59	90	19	32	8	2	7
Dave Andreychuk	Buffalo	78	38	42	80	20	42	10	0	7
Phil Housley	Buffalo	75	31	46	77	4	33	13	2	6
Mike Foligno	Buffalo	70	32	31	63	32	151	6	0	5
Real Cloutier	Buffalo	77	24	36	60	1−	25	9	0	6
Lindy Ruff	Buffalo	58	14	31	45	15	101	3	0	4
Gilles Hamel	Buffalo	75	21	23	44	4	37	4	2	1
Paul Cyr	Buffalo	71	16	27	43	3−	52	5	0	1
Hannu Virta	Buffalo	70	6	30	36	14	12	4	0	0
Ric Seiling	Buffalo	78	13	22	35	10	42	0	3	0
Mike Ramsey	Buffalo	72	9	22	31	26	82	1	0	4
Sean McKenna	Buffalo	78	20	10	30	0	45	0	0	2
Bill Hajt	Buffalo	79	3	24	27	26	32	0	1	0
Craig Ramsay	Buffalo	76	9	17	26	3	17	0	0	0
Brent Peterson	Buffalo	70	9	12	21	3	52	0	0	0
Jim Wiemer	Buffalo	64	5	15	20	1	48	0	1	0
John Tucker	Buffalo	21	12	4	16	2	4	5	0	2
Mike Moller	Buffalo	59	5	11	16	2	27	0	0	1
Larry Playfair	Buffalo	76	5	11	16	4	209	0	0	0
Jerry Korab	Buffalo	48	2	9	11	4	82	1	0	1
Claude Verret	Buffalo	11	2	5	7	3−	2	1	0	0
Steve Patrick	Buffalo	11	1	4	5	2−	6	0	0	0
Adam Creighton	Buffalo	7	2	2	4	0	4	0	0	1
Mark Renaud	Buffalo	10	1	3	4	1	6	0	0	0
Dave Fenyves	Buffalo	10	0	4	4	7	9	0	0	0
Mal Davis	Buffalo	11	2	1	3	1−	4	1	0	0
Tom Barrasso	Buffalo	42	0	2	2	0	20	0	0	0
Chris Langevin	Buffalo	6	1	0	1	2−	2	0	0	0
Bob Sauve	Buffalo	40	0	0	0	0	2	0	0	0
Kent Nilsson	Calgary	67	31	49	80	24−	22	7	9	5
Ed Beers	Calgary	73	36	39	75	7	88	16	0	4

PLAYER	TEAM	GP	G	A	PTS	+/−	PIM	PP	SH	GW
Lanny McDonald......	Calgary	65	33	33	66	15−	64	10	0	1
Hakan Loob.........	Calgary	77	30	25	55	11	22	3	0	2
Dan Quinn.........	Calgary	54	19	33	52	1−	20	11	0	1
Doug Risebrough	Calgary	77	23	28	51	11	161	0	1	3
Mike Eaves	Calgary	61	14	36	50	9	20	3	0	3
Allan MacInnis	Calgary	51	11	34	45	1	42	7	0	2
Kari Eloranta	Calgary	78	5	34	39	12	44	2	0	0
Jim Peplinski.......	Calgary	74	11	22	33	21−	114	0	0	1
Jamie Macoun	Calgary	72	9	23	32	3	97	0	1	0
Colin Patterson.......	Calgary	56	13	14	27	17	15	0	1	1
Paul Baxter	Calgary	74	7	20	27	1−	182	1	0	1
Steve Tambellini	Calgary	73	15	10	25	8−	16	1	0	2
Richard Kromm	Calgary	53	11	12	23	14	27	0	0	3
Paul Reinhart	Calgary	27	6	15	21	10−	10	3	0	1
Steve Bozek.........	Calgary	46	10	10	20	16−	16	0	0	2
Jim Jackson	Calgary	49	6	14	20	1	13	0	1	0
Steve Konroyd	Calgary	80	1	13	14	8−	94	0	1	0
Dave Hindmarch......	Calgary	29	6	5	11	2−	2	0	0	0
Tony Stiles	Calgary	30	2	7	9	14	20	0	0	0
Jamie Hislop	Calgary	27	1	8	9	0	2	0	0	1
Tim Hunter	Calgary	43	4	4	8	0	130	0	0	0
Carey Wilson	Calgary	15	2	5	7	1−	2	0	0	0
Mickey Volcan	Calgary	19	1	4	5	2−	18	0	0	1
Charles Bourgeois.....	Calgary	17	1	3	4	0	35	0	0	0
Bruce Eakin.........	Calgary	7	2	1	3	1−	4	0	0	0
Rejean Lemelin.......	Calgary	51	0	3	3	0	6	0	0	0
Keith Hanson	Calgary	25	0	2	2	13−	77	0	0	0
Don Edwards........	Calgary	41	0	2	2	0	2	0	0	0
Neil Sheehy	Calgary	1	1	0	1	0	2	0	0	0
Danny Bolduc	Calgary	2	0	1	1	1	0	0	0	0
Mike Vernon	Calgary	1	0	0	0	0	0	0	0	0
Jeff Brubaker........	Calgary	4	0	0	0	1−	19	0	0	0
Denis Savard	Chicago	75	37	57	94	13−	71	12	0	5
Steve Larmer........	Chicago	80	35	40	75	1−	34	13	0	3
Doug Wilson	Chicago	66	13	45	58	11−	64	4	1	1
Bill Gardner	Chicago	79	27	21	48	1	12	3	3	3
Bob Murray.........	Chicago	78	11	37	48	1	78	3	1	1
Tom Lysiak	Chicago	54	17	30	47	13−	35	5	1	2
Jeff Larmer	New Jersey	40	6	13	19	17−	8	0	0	0
	Chicago	36	9	13	22	3	20	2	0	1
	Total	76	15	26	41	14−	28	2	0	1
Darryl Sutter	Chicago	59	20	20	40	18−	44	8	0	4
Keith Brown.........	Chicago	74	10	25	35	18−	94	3	0	0
Behn Wilson	Chicago	59	10	22	32	5−	143	3	0	1
Troy Murray	Chicago	61	15	15	30	10	45	0	1	2
Steve Ludzik	Chicago	80	9	20	29	5−	73	0	0	0
Rich Preston	Chicago	75	10	18	28	21−	50	3	1	1
Denis Cyr	Chicago	46	12	13	25	0	19	6	0	1
Curt Fraser	Chicago	29	5	12	17	9	26	1	0	0
Jack O'Callahan	Chicago	70	4	13	17	6−	67	0	0	1
Rick Paterson	Chicago	72	7	6	13	13−	41	0	0	0
Dave Feamster	Chicago	46	6	7	13	8−	42	0	0	0
Ken Yaremchuk	Chicago	47	6	7	13	1−	19	0	0	0

Denis Savard led Black Hawks with 37 goals, 57 assists.

PLAYER	TEAM	GP	G	A	PTS	+/−	PIM	PP	SH	GW
Peter Marsh	Chicago	43	4	6	10	11−	44	0	0	0
Al Secord	Chicago	14	4	4	8	7	77	1	0	3
Don Dietrich	Chicago	17	0	5	5	1−	0	0	0	0
Randy Boyd	Pittsburgh	5	0	1	1	2−	6	0	0	0
	Chicago	23	0	4	4	0	16	0	0	0
	Total	28	0	5	5	2−	22	0	0	0
Tom McMurchy	Chicago	27	3	1	4	7−	42	0	0	0
Jerome Dupont	Chicago	36	2	2	4	11−	116	0	0	0
Murray Bannerman	Chicago	56	0	4	4	0	17	0	0	0
Tony Esposito	Chicago	18	0	3	3	0	0	0	0	0
Darrel Anholt	Chicago	1	0	0	0	2	0	0	0	0
Jim Camazzola	Chicago	1	0	0	0	0	0	0	0	0
Bruce Cassidy	Chicago	1	0	0	0	0	0	0	0	0
Dan Frawley	Chicago	3	0	0	0	1−	0	0	0	0
Perry Pelensky	Chicago	4	0	0	0	0	5	0	0	0
Bob Janecyk	Chicago	8	0	0	0	0	2	0	0	0
Florent Robidoux	Chicago	9	0	0	0	3−	0	0	0	0
Steve Yzerman	Detroit	80	39	48	87	17−	33	13	0	2
Ivan Boldirev	Detroit	75	35	48	83	3	20	12	0	4
Ron Duguay	Detroit	80	33	47	80	26−	34	13	1	1
John Ogrodnick	Detroit	64	42	36	78	16−	14	19	3	5
Reed Larson	Detroit	78	23	39	62	10−	122	10	0	5
Kelly Kisio	Detroit	70	23	37	60	16	34	1	0	2
Brad Park	Detroit	80	5	53	58	29−	85	4	0	0
Lane Lambert	Detroit	73	20	15	35	5−	115	1	0	2
Rick MacLeish	Philadelphia	29	8	14	22	4	4	3	0	2
	Detroit	25	2	8	10	4−	4	0	0	0
	Total	54	10	22	32	0	8	3	0	2
Blake Dunlop	St. Louis	17	1	10	11	1−	4	0	0	0
	Detroit	57	6	14	20	13−	20	1	1	0
	Total	74	7	24	31	14−	24	1	1	0
Danny Gare	Detroit	63	13	13	26	3	147	1	0	2
Ed Johnstone	Detroit	46	12	11	23	3	54	4	0	0
Greg Smith	Detroit	75	3	20	23	6	108	0	0	1
Bob Manno	Detroit	62	9	13	22	1−	60	0	1	4
Dwight Foster	Detroit	52	9	12	21	4−	50	0	2	1
Randy Ladouceur	Detroit	71	3	17	20	12−	58	0	0	0
Claude Loiselle	Detroit	28	4	6	10	4	32	0	0	0
John Barrett	Detroit	78	2	8	10	0	78	0	0	0
Pierre Aubry	Quebec	23	1	1	2	3−	17	0	0	0
	Detroit	14	4	1	5	1−	8	0	0	0
	Total	37	5	2	7	4−	25	0	0	0
Colin Campbell	Detroit	68	3	4	7	0	108	0	0	1
Joe Paterson	Detroit	41	2	5	7	0	148	0	0	0
Paul Woods	Detroit	57	2	5	7	16−	18	0	0	0
Andre St.Laurent	Pittsburgh	8	2	0	2	3−	21	0	1	0
	Detroit	19	1	3	4	3−	17	0	1	0
	Total	27	3	3	6	6−	38	0	2	0
Murray Craven	Detroit	15	0	4	4	2	6	0	0	0
Brad Smith	Detroit	8	2	1	3	2−	36	0	0	0
Ted Nolan	Detroit	19	1	2	3	11−	26	0	0	1
Greg Stefan	Detroit	50	0	3	3	0	14	0	0	0
Corrado Micalef	Detroit	14	0	1	1	0	2	0	0	0

PLAYER	TEAM	GP	G	A	PTS	+/−	PIM	PP	SH	GW
Barry Melrose	Detroit	21	0	1	1	0	74	0	0	0
Eddie Mio	Detroit	24	0	1	1	0	6	0	0	0
Jody Gage	Detroit	3	0	0	0	0	0	0	0	0
Ken Holland	Detroit	3	0	0	0	0	0	0	0	0
Brian Johnson	Detroit	3	0	0	0	3−	5	0	0	0
Wayne Gretzky	Edmonton	74	87	118	205	76	39	20	12	11
Paul Coffey	Edmonton	80	40	86	126	52	104	14	1	4
Jari Kurri	Edmonton	64	52	61	113	38	14	10	5	4
Mark Messier	Edmonton	73	37	64	101	40	165	7	4	7
Glenn Anderson	Edmonton	80	54	45	99	41	65	11	4	11
Ken Linseman	Edmonton	72	18	49	67	30	119	5	1	2
Pat Hughes	Edmonton	77	27	28	55	18	61	2	3	3
Dave Hunter	Edmonton	80	22	26	48	25	90	1	1	3
Kevin Lowe	Edmonton	80	4	42	46	37	59	1	0	1
Charlie Huddy	Edmonton	75	8	34	42	50	43	3	0	0
Randy Gregg	Edmonton	80	13	27	40	40	56	2	1	2
Willy Lindstrom	Edmonton	73	22	16	38	17	38	2	0	3
Kevin McClelland	Pittsburgh	24	2	4	6	7−	62	0	2	0
	Edmonton	52	8	20	28	9	127	0	2	2
	Total	76	10	24	34	2	189	0	4	2
Jaroslav Pouzar	Edmonton	67	13	19	32	17	44	2	0	0
Dave Lumley	Edmonton	56	6	15	21	14	68	0	0	0
Lee Fogolin	Edmonton	80	5	16	21	33	125	0	0 −	2
Don Jackson	Edmonton	64	8	12	20	28	120	0	1	2
Dave Semenko	Edmonton	52	6	11	17	9	118	0	0	2
Grant Fuhr	Edmonton	45	0	14	14	0	6	0	0	0
Pat Conacher	Edmonton	45	2	8	10	2−	31	0	0	0
Rick Chartraw	NY Rangers	4	0	0	0	3−	4	0	0	0
	Edmonton	24	2	6	8	5	21	0	0	0
	Total	28	2	6	8	2	25	0	0	0
Ken Berry	Edmonton	13	2	3	5	6	10	0	1	0
Raimo Summanen	Edmonton	2	1	4	5	4	2	0	0	0
Kari Jalonen	Calgary	9	0	3	3	1−	0	0	0	0
	Edmonton	3	0	0	0	2−	0	0	0	0
	Total	12	0	3	3	3−	0	0	0	0
Jim Playfair	Edmonton	2	1	1	2	4	2	0	0	0
Tom Gorence	Edmonton	12	1	1	2	0	0	0	0	0
Gord Sherven	Edmonton	2	1	0	1	1	0	0	0	0
Marc Habscheid	Edmonton	9	1	0	1	3−	6	0	0	0
Todd Strueby	Edmonton	1	0	1	1	2	2	0	0	0
Andy Moog	Edmonton	38	0	1	1	0	4	0	0	0
Dean Clark	Edmonton	1	0	0	0	0	0	0	0	0
Steve Graves	Edmonton	2	0	0	0	0	0	0	0	0
Reg Kerr	Edmonton	3	0	0	0	3−	0	0	0	0
Ray Cote	Edmonton	13	0	0	0	5−	2	0	0	0
Mark Johnson	Hartford	79	35	52	87	14−	27	13	1	2
Ron Francis	Hartford	72	23	60	83	10−	45	5	0	5
Sylvain Turgeon	Hartford	76	40	32	72	11−	55	18	0	5
Ray Neufeld	Hartford	80	27	42	69	18−	97	5	0	5
Bob Crawford	Hartford	80	36	25	61	1−	32	5	0	3
Greg Malone	Hartford	78	17	37	54	10−	56	3	0	1

PLAYER	TEAM	GP	G	A	PTS	+/-	PIM	PP	SH	GW
Risto Siltanen	Hartford	75	15	38	53	21−	34	12	0	0
Tony Currie	Vancouver	18	3	3	6	1−	2	1	0	0
	Hartford	32	12	16	28	2−	4	6	0	2
	Total	50	15	19	34	3−	6	7	0	2
Mike Zuke...........	Hartford	75	6	23	29	18−	36	1	0	0
Richie Dunn.........	Hartford	63	5	20	25	20−	30	0	0	0
Norm Dupont........	Hartford	40	7	15	22	16−	12	2	0	0
Torrie Robertson	Hartford	66	7	14	21	9−	198	0	0	2
Doug Sulliman	Hartford	67	6	12	18	11−	20	0	0	0
Chris Kotsopoulos.....	Hartford	72	5	13	18	2−	118	3	0	0
Dan Bourbonnais	Hartford	35	0	16	16	3	0	0	0	0
Joel Quenneville	Hartford	80	5	8	13	11−	95	0	2	0
Jack Brownschidle	St. Louis	51	1	7	8	21−	19	1	0	0
	Hartford	13	2	2	4	5−	10	0	0	1
	Total	64	3	9	12	26−	29	1	0	1
Marty Howe..........	Hartford	69	0	11	11	1	34	0	0	0
Randy Pierce	Hartford	17	6	3	9	5	9	0	1	0
Ed Hospodar	Hartford	59	0	9	9	17−	163	0	0	0
Steve Stoyanovich.....	Hartford	23	3	5	8	1−	11	0	0	1
Dave Tippett	Hartford	17	4	2	6	1−	2	0	1	0
Mike Crombeen	Hartford	56	1	4	5	13−	25	0	0	0
Mark Fusco..........	Hartford	17	0	4	4	6−	2	0	0	0
Paul Lawless	Hartford	6	0	3	3	5	0	0	0	0
Greg Millen	Hartford	60	0	3	3	0	10	0	0	0
Mark Paterson	Hartford	9	2	0	2	4	4	0	0	0
Ross Yates	Hartford	7	1	1	2	0	4	0	0	0
Paul MacDermid......	Hartford	3	0	1	1	1	0	0	0	0
Ed Staniowski	Winnipeg	1	0	1	1	0	0	0	0	0
	Hartford	18	0	0	0	0	2	0	0	0
	Total	19	0	1	1	0	2	0	0	0
Bob Hess	Hartford	3	0	0	0	1	0	0	0	0
Gerry McDonald	Hartford	5	0	0	0	3−	4	0	0	0
Reid Bailey	Hartford	12	0	0	0	2−	25	0	0	0
Bernie Nicholls.......	Los Angeles	78	41	54	95	21−	83	8	4	2
Charlie Simmer	Los Angeles	79	44	48	92	7	78	13	1	4
Marcel Dionne	Los Angeles	66	39	53	92	8	28	13	0	2
Jim Fox	Los Angeles	80	30	42	72	12−	26	10	0	5
Dave Taylor	Los Angeles	63	20	49	69	3−	91	6	0	2
Brian MacLellan	Los Angeles	72	25	29	54	21−	45	3	1	1
Mark Hardy..........	Los Angeles	79	8	41	49	30−	122	5	0	1
Doug Smith..........	Los Angeles	72	16	20	36	33−	28	6	0	0
Mike McEwen	NY Islanders	15	0	2	2	5−	6	0	0	0
	Los Angeles	47	10	24	34	12−	14	7	0	0
	Total	62	10	26	36	17−	20	7	0	0
Anders Hakansson	Los Angeles	80	15	17	32	7−	41	0	1	3
Terry Ruskowski......	Los Angeles	77	7	25	32	24−	92	0	2	1
Brian Engblom	Washington	6	0	1	1	4−	8	0	0	0
	Los Angeles	74	2	27	29	9−	59	2	0	0
	Total	80	2	28	30	13−	67	2	0	0
Billy Harris	Toronto	50	7	10	17	20−	14	0	0	0
	Los Angeles	21	2	4	6	3−	6	0	0	0
	Total	71	9	14	23	23−	20	0	0	0
Wes Jarvis	Los Angeles	61	9	13	22	7−	36	1	1	0

PLAYER	TEAM	GP	G	A	PTS	+/-	PIM	PP	SH	GW
J. P. Kelly	Los Angeles	72	7	14	21	34−	73	0	0	0
Jay Wells	Los Angeles	69	3	18	21	10−	141	0	0	0
Russ Anderson	Los Angeles	70	5	12	17	30−	126	0	0	1
Ken Houston	Washington	4	0	0	0	2−	4	0	0	0
	Los Angeles	33	8	8	16	3−	11	0	0	0
	Total	37	8	8	16	5−	15	0	0	0
Steve Christoff	Los Angeles	58	8	7	15	19−	13	0	0	1
Marc Chorney	Pittsburgh	4	0	1	1	4−	8	0	0	0
	Los Angeles	71	3	9	12	24−	58	0	0	0
	Total	75	3	10	13	28−	66	0	0	0
Kevin LaVallee	Los Angeles	19	3	3	6	5−	2	0	0	0
Dean Kennedy	Los Angeles	37	1	5	6	5−	50	0	0	0
Fred Barrett	Los Angeles	15	2	0	2	2−	8	0	0	0
Marco Baron	Los Angeles	21	0	2	2	0	10	0	0	0
Bob Laforest	Los Angeles	5	1	0	1	3−	2	1	0	0
Daryl Evans	Los Angeles	4	0	1	1	1	0	0	0	0
Mike Heidt	Los Angeles	6	0	1	1	1−	7	0	0	0
Mike Blake	Los Angeles	29	0	1	1	0	6	0	0	0
Dan Brennan	Los Angeles	2	0	0	0	1−	0	0	0	0
Warren Holmes	Los Angeles	3	0	0	0	3−	0	0	0	0
Phil Sykes	Los Angeles	3	0	0	0	1−	2	0	0	0
Dean Jenkins	Los Angeles	5	0	0	0	1−	2	0	0	0
Bill O'Dwyer	Los Angeles	5	0	0	0	1	0	0	0	0
Mario Lessard	Los Angeles	6	0	0	0	0	0	0	0	0
Gary Laskoski	Los Angeles	13	0	0	0	0	0	0	0	0
Markus Mattsson	Los Angeles	19	0	0	0	0	0	0	0	0
Neal Broten	Minnesota	76	28	61	89	16	43	8	3	5
Brian Bellows	Minnesota	78	41	42	83	2−	66	14	5	5
Brad Maxwell	Minnesota	78	19	54	73	7−	225	8	0	2
Dino Ciccarelli	Minnesota	79	38	33	71	1	58	16	0	2
Tom McCarthy	Minnesota	66	39	31	70	17	49	16	2	7
Keith Acton	Montreal	9	3	7	10	9−	4	2−	0	0
	Minnesota	62	17	38	55	2	60	4	2	5
	Total	71	20	45	65	3−	64	6	2	5
Dennis Maruk	Minnesota	71	17	43	60	17−	42	7	0	2
Steve Payne	Minnesota	78	28	31	59	2−	49	7	0	2
Gordie Roberts	Minnesota	77	8	45	53	14	132	1	1	
Mark Napier	Montreal	5	3	2	5	0	0	0	0	
	Minnesota	58	13	28	41	2	17	0	0	
	Total	63	16	30	46	2	17	0	0	2
Willi Plett	Minnesota	73	15	23	38	6−	316	1	0	
Al MacAdam	Minnesota	80	22	13	35	5−	23	1	4	1
Brian Lawton	Minnesota	58	10	21	31	0	33	0	0	
Paul Holmgren	Philadelphia	52	9	13	22	1	105	1	0	
	Minnesota	11	2	5	7	2−	46	0	0	
	Total	63	11	18	29	1−	151	1	0	
Curt Giles	Minnesota	70	6	22	28	2	59	2	0	
Craig Levie	Minnesota	37	6	13	19	9	44	0	0	
Lars Lindgren	Vancouver	7	1	2	3	0	4	0	0	
	Minnesota	59	2	14	16	3−	33	0	0	
	Total	66	3	16	19	3−	37	0	0	
Brent Ashton	Minnesota	68	7	10	17	13−	54	0	0	
George Ferguson	Minnesota	63	6	10	16	6−	19	0	0	

PLAYER	TEAM	GP	G	A	PTS	+/-	PIM	PP	SH	GW
Craig Hartsburg	Minnesota	26	7	7	14	2−	37	5	0	0
Dan Mandich	Minnesota	31	2	7	9	6−	77	0	0	0
Dave Richter	Minnesota	42	2	3	5	8−	132	0	0	0
Randy Velischek	Minnesota	33	2	2	4	6−	10	0	0	0
Tom Hirsch	Minnesota	15	1	3	4	3−	20	0	1	0
Dirk Graham	Minnesota	6	1	1	2	1	0	0	0	0
David Jensen	Minnesota	8	0	1	1	2	0	0	0	0
Gilles Meloche	Minnesota	52	0	1	1	0	2	0	0	0
Bob Rouse	Minnesota	1	0	0	0	0	0	0	0	0
Jon Casey	Minnesota	2	0	0	0	0	0	0	0	0
Tim Coulis.	Minnesota	2	0	0	0	1−	4	0	0	0
Jim Craig	Minnesota	3	0	0	0	0	0	0	0	0
Scott Bjugstaad	Minnesota	5	0	0	0	1−	2	0	0	0
Don Beaupre	Minnesota	33	0	0	0	0	17	0	0	0
Bobby Smith	Minnesota	10	3	6	9	1−	9	1	0	0
	Montreal	70	26	37	63	7−	62	6	1	3
	Total	80	29	43	72	8−	71	7	1	3
Guy Lafleur	Montreal	80	30	40	70	14−	19	6	0	6
Mats Naslund.	Montreal	77	29	35	64	5	4	3	0	1
Guy Carbonneau	Montreal	78	24	30	54	5	75	3	7	2
Ryan Walter.	Montreal	73	20	29	49	11−	83	7	1	4
John Chabot	Montreal	56	18	25	43	2−	13	4	1	2
Larry Robinson	Montreal	74	9	34	43	4	39	4	0	1
Bob Gainey	Montreal	77	17	22	39	10	41	0	0	3
Mario Tremblay	Montreal	67	14	25	39	2	112	3	0	3
Pierre Mondou	Montreal	52	15	22	37	9	8	3	1	1
Steve Shutt	Montreal	63	14	23	37	18−	29	4	0	2
Perry Turnbull	St. Louis	32	14	8	22	2−	81	1	0	0
	Montreal	40	6	7	13	12−	59	2	0	1
	Total	72	20	15	35	14−	140	3	0	1
Chris Nilan	Montreal	76	16	10	26	4−	338	4	0	1
Craig Ludwig	Montreal	80	7	18	25	10−	52	0	0	0
Bill Root	Montreal	72	4	13	17	26	45	1	1	0
Alfie Turcotte	Montreal	30	7	7	14	9−	10	5	0	0
Jean Hamel	Montreal	79	1	12	13	7	92	0	0	0
Ric Nattress.	Montreal	34	0	12	12	11−	15	0	0	0
Mark Hunter	Montreal	22	6	4	10	2−	42	1	0	0
Kent Carlson	Montreal	65	3	7	10	15−	73	0	0	2
Mike McPhee	Montreal	14	5	2	7	4	41	0	0	0
Rick Wamsley	Montreal	42	0	3	3	0	6	0	0	0
Claude Lemieux	Montreal	8	1	1	2	2−	12	0	0	0
Chris Chelios	Montreal	12	0	2	2	5−	12	0	0	0
Rick Green	Montreal	7	0	1	1	5−	7	0	0	0
Mark Holden	Montreal	1	0	0	0	0	0	0	0	0
Sergio Momesso	Montreal	1	0	0	0	1	0	0	0	0
Jocelyn Gauvreau	Montreal	2	0	0	0	2−	0	0	0	0
Larry Landon	Montreal	2	0	0	0	2	0	0	0	0
Dave Allison	Montreal	3	0	0	0	2−	12	0	0	0
Bill Kitchen	Montreal	3	0	0	0	0	2	0	0	0
John Newberry.	Montreal	3	0	0	0	0	0	0	0	0
Normand Baron	Montreal	4	0	0	0	2−	12	0	0	0
Steve Penney.	Montreal	4	0	0	0	0	0	0	0	0
Richard Sevigny	Montreal	40	0	0	0	0	12	0	0	0

PLAYER	TEAM	GP	G	A	PTS	+/-	PIM	PP	SH	GW
Mel Bridgman	New Jersey	79	23	38	61	27-	121	9	1	0
Jan Ludvig	New Jersey	74	22	32	54	18-	70	7	0	2
Pat Verbeek.	New Jersey	79	20	27	47	19-	158	5	1	2
Joe Cirella.	New Jersey	79	11	33	44	43-	137	6	0	0
Bob MacMillan	New Jersey	71	17	23	40	21-	23	2	0	2
Aaron Broten	New Jersey	80	13	23	36	28-	36	3	0	1
Tim Higgins.	Chicago	32	1	4	5	1	21	0	0	1
	New Jersey	37	18	10	28	4-	27	3	1	3
	Total	69	19	14	33	3-	48	3	1	4
Don Lever	New Jersey	70	14	19	33	21-	44	3	0	2
Paul Gagne	New Jersey	66	14	18	32	22-	33	3	0	1
Phil Russell	New Jersey	76	9	22	31	27-	96	0	0	0
Rick Meagher	New Jersey	52	14	14	28	9-	16	2	0	2
Gary McAdam	New Jersey	6	2	0	2	3-	2	0	0	0
	Washington	24	1	5	6	0	12	0	0	1
	New Jersey	32	7	6	13	4-	13	0	2	1
	NJ Total	38	9	6	15	7-	15	0	2	1
	Total	62	10	11	21	7-	27	0	2	2
Dave Cameron	New Jersey	67	9	12	21	11-	85	2	0	0
Murray Brumwell	New Jersey	42	7	13	20	5-	14	5	0	0
Bob Hoffmeyer	New Jersey	58	4	12	16	20-	61	0	0	0
Bob Lorimer	New Jersey	72	2	10	12	28-	62	1	0	0
Mike Antonovich.	New Jersey	38	3	5	8	15-	16	0	0	0
Yvon Vautour.	New Jersey	42	3	4	7	18-	78	0	0	1
Dave Lewis	New Jersey	66	2	5	7	19-	63	0	0	0
Ken Daneyko	New Jersey	11	1	4	5	1-	17	0	0	0
Mike Kitchen	New Jersey	43	1	4	5	15-	24	0	0	0
Rob Palmer	New Jersey	38	0	5	5	10-	10	0	0	0
Hector Marini	New Jersey	32	2	2	4	2-	47	0	0	0
Larry Floyd	New Jersey	7	1	3	4	4-	7	0	0	0
Rich Chernomaz	New Jersey	7	2	1	3	3-	2	0	0	0
Grant Mulvey	New Jersey	12	1	2	3	5-	19	0	0	0
Kevin Maxwell	New Jersey	14	0	3	3	9-	2	0	0	0
Rocky Trottier	New Jersey	5	1	1	2	1-	0	0	0	0
Bruce Driver	New Jersey	4	0	2	2	2-	0	0	0	0
Glenn Resch	New Jersey	51	0	2	2	0	12	0	0	0
Glenn Merkosky	New Jersey	5	1	0	1	0	0	0	0	0
John MacLean	New Jersey	23	1	0	1	7-	10	0	0	0
Alan Hepple	New Jersey	1	0	0	0	1-	7	0	0	0
John Johannson	New Jersey	5	0	0	0	2-	0	0	0	0
Garry Howatt	New Jersey	6	0	0	0	1-	14	0	0	0
Ron Low.	New Jersey	44	0	0	0	0	4	0	0	0
Mike Bossy	NY Islanders	67	51	67	118	66	8	6	0	11
Bryan Trottier.	NY Islanders	68	40	71	111	70	59	7	3	4
Denis Potvin	NY Islanders	78	22	63	85	55	87	11	1	3
John Tonelli.	NY Islanders	73	27	40	67	21	66	5	1	7
Greg Gilbert.	NY Islanders	79	31	35	66	51	59	6	0	2
Bob Bourne.	NY Islanders	78	22	34	56	12	75	5	5	2
Brent Sutter.	NY Islanders	69	34	15	49	4	69	7	0	6
Tomas Jonsson	NY Islanders	72	11	36	47	12	54	2	0	1
Butch Goring	NY Islanders	71	22	24	46	8	8	0	5	3
Bob Nystrom	NY Islanders	74	15	29	44	9	80	1	0	1
Duane Sutter	NY Islanders	78	17	23	40	2	94	2	0	1

PLAYER	TEAM	GP	G	A	PTS	+/−	PIM	PP	SH	GW
Stefan Persson	NY Islanders	75	9	24	33	30	65	4	0	2
Clark Gillies	NY Islanders	76	12	16	28	5	65	3	0	2
Anders Kallur	NY Islanders	65	9	14	23	0	24	2	3	1
Pat Lafontaine	NY Islanders	15	13	6	19	9	6	1	0	0
Dave Langevin	NY Islanders	69	3	16	19	26	53	0	0	1
Ken Morrow	NY Islanders	63	3	11	14	26	45	0	0	1
Gord Dineen	NY Islanders	43	1	11	12	10	32	0	0	0
Wayne Merrick	NY Islanders	31	6	5	11	2	10	0	0	0
Paul Boutilier	NY Islanders	28	0	11	11	18	36	0	0	0
Pat Flatley	NY Islanders	16	2	7	9	3	6	1	0	0
Billy Carroll	NY Islanders	39	5	2	7	1−	12	0	0	2
Mats Hallin	NY Islanders	40	2	5	7	2−	27	0	0	0
Gord Lane	NY Islanders	38	0	3	3	6	70	0	0	0
Roland Melanson	NY Islanders	37	0	2	2	0	10	0	0	0
Billy Smith	NY Islanders	42	0	2	2	0	23	0	0	0
Garth MacGuigan	NY Islanders	3	0	1	1	0	0	0	0	0
Darcy Regier	NY Islanders	5	0	1	1	2	0	0	0	0
Bruce Affleck	NY Islanders	1	0	0	0	1−	0	0	0	0
Kelly Hrudey	NY Islanders	12	0	0	0	0	0	0	0	0
Mark Pavelich	NY Rangers	77	29	53	82	11	96	12	1	2
Pierre Larouche	NY Rangers	77	48	33	81	15−	22	19	0	4
Anders Hedberg	NY Rangers	79	32	35	67	18	16	6	0	2
Don Maloney	NY Rangers	79	24	42	66	5−	62	5	3	5
Mike Rogers	NY Rangers	78	23	38	61	24−	45	6	3	2
Reijo Ruotsalainen	NY Rangers	74	20	39	59	17	26	5	0	4
Ron Greschner	NY Rangers	77	12	44	56	5	117	5	0	0
Mark Osborne	NY Rangers	73	23	28	51	1	88	6	0	5
Blaine Stoughton	Hartford	54	23	14	37	13−	4	7	0	2
	NY Rangers	14	5	2	7	12−	4	1	0	1
	Total	68	28	16	44	25−	8	8	0	3
Peter Sundstrom	NY Rangers	77	22	22	44	3	24	0	2	4
Barry Beck	NY Rangers	72	9	27	36	12	132	2	1	0
Dave Maloney	NY Rangers	68	7	26	33	11	168	2	0	1
Jan Erixon	NY Rangers	75	5	25	30	14	16	1	0	0
Mikko Leinonen	NY Rangers	28	3	23	26	4	28	0	0	1
Willie Huber	NY Rangers	42	9	14	23	14−	60	4	1	1
Mike Allison	NY Rangers	45	8	12	20	5	64	0	0	2
K.E. Andersson	NY Rangers	63	5	15	20	5	8	0	0	1
Tom Laidlaw	NY Rangers	79	3	15	18	10−	62	0	0	1
Rob McClanahan	NY Rangers	41	6	8	14	0	21	0	0	2
Nick Fotiu	NY Rangers	40	7	6	13	8	115	0	0	2
Mike Blaisdell	NY Rangers	36	5	6	11	0	31	0	0	1
Jim Patrick	NY Rangers	12	1	7	8	6	2	0	0	0
Steve Richmond	NY Rangers	26	2	5	7	6	110	0	0	0
Robbie Ftorek	NY Rangers	31	3	2	5	2	22	0	0	1
Larry Patey	St. Louis	17	0	1	1	12−	8	0	0	0
	NY Rangers	9	1	2	3	0	4	0	1	0
	Total	26	1	3	4	12−	12	0	1	0
Bob Brooke	NY Rangers	9	1	2	3	1	4	0	0	0
George McPhee	NY Rangers	9	1	1	2	0	11	0	0	0
Scot Kleinendorst	NY Rangers	23	0	2	2	10−	35	0	0	0
Glen Hanlon	NY Rangers	50	0	2	2	0	30	0	0	0
Chris Kontos	NY Rangers	6	0	1	1	0	8	0	0	0

PLAYER	TEAM	GP	G	A	PTS	+/-	PIM	PP	SH	GW
Mike Backman	NY Rangers	8	0	1	1	1-	8	0	0	0
Mark Morrison	NY Rangers	1	0	0	0	0	0	0	0	0
John Vanbiesbrouck	NY Rangers	3	0	0	0	0	2	0	0	0
Ron Scott	NY Rangers	9	0	0	0	0	0	0	0	0
Steve Weeks	NY Rangers	26	0	0	0	0	4	0	0	0
Tim Kerr	Philadelphia	79	54	39	93	30	29	9	0	5
Brian Propp	Philadelphia	79	39	53	92	49	37	11	1	4
Dave Poulin	Philadelphia	73	31	45	76	31	47	6	3	6
Darryl Sittler	Philadelphia	76	27	36	63	13	38	11	1	3
Bobby Clarke	Philadelphia	73	17	43	60	23	70	3	1	1
Bill Barber	Philadelphia	63	22	32	54	4	36	3	0	1
Mark Howe	Philadelphia	71	19	34	53	30	44	3	3	2
Ron Sutter	Philadelphia	79	19	32	51	4	101	5	3	3
Ilkka Sinisalo	Philadelphia	73	29	17	46	22	29	2	3	4
Thomas Eriksson	Philadelphia	68	11	33	44	28	37	2	0	1
Doug Crossman	Philadelphia	78	7	28	35	23	63	2	0	2
Len Hachborn	Philadelphia	38	11	21	32	8	4	1	0	2
Miroslav Dvorak	Philadelphia	66	4	27	31	19	27	0	1	0
Rich Sutter	Pittsburgh	5	0	0	0	2-	0	0	0	0
	Philadelphia	70	16	12	28	10	93	2	0	1
	Total	75	16	12	28	8	93	2	0	1
Brad McCrimmon	Philadelphia	71	0	24	24	19	76	0	0	0
Glen Cochrane	Philadelphia	67	7	16	23	16	225	0	0	3
Ray Allison	Philadelphia	37	8	13	21	11	47	0	0	0
Brad Marsh	Philadelphia	77	3	14	17	24	83	0	0	0
Paul Guay	Philadelphia	14	2	6	8	1	14	0	0	0
Ross Fitzpatrick	Philadelphia	12	4	2	6	4	0	0	0	1
Dave Brown	Philadelphia	19	1	5	6	4	98	0	0	0
Darryl Stanley	Philadelphia	23	1	4	5	4	71	0	0	1
Lindsay Carson	Philadelphia	16	1	3	4	7-	10	0	0	1
Bob Froese	Philadelphia	48	0	2	2	0	10	0	0	0
Pelle Lindbergh	Philadelphia	36	0	1	1	0	6	0	0	0
Randy Holt	Philadelphia	26	0	0	0	1-	74	0	0	0
Mike Bullard	Pittsburgh	76	51	41	92	33-	57	15	0	0
Doug Shedden	Pittsburgh	67	22	35	57	38-	20	6	1	1
Mark Taylor	Philadelphia	1	0	0	0	0	0	0	0	0
	Pittsburgh	59	24	31	55	20-	24	9	1	1
	Total	60	24	31	55	20-	24	9	1	1
Ron Flockhart	Philadelphia	8	0	3	3	1	4	0	0	0
	Pittsburgh	68	27	18	45	19-	40	5	0	1
	Total	76	27	21	48	18-	44	5	0	1
Rick Kehoe	Pittsburgh	57	18	27	45	20-	8	7	0	3
Tom Roulston	Edmonton	24	5	7	12	0	16	1	0	0
	Pittsburgh	53	11	17	28	31-	8	3	0	0
	Total	77	16	24	40	31-	24	4	0	0
Pat Boutette	Pittsburgh	73	14	26	40	58-	142	10	0	1
Andy Brickley	Pittsburgh	50	18	20	38	7-	9	7	1	2
Kevin McCarthy	Vancouver	47	2	14	16	8-	61	0	0	0
	Pittsburgh	31	4	16	20	32-	52	1	0	0
	Total	78	6	30	36	40-	113	1	0	0
Greg Hotham	Pittsburgh	76	5	25	30	25-	59	3	0	0

PLAYER	TEAM	GP	G	A	PTS	+/-	PIM	PP	SH	GW
Bob Errey	Pittsburgh	65	9	13	22	20−	29	1	0	0
Norm Schmidt	Pittsburgh	34	6	12	18	1−	12	0	0	0
Bryan Maxwell	Winnipeg	3	0	3	3	1	27	0	0	0
	Pittsburgh	45	3	12	15	2	84	0	0	0
	Total	48	3	15	18	3	111	0	0	0
Gary Rissling	Pittsburgh	47	4	13	17	9−	297	1	0	1
Tom O'Regan	Pittsburgh	51	4	10	14	22−	8	0	0	0
Greg Fox	Chicago	24	0	5	5	0	31	0	0	0
	Pittsburgh	49	2	5	7	42−	66	0	0	0
	Total	73	2	10	12	42−	97	0	0	0
Tim Hrynewich	Pittsburgh	25	4	5	9	10−	34	0	0	2
Marty McSorley	Pittsburgh	72	2	7	9	39−	224	0	0	0
Tom Thornbury	Pittsburgh	14	1	8	9	19−	16	0	0	0
Warren Young	Pittsburgh	15	1	7	8	2−	19	0	0	0
Steve Gatzos	Pittsburgh	23	3	3	6	9−	15	0	0	1
Rod Buskas	Pittsburgh	47	2	4	6	18−	60	1	0	0
Bob Gladney	Pittsburgh	13	1	5	6	1−	2	0	0	0
Ted Bulley	Pittsburgh	26	3	2	5	14−	12	0	0	1
Dave Hannan	Pittsburgh	24	2	3	5	2−	33	0	1	1
Paul Gardner	Pittsburgh	16	0	5	5	4−	6	0	0	0
Jim Hamilton	Pittsburgh	11	2	2	4	2	4	1	0	0
Rod Schutt	Pittsburgh	11	1	3	4	0	4	0	0	0
Rocky Saganiuk	Pittsburgh	29	1	3	4	12−	37	0	0	0
Darren Lowe	Pittsburgh	8	1	2	3	5−	0	0	0	0
Mitch Lamoureux	Pittsburgh	8	1	1	2	6−	6	0	0	0
Tim Tookey	Pittsburgh	8	0	2	2	2−	2	0	0	0
Dean Defazio	Pittsburgh	22	0	2	2	11−	28	0	0	0
Greg Tebbutt	Pittsburgh	24	0	2	2	26−	31	0	0	0
Phil Bourque	Pittsburgh	5	0	1	1	2−	12	0	0	0
Michel Dion	Pittsburgh	30	0	1	1	0	2	0	0	0
Grant Sasser	Pittsburgh	3	0	0	0	2−	0	0	0	0
Vincent Tremblay	Pittsburgh	4	0	0	0	0	2	0	0	0
Todd Charlesworth	Pittsburgh	10	0	0	0	7−	8	0	0	0
Troy Loney	Pittsburgh	13	0	0	0	7−	9	0	0	0
Roberto Romano	Pittsburgh	18	0	0	0	0	0	0	0	0
Denis Herron	Pittsburgh	38	0	0	0	0	21	0	0	0
Michel Goulet	Quebec	75	56	65	121	62	76	11	2	16
Peter Stastny	Quebec	80	46	73	119	22	73	11	0	4
Dale Hunter	Quebec	77	24	55	79	35	232	7	2	1
Wilf Paiement	Quebec	80	39	37	76	28	121	8	3	3
Anton Stastny	Quebec	69	25	37	62	12	14	7	0	0
Marian Stastny	Quebec	68	20	32	52	1	26	4	0	5
Tony McKegney	Quebec	75	24	27	51	4	23	4	0	2
Mario Marois	Quebec	80	13	36	49	51	151	4	0	0
Andre Savard	Quebec	60	20	24	44	17	38	0	2	2
Alain Cote	Quebec	77	19	24	43	21	41	0	1	1
Bo Berglund	Quebec	75	16	27	43	6	20	1	0	1
Louis Sleigher	Quebec	44	15	19	34	23	32	3	1	1
Andre Dore	St. Louis	55	3	12	15	3	58	0	0	1
	Quebec	25	1	16	17	1	25	0	0	0
	Total	80	4	28	32	4	83	0	0	1
Pat Price	Quebec	72	3	25	28	20	188	0	0	2
J. F. Sauve	Quebec	39	10	17	27	4	2	5	0	0

PLAYER	TEAM	GP	G	A	PTS	+/−	PIM	PP	SH	GW
Normand Rochefort....	Quebec	75	2	22	24	41	47	0	0	1
Randy Moller........	Quebec	74	4	14	18	26	147	0	0	1
Paul Gillis	Quebec	57	8	9	17	10	59	0	0	1
Rick Lapointe........	Quebec	22	2	10	12	9	12	0	0	0
Blake Wesley	Quebec	46	2	8	10	14	75	0	0	0
John Van Boxmeer	Quebec	18	5	3	8	1−	12	4	0	0
Wally Weir	Quebec	25	2	3	5	5	17	0	0	1
Gord Donnelly	Quebec	38	0	5	5	1−	60	0	0	0
Jimmy Mann	Winnipeg	16	0	1	1	0	54	0	0	0
	Quebec	22	1	1	2	3−	42	0	0	0
	Total	38	1	2	3	3−	96	0	0	0
Dan Bouchard	Quebec	57	0	3	3	0	19	0	0	0
Clint Malarchuk	Quebec	23	0	1	1	0	9	0	0	0
Jim Dobson.........	Quebec	1	0	0	0	1−	0	0	0	0
Jean Marc Gaulin	Quebec	2	0	0	0	1−	0	0	0	0
Brian Ford.........	Quebec	3	0	0	0	0	0	0	0	0
Mario Gosselin.......	Quebec	3	0	0	0	0	2	0	0	0
David Shaw.........	Quebec	3	0	0	0	2	0	0	0	0
Bernie Federko	St. Louis	79	41	66	107	3−	43	14	0	4
Joe Mullen	St. Louis	80	41	44	85	8−	19	13	0	6
Brian Sutter.........	St. Louis	76	32	51	83	6−	162	14	2	3
Jorgen Pettersson.....	St. Louis	77	28	34	62	2−	29	7	0	7
Rob Ramage	St. Louis	80	15	45	60	11−	121	9	0	3
Doug Gilmour	St. Louis	80	25	28	53	6	57	3	1	1
Guy Chouinard	St. Louis	64	12	34	46	15−	10	4	0	2
Wayne Babych	St. Louis	70	13	29	42	1	52	3	0	0
Doug Wickenheiser	Montreal	27	5	5	10	1	6	0	0	1
	St. Louis	46	7	21	28	10	19	2	0	1
	Total	73	12	26	38	11	25	2	0	2
Mark Reeds.........	St. Louis	65	11	14	25	3−	23	3	1	0
Pat Hickey..........	St. Louis	67	9	11	20	3−	24	0	0	1
Dave Pichette........	Quebec	23	2	7	9	2	12	0	0	0
	St. Louis	23	0	11	11	5−	6	0	0	0
	Total	46	2	18	20	3−	18	0	0	0
Greg Paslawski.......	Montreal	26	1	4	5	5−	4	0	0	0
	St. Louis	34	8	6	14	4	17	1	0	0
	Total	60	9	10	19	1−	21	1	0	0
Rik Wilson	St. Louis	48	7	11	18	4	53	2	0	1
Tim Bothwell	St. Louis	62	2	13	15	22	65	1	0	0
Jack Carlson	St. Louis	58	6	8	14	9	95	0	0	0
Dwight Schofield	St. Louis	70	4	10	14	3−	219	0	0	1
Gilbert Delorme	Montreal	27	2	7	9	4−	8	0	0	0
	St. Louis	44	0	5	5	7−	41	0	0	0
	Total	71	2	12	14	11−	49	0	0	0
Perry Anderson	St. Louis	50	7	5	12	13−	195	0	0	1
Alain Lemieux	St. Louis	17	4	5	9	0	6	1	0	0
Terry Johnson	St. Louis	65	2	6	8	5	141	0	0	0
Mike Liut	St. Louis	58	0	4	4	0	0	0	0	0
Jim Pavese	St. Louis	4	0	1	1	1−	19	0	0	0
Perry Ganchar	St. Louis	1	0	0	0	1	0	0	0	0
John Markell	St. Louis	2	0	0	0	4−	0	0	0	0
Ralph Klassen	St. Louis	5	0	0	0	5−	0	0	0	0
Michel Larocque......	St. Louis	5	0	0	0	0	2	0	0	0

PLAYER	TEAM	GP	G	A	PTS	+/−	PIM	PP	SH	GW
Dave Barr	NY Rangers	6	0	0	0	0	2	0	0	0
	St. Louis	1	0	0	0	1−	0	0	0	0
	Total	7	0	0	0	1−	2	0	0	0
Rick Heinz	St. Louis	22	0	0	0	0	4	0	0	0
Rick Vaive	Toronto	76	52	41	93	14−	114	17	0	6
Dan Daoust	Toronto	78	18	56	74	16−	88	8	0	1
John Anderson	Toronto	73	37	31	68	12−	22	14	0	5
Bill Derlago	Toronto	79	40	20	60	7−	50	8	2	3
Jim Benning	Toronto	79	12	39	51	4−	66	6	0	1
Dale McCourt	Buffalo	5	1	3	4	2−	0	0	0	0
	Toronto	72	19	24	43	16−	10	8	2	1
	Total	77	20	27	47	18−	10	8	2	1
Borje Salming	Toronto	68	5	38	43	34−	92	2	1	0
Greg Terrion	Toronto	79	15	24	39	6−	36	0	2	2
Stewart Gavin	Toronto	80	10	22	32	6−	90	0	1	3
Gaston Gingras	Toronto	59	7	20	27	30−	16	4	0	0
Jim Korn	Toronto	65	12	14	26	33−	257	0	0	1
Miroslav Frycer	Toronto	47	10	16	26	23−	55	1	0	2
Terry Martin	Toronto	63	15	10	25	8−	51	1	2	1
Walt Poddubny	Toronto	38	11	14	25	12−	48	4	0	0
Peter Ihnacak	Toronto	47	10	13	23	21−	24	5	0	0
Dave Farrish	Toronto	59	4	19	23	13−	57	1	0	0
Bill Stewart	Toronto	56	2	17	19	1−	116	0	0	0
Gary Nylund	Toronto	47	2	14	16	27−	103	0	0	0
Gary Leeman	Toronto	52	4	8	12	14−	31	1	0	0
Russ Courtnall	Toronto	14	3	9	12	0	6	1	0	0
Pat Graham	Toronto	41	4	4	8	8−	65	0	0	0
Frank Nigro	Toronto	17	2	3	5	4−	16	0	0	0
Rich Costello	Toronto	10	2	1	3	5−	2	1	0	0
Dave Hutchison	Toronto	47	0	3	3	5	137	0	0	0
Ken Strong	Toronto	2	0	2	2	0	2	0	0	0
Bob McGill	Toronto	11	0	2	2	1	51	0	0	0
Mike Palmateer	Toronto	34	0	2	2	0	28	0	0	0
Fred Perlini	Toronto	1	0	0	0	0	0	0	0	0
Gary Yaremchuk	Toronto	1	0	0	0	1−	0	0	0	0
Bruce Dowie	Toronto	2	0	0	0	0	0	0	0	0
Basil McRae	Toronto	3	0	0	0	3−	19	0	0	0
Ken Wregget	Toronto	3	0	0	0	0	0	0	0	0
Greg Britz	Toronto	6	0	0	0	1−	2	0	0	0
Rick St. Croix	Toronto	20	0	0	0	0	0	0	0	0
Allan Bester	Toronto	32	0	0	0	0	6	0	0	0
Patrik Sundstrom	Vancouver	78	38	53	91	11−	37	7	0	7
Tony Tanti	Vancouver	79	45	41	86	12−	50	19	1	6
Thomas Gradin	Vancouver	75	21	57	78	2−	32	11	1	5
Stan Smyl	Vancouver	80	24	43	67	21−	136	8	0	4
Rick Lanz	Vancouver	79	18	39	57	3−	45	14	0	3
Darcy Rota	Vancouver	59	28	20	48	12−	73	6	0	0
Gary Lupul	Vancouver	69	17	27	44	16−	51	6	0	2
Jiri Bubla	Vancouver	62	6	33	39	10−	43	2	0	1
Peter McNab	Boston	52	14	16	30	7	10	2	0	3
	Vancouver	13	1	6	7	2−	10	1	0	0
	Total	65	15	22	37	5	20	3	0	3

PLAYER	TEAM	GP	G	A	PTS	+/-	PIM	PP	SH	GW
Cam Neely	Vancouver	56	16	15	31	0	57	3	0	1
Dave Williams	Vancouver	67	15	16	31	11−	294	2	0	1
Moe Lemay	Vancouver	56	12	18	30	4	38	1	0	1
Doug Halward	Vancouver	54	7	16	23	1	35	2	0	1
Jere Gillis	Vancouver	37	9	13	22	2	7	0	1	0
Neil Belland	Vancouver	44	7	13	20	8−	24	2	0	0
Harold Snepsts	Vancouver	79	4	16	20	19−	152	0	0	0
Michel Petit	Vancouver	44	6	9	15	6−	53	5	0	0
Lars Molin	Vancouver	42	6	7	13	9−	4	0	1	0
Andy Schliebener	Vancouver	51	2	10	12	9−	48	0	0	0
Mark Kirton	Vancouver	26	2	3	5	8−	2	0	0	0
Ron Delorme	Vancouver	64	2	2	4	2−	68	0	0	0
Jean-Marc Lanthier	Vancouver	11	2	1	3	2−	2	0	0	0
Garth Butcher	Vancouver	28	2	0	2	12−	34	0	0	0
Grant Martin	Vancouver	12	0	2	2	2−	6	0	0	0
Richard Brodeur	Vancouver	36	0	2	2	0	0	0	0	0
Taylor Hall	Vancouver	4	1	0	1	2−	0	0	0	0
Marc Crawford	Vancouver	19	0	1	1	0	9	0	0	0
Doug Lidster	Vancouver	8	0	0	0	7−	4	0	0	0
Gerry Minor	Vancouver	9	0	0	0	0	0	0	0	0
Frank Caprice	Vancouver	19	0	0	0	0	2	0	0	0
John Garrett	Vancouver	29	0	0	0	0	9	0	0	0
Mike Gartner	Washington	80	40	45	85	22	90	8	0	7
Dave Christian	Washington	80	29	52	81	26	28	9	0	6
Bengt Gustafsson	Washington	69	32	43	75	29	16	8	0	5
Bob Carpenter	Washington	80	28	40	68	0	51	8	0	5
Alan Haworth	Washington	75	24	31	55	14	52	7	0	5
Craig Laughlin	Washington	80	20	32	52	4	69	7	0	3
Larry Murphy	Los Angeles	6	0	3	3	4−	0	0	0	0
	Washington	72	13	33	46	12	50	2	0	2
	Total	78	13	36	49	8	50	2	0	2
Scott Stevens	Washington	78	13	32	45	26	201	7	0	2
Doug Jarvis	Washington	80	13	29	42	7	12	0	2	0
Bobby Gould	Washington	78	21	19	40	2−	74	4	0	4
Gaetan Duchesne	Washington	79	17	19	36	15	29	3	2	1
Glen Currie	Washington	80	12	24	36	9	20	0	2	2
Rod Langway	Washington	80	9	24	33	14	61	1	2	2
Bryan Erickson	Washington	45	12	17	29	10	16	4	0	2
Darren Veitch	Washington	46	6	18	24	0	17	4	0	0
Timo Blomqvist	Washington	65	1	19	20	17	84	0	0	0
Dave Shand	Washington	72	4	15	19	23	124	0	0	0
Chris Valentine	Washington	22	6	5	11	8−	21	2	0	1
Peter Andersson	Washington	42	3	7	10	12	20	2	0	0
Greg Adams	Washington	57	2	6	8	1	133	0	0	0
Greg Theberge	Washington	13	1	2	3	4−	4	1	0	0
Gary Sampson	Washington	15	1	1	2	1	6	0	0	0
Paul MacKinnon	Washington	12	0	1	1	7−	4	0	0	0
Andre Hidi	Washington	1	0	0	0	0	0	0	0	0
Dave Parro	Washington	1	0	0	0	0	0	0	0	0
Dean Evason	Washington	2	0	0	0	0	2	0	0	0
Lou Franceschetti	Washington	2	0	0	0	2−	0	0	0	0
Bob Mason	Washington	2	0	0	0	0	0	0	0	0
Pat Riggin	Washington	41	0	0	0	0	4	0	0	0
Al Jensen	Washington	43	0	0	0	0	22	0	0	0

PLAYER	TEAM	GP	G	A	PTS	+/−	PIM	PP	SH	GW
Dale Hawerchuk	Winnipeg	80	37	65	102	14−	73	10	0	4
Lucien Deblois	Winnipeg	80	34	45	79	14−	50	8	1	2
Laurie Boschman	Winnipeg	61	28	46	74	4−	234	9	0	3
Paul MacLean	Winnipeg	76	40	31	71	15−	155	13	0	5
Thomas Steen	Winnipeg	78	20	45	65	5−	69	5	3	2
Brian Mullen	Winnipeg	75	21	41	62	11−	28	4	4	1
Dave Babych	Winnipeg	66	18	39	57	31−	62	10	0	4
Scott Arniel	Winnipeg	80	21	35	56	10−	68	6	0	2
Morris Lukowich	Winnipeg	80	30	25	55	10	71	4	0	1
Moe Mantha	Winnipeg	72	16	38	54	14−	67	3	0	1
Doug Smail	Winnipeg	66	20	17	37	5−	62	1	4	2
Tim Young	Winnipeg	44	15	19	34	11−	25	3	0	0
Andrew McBain	Winnipeg	78	11	19	30	6−	37	0	0	0
Randy Carlyle	Pittsburgh	50	3	23	26	25−	82	0	0	1
	Winnipeg	5	0	3	3	2	2	0	0	0
	Total	55	3	26	29	23−	84	0	0	1
Robert Picard	Montreal	7	0	2	2	1−	0	0	0	0
	Winnipeg	62	6	16	22	9	34	1	1	1
	Total	69	6	18	24	8	34	1	1	1
Tim Watters	Winnipeg	74	3	20	23	7	169	1	0	1
Wade Campbell	Winnipeg	79	7	14	21	2−	147	0	0	0
Bengt Lundholm	Winnipeg	57	5	14	19	7−	20	1	0	0
Ron Wilson	Winnipeg	51	3	12	15	3−	12	0	0	1
Jordy Douglas	Minnesota	14	3	4	7	2−	10	0	0	1
	Winnipeg	17	4	2	6	9−	8	1	0	1
	Total	31	7	6	13	11−	18	1	0	2
Don Spring	Winnipeg	21	0	4	4	5−	4	0	0	0
Jim Kyte	Winnipeg	58	1	2	3	7−	55	0	0	0
Doug Soetaert	Winnipeg	47	0	3	3	0	14	0	0	0
Jyrki Seppa	Winnipeg	13	0	2	2	9−	6	0	0	0
Mike Lauen	Winnipeg	3	0	1	1	0	0	0	0	0
Brian Hayward	Winnipeg	28	0	1	1	0	2	0	0	0
Bobby Dollas	Winnipeg	1	0	0	0	2−	0	0	0	0
Murray Eaves	Winnipeg	2	0	0	0	0	0	0	0	0
Tim Trimper	Winnipeg	5	0	0	0	1	0	0	0	0
Marc Behrend	Winnipeg	6	0	0	0	0	0	0	0	0
John Gibson	Winnipeg	11	0	0	0	2	14	0	0	0
Mike Veisor	Hartford	4	0	0	0	0	0	0	0	0
	Winnipeg	8	0	0	0	0	0	0	0	0
	Total	12	0	0	0	0	0	0	0	0

GOALTENDERS' RECORDS

ALL GOALS AGAINST A TEAM IN ANY GAME ARE CHARGED TO THE INDIVIDUAL GOALTENDER OF THAT GAME FOR PURPOSES OF AWARDING THE BILL JENNINGS TROPHY.

WON-LOST-TIED RECORD IS BASED ON WHICH GOALTENDER WAS PLAYING WHEN WINNING OR TYING GOAL WAS SCORED.

CODE: GPI—GAMES PLAYED IN. MINS—MINUTES PLAYED. AVG—60-MINUTE AVERAGE. EN—EMPTY-NET GOALS (NOT COUNTED IN PERSONAL AVERAGES BUT INCLUDED IN TEAM TOTALS). SO—SHUTOUTS. GA—GOALS-AGAINST. SA—SHOTS AGAINST.

GOALTENDERS	TEAM	GPI	MINS	AVG	W	L	T	EN	SO	GA	SA
Parro	Washington	1	1	.00	0	0	0	0	0	0	0
Mason	Washington	2	120	1.50	2	0	0	0	0	3	46
Riggin	Washington	41	2299	2.66	21	14	2	1	4	102	924
Jensen	Washington	43	2414	2.91	25	13	3	3	4	117	995
WASHINGTON	**TOTALS**	**80**	**4834**	**2.81**	**48**	**27**	**5**		**8**	**226**	**1965**
Barrasso	Buffalo	42	2475	2.84	26	12	3	2	2	117	1098
Sauve	Buffalo	40	2375	3.49	22	13	4	0	0	138	1050
BUFFALO	**TOTALS**	**80**	**4850**	**3.18**	**48**	**25**	**7**		**2**	**257**	**2148**
Keans	Boston	33	1779	3.10	19	8	3	2	2	92	791
Peeters	Boston	50	2868	3.16	29	16	2	1	0	151	1222
Moffat	Boston	4	186	4.84	1	1	1	0	0	15	81
BOSTON	**TOTALS**	**80**	**4833**	**3.24**	**49**	**25**	**6**		**2**	**261**	**2094**
Hrudey	NY Islanders	12	535	3.14	7	2	0	0	0	28	289
Melanson	NY Islanders	37	2019	3.27	20	11	2	1	0	110	1129
Smith	NY Islanders	42	2279	3.42	23	13	2	0	2	130	1252
ISLANDERS	**TOTALS**	**80**	**4833**	**3.34**	**50**	**26**	**4**		**2**	**269**	**2670**
Gosselin	Quebec	3	148	1.22	2	0	0	0	1	3	67
Bouchard	Quebec	57	3373	3.20	29	18	8	2	1	180	1523
Malarchuk	Quebec	23	1215	3.95	10	9	2	0	0	80	591
Ford	Quebec	3	123	6.34	1	1	0	0	0	13	70
QUEBEC	**TOTALS**	**80**	**4859**	**3.43**	**42**	**28**	**10**		**2**	**278**	**2251**
Froese	Philadelphia	48	2863	3.14	28	13	7	2	2	150	1326
Lindbergh	Philadelphia	36	1999	4.05	16	13	3	3	1	135	966
PHILADELPHIA	**TOTALS**	**80**	**4862**	**3.58**	**44**	**26**	**10**		**3**	**290**	**2292**
Sevigny	Montreal	40	2203	3.38	16	18	2	3	1	124	946
Wamsley	Montreal	42	2333	3.70	19	17	3	1	2	144	977
Holden	Montreal	1	52	4.62	0	1	0	0	0	4	17
Penney	Montreal	4	240	4.75	0	4	0	0	0	19	115
MONTREAL	**TOTALS**	**80**	**4828**	**3.67**	**35**	**40**	**5**		**3**	**295**	**2055**
Vanbiesbrouck	NY Rangers	3	180	3.33	2	1	0	1	0	10	85
Hanlon	NY Rangers	50	2837	3.51	28	14	4	5	1	166	1508
Scott	NY Rangers	9	485	3.59	2	3	3	1	0	29	254
Weeks	NY Rangers	26	1361	3.97	10	11	2	2	0	90	667
RANGERS	**TOTALS**	**80**	**4863**	**3.75**	**42**	**29**	**9**		**1**	**304**	**2514**

Montreal's Steve Penney emerged in Stanley Cup play.

GOALTENDERS	TEAM	GPI	MINS	AVG	W	L	T	EN	SO	GA	SA
Bannerman	Chicago	56	3335	3.38	23	29	4	4	2	188	1667
Janecyk.......	Chicago	8	412	4.08	2	3	1	0	0	28	237
Esposito	Chicago	18	1095	4.82	5	10	3	3	1	88	622
CHICAGO......	**TOTALS**	80	4842	3.85	30	42	8		3	311	2526
Lemelin.......	Calgary	51	2568	3.50	21	12	9	0	0	150	1405
Edwards	Calgary	41	2303	4.09	13	19	5	3	0	157	1217
Vernon	Calgary	1	11	21.82	0	1	0	0	0	4	6
CALGARY	**TOTALS**	80	4882	3.86	34	32	14		0	314	2628
Moog	Edmonton	38	2212	3.77	27	8	1	2	1	139	1179
Fuhr.........	Edmonton	45	2625	3.91	30	10	4	2	1	171	1463
EDMONTON	**TOTALS**	80	4837	3.89	57	18	5		2	314	2642
Liut	St Louis	58	3425	3.45	25	29	4	6	3	197	1697
Heinz	St Louis	22	1118	4.29	7	7	3	1	0	80	539
Larocque......	St Louis	5	300	6.20	0	5	0	1	0	31	164
ST. LOUIS.....	**TOTALS**	80	4843	3.91	32	41	7		3	316	2400
Millen........	Hartford	60	3583	3.70	21	30	9	5	2	221	1817
Staniowski.....	Hartford	18	1041	4.27	6	9	1	0	0	74	556
Veisor........	Hartford	4	240	5.00	1	3	0	0	0	20	114
HARTFORD	**TOTALS**	80	4864	3.95	28	42	10		2	320	2487
Stefan........	Detroit	50	2600	3.51	19	22	2	5	2	152	1223
Micalef	Detroit	14	808	3.86	5	8	1	4	0	52	361
Holland.......	Detroit	3	146	4.11	0	1	1	2	0	10	53
Mio	Detroit	24	1295	4.40	7	11	3	3	1	95	677
DETROIT......	**TOTALS**	80	4849	4.00	31	42	7		3	323	2314
Caprice	Vancouver	19	1099	3.38	8	8	2	2	1	62	525
Brodeur.......	Vancouver	36	2107	4.02	10	21	5	7	1	141	1067
Garrett	Vancouver	29	1652	4.10	14	10	2	3	0	113	758
VANCOUVER ...	**TOTALS**	80	4858	4.05	32	39	9		2	328	2350
Beaupre	Minnesota	33	1791	4.12	16	13	2	2	0	123	971
Meloche	Minnesota	52	2883	4.18	21	17	8	3	2	201	1524
Casey	Minnesota	2	84	4.29	1	0	0	0	0	6	59
Craig	Minnesota	3	110	4.91	1	1	0	0	0	9	56
MINNESOTA....	**TOTALS**	80	4868	4.24	39	31	10		2	344	2610
Resch........	New Jersey	51	2641	4.18	9	31	3	4	1	184	1426
Low	New Jersey	44	2218	4.36	8	25	4	1	0	161	1133
NEW JERSEY ...	**TOTALS**	80	4859	4.32	17	56	7		2	350	2559

(Low and Resch shared shutout against Detroit, Dec. 4, 1983)

Veisor........	Winnipeg	8	420	3.71	4	1	2	0	0	26	172
Soetaert	Winnipeg	47	2536	4.31	18	15	7	1	0	182	1385
Hayward	Winnipeg	28	1530	4.86	7	18	2	1	0	124	860
Behrend	Winnipeg	6	351	5.47	2	4	0	0	0	32	184
Staniowski	Winnipeg	1	40	12.00	0	0	0	0	0	8	20
WINNIPEG.....	**TOTALS**	80	4877	4.60	31	38	11		0	374	2621

GOALTENDERS	TEAM	GPI	MINS	AVG	W	L	T	EN	SO	GA	SA
Baron	Los Angeles	21	1211	4.31	3	14	4	5	0	87	633
Mattsson	Los Angeles	19	1101	4.31	7	8	2	1	1	79	530
Blake	Los Angeles	29	1634	4.33	9	11	5	1	0	118	891
Laskoski	Los Angeles	13	665	4.96	4	7	1	2	0	55	321
Lessard	Los Angeles	6	266	5.86	0	4	1	2	0	26	160
LOS ANGELES	**TOTALS**	80	4877	4.63	23	44	13		1	376	2535
Dowie	Toronto	2	72	3.33	0	1	0	0	0	4	43
Bester	Toronto	32	1848	4.35	11	16	4	1	0	134	1144
Palmateer	Toronto	34	1831	4.88	9	17	4	3	0	149	986
Wregget	Toronto	3	165	5.09	1	1	1	0	0	14	128
St. Croix	Toronto	20	939	5.11	5	10	0	2	0	80	531
TORONTO	**TOTALS**	80	4855	4.78	26	45	9		0	387	2832
Herron	Pittsburgh	38	2028	4.08	8	24	2	7	1	138	1200
Romano	Pittsburgh	18	1020	4.59	6	11	0	0	1	78	629
Dion	Pittsburgh	30	1553	5.33	2	19	4	4	0	138	937
Tremblay	Pittsburgh	4	240	6.00	0	4	0	1	0	24	142
PITTSBURGH	**TOTALS**	80	4841	4.83	16	58	6		2	390	2908

All-Time NHL Records

Tony Esposito set modern mark for shutouts (15) in 1969-70.

Game

MOST GOALS: 7, Joe Malone, Quebec Bulldogs, Jan. 31, 1920 vs. Toronto St. Pats; (Modern) 6, Syd Howe, Detroit Red Wings, Feb. 3, 1944 vs. New York Rangers; 6, Red Berenson, St. Louis Blues, Nov. 7, 1968 vs. Philadelphia Flyers; 6, Darryl Sittler, Toronto Maple Leafs, Feb. 7, 1976 vs. Boston Bruins

MOST ASSISTS: 7, Bill Taylor, Detroit Red Wings, Mar. 16, 1947 vs. Chicago Black Hawks; Wayne Gretzky, Edmonton, Feb. 15, 1980 vs. Washington Capitals

MOST POINTS: 10, Darryl Sittler, Toronto Maple Leafs, Feb. 7, 1976 vs. Boston Bruins (six goals, four assists)

MOST PENALTY MINUTES: 67, Randy Holt, Los Angeles Kings, Mar. 11, 1979 vs. Philadelphia Flyers

Season

MOST GOALS: 92, Wayne Gretzky, Edmonton Oilers, 1981-82

MOST ASSISTS: 125, Wayne Gretzky, Edmonton Oilers, 1982-83

MOST POINTS: 212, Wayne Gretzky, Edmonton Oilers, 1981-82

MOST SHUTOUTS: 22, George Hainsworth, Montreal Canadiens, 1928-29; (Modern) 15, Tony Esposito, Chicago Black Hawks, 1969-70

MOST PENALTY MINUTES: 472, Dave Schultz, Philadelphia Flyers, 1974-75

MOST POINTS BY A ROOKIE: 109, Peter Stastny, Quebec, 1980-81

MOST ASSISTS BY A GOALIE: 8, Mike Palmateer, Washington Capitals, 1980-81

Career

MOST SEASONS: 26, Gordie Howe, Detroit Red Wings, Hartford Whalers, 1946-47 to 1970-71, 1979-80

MOST GAMES: 1,767, Gordie Howe, Detroit Red Wings, Hartford Whalers

MOST GOALS: 801, Gordie Howe, Detroit Red Wings, Hartford Whalers

MOST POINTS: 1,850, Gordie Howe, Detroit Red Wings, Hartford Whalers

MOST PENALTY MINUTES: 2,994, Dave Williams, Toronto, Vancouver, 1974-84

MOST SHUTOUTS: 103, Terry Sawchuk, Detroit, Boston, Toronto, Los Angeles, New York Rangers

MOST CONSECUTIVE GAMES: 914, Garry Unger, Toronto, Detroit, St. Louis, Atlanta, Feb. 24, 1968 through Dec. 21, 1979

NHL Trophy Winners

HART MEMORIAL TROPHY

Awarded to the league's Most Valuable Player. Selected in a vote of hockey writers and broadcasters in each of the 21 NHL cities. The award was presented by the National Hockey League in 1960 after the original Hart Trophy was retired to the Hockey Hall of Fame. The original Hart Trophy was donated in 1923 by Dr. David A. Hart, father of Cecil Hart, former manager-coach of the Montreal Canadiens.

1923-24 Frank Nighbor, Ottawa
1924-25 Billy Burch, Hamilton
1925-26 Nels Stewart, Montreal M.
1926-27 Herb Gardiner, Montreal C.
1927-28 Howie Morenz, Montreal C.
1928-29 Roy Worters, New York A.
1929-30 Nels Stewart, Montreal M.
1930-31 Howie Morenz, Montreal C.
1931-32 Howie Morenz, Montreal C.
1932-33 Eddie Shore, Boston
1933-34 Aurel Joliat, Montreal C.
1934-35 Eddie Shore, Boston
1935-36 Eddie Shore, Boston
1936-37 Babe Siebert, Montreal C.
1937-38 Eddie Shore, Boston
1938-39 Toe Blake, Montreal C.
1939-40 Eddie Goodfellow, Detroit
1940-41 Bill Cowley, Boston
1941-42 Tommy Anderson, New York A.
1942-43 Bill Cowley, Boston
1943-44 Babe Pratt, Toronto
1944-45 Elmer Lach, Montreal C.
1945-46 Max Bentley, Chicago
1946-47 Maurice Richard, Montreal
1947-48 Buddy O'Conner, New York R.
1948-49 Sid Abel, Detroit
1949-50 Charlie Rayner, New York R.
1950-51 Milt Schmidt, Boston
1951-52 Gordie Howe, Detroit
1952-53 Gordie Howe, Detroit
1953-54 Al Rollins, Chicago

1954-55 Ted Kennedy, Toronto
1955-56 Jean Beliveau, Montreal
1956-57 Gordie Howe, Detroit
1957-58 Gordie Howe, Detroit
1958-59 Andy Bathgate, New York R.
1959-60 Gordie Howe, Detroit
1960-61 Bernie Geoffrion, Montreal
1961-62 Jacques Plante, Montreal
1962-63 Gordie Howe, Detroit
1963-64 Jean Beliveau, Montreal
1964-65 Bobby Hull, Chicago
1965-66 Bobby Hull, Chicago
1966-67 Stan Mikita, Chicago
1967-68 Stan Mikita, Chicago
1968-69 Phil Esposito, Boston
1969-70 Bobby Orr, Boston
1970-71 Bobby Orr, Boston
1971-72 Bobby Orr, Boston
1972-73 Bobby Clarke, Philadelphia
1973-74 Phil Esposito, Boston
1974-75 Bobby Clarke, Philadelphia
1975-76 Bobby Clarke, Philadelphia
1976-77 Guy Lafleur, Montreal
1977-78 Guy Lafleur, Montreal
1978-79 Bryan Trottier, New York I.
1979-80 Wayne Gretzky, Edmonton
1980-81 Wayne Gretzky, Edmonton
1981-82 Wayne Gretzky, Edmonton
1982-83 Wayne Gretzky, Edmonton
1983-84 Wayne Gretzky, Edmonton

VEZINA TROPHY

Awarded to the goalie voted most valuable by the Professional Hockey Writers' Association. Up until the 1981-82 season, the trophy was awarded to the goalie or goalies for the team which gives up the fewest goals during the regular season.

The trophy was presented to the NHL in 1926-27 by the owners of the Montreal Canadiens in memory of Georges Vezina, former Canadien goalie.

1926-27 George Hainsworth, Montreal C.
1927-28 George Hainsworth, Montreal C.
1928-29 George Hainsworth, Montreal C.
1929-30 Tiny Thompson, Boston
1930-31 Roy Worters, New York A.
1931-32 Charlie Gardiner, Chicago
1932-33 Tiny Thompson, Boston
1933-34 Charlie Gardiner, Chicago
1934-35 Lorne Chabot, Chicago
1935-36 Tiny Thompson, Boston
1936-37 Normie Smith, Detroit
1937-38 Tiny Thompson, Boston
1938-39 Frank Brimsek, Boston
1939-40 Davey Kerr, New York R.
1940-41 Turk Broda, Toronto
1941-42 Frank Brimsek, Boston
1942-43 Johnny Mowers, Detroit
1943-44 Bill Durnan, Montreal
1944-45 Bill Durnan, Montreal
1945-46 Bill Durnan, Montreal
1946-47 Bill Durnan, Montreal
1947-48 Turk Broda, Toronto
1948-49 Bill Durnan, Montreal
1949-50 Bill Durnan, Montreal
1950-51 Al Rollins, Toronto
1951-52 Terry Sawchuk, Detroit
1952-53 Terry Sawchuk, Detroit
1953-54 Harry Lumley, Toronto
1954-55 Terry Sawchuk, Detroit
1955-56 Jacques Plante, Montreal
1956-57 Jacques Plante, Montreal
1957-58 Jacques Plante, Montreal
1958-59 Jacques Plante, Montreal
1959-60 Jacques Plante, Montreal
1960-61 Johnny Bower, Toronto
1961-62 Jacques Plante, Montreal

1962-63 Glenn Hall, Chicago
1963-64 Charlie Hodge, Montreal
1964-65 Terry Sawchuk, Toronto
        Johnny Bower, Toronto
1965-66 Lorne Worsley, Montreal
        Charlie Hodge, Montreal
1966-67 Glenn Hall, Chicago
        Denis DeJordy, Chicago
1967-68 Lorne Worsley, Montreal
        Rogatien Vachon, Montreal
1968-69 Glenn Hall, St. Louis
        Jacques Plante, St. Louis
1969-70 Tony Esposito, Chicago
1970-71 Ed Giacomin, New York R.
        Gilles Villemure, New York R.
1971-72 Tony Esposito, Chicago
        Gary Smith, Chicago
1972-73 Ken Dryden, Montreal
1973-74 Bernie Parent, Philadelphia
        Tony Esposito, Chicago
1974-75 Bernie Parent, Philadelphia
1975-76 Ken Dryden, Montreal
1976-77 Ken Dryden, Montreal
        Michel Larocque, Montreal
1977-78 Ken Dryden, Montreal
        Michel Larocque, Montreal
1978-79 Ken Dryden, Montreal
        Michel Larocque, Montreal
1979-80 Bob Sauve, Buffalo
        Don Edwards, Buffalo
1980-81 Richard Sevigny, Montreal
        Denis Herron, Montreal
        Michel Larocque, Montreal
1981-82 Billy Smith, New York I.
1982-83 Pete Peeters, Boston
1983-84 Tom Barrasso, Buffalo

ART ROSS TROPHY

Awarded to the player who compiles the highest number of scoring points during the regular season.

If players are tied for the lead, the trophy is awarded to the one with the most goals. If still tied, it is given to the player with the fewer number of games played. If these do not break the deadlock, the trophy is presented to the player who scored his first goal of the season at the earliest date.

The trophy was presented by Art Ross, the former manager-coach of the Boston Bruins, to the NHL in 1947.

Season	Player and Clubs	Games Played	Goals	Assists	Points
1917-18	Joe Malone, Mtl. Canadiens	20	44	–	44
1918-19	Newsy Lalonde, Mtl. Canadiens	17	23	9	32
1919-20	Joe Malone, Quebec	24	39	9	48
1920-21	Newsy Lalonde, Mtl. Canadiens	24	33	8	41
1921-22	Punch Broadbent, Ottawa	24	32	14	46
1922-23	Babe Dye, Toronto	22	26	11	37
1923-24	Cy Denneny, Ottawa	21	22	1	23
1924-25	Babe Dye, Toronto	29	38	6	44
1925-26	Nels Stewart, Montreal	36	34	8	42
1926-27	Bill Cook, N.Y. Rangers	44	33	4	37
1927-28	Howie Morenz, Mtl. Canadiens	43	33	18	51
1928-29	Ace Bailey, Toronto	44	22	10	32
1929-30	Cooney Weiland, Boston	44	43	30	73
1930-31	Howie Morenz, Mtl. Canadiens	39	28	23	51
1931-32	Harvey Jackson, Toronto	48	28	25	53
1932-33	Bill Cook, N.Y. Rangers	48	28	22	50
1933-34	Charlie Conacher, Toronto	42	32	20	52
1934-35	Charlie Conacher, Toronto	48	36	21	57
1935-36	Dave Schriner, N.Y. Americans	48	19	26	45
1936-37	Dave Schriner, N.Y. Americans	48	21	25	46
1937-38	Gordie Drillon, Toronto	48	26	26	52
1938-39	Toe Blake, Mtl. Canadiens	48	24	23	47
1939-40	Milt Schmidt, Boston	48	22	30	52
1940-41	Bill Cowley, Boston	46	17	45	62
1941-42	Bryan Hextall, N.Y. Rangers	48	24	32	56
1942-43	Doug Bentley, Chicago	50	33	40	73
1943-44	Herbie Cain, Boston	48	36	46	82
1944-45	Elmer Lach, Montreal	50	26	54	80
1945-46	Max Bentley, Chicago	47	31	30	61
1946-47	Max Bentley, Chicago	60	29	43	72
1947-48	Elmer Lach, Montreal	60	30	31	61
1948-49	Roy Conacher, Chicago	60	26	42	68
1949-50	Ted Lindsay, Detroit	69	23	55	78
1950-51	Gordie Howe, Detroit	70	43	43	86
1951-52	Gordie Howe, Detroit	70	47	39	86

Season	Player and Clubs	Games Played	Goals	Assists	Points
1952-53	Gordie Howe, Detroit	70	49	46	95
1953-54	Gordie Howe, Detroit	70	33	48	81
1954-55	Bernie Geoffrion, Montreal	70	38	37	75
1955-56	Jean Beliveau, Montreal	70	47	41	88
1956-57	Gordie Howe, Detroit	70	44	45	89
1957-58	Dickie Moore, Montreal	70	36	48	84
1958-59	Dickie Moore, Montreal	70	41	55	96
1959-60	Bobby Hull, Chicago	70	39	42	81
1960-61	Bernie Geoffrion, Montreal	64	50	45	95
1961-62	Bobby Hull, Chicago	70	50	34	84
1962-63	Gordie Howe, Detroit	70	38	48	86
1963-64	Stan Mikita, Chicago	70	39	50	89
1964-65	Stan Mikita, Chicago	70	28	59	87
1965-66	Bobby Hull, Chicago	65	54	43	97
1966-67	Stan Mikita, Chicago	70	35	62	97
1967-68	Stan Mikita, Chicago	72	40	47	87
1968-69	Phil Esposito, Boston	74	49	77	126
1969-70	Bobby Orr, Boston	76	33	87	120
1970-71	Phil Esposito, Boston	76	76	76	152
1971-72	Phil Esposito, Boston	76	66	67	133
1972-73	Phil Esposito, Boston	78	55	75	130
1973-74	Phil Esposito, Boston	78	68	77	145
1974-75	Bobby Orr, Boston	80	46	89	135
1975-76	Guy Lafleur, Montreal	80	56	69	125
1976-77	Guy Lafleur, Montreal	80	56	80	136
1977-78	Guy Lafleur, Montreal	78	60	72	132
1978-79	Bryan Trottier, New York I.	76	47	87	134
1979-80	Marcel Dionne, Los Angeles	80	53	84	137
1980-81	Wayne Gretzky, Edmonton	80	55	109	164
1981-82	Wayne Gretzky, Edmonton	80	92	120	212
1982-83	Wayne Gretzky, Edmonton	80	71	125	196
1983-84	Wayne Gretzky, Edmonton	74	87	118	205

JACK ADAMS AWARD

Awarded by the National Hockey League Broadcasters' Association to the "NHL coach adjudged to have contributed the most to his team's success." It is presented in memory of the late Jack Adams, longtime coach and general manager of the Detroit Red Wings.

1973-74 Fred Shero, Philadelphia
1974-75 Bob Pulford, Los Angeles
1975-76 Don Cherry, Boston
1976-77 Scotty Bowman, Montreal
1977-78 Bobby Kromm, Detroit
1978-79 Al Arbour, New York I.

1979-80 Pat Quinn, Philadelphia
1980-81 Red Berenson, St. Louis
1981-82 Tom Watt, Winnipeg
1982-83 Orval Tessier, Chicago
1983-84 Bryan Murray, Washington

FRANK J. SELKE TROPHY

Awarded to the forward "who best excels in the defensive aspects of the game."

The trophy was presented to the NHL in 1977 by the Board of Governors in honor of Frank J. Selke, a "Builder" member of the Hall of Fame who spent more than 60 years in the game as coach, manager and front-office executive.

1977-78 Bob Gainey, Montreal
1978-79 Bob Gainey, Montreal
1979-80 Bob Gainey, Montreal
1980-81 Bob Gainey, Montreal

1981-82 Steve Kasper, Boston
1982-83 Bobby Clarke, Philadelphia
1983-84 Doug Jarvis, Washington

WILLIAM M. JENNINGS AWARD

Awarded to the goalie or goalies for the team which gives up the fewest goals during the regular season. To be eligible, a goalie must play at least 25 games.

The trophy was presented to the NHL in 1982 in memory of William M. Jennings, an architect of the league's expansion from six teams to the present 21.

1981-82 Denis Herron, Montreal
       Rick Wamsley, Montreal
1982-83 Billy Smith, New York I.
       Roland Melanson, New York I.

1983-84 Al Jensen, Washington
       Pat Riggin, Washington

BILL MASTERTON TROPHY

Awarded by the Professional Hockey Writers' Association to "the NHL player who exemplifies the qualities of preseverance, sportsmanship and dedication to hockey." Named for the late Minnesota North Star player.

1967-68 Claude Provost, Montreal
1968-69 Ted Hampson, Oakland
1969-70 Pit Martin, Chicago
1970-71 Jean Ratelle, New York R.
1971-72 Bobby Clarke, Philadelphia
1972-73 Lowell MacDonald, Pittsburgh
1973-74 Henri Richard, Montreal
1974-75 Don Luce, Buffalo
1975-76 Rod Gilbert, New York R.

1976-77 Ed Westfall, New York I.
1977-78 Butch Goring, Los Angeles
1978-79 Serge Savard, Montreal
1979-80 Al MacAdam, Minnesota
1980-81 Blake Dunlop, St. Louis
1981-82 Glenn Resch, Colorado
1982-83 Lanny McDonald, Calgary
1983-84 Brad Park, Detroit

JAMES NORRIS MEMORIAL TROPHY

Awarded to the league's best defenseman. Selected by a vote of hockey writers and broadcasters in each of the 21 NHL cities.

It was presented in 1953 by the four children of the late James Norris Sr., in memory of the former owner-president of the Detroit Red Wings.

1953-54 Red Kelly, Detroit
1954-55 Doug Harvey, Montreal
1955-56 Doug Harvey, Montreal
1956-57 Doug Harvey, Montreal
1957-58 Doug Harvey, Montreal
1958-59 Tom Johnson, Montreal
1959-60 Doug Harvey, Montreal
1960-61 Doug Harvey, Montreal
1961-62 Doug Harvey, New York R.
1962-63 Pierre Pilote, Chicago
1963-64 Pierre Pilote, Chicago
1964-65 Pierre Pilote, Chicago
1965-66 Jacques Laperriere, Montreal
1966-67 Harry Howell, New York R.
1967-68 Bobby Orr, Boston
1968-69 Bobby Orr, Boston
1969-70 Bobby Orr, Boston
1970-71 Bobby Orr, Boston
1971-72 Bobby Orr, Boston
1972-73 Bobby Orr, Boston
1973-74 Bobby Orr, Boston
1974-75 Bobby Orr, Boston
1975-76 Denis Potvin, New York I.
1976-77 Larry Robinson, Montreal
1977-78 Denis Potvin, New York I.
1978-79 Denis Potvin, New York I.
1979-80 Larry Robinson, Montreal
1980-81 Randy Carlyle, Pittsburgh
1981-82 Doug Wilson, Chicago
1982-83 Rod Langway, Washington
1983-84 Rod Langway, Washington

CONN SMYTHE TROPHY

Awarded to the Most Valuable Player in the Stanley Cup play-offs. Selected in a vote of the League Governors.

The trophy was presented by Maple Leaf Gardens Ltd. in 1964 to honor the former coach, manager, president and owner of the Toronto Maple Leafs.

1964-65 Jean Beliveau, Montreal
1965-66 Roger Crozier, Detroit
1966-67 Dave Keon, Toronto
1967-68 Glenn Hall, St. Louis
1968-69 Serge Savard, Montreal
1969-70 Bobby Orr, Boston
1970-71 Ken Dryden, Montreal
1971-72 Bobby Orr, Boston
1972-73 Yvan Cournoyer, Montreal
1973-74 Bernie Parent, Philadelphia
1974-75 Bernie Parent, Philadelphia
1975-76 Reggie Leach, Philadelphia
1976-77 Guy Lafleur, Montreal
1977-78 Larry Robinson, Montreal
1978-79 Bob Gainey, Montreal
1979-80 Bryan Trottier, New York I.
1980-81 Butch Goring, New York I.
1981-82 Mike Bossy, New York I.
1982-83 Billy Smith, New York I.
1983-84 Mark Messier, Edmonton

CALDER MEMORIAL TROPHY

Awarded to the league's outstanding rookie. Selected by a vote of hockey writers and broadcasters in each of the 21 NHL cities. It was originated in 1937 by Frank Calder, first president of the NHL. After his death in 1943, the league presented the Calder Memorial Trophy in his memory.

To be eligible to receive the trophy, a player cannot have participated in more than 20 games in any preceding season or in six or more games in each of any two preceding seasons.

Prior to 1937-37, top rookies were named but there was no trophy.

1932-33 Carl Voss, Detroit	1958-59 Ralph Backstrom, Montreal
1933-34 Russ Blinco, Montreal M.	1959-60 Bill Hay, Chicago
1934-35 Dave Schriner, New York A.	1960-61 Dave Keon, Toronto
1935-36 Mike Karakas, Chicago	1961-62 Bobby Rousseau, Montreal
1936-37 Syl Apps, Toronto	1962-63 Kent Douglas, Toronto
1937-38 Cully Dahlstrom, Chicago	1963-64 Jacques Laperriere, Montreal
1938-39 Frank Brimsek, Boston	1964-65 Roger Crozier, Detroit
1939-40 Kilby MacDonald, New York R.	1965-66 Brit Selby, Toronto
1940-41 Johnny Quilty, Montreal C.	1966-67 Bobby Orr, Boston
1941-42 Grant Warwick, New York R.	1967-68 Derek Sanderson, Boston
1942-43 Gaye Stewart, Toronto	1968-69 Danny Grant, Minnesota
1943-44 Gus Bodnar, Toronto	1969-70 Tony Esposito, Chicago
1944-45 Frank McCool, Toronto	1970-71 Gil Perreault, Buffalo
1945-46 Edgar Laprade, New York R.	1971-72 Ken Dryden, Montreal
1946-47 Howie Meeker, Toronto	1972-73 Steve Vickers, New York R.
1947-48 Jim McFadden, Detroit	1973-74 Denis Potvin, New York I.
1948-49 Pentti Lund, New York R.	1974-75 Eric Vail, Atlanta
1949-50 Jack Gelineau, Boston	1975-76 Bryan Trottier, New York I.
1950-51 Terry Sawchuk, Detroit	1976-77 Willi Plett, Atlanta
1951-52 Bernie Geoffrion, Montreal	1977-78 Mike Bossy, New York I.
1952-53 Lorne Worsley, New York R.	1978-79 Bobby Smith, Minnesota
1953-54 Camille Henry, New York R.	1979-80 Ray Bourque, Boston
1954-55 Ed Litzenberger, Chicago	1980-81 Peter Stastny, Quebec
1955-56 Glenn Hall, Detroit	1981-82 Dale Hawerchuk, Winnipeg
1956-57 Larry Regan, Boston	1982-83 Steve Larmer, Chicago
1957-58 Frank Mahovlich, Toronto	1983-84 Tom Barrasso, Buffalo

LADY BYNG TROPHY

Awarded to the player combining the highest type of sportsmanship and gentlemanly conduct plus a high standard of playing ability. Selected by a vote of hockey writers and broadcasters in the 21 NHL cities.

Lady Byng, the wife of the Governor-General of Canada in 1925, presented the trophy to the NHL during that year.

1924-25 Frank Nighbor, Ottawa	1954-55 Sid Smith, Toronto
1925-26 Frank Nighbor, Ottawa	1955-56 Earl Reibel, Detroit
1926-27 Billy Burch, New York A.	1956-57 Andy Hebenton, New York R.
1927-28 Frank Boucher, New York R.	1957-58 Camille Henry, New York R.
1928-29 Frank Boucher, New York R.	1958-59 Alex Delvecchio, Detroit
1929-30 Frank Boucher, New York R.	1959-60 Don McKenney, Boston
1930-31 Frank Boucher, New York R.	1960-61 Red Kelly, Toronto
1931-32 Joe Primeau, Toronto	1961-62 Dave Keon, Toronto
1932-33 Frank Boucher, New York R.	1962-63 Dave Keon, Toronto
1933-34 Frank Boucher, New York R.	1963-64 Ken Wharram, Chicago
1934-35 Frank Boucher, New York R.	1964-65 Bobby Hull, Chicago
1935-36 Doc Romnes, Chicago	1965-66 Alex Delvecchio, Detroit
1936-37 Marty Barry, Detroit	1966-67 Stan Mikita, Chicago
1937-38 Gordie Drillon, Toronto	1967-68 Stan Mikita, Chicago
1938-39 Clint Smith, New York R.	1968-69 Alex Delvecchio, Detroit
1939-40 Bobby Bauer, Boston	1969-70 Phil Goyette, St. Louis
1940-41 Bobby Bauer, Boston	1970-71 Johnny Bucyk, Boston
1941-42 Syl Apps, Toronto	1971-72 Jean Ratelle, New York R.
1942-43 Max Bentley, Chicago	1972-73 Gil Perreault, Buffalo
1943-44 Clint Smith, Chicago	1973-74 John Bucyk, Boston
1944-45 Bill Mosienko, Chicago	1974-75 Marcel Dionne, Detroit
1945-46 Toe Blake, Montreal	1975-76 Jean Ratelle, NYR-Boston
1946-47 Bobby Bauer, Boston	1976-77 Marcel Dionne, Los Angeles
1947-48 Buddy O'Connor, New York R.	1977-78 Butch Goring, Los Angeles
1948-49 Bill Quackenbush, Detroit	1978-79 Bob MacMillan, Atlanta
1949-50 Edgar Laprade, New York R.	1979-80 Wayne Gretzky, Edmonton
1950-51 Red Kelly, Detroit	1980-81 Rick Kehoe, Pittsburgh
1951-52 Sid Smith, Toronto	1981-82 Rick Middleton, Boston
1952-53 Red Kelly, Detroit	1982-83 Mike Bossy, New York I.
1953-54 Red Kelly, Detroit	1983-84 Mike Bossy, New York I.

STANLEY CUP WINNERS

Season	Champions	Coach
1892-93	Montreal A.A.A.	
1894-95	Montreal Victorias	Mike Grant*
1895-96	Winnipeg Victorias	
1896-97	Montreal Victorias	Mike Grant*
1897-98	Montreal Victorias	F. Richardson
1898-99	Montreal Shamrocks	H. J. Trihey*
1899-00	Montreal Shamrocks	H. J. Trihey*
1900-01	Winnipeg Victorias	
1901-02	Montreal A.A.A.	R. R. Boon*
1902-03	Ottawa Silver Seven	A. T. Smith
1903-04	Ottawa Silver Seven	A. T. Smith
1904-05	Ottawa Silver Seven	A. T. Smith
1905-06	Montreal Wanderers	
1906-07	Kenora Thistles (January)	Tommy Phillips*
1906-07	Montreal Wanderers (March)	Cecil Blachford
1907-08	Montreal Wanderers	Cecil Blachford
1908-09	Ottawa Senators	Bruce Stuart*
1909-10	Montreal Wanderers	Pud Glass*
1910-11	Ottawa Senators	Bruce Stuart*
1911-12	Quebec Bulldogs	C. Nolan
1912-13	Quebec Bulldogs	Joe Marlowe*
1913-14	Toronto Blue Shirts	Scotty Davidson*
1914-15	Vancouver Millionaires	Frank Patrick
1915-16	Montreal Canadiens	George Kennedy
1916-17	Seattle Metropolitans	Pete Muldoon
1917-18	Toronto Arenas	Dick Carroll
1918-19	No decision.	
1919-20	Ottawa Senators	Pete Green
1920-21	Ottawa Senators	Pete Green
1921-22	Toronto St. Pats	Eddie Powers
1922-23	Ottawa Senators	Pete Green
1923-24	Montreal Canadiens	Leo Dandurand
1924-25	Victoria Cougars	Lester Patrick
1925-26	Montreal Maroons	Eddie Gerard
1926-27	Ottawa Senators	Dave Gill
1927-28	New York Rangers	Lester Patrick
1928-29	Boston Bruins	Cy Denneny
1929-30	Montreal Canadiens	Cecil Hart

* In the early years the teams were frequently run by the Captain.
** Victoria defeated Quebec in challenge series. No official recognition.
*** In the spring of 1919 the Montreal Canadiens traveled to Seattle to meet Seattle, PCHL champions. After five games had been played—teams were tied at 2 wins each and 1 tie—the series was called off by the local Department of Health because of the influenza epidemic and the death from influenza of Joe Hall.

1984: Islander Duane Sutter, 12, vs. Oiler Kevin McClelland.

Season	Champions	Coach
1930-31	Montreal Canadiens	Cecil Hart
1931-32	Toronto Maple Leafs	Dick Irvin
1932-33	New York Rangers	Lester Patrick
1933-34	Chicago Black Hawks	Tommy Gorman
1934-35	Montreal Maroons	Tommy Gorman
1935-36	Detroit Red Wings	Jack Adams

Season	Champions	Coach
1936-37	Detroit Red Wings	Jack Adams
1937-38	Chicago Black Hawks	Bill Stewart
1938-39	Boston Bruins	Art Ross
1939-40	New York Rangers	Frank Boucher
1940-41	Boston Bruins	Cooney Weiland
1941-42	Toronto Maple Leafs	Hap Day
1942-43	Detroit Red Wings	Jack Adams
1943-44	Montreal Canadiens	Dick Irvin
1944-45	Toronto Maple Leafs	Hap Day
1945-46	Montreal Canadiens	Dick Irvin
1946-47	Toronto Maple Leafs	Hap Day
1947-48	Toronto Maple Leafs	Hap Day
1948-49	Toronto Maple Leafs	Hap Day
1949-50	Detroit Red Wings	Tommy Ivan
1950-51	Toronto Maple Leafs	Joe Primeau
1951-52	Detroit Red Wings	Tommy Ivan
1952-53	Montreal Canadiens	Dick Irvin
1953-54	Detroit Red Wings	Tommy Ivan
1954-55	Detroit Red Wings	Jimmy Skinner
1955-56	Montreal Canadiens	Toe Blake
1956-57	Montreal Canadiens	Toe Blake
1957-58	Montreal Canadiens	Toe Blake
1958-59	Montreal Canadiens	Toe Blake
1959-60	Montreal Canadiens	Toe Blake
1960-61	Chicago Black Hawks	Rudy Pilous
1961-62	Toronto Maple Leafs	Punch Imlach
1962-63	Toronto Maple Leafs	Punch Imlach
1963-64	Toronto Maple Leafs	Punch Imlach
1964-65	Montreal Canadiens	Toe Blake
1965-66	Montreal Canadiens	Toe Blake
1966-67	Toronto Maple Leafs	Punch Imlach
1967-68	Montreal Canadiens	Toe Blake
1968-69	Montreal Canadiens	Claude Ruel
1969-70	Boston Bruins	Harry Sinden
1970-71	Montreal Canadiens	Al MacNeil
1971-72	Boston Bruins	Tom Johnson
1972-73	Montreal Canadiens	Scotty Bowman
1973-74	Philadelphia Flyers	Fred Shero
1974-75	Philadelphia Flyers	Fred Shero
1975-76	Montreal Canadiens	Scotty Bowman
1976-77	Montreal Canadiens	Scotty Bowman
1977-78	Montreal Canadiens	Scotty Bowman
1978-79	Montreal Canadiens	Scotty Bowman
1979-80	New York Islanders	Al Arbour
1980-81	New York Islanders	Al Arbour
1981-82	New York Islanders	Al Arbour
1982-83	New York Islanders	Al Arbour
1983-84	Edmonton Oilers	Glen Sather

NHL TV/Radio Roundup

Plans for cable network television had not been determined at press time.

BOSTON BRUINS
Bruins' games are carried over WSBK-TV (Channel 38) with Fred Cusick and John Peirson at the mike. Bob Wilson and Johnny Bucyk handle the radio calls on WPLM (1390).

BUFFALO SABRES
Ted Darling telecasts on WGRZ-TV (Channel 2) with Ed Kilgore as host and Jim Lorentz handling color. Darling provides play-by-play on Cable TV with Mike Robitaille on color and Gerry Meehan as host. When games are not telecast, Darling does the play-by-play on WBEN radio (930), with Rick Jenneret the color man. Jenneret also fills in on play-by-play, and Mike Robitaille and Jim Lorentz handle color.

CALGARY FLAMES
Flames' games can be found on CFAC-TV (Channels 2 and 7), with Ed Whalen and Jim Van Horne describing the action. Peter Maher and Doug Barkley are the radio voices on CHQR (810).

CHICAGO BLACK HAWKS
Plans were uncertain at press time.

DETROIT RED WINGS
Bruce Martyn does the play-by-play and Sid Abel the color for the Red Wings on WKBD-TV (Channel 50) and WJR radio (760).

EDMONTON OILERS
The Oilers are heard on CFRN radio (1260), with Rod Phillips and Ken Brown doing the honors. The television outlets are CITV (Channel 13), with Bruce Buchanan announcing, and CBXT (Channel 5).

HARTFORD WHALERS
Whalers' games are carried over WTIC radio (1080) and WVIT-TV (Channel 30). Cable TV station Sportschannel also carries Whaler games. Chuck Kaiton handles radio play-by-play and Mike Fornes handles TV and cable play-by-play.

LOS ANGELES KINGS

Bob Miller and Nick Nickson handle Kings' action on KHJ-TV (Channel 9) and KFOX-FM (93.5).

MINNESOTA NORTH STARS

The Stars shine on KITN-TV (Channel 29), announcers un-named at press time. Al Shaver and Russ Small are on radio at KSTP (1500).

MONTREAL CANADIENS

The Canadiens are covered in English on CBMT (Channel 6) and French on CBFT (Channel 2) and CFMT (Channel 10). Danny Gallivan and Dick Irvin handle telecasts in English while Lionel Duval, Rene Lecavalier, Jacques Moreau, Bert Raymond and Gilles Tremblay say it in French. English language radio broadcasts are carried on CBM (940) and CFCF (600) with Irvin and Ron Reusch, and Richard Garneau teams with Duval to provide French radio coverage on CBF (690).

NEW JERSEY DEVILS

The Devils' action can be seen on Madison Square Garden network and WOR-TV (Channel 9), with Mike Emrick, and heard on WMCA radio (570), with Larry Hirsch and Fred Shero.

NEW YORK ISLANDERS

Islander outlets WOR-TV (Channel 9), SportsChannel and WOR radio (710). Jiggs McDonald and Eddie Westfall call the shots on TV while Barry Landers (play-by-play) and Jean Potvin (color) handle radio.

NEW YORK RANGERS

Jim Gordon, Phil Esposito and John Davidson handle Ranger telecasts on WOR-TV (Channel 9). Marv Albert and Sal Messina are the voices of the Rangers on WNEW radio (1130)

PHILADELPHIA FLYERS

Gene Hart and Bobby Taylor cover the Flyers on WIP radio (610) and WTAF-TV (Channel 29).

PITTSBURGH PENGUINS

Penguin games can be heard on KQV (1410) and seen on WPGH-TV (Channel 53), with Mike Lange and Terry Schiffhauer describing the action.

QUEBEC NORDIQUES
The Nordiques are carried on CKCV radio (1280) with Andre Cote and Jos Hardy and CFCM-TV (Channel 4) with Claude Bedard and Pierre Bouchard.

ST. LOUIS BLUES
Dan Kelly is the anchor man for Blues' games on KDNL-TV (Channel 30) and KMOX radio (1120).

TORONTO MAPLE LEAFS'
Dave Hodge, Jim Hughson, Bob Cole and Joe Bowen cover the Maple Leafs on CBLT-TV (Channel 5) and CHCH-TV (Channel 11) and a radio network.

VANCOUVER CANUCKS
All games are carried on CKNW radio (980), with Jim Robson doing the play-by-play. Robson calls the action on CBC (Channel 2) and Bernie Pascall is on CHAN-TV (Channel 8).

WASHINGTON CAPITALS
Ron Weber covers Capital games on WTOP radio (1500). The TV voices on WDCA (Channel 20) were undecided at press time.

WINNIPEG JETS
Jets' games are carried on CKY radio (580) and CKND-TV (Channel 9). Ken Nicholson and Curt Keilback do the radio and Brian Swain and Dave Richardson are on the tube.

Official 1984–85 NHL Schedule

SUBJECT TO CHANGE   *Afternoon Game

Thur Oct 11
Pitt at Bos
Hart at NYR
Mont at Buff
Que at Van
Wash at Phil
Tor at Minn
Det at Chi
StL at Calg
Edm at LA

Fri Oct 12
NYI at NJ
StL at Edm

Sat Oct 13
Bos at Hart
Buff at Tor
Pitt at Mont
Que at Calg
Chi at NYI
NYR at Minn
NJ at Det
Phil at Wash
Van at LA

Sun Oct 14
Hart at Bos
Det at Buff
Que at Edm
Minn at NYR
Wash at Chi
Tor at Winn
StL at LA
Calg at Van

Mon Oct 15
Phil at Mont

Tues Oct 16
Bos at Edm
NJ at NYI
LA at Wash

Wed Oct 17
Hart at Tor
Buff at Que
NYI at Det
Van at Pitt
StL at Chi
Winn at Calg

Thur Oct 18
Det at Hart

LA at Mont
Van at Phil
Edm at Minn

Fri Oct 19
Bos at Calg
Que at Buff
Tor at NJ
Edm at Winn

Sat Oct 20
Van at Hart
Minn at Mont
Que at Tor
LA at NYI
NYR at Wash
NJ at StL
Phil at Pitt
Chi at Det

Sun Oct 21
Bos at Winn
Minn at Buff
NYI at NYR
Pitt at Phil
LA at Chi
Calg at Edm

Tues Oct 23
Hart at Calg
Mont at Que
Van at NYI
Phil at Minn

Wed Oct 24
Bos at StL
Hart at Winn
NJ at Pitt
Wash at Edm
Det at Tor
Van at Chi

Thur Oct 25
Buff at Mont
NYR at NJ
StL at Phil
Wash at Calg

Fri Oct 26
Buff at Det
Tor at Que
LA at Edm

Sat Oct 27
Bos at NYI

Hart at Minn
Mont at Pitt
NYR at Que
Phil at NJ
Calg at Tor
Chi at StL
LA at Winn

Sun Oct 28
Bos at NYR
Hart at Chi
Calg at Buff
Wash at Van

Mon Oct 29
Que at Mont
LA at Winn

Tues Oct 30
NYR at NYI
Det at Pitt
Chi at Minn
Van at Edm

Wed Oct 31
Que at Hart
Phil at Buff
Pitt at NJ
Calg at Wash
Tor at StL
LA at Van

Thur Nov 1
Que at Bos
NYI at Mont
Winn at Phil
Calg at Det

Fri Nov 2
Hart at Buff
Minn at NJ
Winn at Det
Chi at Edm

Sat Nov 3
Bos at Mont
Buff at Hart
NYI at Que
NYR at Pitt
NJ at Wash
Minn at Phil
Tor at LA
Chi at Van
Calg at StL

Sun Nov 4
NYI at Bos
Edm at Winn

Mon Nov 5
Tor at Minn
Chi at LA

Tues Nov 6
Mont at Det
Winn at Que
StL at NYI
Edm at Pitt

Wed Nov 7
Winn at Hart
Buff at Minn
Wash at NYR
Van at Tor
Chi at Calg

Thur Nov 8
Det at Bos
Edm at NJ
StL at Pitt

Fri Nov 9
Buff at LA
NYI at NYR
StL at Phil
Edm at Wash
Van at Winn

Sat Nov 10
Bos at Det
Hart at Que
Mont at Calg
Pitt at NYI
Wash at NJ
Chi at Tor
Van at Minn

Sun Nov 11
StL at Bos
Buff at Winn
LA at NYR
Edm at Phil
Minn at Tor

Mon Nov 12
Mont at Van

Tue Nov 13
LA at Que
Minn at Wash
Det at Calg

Wed Nov 14
Bos at Buff
Mont at Edm
Que at StL
NYR at Chi
Pitt at Winn
LA at Tor
Det at Van

Thur Nov 15
NJ at Bos
Hart at Phil
Minn at NYI
Edm at Calg

Fri Nov 16
Wash at Buff
Que at StL
Pitt at Van
Calg at Winn

Sat Nov 17
Phil at Bos
Chi at Hart
Buff at Wash
NJ at Mont
NYR at NYI
Pitt at LA
Winn at Tor
Det at Minn
Van at Edm

Sun Nov 18
Que at Chi
NYI at Phil
NJ at NYR

Mon Nov 19
Tor at Mont
Calg at LA

Tues Nov 20
Chi at Que
Wash at NYI
StL at Van

Wed Nov 21
Bos at Phil
Hart at Det
Buff at NYR

Copyright © 1984 by the National Hockey League. All rights reserved.

NJ at LA
Wash at Pitt
Tor at Minn
Winn at Edm
Van at Calg

Thur Nov 22
Pitt at Hart
Chi at Mont

Fri Nov 23
Phil at Buff
NYI at Wash
NJ at Minn
Tor at Det
StL at Calg
Winn at Van

Sat Nov 24
Chi at Bos
Phil at Hart
Buff at NYI
Det at Mont
NYR at Que
NJ at Pitt
Minn at Tor
StL at Edm
Winn at LA

Sun Nov 25
Mont at Bos
Que at NYR
Chi at Wash
Calg at Van

Tues Nov 27
Buff at Pitt
Wash at Que
Minn at NJ
Chi at Phil
Edm at Tor
StL at Van
Winn at LA

Wed Nov 28
Minn at Hart
Mont at Det
NYI at Calg
Wash at NYR

Thur Nov 29
Edm at Bos
NJ at Phil
Chi at Pitt
Van at LA

Fri Nov 30
Edm at Hart
Mont at Buff
NYI at Winn
Tor at NYR
StL at Det

Sat Dec 1
Wash at Bos
Hart at Que

Buff at Mont
NYR at Tor
*Chi at NJ
*Pitt at Phil
Det at StL
Calg at Minn
Van at LA

Sun Dec 2
Pitt at Wash
Calg at Winn

Mon Dec 3
Bos at Que
Hart at Mont
NYI at Van
Phil at NYR

Tues Dec 4
NJ at Wash
Tor at Det
Winn at StL
LA at Minn

Wed Dec 5
Bos at Buff
Mont at Hart
NYI at Edm
Calg at NYR
StL at Pitt
Det at Tor
LA at Chi

Thur Dec 6
Mont at Bos
Que at Phil

Fri Dec 7
Pitt at NYR
Calg at NJ
Winn at Wash
Chi at Det
Minn at Edm

Sat Dec 8
*Buff at Bos
Hart at NYI
LA at Mont
NJ at Que
NYR at Phil
Calg at Pitt
Tor at StL
Edm at Van

Sun Dec 9
Que at Buff
*Det at Wash
Tor at Chi
Minn at Winn

Mon Dec 10
LA at NYR
Det at Minn

Tues Dec 11
Van at Que
NJ at NYI
Phil at Winn
Wash at StL

Wed Dec 12
Bos at NYR
Buff at Hart
NYI at Pitt
Phil at Tor
Wash at Minn
Det at Chi
Winn at Calg

Thur Dec 13
Que at Bos
Van at Mont
StL at NJ
Edm at LA

Fri Dec 14
Det at Buff
Tor at Winn

Sat Dec 15
*Van at Bos
Mont at Hart
Que at NJ
Phil at NYI
NYR at Wash
Pitt at Tor
Chi at Minn
Edm at StL
Calg at LA

Sun Dec 16
Van at Buff
Mont at Phil
Wash at NYR
Det at Winn
Minn at Chi

Mon Dec 17
Edm at NJ
StL at Tor

Tues Dec 18
Bos at Mont
Wash at Que
Winn at NYI
LA at Calg

Wed Dec 19
Bos at Hart
Buff at Chi
Winn at NYR
NJ at Pitt
Minn at StL
LA at Edm

Thur Dec 20
Wash at Mont
Que at Det
NJ at Phil
Van at Calg

Fri Dec 21
NYI at Hart
Phil at Pitt
Tor at Chi
Van at Edm

Sat Dec 22
Bos at Tor
Hart at Mont
Buff at Que
Pitt at NYI
NYR at NJ
StL at Wash
Minn at Det
LA at Winn
Calg at Edm

Sun Dec 23
Minn at Bos
StL at Buff
Mont at NYR
Que at Chi
Wash at Phil
LA at Winn
Calg at Van

Wed Dec 26
NJ at Hart
Tor at Buff
NYI at Pitt
NYR at Det
Phil at Wash
Chi at StL
Winn at Minn
Edm at Calg
LA at Van

Thur Dec 27
Bos at LA
Mont at Que
Wash at NYI
Tor at NJ

Fri Dec 28
Hart at Pitt
Winn at Buff
Phil at Van
Det at Calg

Sat Dec 29
*Bos at Minn
Hart at Wash
Buff at NJ
NYR at Mont
Pitt at Que
NYI at StL
Chi at Tor
Det at Edm

Sun Dec 30
Bos at Winn
StL at NYR
Phil at LA
Calg at Chi
Edm at Van

Mon Dec 31
NJ at Buff
Que at Mont
NYI at Minn
Pitt at Det

Tues Jan 1
*Bos at Wash
*Calg at Winn

Wed Jan 2
Hart at Que
Mont at Chi
NYI at Det
Van at NYR
Phil at Edm
Pitt at Tor

Thur Jan 3
Det at Hart
Mont at StL
Van at NJ
Phil at Calg
Minn at LA

Fri Jan 4
Pitt at Buff
Que at Wash
Winn at Edm

Sat Jan 5
*NYR at Bos
Chi at Hart
Buff at NYI
*Mont at NJ
Que at Pitt
Phil at StL
Van at Tor
LA at Det
Minn at Calg

Sun Jan 6
NJ at NYR
StL at Chi
Edm at Winn

Mon Jan 7
LA at Bos
Hart at Tor

Tues Jan 8
Hart at Buff
Mont at NYI
Edm at Que
Van at Phil
Wash at Det

Wed Jan 9
Bos at Tor
NYR at Winn
Van at Pitt
Wash at StL
Minn at Chi
LA at Calg

Thur Jan 10
Buff at Bos
Edm at Mont
NYI at NJ
Chi at Phil
StL at Minn

Fri Jan 11
Calg at Que

Sat Jan 12
*Det at Bost
Hart at Minn
Buff at Mont
Phil at NYI
NYR at StL
*Wash at NJ
Edm at Pitt
Winn at LA

Sun Jan 13
Edm at Buff
Det at Que
NYI at Chi
*Calg at Phil
Tor at Van
Winn at LA

Mon Jan 14
NJ at NYR
Minn at Wash

Tues Jan 15
Bos at NJ
Calg at Hart
Mont at Que
NYI at Van

Wed Jan 16
Buff at NYR
NYI at Edm
Phil at Det
Wash at Pitt
Tor at LA
Winn at Chi
StL at Minn

Thur Jan 17
Calg at Bos
Hart at Mont
Det at Phil
Pitt at Wash

Fri Jan 18
Chi at Buff
NYR at NJ
StL at Winn
Edm at Van

Sat Jan 19
Bos at Que
Buff at Hart
NJ at Mont
NYI at LA
NYR at Wash
Phil at Minn

Chi at Pitt
StL at Tor
Winn at Det
Van at Edm

Mon Jan 21
Mont at Bos
Pitt at Winn
StL at Det
Minn at Chi
Calg at Van
LA at Edm

Tues Jan 22
Mont at Hart
NYR at Buff
Tor at Que
Det at NYI

Wed Jan 23
NJ at Calg
Phil at LA
Pitt at Minn
Wash at Chi
Winn at Van

Thur Jan 24
Buff at Bos
Que at Mont
Tor at NYI
Det at NYR

Fri Jan 25
Buff at Que
NJ at Edm
Pitt at Calg
LA at StL
Winn at Van

Sat Jan 26
*Hart at Bos
NYR at Mont
Wash at NYI
Pitt at Edm
Chi at Tor
Det at Minn
LA at StL
Van at Calg

Sun Jan 27
*Bos at Hart
Que at Buff
*NYI at Wash
Minn at NYR
*Phil at Winn
Tor at Chi

Mon Jan 28
Calg at Edm

Tues Jan 29
Minn at NYI
NJ at LA
Wash at Det
Winn at StL
Edm at Calg

Wed Jan 30
Bos at Buff
Mont at Minn
Tor at Pitt
Winn at Chi

Thur Jan 31
Que at Bos
Hart at LA
NYR at Calg
NJ at Phil
Det at StL

Fri Feb 1
Hart at Van
NYI at NJ
Tor at Wash

Sat Feb 2
*Winn at Bos
*Buff at Phil
Mont at LA
*Que at Det
NYI at Pitt
NYR at Edm
Minn at Tor
Chi at StL

Sun Feb 3
Hart at Edm
Calg at Buff
Minn at Que
NYR at Van
Det at NJ
*Winn at Wash
*StL at Chi

Tues Feb 5
Calg at Mont
Phil at NYI
NYR at LA
Wash at Tor

Wed Feb 6
Calg at Hart
Buff at Minn
Tor at Chi
Van at StL
Edm at Winn

Thur Feb 7
Hart at Bos
Mont at Que
NYR at NYI
Pitt at NJ
LA at Phil
StL at Det

Fri Feb 8
LA at Wash
Edm at Minn
Van at Winn

Sat Feb 9
*Chi at Bos
NYR at Hart

Buff at Calg
Tor at Mont
*NJ at Que
Pitt at NYI
Phil at Wash
Edm at Det
Minn at StL

Sun Feb 10
*Bos at Chi
*Que at Hart
Mont at Tor
NYR at Phil
LA at Pitt
*Van at Winn

Tues Feb 12
All-Star Game
at Calgary

Wed Feb 13
Wash at Winn

Thur Feb 14
Bost at LA
Hart at NJ
Que at Phil
Pitt at Chi
Wash at Calg
Tor at StL
Minn at Det

Fri Feb 15
Mont at Buff
Edm at NYR

Sat Feb 16
Bos at Van
Hart at NYI
Buff at Mont
Que at Pitt
NJ at Tor
Edm at Phil
Wash at LA
*Chi at Det
Minn at StL
Winn at Calg

Sun Feb 17
*Tor at Hart
Que at Minn
NYI at NYR
NJ at Winn
*Det at Chi

Mon Feb 18
Edm at Buff
*Pitt at Phil

Tues Feb 19
Hart at Winn
Mont at StL
LA at Que
Calg at NYI
NJ at Van
Edm at Tor

Wed Feb 20
Bos at Minn
Mont at Chi
Calg at Pitt
StL at Det

Thur Feb 21
Hart at NYR
Winn at NYI
LA at NJ
Tor at Phil
Wash at Van

Fri Feb 22
StL at Buff
Que at Edm
NYR at Pitt
Chi at Minn

Sat Feb 23
Bos at NYI
LA at Hart
Winn at Mont
Que at Van
*Calg at NJ
Pitt at Minn
Wash at Edm
*Tor at Det

Sun Feb 24
*StL at Hart
LA at Buff
NYI at Mont
Calg at Phil
*Det at Chi

Mon Feb. 25
Winn at NYR
Minn at Pitt
Chi at Tor

Tues Feb 26
Phil at Hart
Buff at NJ
Van at Wash

Wed Feb 27
Buff at StL
Mont at Bos
Que at LA
NYI at Calg
NJ at Chi
Winn at Pitt
Minn at Tor
Van at Det

Thur Feb 28
Phil at Bos
Wash at NYR

Fri Mar 1
Hart at NJ
Mont at Calg
Minn at Det
LA at Edm

Sat Mar 2
*Van at Bos
Buff at Wash
Phil at Que
NYI at Tor
NYR at Pitt
Det at Minn
Chi at StL

Sun Mar 3
*Van at Hart
NYI at Buff
Pitt at NYR
Phil at NJ
StL at Chi
Winn at Edm
LA at Calg

Mon Mar 4
Mont at Minn

Tues Mar 5
Bos at Que
Hart at Buff
Phil at NYI
NJ at Wash
Pitt at LA
Tor at StL
Edm at Calg

Wed Mar 6
Mont at Winn
NYR at Van
Det at Tor
Chi at Minn

Thur Mar 7
Hart at Bos
NYI at NJ
NYR at Calg
Wash at Phil
Pitt at StL

Fri Mar 8
Chi at Buff
Que at Winn
Phil at Wash
LA at Van

Sat Mar 9
*Pitt at Bos
Hart at Mont
Que at Calg
Tor at NYI
NYR at Edm
*NJ at Det
*StL at Minn

Sun Mar 10
*Bos at Wash
Mont at Hart
Buff at LA
*NJ at Winn
Pitt at Phil

Det at StL
*Minn at Chi
Edm at Van

Mon Mar 11
Chi at NYR

Tues Mar 12
NYI at StL
Winn at NJ

Wed Mar 13
Bos at Pitt
Hart at LA
Buff at Van
Minn at Que
NYI at Chi
Phil at NYR
Calg at Tor
Det at Edm

Thur Mar 14
Bos at NJ
Winn at Mont
Tor at Wash

Fri Mar 15
Buff at Edm
Winn at Que
Det at Van

Sat Mar 16
*Calg at Bos
Hart at StL
Minn at Mont
Wash at NYI
*NYR at Pitt
Phil at Tor
Det at LA

Sun Mar 17
Pitt at Hart
*Buff at Winn
*NYI at Phil
NJ at NYR
Chi at Van
Edm at LA

Mon Mar 18
Que at Bos
StL at Tor
Calg at Minn

Tues Mar 19
LA at NYI
NJ at Wash
Phil at Pitt

Wed Mar 20
StL at Hart
Van at Buff
Tor at Calg
LA at Det
Chi at Edm
Minn at Winn

Thur Mar 21
StL at Bos
Wash at Mont
Que at NYI
NYR at Phil
Van at NJ

Fri Mar 22
Pitt at Buff
Mont at Wash
NYR at Det
Tor at Edm
Chi at Calg

Sat Mar 23
Bos at Hart
*Phil at NJ
Minn at StL
Van at Winn
Calg a LA

Sun Mar 24
Bos at Buff
*Que at Hart
Mont at Phil
NYI at NYR
*Pitt at Wash
Tor at Det

Mon Mar 25
Van at Minn

Tues Mar 26
Bos at Mont
Buff at Que
Edm at NYI
Pitt at NYR
Minn at Det

Wed Mar 27
Hart at Wash
NJ at Pitt
Phil at Chi
StL at Tor
Winn at Van
Calg at LA

Thur Mar 28
Edm at Bos
StL at Mont
NYI at Que
Wash at NJ
Det at Phil

Fri Mar 29
Edm at Hart
Chi at Winn
LA at Calg

Sat Mar 30
*Mont at Bos
Buff at Hart
StL at Que
NYI at Wash
*NYR at Phil

*Pitt at NJ
Det at Tor
Minn at LA

Sun Mar 31
Que at Buff
Mont at Pitt
Tor at NYR
*Edm at Chi
Minn at Van
*Calg at Winn

Tues Apr 2
Bos at Que
Hart at Buff
Pitt at NYI
Phil at NYR
NJ at StL
Edm at LA

Wed Apr 3
NJ at Chi
Det at Pitt
Tor at Minn
Van at Calg

Thur Apr 4
Buff at Bos
Wash at Hart
Que at Mont
NYI at Phil
NYR at StL

Fri Apr 5
Calg at Edm
LA at Van

Sat Apr 6
Bos at Mont
Que at Hart
Buff at Tor
NJ at NYI
Wash at Pitt
*Chi at Det
StL at Minn
Winn at Edm
Van at LA

Sun Apr 7
Tor at Bos
Hart at Que
Mont at Buff
*NYR at Chi
Phil at NJ
Pitt at Wash
Det at StL
Winn at Calg

THE COMPLETE ENCYCLOPEDIA OF
HOCKEY

EDITED BY ZANDER HOLLANDER
AND HAL BOCK

All the vital facts, figures and drama in this revised,
updated third edition:

Illustrated with more than 200 historic photos, this mammoth
work contains:

- Lifetime year-by-year records of more than 3,000 NHL players
- Reviews of every NHL season • Profiles of the greatest players
- Hockey Hall of Fame • NHL and Stanley Cup all-time records
- Official Rules • Color photo insert

"A valuable and welcome addition to the reference library of
any hockey collector, fan or journalist."
>   —From the foreword by John A. Ziegler, Jr.
>   President, NHL

"An outstanding reference book."
>   —American Library Association

"A great book about a great game."
>   —Bill Chadwick, Member of the Hall of Fame

An Associated Features Book

NAL Hardcover (0453-00449-0) $24.95 U.S. only

Buy it at your local bookstore or use this convenient coupon for ordering.

THE NEW AMERICAN LIBRARY, INC.
P.O. Box 999, Bergenfield, New Jersey 07521

Please send me _____ hardbound copies of THE COMPLETE ENCYCLOPEDIA
OF HOCKEY (004490—$24.95). I am enclosing $_____ (Please add $1.50 to
this order to cover postage and handling). Send check or money order—no cash
or C.O.D.'s. Price and number are subject to change without notice.

Name _____

Address _____

City _____ State _____ Zip Code _____

Allow 4–6 weeks for delivery.
This offer is subject to withdrawal without notice.